HOTEL ORGANISATION

Hotel Organisation

M.N. Ahmed

ANMOL PUBLICATIONS PVT. LTD.
NEW DELHI - 110 002 (INDIA)

ANMOL PUBLICATIONS PVT. LTD.
4374/4B, Ansari Road, Daryaganj
New Delhi - 110 002
Ph.: 23261597, 23278000
Visit us at: www.anmolpublications.com

Hotel Organisation

First Published, 2005

ISBN 81-261-2293-5

PRINTED IN INDIA

Published by J.L. Kumar for Anmol Publications Pvt. Ltd., New Delhi - 110 002 and Printed at Mehra Offset Press, Delhi.

Contents

Preface

Tourism and Hotel Industry are the two significant sectors of modern day economy and are complimentary to each other. The new world order has turned the whole mankind into one family or society. Today's world is a global village, where distances have no meaning. Although, tourism and travelling are the two phenomena, as old as the civilized world, yet, tourism evolved into a regular and well-organised industry, during the last century only.

Hotel industry is part and parcel of tourism sector. The tourists are honoured guests and the hotels offer them the demanded hospitality. Hence, the two form a correlated industrial sector, which is growing and flourishing fast, with promises for future.

Extension of education and expansion of knowledge have created a new anxiety, among the members of the new generation, regarding the above said two areas. In fact, the two sectors offer high profile career avenues and good opportunities for aspirants and job-seekers. However, like other disciplines, Tourism and Hotel Management also require proper training for professionals. Hence, a large room for exhaustive and exclusive books on the subject, is there.

This series of comprehensive books has been outlined within the parameters of the syllabi of various universities and institutes, in a broad-based manner, in order to cover all streams of the discipline and for the benefit of students at graduate and post-graduate levels.

The undersigned is confident of a due recognition and proper acknowledgement from concerned circles. Further expectation is that this series of useful books would prove to be practically helpful to the professionals and students equally.

— Editor

1

Introduction

Among the important inputs which flow into the tourist system is tourist accommodation. Accommodation facilities constitute a vital and fundamental part of tourist supply and an important feature of the total tourist image of a country. Many countries have recognised the vital importance of accommodation industry in relation to tourism and their governments have coordinated their activities with the industry by way of providing attractive incentives and concessions to suppliers of tourist accommodation, which have resulted in the building up of various types of accommodation. For instance, availability of sites for tourist accommodation on liberal payment terms, special concessions in the form of long-term loans, liberal import licences and tax relief, cash grants for construction and renovation of buildings, and other similar concessions are provided to the accommodation industry.

The United Nations Conference on International Travel and Tourism held in Rome in 1963 considered, in particular, problems relating to means of accommodation. The Conference acknowledged the importance of means of accommodation, both traditional (hotels, motels) and supplementary (camps, youth hostels, etc..) as incentives to international tourism. The Conference recommended that governments should consider the possibility of including tourism projects, and particularly those relating to accommodation on the list of projects eligible for loans from their industrial or other corporations, and that, where required, they should establish special financial corporations for tourism. It also recommended that governments should give sympathetic consideration to the possibility of granting special facilities and incentives for accommodation projects. An adequate supply of accommodation suitably tailored to the requirements of the tourist market is one of the basic conditions of tourism development. The provision of accommodation facilities and their growth should, at the same time, be regarded in a much broader context as they make an important contribution to the economy as a whole, by stimulating economic development, social contacts and commercial activities.

In the promotion of tourism, of all the constituents of the tourist industry, the accommodation sector thus constitutes the most important segment. Tourism is, to a great extent, dependent on the type and quantity of accommodation available. Accommodation is a very important part of the tourism infrastructure and the expansion of tourism inevitably brings about the development of accommodation. It is rather the core of the tourist industry. Accommodation is, in other words, the matrix of tourism, and is thus the obvious choice to play a distinctive role in the development of this expanding industry.

According to the World Tourism Organisation, WTO Report on 'The Development of the Accommodation Sector, tourist accommodation is used to denote the facilities operated for short term accommodation of guests, either with or without service, against payment and according to fixed rates. For the purposes of classification, all tourist accommodation has been divided into the following groups: (i) hotels and similar establishments (the hotel industry proper) and, (ii) supplementary means of accommodation.

The first group usually includes hotels, motels, boarding houses and inns, while the second includes registered private accommodation (rented rooms; apartments, houses), camping and caravan sites, youth hostels, recreation centres for children, mountain huts and shelters as well as health establishments, that is, sanatoria and convalescent homes.

The Backdrop

The early history of accommodation for travellers can be said to have its origin in the Greek Word 'Xenia'. By this word ancient Greeks meant not only hospitality but also all forms of protection given to a visiting stranger. In ancient Greece, hospitality was a sort of divine order. The city or a town itself was bound to offer hospitality to a visitor and protect him from any discomfort. This was a custom. In the city of Sparta, whose extremely rigorous customs did not attract many visitors, it was the goddess Athena who was considered as protector of strangers, and hence her name 'Xenia Athena'.

Travelling during this period was not an easy affair. Travellers were mainly diplomats, philosophers, intellectuals and researchers. There were no lodgings specially designed to receive visitors. Guests were invited to stay in the dwellings of noblemen. This was rather a gift comprising a place to stay, food, care and bath. This explains the presence of baths in most archaeological finds. In ancient Olympia one can find one of the first buildings constructed with the aim of accommodating strangers, called the "Leonidio", built in 4th century B.C.

As travelling became more frequent, accommodation for travellers was viewed in two ways. The traveller who left his home required accommodation at his destination and, during journeys which could be completed in a single day, he needed overnight accommodation. The institution of 'inns' came into being. Inns can perhaps be considered to be the first of such accommodation units which catered to the needs of travellers in early times. During the Roman Empire many such inns were established which provided food, drink and also entertainment to weary travellers. However, with the decline of the Roman Empire by about A.D. 500, the institution of inn-keeping lost its importance and for many years there was not much development since people travelled very infrequently and there being not much trading activity, there was not much need felt for inn-keeping.

Later, when travelling began to be undertaken in coaches, travellers were lodged in 'Hostelries' situated at the relay stations where both the traveller and their horses found rest and food.

From this time onwards, hospitality was not always offered free. Payment for accommodation used was being resorted to.

After the advent of Christianity, it was the Church which came to the rescue of the travellers. Travel grew again for religious pilgrimage purposes. Travellers in thousands visited religious centres. Monasteries took over the role of providing lodgings and facilities to travellers who were mainly pilgrims. These welcomed the travellers and made their stay a comfortable experience. Every large monastery had a person responsible for reception of visitors and their well-being. The accommodation and the hospitality provided were free.

By the 15th century, the institution of the 'inn' once again developed in several countries in Europe, specially in England and France. During the seventeenth and eighteenth centuries, the facilities provided in the inns were expanded. Some of the inns had as many as 30 or more rooms. The English Common Law declared the inn to be a public house and imposed social responsibility in the innkeeper for the well-being of the traveller. Even today over one hundred odd inns are still operating in England as hotels as part of Trust House Limited. Some of these were built about four hundred years ago.

In the United States of America another type of accommodation unit, known as the 'tavern', was opened in the year 1634 by a man called Samuel Coles who had come by ship to the New World in search of a fortune in the year 1630. By 1780, taverns were popular meeting places where people used to come for eating, drinking and entertainment. Many important events were associated with taverns. In the year 1783, General George Washington bid farewell to his top ranking officers at the Frances Tavern in New York city. The famous Boston Tea Party was planned in a tavern called Green Dragon.

In India the concept of shelter for travellers is not new. In fact, it is as old as its recorded history. The historical records are replete with the mention/references of *viharas, dharamshalas, sarais, musafirkhanas,* etc. These establishments provided a home to all wayfarers, be they pilgrims, scholars, adventurers or merchants. The shelter under various names has always been a part of India's culture as a valuable institution, providing a vital service. The ancient Buddhist monks were probably the first to institutionalise the concept of a shelter in India. The cave temples scattered all over the south-western region of India have both a *chaitya* (sanctuary) for worship and prayer and a *vihara* (monastery). These monks, although living in their quiet retreats, away from towns and villages, were nevertheless mindful of the needs of travellers and pilgrims who found shelter and food at these monasteries. It is interesting to note that these monasteries were located on the ancient trade routes between important centres of pilgrimage of the region. It is gathered from some inscriptions that merchants gave liberal donations for the construction and maintenance of these establishments. Mere charity was obviously not the motivation in these displays of generosity. The trader travelled with their merchandise and money on these routes and the *viharas* were their 'hotels'.

In the medieval period this ancient institution gradually assumed a more secular character. Although religious centres invariably had *dharamshalas* and *musafirkhanas* attached to them, the caravan *sarai* appeared as an exclusive traveller's lodge with a *Nanbai* or the cook attached with it. Sher Shah Suri, the Great Afghan Emperor and the builder of the Grand Trunk Road, is credited with having built caravan sarais at regular intervals all along this highway creating favourable conditions for commerce and travel. However, he was not alone in this venture. The Mughals built such facilities all over their empire. Later kings, rajas, nawabs, rich businessmen and philanthropists built *sarais* making travel less arduous.

At approximately the same point in time, the inn was the western counterpart of India's *sarais*. With the expansion of commerce, travelling became profitable and with it emerged the business of providing comfortable shelter and good food to the growing number of travellers. The *sarais* in India, like the inns in Europe, or the stage coach stations in the USA of the 18th and 19th centuries, stood all along the well-travelled routes. They provided food and shelter to the travellers and fodder to their horses. The amenities these early hotels offered would seem to us to be primitive but they conformed to the life-style of that age.

However, with the passage of time, the age-old institution of the *sarai* or the inn adapted itself to the ever changing and constantly growing requirements of the market.

Institution of Hotel

The institution of hotel had its beginning in the early fourteenth century. The first hotel in the classical sense, the forerunner of the present day existing complex unit, is said to have been created in Paris, in the year 1312. Other similar hotels were soon established in France, Holland, Italy, Germany and many other countries.

With the growth of travel in the eighteenth century, there appeared in London the prototype of the modern hotel with the opening by one David Low in 1774. The next fifty years saw a gradual increase in the hotels and resorts in many countries of Europe. In the United States of America, hotels emerged from institutions known as 'Tavern' by the simple expedient of a change of name. By about the beginning of the nineteenth century, the terms tavern and hotel were used to describe the same thing. By the year 1820, 'hotel' became the accepted term to describe a place where people stayed for the night and took their meals on payment. In the 1820s the first tourist hotel appeared in Switzerland. The period preceding World War I also saw many hotels coming up in Europe especially in resorts of France, Italy, Switzerland and Germany. The hotels in fashionable resorts such as Vichy and Evian in France, Montecatine in Italy, Baden-Baden in Germany became very popular with tourists. In the same way hotels also came up in summer resorts along the French and Italian Riviera.

From the age of carriage and horses through the age of rail-road into the era of jumbo jet, the hotel industry developed with the simultaneous development of transportation systems. In the field of mass passenger transport, railways could perhaps be credited with being the pioneers. The evolution of the railway system in the eighteenth century greatly affected the quality and the quantity of accommodation used in conjunction with travel. The growth of the railways also brought in a speedy network of stage coach services. By the mid-nineteenth century the use of the stage coach as a means of travel had almost ceased. The industrialisation in its wake brought increased urbanisation. The great number of people who flocked to various urban towns in search of employment and also entertainment needed some kind of accommodation. This need for accommodation enabled promising and enterprising people to build hotels and inns in many such urban towns to cater to an increasingly local market and also to serve the large number of travellers carried by the railways. Until about the middle of the nineteenth century, the bulk of the journeys were undertaken for business and vocational reasons, by road and within the boundaries of individual countries. The volume of travel was relatively small and was confined to a fraction of the rich segment of the population in any country. Inns and similar establishments along the main highways and in the principal towns grew tc become the hallmark of the accommodation for the travellers. The traveller could reasonably expect, at most inns, a clean and comfortable stay when he wished to eat or spend the night. It provided the bulk of accommodation *en route*. This trend continued until the end of the nineteenth century, as most people travelled by coach.

***Emergence of the Hotel*:** Although the earliest hotels date back to the eighteenth century, their growth on any scale occurred only in the following century when the railways created sufficiently large markets to make large hotels possible. During this period a large number of hotels grew up at important destinations. The hotels were developed along the main railway and highway routes in major towns. Substantial development of the hotels thus awaited the volume and the type of traffic only the railways could bring. With the development of railway systems in many other countries within and outside Europe, the number of hotels also increased. These hotels catered to the increasing volume of traffic. The 1860s also saw the introduction of Thomas Cook's railway and hotel coupons. Starting in 1868 Cook arranged regular circular tours of Switzerland and Northern Italy from England. By the 1890s, 1,200 hotels throughout the world accepted hotel coupons. Thus we find that railways greatly influenced the development of hotels during the early twentieth century.

The demand for accommodation of tourists was thus met by a variety of facilities ranging from inns, taverns, private houses to hotels. The main changes in the demand for tourist accommodation have come about from changes in tourist transportation and in the popularity of different forms of holidays. After the introduction of the motor car and the aircraft, a large number of hotels sprang up at various tourist areas and destinations. The growth of hotels continued until the 1950s. Hotels as a unit of accommodation dominated the scene all over the world.

Definitions : Hotels provide accommodation, meals and refreshments for irregular periods of time for those who may reserve their accommodation either in advance or on the premises. In broad terms, hotels provide facilities to meet the needs of the modern traveller. The dictionaries define hotel in several ways: 'a place which supplies board and lodging', 'a place for the entertainment of the travellers', 'large city house of distinction', and 'a public building.'

The common law states that a hotel is "A place where all who conduct themselves properly, and who, being able and ready to pay for their entertainment, are received, if there be accommodation for them, and who without any stipulated engagement as to the duration of their stay or as to the rate of compensation, are, while there, supplied at a reasonable cost with their meals, lodging, and such services and attention as are necessarily incident to the use of the house as a temporary home."

A definition of the hotel as a business entity worthy of study was presented by hotel operators during the consideration of the hotel business to authorities of the National Recovery Administration, in Washington in 1933. This definition, as formulated by Stuart McNamara, was:

> "Primarily and fundamentally a hotel is an establishment which provides board and lodging, not engaged in interstate commerce, competitive with or affecting interstate commerce (or so related thereto that the regulation of the one involves the control of the other), but is a quasi-domestic institution retaining from its ancient origin certain traditional, and acquiring, in its modern development, certain statutory rights and obligations to the public, where all persons, not disqualified by condition or conduct, prepared to

pay for their accommodation, are to be received and furnished with a room or place to sleep or occupy if such accommodations are available, and with such services and attention as are incident to their use of the hotel as a home, and/or with food, at stipulated prices, and with or without contract as to duration of visit, and which conducts, within the confines of its physical locations, this business of supplying personal services of individuals for profit. Incidental to such fundamental and principal business, the hotel may furnish quarters and facilities for the assemblage of people for social, business or entertainment purposes, and may engage in renting portions of its premises for shops and business whose contiguity is deemed appropriate to an hotel".

Categories of Accommodation : Accommodation can be categorized in different ways. These could be categorized by location, price, by type of visitors and by type of facilities they offer. Luxury hotels are at one end of the scale while budget or economy hotels are at the other end. Some are within the city limits or in city centre while others may be in suburban areas. Some properties may cater to business travellers while others may cater to families on holiday. Yet another way to categorise them is on the basis of whether they are fully serviced, partially serviced or non-serviced. It is however, difficult to place international lodging accommodation into strict, exclusive categories.

According to the organisation for Economic Cooperation and Development (OECD) there are eleven different types of accommodation plus two 'other' categories. The 'other' categories refer to other "hotels and similar establishments" and "supplementary means of accommodation". Following are the main categories of accommodation:

Hotels

(i) International Hotels

(ii) Commercial Hotels

(iii) Residential Hotels

(iv) Resort Hotels

(v) Floating Hotels

(vi) Capsule Hotels

(vii) Airport Hotels

World Class Hotels

International hotels are the modern western-style hotels located in almost all metropolitan and other large cities as well as principal tourist centres. These hotels are luxury hotels and reclassified on the basis of an internationally accepted system of classification. The hotels are placed in various star categories. There are five such categories ranging from five star to one star, depending upon the facilities and services provided. These hotels provide, in addition to accommodation, all the other facilities which make the stay a very comfortable and interesting experience. These facilities include well-appointed reception and information counter, banquet halls, conference facilities, etc. There are also a number of shops, travel agency, money changing and safe deposit facilities. Restaurant facilities, bars and banqueting are an integral part of the business of a hotel. The various services provided in these hotels include international and local cuisine, food and beverage service and speciality restaurant service. These hotels also provide entertainment for the guests in the form of various dance and music programmes, sports and games.

A number of these hotels belong to the luxury category. There are some international chains which own a large number of such luxury hotels. Hotels belonging to international chains are mostly owned by public companies and controlled by a Board of Directors. These hotels have various departments which are managed by persons qualified and experienced in the field of hoteliering. The chief of the hotel designated as General Manager is responsible for the overall management and operation of the hotel through his departmental heads. International hotels are suitable for metropolitan cities and for other large business and commercial towns and principal tourist centres. The potential of these hotels is therefore limited to these areas. A number of this type of hotels have conference/convention facilities and are suitable for holding meetings, conventions and conferences.

Resort Hotels : Resort hotels cater to the needs of the holiday-maker, the tourist and those, who by reasons of health, desire a change of atmosphere. Resort hotels are located near the sea, mountain and other areas abounding in natural beauty. Rest, relaxation and entertainment are the key factors around which resorts are built. The primary motive of a person visiting them is rest and relaxation which he is looking for, away from his routine, busy work life. The resort hotels, in order to provide special services to the visitors, are built to give a visitor special welcome and an atmosphere of informality. The type of services and amenities located in resort property include recreation facilities such as swimming pool, golf course, tennis courts, skiing, boating, surf-riding and various indoor sports. Other important amenities include coffee shops, restaurants, conference rooms, lounge, shopping arcade and entertainment. Emphasis in resort hotels, however, is on recreational facilities. The clientele of resort hotels is mostly persons with considerable income looking for relaxation and recreation. Resort hotels rarely attract commercial patronage.

Resorts can be of various types and can be classified on the basis of climate and topography. Broadly they fall in the following categories: (i) Summer resorts, (ii) Winter resorts (iii) Hill resorts, (iv) All season resorts, and (v) Health resorts.

A majority of the resort hotels are seasonal establishments which work to capacity during the high tourist season. Generally the high tourist season is the period when there are holidays at educational institutions. However, in recent years many of the resort hotels, with a view to extend the season, provide certain special facilities and various other concessions to the guests. The concessions provided include reduced tariffs, free entertainment, sightseeing, gifts, etc.

Commercial Hotels : The commercial hotels direct their appeal primarily to the individual traveller as compared to international or resort hotel where the focus is on group travel. Most of the commercial hotels receive guests who are on business although some have permanent guests. As the hotel caters primarily to people who are visiting a place for commerce or business, these are located in important commercial and industrial centres of large towns and cities. These hotels are generally run by the owners and their success depends on their efficient running and the comfort and facilities they provide. In some of the large industrial towns, fully licensed commercial hotels exist complete with restaurants, grill room, functional accommodation and a garage for those travelling by automobile.

Residential Hotels : These hotels can be described as apartment houses complete with hotel services. These are often referred to as apartment hotels. The tariff of rooms in these hotels is charged on monthly, half-yearly or yearly basis and is charged for either furnished or unfurnished accommodation. These hotels, which are located mostly in big cities, operate exclusively under the European plan where no meals are provided to the guests. These hotels were developed in the United States of America where people discovered that permanent living in hotels offers many advantages. Services and amenities provided in these hotels are comparable to those of an average well-regulated home. These are very popular in the United States and western Europe where these are also popularly known as Pension.

Floating Hotels : As the name suggests, these hotels are located on the surface of the water. It may be on the sea or on a lake. All the facilities and services of a hotel are provided here and these are very popular in many countries. In some countries old luxury ships have been converted into floating hotels and are very popular among tourists. The atmosphere they provide is exclusive and exotic. In India, floating hotels in the form of houseboats are very popular with tourists.

Capsule Hotels : Capsule hotel is the newest innovation in the budget hotel market. The first of its kind was opened in Osaka in Japan in the year 1979, as a spin-off of the 1970s fashion in Japanese architecture for capsules. These have now sprung up in increasing numbers in big cities of Japan.

The capsule is a box made of glass-reinforced plastic or cement, open either at one side or one end, in which are concentrated some of the functions of a traditional hotel room — bed, a clock, radio, TV, flexible lighting, a box for valuables and a miniature table for writing. Rooms in a capsule hotel generally are lined up in double-decker fashion along a central aisle as in a sleeping compartment of a train. Toilets and washrooms, vending machine room, and lounge are close by on each floor, of the hotel. The functions of each capsule are controlled and monitored by a central computer system and the security is controlled by close circuit TV cameras. The hotels cater mainly to business travellers. The low tariff and vintage locations are the major factors for their popularity. The hotels are well located near major transportation centres in Japan's largest cities.

Airport Hotels : Airport hotels, as the name suggests, are located near the airports primarily to cater to the needs of transit passengers, airport crew as also passengers of delayed or cancelled flights. The various facilities provided in these hotels are designed to offer comfort and convenience to the air travellers. The various services may include parking and shuttle service to and from the airport terminal. The hotels may also provide services for business travellers for organising meetings, conferences and conventions etc.

Space Hotels : Space tourism is probably just another decade or so away. A brand new phenomenon in the hotel stay to be available in space travel would be called 'Skotel'. It would perhaps be the world's first airborne hotel. In the initial stages, space travel may start off as suborbital flights which would mean taking off in a shuttle and staying put in space for a few days. It may limit to flying off from an airport orbiting the earth once and then landing back on it. According to the International Institute of Tourism Studies, space tourism is broadly applied to the concept of paying customers travelling beyond earth's atmosphere. It can include parabolic flight, vertical suborbital flights, orbital flights lasting upto three days or week-long stays at a floating space hotel, including participatory educational, research and entertainment experiences as well as space sports competitions.

Many experts have conceived different designs and ideas regarding the structure of space hotels. Some experts feel that space hotels wouldn't be anything more than clusters of pre-fabricated cylindrical modules. Inside these cylinders there could be lots of fun. Since there would be zero gravity one may find the bar of the hotel merrily perched on the ceiling, while the other guests laze on the ground below. Studies are, however, going ahead on Space Hotel concepts. Some of these concept hotels including one called space Hotel Europe can room around 50 guests. Most travel specialists would advertise them as elevated or uplifted establishments, since space hotels would be above earth hotels simply because of the physical reality of being airborne or floating in space.

Supplementary Accommodation : Supplementary accommodation may be of various types other than the conventional hotel type. Although hotels have been and still are the principal form of accommodation, there has been a growth and development of some other forms in various parts at the world. Supplementary accommodation can be classified on the basis of its location, type of construction, type of management, etc. A study of these indicates that their diversity is a reflection of the specific nature of each one and their names simply indicate various ways in which one and the same function can be fulfilled or a need can be satisfied.

Supplementary accommodation may be described as the premises which offer accommodation, but not the services, of a hotel. Services provided here is minimal and not comprehensive as in the case of hotel establishments.

All establishments under the heading of supplementary accommodation are designed to offer the possibility of stay overnight and meals in return for cash payment per day and on the basis of services provided. The standard of comforts is modest compared to that of a hotel. On the other hand, however, there are certain inherent advantages in this type of accommodation. The biggest advantage is that of price. It is moderately priced. In addition, the atmosphere is informal and there is more freedom with regard to dress, etc. There is also more emphasis on entertainment and sports resulting in increased social contact among the guests.

Supplementary accommodation plays a very important role in the total available tourist accommodation in a country and can cater to both international as well as domestic tourist traffic. In fact, in some countries more tourists utilise this type of accommodation than hotels. In France and Italy as also in some other countries in Europe and elsewhere there are more campers than there are hotel clients. The following are some of the principal forms of supplemental accommodation:

(i) Motel

(ii) Youth Hostel
(iii) Camping Sites
(iv) Pension
(v) Bed and Breakfast Establishments and
(vi) Tourist Holiday Villages.

Motel : The concept of motel and motel-hotel originated in the United States of America. Motel was meant for local motorists and foreign tourists travelling by road. Primarily designed to serve the needs of motorists, motels almost exclusively meet the demand for transit accommodation. They serve the function of a transit hotel except that they are geared to accommodate motor travelling guests for overnight stay. The important services provided by motels include parking, garage facilities, accommodation, restaurant facilities, public catering and recreational facilities. Hence all motels are equipped with filling stations, repair services, accessories, garages, parking space, "elevator service to the automobile, restaurants, etc. There are also equipment and tools available which the guest can use himself if he wishes to repair his vehicle. The price charged for accommodation and meals/refreshments is much cheaper as compared to that in hotels.

Motels are mostly located outside the city limits in the countryside along the main highway and preferably at an important road junction. Since these establishments cater mainly for persons travelling by road, their development is linked with the development of new motorways along which these are necessarily located. Motels are of different types. Some provide just the minimum services while others are well-furnished, with comfortable accommodation and excellent facilities. The accommodation provided is of a chalet type, which is furnished, having a dining hall and a fixed menu. Shopping facilities for travelling public are also provided.

In many countries, especially the United States of America, motel accommodation is ranked with hotel accommodation and subject to general standards applicable to the hotel industry. In countries like Norway, France, Ireland, Turkey, etc., specific legislation has been introduced for motels. This includes requirements for the approval of plans, easy access of cars, minimum capacity, provision of restaurant where necessary, minimum standards for facilities and provision of petrol pump or service station where they exist and model classification standards similar to those for hotels. For instance, in France, there are three categories designated by stars, the classification being based on location, sanitary fittings and collective amenities. An increasingly important segment of the accommodation industry, motels are looked upon as a distinct asset, as these have enabled the industry to meet the changes in travel patterns and personal preferences of the modern day traveller.

Youth Hostels : Youth hostels made their first appearance in Germany in the form of a movement in about the year 1900. The movement which spread rapidly all over the world was based on the need of city youth to travel throughout the country. In order to provide some sort of accommodation and services the dormitories in the inns were equipped with cots, mattresses, sheets and blankets. Large rooms in inns were used as dining and living places providing full board at low cost to the guests. There was also provision of additional kitchen where travellers could prepare their own meals. Since the movement was started with a view to encouraging youth to travel - in order to learn and know more about the country and also to socialise, it had an educational value. As such, no service was provided in the inn. The persons staying in the inn were themselves required to look after the inn. Subsequently, exclusive youth hostel buildings were constructed to accommodate young travellers.

A Youth hostel can be defined as a building which offers clean, moderate and inexpensive shelter to young people exploring their own country or other countries and travelling independently or in groups on holiday or for educational purposes. It is a place where young people of different social backgrounds and nationalities meet and come to know each other. The objective of youth hostels, therefore, is not merely to provide accommodation and board, but also to serve as centres which offer an opportunity to young people coming from different parts of the country, as also young travellers from abroad, to know and understand each other. It is a place of friendship, recreation and out-of-school and college education.

The youth hostels are equipped to accommodate young men and women who travel on foot, by bicycle or other means of locomotion and who, at very little cost, are provided with a place to sleep, eat or to make their own meal. The services provided include accommodation, meals and also recreation. The charges for these services are very modest. The hostels are also equipped to enable the users to prepare their own meals if they so desire. The accommodation provided in the hostels is for a limited number of days.

In most countries, youth hostels are developed and managed by non-commercial organisations whose main aim is the development of youth tourism. Since World War II, the number of such hostels has increased greatly. These hostels are now planned to provide comfortable accommodation as also such other services and facilities which are required by youth. Also the number of those using these hostels has grown tremendously. Many hostels receive an increasing number of groups and organise stays for winter sports or sailing.

The construction of youth hostels is based on certain norms laid down from time to time all over the world. International requirements for these include provision of separate dormitories for men and women, appropriate and clean toilets, washrooms for both men and women, a kitchen where hostelers can prepare their own meals, common rooms, living accommodation for warden and a left-luggage room. There is also a provision of a kitchen where warden and staff can prepare meals to supply to hostelers, separate small room for instructors, a dining room and classroom for school parties and a warden's office. Some youth hostels have playgrounds attached for the use of hostelers.

The International Youth Hostel Federation has laid down certain minimum requirements for accommodation in the youth hostels. These include:

(i) Separate dormitories for men and women with separate entrances;

(ii) Separate toilets and washrooms for men and women with separate entrances;

(iii) A members' kitchen where hostelers can prepare their own meals;

(iv) A common room, separate from members' kitchen, wherever possible;

(v) Living accommodation for warden(s), on the premises wherever possible.

Caravan and Camping Sites : Caravan and camping sites constitute a significant accommodation category in many holiday areas. These are very popular in some European countries as in the United States of America. These are also known as open-air hostels, tourist camps or camping grounds. Camping, originally practised by hikers on foot, is increasingly giving way to car camping. The sites are usually located within the large cities in open spaces. Equipped to receive mobile accommodation in the form of caravans, the camping sites provide facilities for parking, tent pitching, water, electricity, toilet, etc. Though the services provided generally include restaurants, recreational rooms, toilets and at certain places a grocers shop, the type of services often vary from place to place. Some countries have enacted legislation establishing the minimum facilities that must be provided and these include health and sanitation standards, prices to be charged for parking and use of various services and facilities.

Pension : This type of accommodation is very popular in certain European countries. Particularly in Italy, Austria, Germany and Switzerland these establishments are used extensively by the tourists. Pension is also described as a private hotel, a guest house or a boarding house. Catering facilities are optional and are usually restricted to the residents. Many of them stay for longer and definite periods such as a week or a fortnight. The reservation of accommodation is made in advance. Mostly managed by a family, a pension is much cheaper than a hotel.

Bed and Breakfast Establishments : Also known in some countries as apartment hotels and hotel garnis, they represent a growing form of accommodation units catering for holiday as well as business travellers. These establishments provide only accommodation and breakfast but not the principal meals. These are usually located in large towns and cities, along commercial and holiday routes and also resort areas and are used by en route travellers. Some of these are very popular with holidaymakers.

Tourist Holiday Villages : Tourist villages were established in some European countries after World War II. These are situated at warm seasides and in the regions which offer certain facilities for tourists. In Italy and Spain, tourist villages are located in the regions not economically developed, thereby helping the region economically. The villages are mostly promoted by important clubs, social and tourist organisations.

The village complex is a centre of accommodation providing extensive sports and recreation facilities, riding, swimming, tennis, volleyball, football, sauna, mini-golf, badminton, table tennis and yoga. These provide both board and lodging. The atmosphere in these villages is kept as informal as possible. Telephones, radios, newspapers and TV are banned unless there is an emergency. Wallets and other valuables are locked away at the beginning of one's stay. The staff are chiefly educated young people who live on an equal basis with the holiday-makers. The accommodation provided is usually in multiple units and many provide for self-catering. The furnishing provided in the rooms is minimal. The easy mixing of guests is encouraged by the banning of advance booking of tables in the village restaurants. One rarely finds oneself sitting with the same group twice.

The holiday villages are usually based on family units, each providing a convertible living room, bath/shower and sometimes a kitchen. The villages are self-sufficient, providing almost all necessities required by the residents. There is also a small shopping complex where one can buy articles of daily need. The services of a doctor are available. The accommodation is sold for a week or a fortnight at an all-inclusive price. In Spain and Italy, these are classified into three categories according to the services and amenities provided.

Time-share and Resort Condominiums : Through time-share and condominium concepts a tourist has a unique range of options for resort holiday and lodging. In the case of condominiums, a tourist owns a room or a suite within a condominium or hotel complex and uses the same as required by him or it can be rented to other tourists. The owned condominiums usually are within the complex of rooms or suites that are rented as regular hotel or resort rooms. It is difficult of tell the difference between an owned and a rented room.

Time-share on the other hand is a modification of condominium ownership. The units are owned partially. The time-share owner may own one-fifth of a unit thereby sharing the unit's use and costs. In some cases the owner may only purchase a certain set of weeks to use the unit. In other cases, a group of investors may jointly own a property through actual deeds. The time-share title implies that the unit is shared with others throughout the year.

Time-share began in the French Alps during the mid sixties. However, it was in USA that the concept began to take a proper shape. It is said that Time-share was born when distressed real estate developers of United States in the Florida region, could not sell their second homes in the mid-seventies and decided to sell one apartment fifty times over for each week of the year. Holiday time-share brings a number of benefits not only to the buyer and developer but also to the holiday resort areas and the traditional suppliers of services to the holiday industry.

Today, time-share owners have the choice of trading the use of their units with others. This provides the owners a unique opportunity to vacation at comparable prices at destinations throughout the world. May time-share companies are available to help time-share owners locate others interested in exchanging units.

Time-share today has become quite popular with holiday-makers especially with families. It offers high quality accommodation and associated amenities ideal for repeat visitors. It also offers better price and value than a hotel room for extended stays and is a hedge against room rate inflation. Time-share offers flexibility of use and a variety of experiences through exchange options as also peripheral benefits offered through an exchange company.

Regulation of Accommodation : Tourist accommodation is an important component of a tourist plant. As an individual product it is intangible, often bought in advance of its use. The tourist at the time of making purchases thus cannot inspect or accept or reject. Accommodation as such, raises some issues in its development and in its marketing, both as an individual product and as a part of a package. It creates a need for reliable and accurate information for both the tourists and the travel agents, and therefore, may require supervision and control. An individual operator needs to bring information about his accommodation to the tourist before he sets off on his journey and also when he reaches his destination. Similarly the tourist on the other hand, needs to know in detail what accommodation is available at what price in a particular destination from which he can make a choice about where to stay. Schemes of classification, registration and grading of the tourist accommodation are intended to meet these requirements.

The United Nations Conference on International Travel and Tourism held in Rome in the year 1963 also emphasised the need for some sort of regulation of accommodation with a view to safeguard the interests of the users. Considering that special attention should be given to relations between the public authorities and the operators of tourist accommodation facilities, the conference advocated the adoption of a hotel trade charter codifying the regulations applicable to the hotel industry and, in particular, giving official tourist organisations powers enabling them to perform the activities devolving on the state in that field. The conference observed that many states classify tourist hotels or are considering doing so. Acting upon the recommendations put forward by the International Chamber of Commerce, the conference advocated the standardisation of methods of classification and in particular the subdivision of hotels into five categories, each identified by a conventional sign (stars) in conformity with the sets of standards appropriate to different climatic conditions. The conference also considered the question of classifying supplementary means of accommodation such as tourist bungalows and camps.

Registration : The aim of registration is to provide a complete list or register of tourist accommodation within a particular definition. A registration scheme results in an inventory of accommodation which can be kept up-to-date. In order to be comprehensive, it normally has to have statutory legal authority and is administered by a government authority or a statutory body. Because of the wider range of accommodation used by the tourists, a scheme of registration should normally cover all forms of accommodation used by them.

Gradation : Grading separates accommodation into different categories or grades, on the basis of judgements such as standards of amenities and service. A grading scheme provides qualitative judgements on the amenities and facilities of a particular accommodation unit in a form which enables the user to choose the quality of accommodation he requires. This may refer to the physical facilities, food and other services of the establishment, various amenities provided, etc. The establishments are graded individually or collectively by way of giving them numbers, letters or symbols.

Classification : The chief aim of classification is to maintain standardisation of services and security for tourists. By establishing uniform standards of classification, it is easier for all concerned with tourism (tour operators, travel agents, tourist enterprise and tourists themselves) to know exactly what standard of services is offered by each hotel (according to the number of stars) thus leading to more effective uniformity both in statistics and in regulatory and control standards. The adopted scheme envisages that hotel establishments are to be divided into five categories, symbolised by stars, and based on objective standards. The categories are assigned on the basis of two types of requirements:

(i) minimum requirements common to all categories, as stated in the classification scheme, concerning health, sanitary, material and staff standards;

(ii) minimum requirements for each category, expressed as specific conditions for the hotel (as a building), the rooms, additional accommodation, facilities and guest service. The classification scheme is intended as a guide for National Tourism Administrations in their efforts to perfect a classifications system in collaboration with the hotel sector, on the basis of the principles set forth in the scheme. The classification system is to be adopted in a flexible manner so that any establishment failing to comply with a particular, though not fundamental requirement, would not be downgraded provided it complied with all other requirements.

International Hotel Association (IHA) : Founded on 18th March, 1946 in London on the initiative of Societe Suisse des Hoteliers, the International Hotel Association (IHA) replaced the International Hotel Mens Association set up in June 1869 and International Hotel Alliance set up in April 1925. The main aim of the new association was to bring together members who could be of mutual benefit to each other. The IHA was registered by a French Ministerial Decree of 23 September 1949 having its headquarters in Paris.

The priority objectives of IHA include the protection and coordination of hotel interests in their relations with travel agencies who often play an important intermediary role between hotels and clients. Through the IHA/UFTAA Convention, there is a formal codification and confirmation of international practice governing relations between hoteliers and travel agencies. It informs hoteliers on their rights concerning payment, commission, cancellation, late arrival or no-show and relevant compensations.

Membership : IHA has a membership spanning 160 countries, comprising hotels and restaurants whether chains, both national or international, or individual establishments, who wish to participate directly in the Associations activities, even whilst being represented by their National Associations.

In addition, there are hotels and tourist personalities as individual members. Affiliates like hotel schools, training centres, tourist organisations, suppliers and services companies etc. also participate in IHA activities. The Association today represents more than 700,000 hotels and restaurants throughout 160 countries and more than seven million hotel industry wage earners.

There are over 90 National Hotel Association members of the IHA. Each Association has the right to send delegates to vote their numbers being determined by the number of hotels who are members of the Association in the respective country. Independent hotels, which constitute about 80 per cent of IHA membership, are entitled to the numerous services offered to IHA. All members receive a personalised membership card which entities them to 25 per cent discount on accommodation in IHA member hotels.

Objectives and Aims : The aims of IHA include the following:

(i) to federate National Hotel Association of all countries;

(ii) to study problems affecting the international hotel industry and international tourist traffic including re-establishment of free traffic, economic policy for hotels and restaurants, hotel guides, international currency exchange, hotel insurance and conditions of work and personnel;

(iii) to create an international employment service for qualified hotel personnel and for the exchange of apprentices;

(iv) to inform members of international problems concerning hotels; and

(v) to give commercial information concerning travel agencies.

The Structure : The association has a General Congress which meets at least every two years, an Executive Committee consisting of 30 members and a Council having 180 members. The Association is headed by the President and assisted by a Deputy President and five Vice Presidents. There is a General Secretariat responsible for looking after administrative and personnel matters. Planning and Finance Committee looks after all matters pertaining to finances including membership. Publications Committee is responsible for various publications of the association and their distribution. In addition, the following Functional Committees look after various subjects of the Association:

(a) Industry Economic Committee

(b) Sub-Committee on Computerisation

(c) Travel Agencies and Commercial Relations Committee

(d) Seasonal and Resort Hotels Sub-Committee

(e) Legal Committee; and

(f) Labour Relations and Training Committee.

One of the most important activities of IHA is, however, the provision of a wide range of practical services for hoteliers interested in attracting business from all over the world. The services include the following:

> Annual IHA international meetings are held where the most pressing issues confronting the large hotel chains", individual hotel owners, and service and supply companies are addressed. These meetings provide an ideal environment in which members can exchange valuable ideas, promote individual properties, and discuss specific problems and concerns of the industry.

International Hotel Guidebook **:** An annual listing of all IHA members is provided to members free of charge. The guide is an automatic sales tool: used by travel agents, hoteliers, airlines, international corporations and business and professional offices worldwide promoting all the properties and services listed. *Hotels & Restaurants International,* a bimonthly magazine published in the US, with a special IHA section in every issue. This magazine keeps the industry well informed of all the activities of the IHA, its members and councils.

International Bibliography : A publication listing books in western languages concerning hotel-related information, administration, proper management, hotel catering, etc. available to members upon request.

The World Directory of Travel Agents, a valuable reference book for hoteliers, listing 6,000 reliable travel agencies approved by the IHA. All listed agencies must belong to their national association, and must be in business for at least one year.

Debt Recovery Service is available to members upon request. The IHA intervenes and assists member hotels to claim payments overdue from foreign travel agencies.

Statistical Service on Payment Incidents, is a subscription service offered to members. Monthly lists are provided of at least 100 slow-paying travel agencies worldwide. Confidential information concerning travel agents is available upon request.

International Hotel Training and Staff Placement: The IHA brings together hoteliers and distinguished specialists in hotel education. The IHA offers a hotel trainee network that facilitates the mobility and coordination of hotel training worldwide. The network also organises introductions for the placing of upper management.

Documentation Centre: The IHA provides members with a wide and varied range of information on the hotel and tourism industries. For example, the IHA member may obtain lists of hotel publications, information on public utility charges, tariffs and all relevant hotel and industry material.

Address Labels of travel agencies worldwide are available to members for promotion and sales use at a small fee.

IHA Membership Card: This card entitles the member to a 25 per cent discount on accommodations in other IHA member hotels worldwide. It encourages referral business the year round and is a valuable sales tool in low seasons.

Accommodation Volume and Use : The number of rooms that are available to the travelling public within lodging facilities varies from country to country and from region to region. Within a country most of the accommodation units will be located where the demand for these is very big. The demand will be more near the location of tourist attractions both natural or man made. Internationally the demand for accommodation will be more pressing in the regions which receive more tourists. Today Europe and America are the regions which receive maximum share of world tourists and it is here that the largest number of accommodation units are located.

According to World Tourism Organisation (WTO) estimates, or a survey conducted by them, the total capacity of hotels and similar establishments like motels, boarding houses and inns is over 20 million bed places. The largest accommodation capacity is, however, available in the continent Europe which is about 10 million bed places in the hotel industry proper. This constitutes about half of the total bed places available all over the world. The explanation for this is that the demand for both international and domestic tourists in Europe is maximum.

In several European countries, hotel development is concentrated in small and medium-sized hotel constructions. In many countries, within the framework of general expansion of the accommodation sector, the increase in hotel accommodation was outstripped by the increase in supplementary means of accommodation, such as camping and caravan sites, rented rooms, apartments, etc. This type of accommodation has become the main provider of lodging for domestic tourism and has also started to play a very-significant role in international tourism. In America the total capacity of hotels and similar establishments increased significantly in several countries of the regions.

In East Asia and the Pacific region, several countries are currently enjoying a hotel-building boom. In South Asia, the countries of the region are undertaking great efforts to develop the accommodation sector. In the Middle East, hotel construction in the region is mainly concentrated on luxury-class hotels intended chiefly to cater to business travellers. In view of the high profitability, there are many hotel projects which are under construction. In the African region, accommodation facilities are concentrated in the northern part of the continent.

Changing Profile

The accommodation sector has undergone substantial changes in recent years. New developments in tourism and transportation, changes in the organisation of travel and technological innovations are some of the factors which are responsible for these changes. In addition, increasing consumer demand among tourists, due in turn to the improvement in living standards and economic conditions, has also changed the profile of the accommodation sector. All the above factors seem to have influenced the structure of the hotel industry as a whole. The tendency among middle-income groups to take a holiday at any time of the year has encouraged accommodation operators to offer novel kinds of arrangements which are now available in addition to traditional hotel accommodation.

New types of accommodation, particularly holiday villages suitable for family-type tourists, condominiums and apartment houses, private villas and camping facilities have proved very successful and to a certain degree are replacing traditional hotels and boarding houses. These changes reflect changes in demand with new, often younger, groups entering the international travel market and also new approaches to the problem of providing facilities in every competitive industry with a highly seasonal demand. The probable future developments in the accommodation sector were the subject of study undertaken in WTO's research programme. Some conclusions which emerge from the study are as follows:

(a) a significant growth in accommodation supply will continue to be contributed by chain operators, including airlines. This expansion will result mainly from the further development of management contracts and franchise agreements;

(b) there will be a continuing move towards the further diversification of accommodation. The development of budget accommodation, covering budget hotels, and also supplementary means of accommodation, is likely to continue as mass tourism stimulates new demands for competitively- priced accommodation;

(c) rising building and operating costs, growing environment and conservation pressures, as well as the need to keep staffing levels at a minimum, will influence design and construction of accommodation units;

(d) the standard of accommodation will continue to rise. Demand for recreational and sporting facilities will increase in both business and leisure accommodation;

(e) advances in technology will both influence the traditional construction methods, for example, more frequent use of prefabricated building techniques, as well as traditional methods of hotel operations.

In recent times, several environmental problems have come to be recognised in the accommodation sector. Several environmentalists as well as users of accommodation are demanding that environmental issues associated with accommodation industry should be addressed properly. Tourists visit different places of tourist interest and consume various products they buy. The consequences of the pressure of consumers on tourist services results in putting pressure on the environment. However, with few exceptions, industry owners are taking various steps to address the environmental issue in its proper perspective.

The various policies for the accommodation industry cover areas like environmental protection, energy conservation, waste reduction, emission reduction, recycling of waste, reduction of chemical usage and awareness and education of employees and the guests about environment. The best possible arrangement is that the commitment for environment should have full support of the top management and that it should start with them. It should be an integral part of management practice and be communicated to all personnel. Once this is agreed, corporate policies can be implemented through management techniques such as environmental audits. A proper and formal monitoring system that can be adopted to achieve the best possible results.

Hotel Industry

Definition : "Hotel" or "Inn" is defined by British law as a "place where a bonafide traveller can receive food and shelter, provided he is in a position to pay for it and is in a fit condition to be received." Hence, a Hotel *must provide* food (and beverage) and lodging to travellers on payment and has, in turn, the right to refuse if the traveller is drunk, disorderly, unkempt, or is not in a position to pay for the services.

Origin : The hotel industry is, perhaps, one of the oldest commercial endeavours in the world. The first inns go back to the sixth century B.C. and were the products of the urge to travel, spurred by the invention of the 'wheel'. The earliest inns were ventures by husband and wife teams who provided large halls for travellers to make their own beds and sleep on the floor. They also provided modest wholesome food, thirst-quenchers like wine, port, ale, etc. and stabling facilities. Entertainment and recreation were provided by the host's wife or his wench. The entire cooking service, and recreation was provided by the husband and wife team and his family.

These conditions prevailed for several hundred years. The advent of the Industrial Revolution in England brought ideas and progress in the business of inn-keeping. The development of railways and steamships made travelling more prominent. The Industrial Revolution also changed travel from social or government travel to business travel. There was a need for quick and clean service.

The lead in hotel-keeping was taken by the emerging nations of Europe, especially Switzerland. It was in Europe that the birth of an organised hotel industry took place in the shape of chalets and small hotels which provided a variety of services and were mainly patronised by the aristocracy of the day.

In early England, public houses were normally called "inns" or "taverns". Normally, the name "inn" was reserved for the finer establishments catering to the nobility and clergy. The houses frequented by the common man were known as "taverns". In France, a similar distinction was made with the finer establishments known as "hoteleries" and the less pretentious houses called "cabarets". The word "hostel" was used after the Norman invasion derived from "host". The "hosteler" was the head of the hostel whereas the same position was called the "innkeeper" in England. The word "hotel" was used in England in about 1760 after a passage of over 80 years. In America lodging houses were called "inn" or "coffee house".

The real growth of the modern hotel industry took place in the USA beginning with the opening of City Hotel in New York in 1794. This was the first building specially erected for hotel purposes. This eventually led to great competition between different cities and resulted in frenzied hotel building activity. Some of the finest hotels of the USA were built in this era, but the real boom in hotel building came in the early twentieth century. This period also saw the beginning of chain operations under the guidance of E.M. Statler. It involved big investments, big profits and trained professionals to manage the business.

The Depression in 1930 had a disastrous effect on the hotel industry. It was felt that the hotel would never recover; but the outbreak of World War II brought a tremendous upsurge. This prosperity continued through the war years into the fifties, when two new concepts emerged:

(1) Motels

(2) International chain operations

While the growth of motels was restricted to the North

American continent, international chain operations spread into all continents. Individual entrepreneurs found themselves crushed in this race for a multi-dimensional, multi-national industry. International chains could provide the expertise technology and marketing thrust that individual owners could not provide. Individual owners thus merged themselves with large international chains such as Sheratons, Hiltons, Hyatt, Holiday Inn, Ramada Inn, etc. These international chains provided the following services to individual owners:

1. Partnership—sharing equity and profits.
2. Franchise—providing "name" and "association" and marketing services in exchange for franchise and marketing fees.
3. Management—expertise in management, professional managers, technicians, manuals, systems, etc. on the basis of management fees and share of profits as "incentive" payment.
4. Marketing—active selling, chain benefits, reservation tie-ups, etc. on payment for marketing fees and incentive payment.

Today's hotel caters to all the needs and wishes of a guest and the future holds promise for a further mushrooming of modern hotels.

Types of Hotels

Hotels may be categorised depending upon factors such as:

1. Location
2. Number of rooms
3. Type of plan room rates that are quoted
4. Type of clientele
5. Length of guest stay
6. Facilities that it offers

Categorisation by Locations

Downtown Hotel : It is located in the heart of the city within a short distance of the business centre, shopping areas, theatres, public buildings, etc. Rates in these hotels are normally high due to their locational advantage and also due to the fact that the rate of return on investment (ROI) computed on these capital intensive hotels is substantially high. Normally business clientele prefer such hotels.

Suburban Hotel : Located in the suburbs, it has the advantage of quieter surroundings. Rates quoted are moderately low. Such hotels are ideal for limited budget travellers and also organisations who find the quiet setting ideal for conferences, seminars, educational programmes, etc.

Resort Hotel : This type of hotel is located in the hills or at beaches. It is mainly patronised by vacationers. Basic facilities are provided and the rates offered are often on American Plan, i.e. room plus all meals included.

Airport Hotel : As the name suggests, these hotels are situated at the airport and are ideal for transit passengers who have only a few hours in the city making it impossible for them to stay in a downtown hotel. Rates are on European plan, i.e. charges for room only.

Motel : This term is derived from the phrase, "motor hotels", which are located principally on highways. They provide modest boarding and lodging to highway travellers. The length of stay is usually overnight, thus rates quoted are on European plan. i.e. room only.

Inns : They are smaller in size with modest board and lodging facilities. They may be located anywhere within or outside the city. They are the forerunners of the modern motel.

Categorisation by Number of Rooms : The capacity of a hotel in terms of the number of rooms is a yardstick for the categorisation of the hotel by "Size". Hotels with 25 rooms and less may be termed "small"; those with 25 to 100 may be called "medium"; those with 101 to 300 are called "large". Hotels with over 300 rooms which are very common these days, may be termed "very" large.

Categorisation by Type of Plan : Hotels are categorised according to the type of plan, they offer. We thus have hotels on

European plan. American plan or Continental Plan for a discussion of plans. These plans are decided by the hotel on a variety of factors including type of clientele, length of stay and average customer preference.

Categorisation by Type of Clientele : We often hear in hotel parlance, the terms such as Group hotel, Commercial hotel, Family hotel, etc. This categorisation is based on the type of patronage. Group hotels cater to groups and thus their rates would be on American Plan. Commercial hotels cater to mostly businessmen and are on European Plan. A family hotel would again be on American plan. Such hotels are normally situated in resort cities.

Categorisation by Length of Guest Stay : This categorisation of hotels further be divided into three sub-groups: (1) Transient hotels where a guest can register for a day or even less (airport hotels could be termed thus); (2) Residential hotels where guests stay for a minimum period of one month the hotel signs a detailed lease with the customer; (3) Semi-residential hotels which incorporate the features of both the transient and residential hotels.

Categorisation by Facilities the Hotel Offers : Facilities offered by hotels may be the most important criteria for classifying hotels. Some countries adopt the star rating system. Thus, a five star hotel which is the highest rating will provide facilities such as central airconditioning, attached bathrooms with hot and cold water, channel music, wall-to-wall carpeting, shopping arcade, health club, swimming pool, sports facilities and a variety of restaurants and bars including a coffee shop, speciality restaurant, grill room, etc. These are just some of the criteria for star rating. Certain such facilities are denied as the star rating of the hotels goes lower and lower. They may be excluded for a variety of reasons such as cost, level of business, etc.

2

The Hospitality

Hospitality is treating people like you would want to be treated when you are travelling. In other words, it means making a tourist feel totally welcome as not only your guest, but also the guest of the complete family of the Hotel. Hospitality is genuine smiling face.

Hospitality can be termed as deliberate, planned and sustained effort to establish and maintain mutual understanding between an organization and public i.e. business of making and keeping friends, and promoting an atmosphere of better understanding.

Very frequently we hear phrases like "He is always hospitable to visitors", "We are grateful to friends for their hospitality in putting us up while we were on holiday", "She is so inhospitable that she grudges giving us any thing to eat or drink when we visit her" etc. All such statements are suggesting the positive or negative attitude of welcome towards visitors, friends or strangers. Hospitality activity covers everything i.e. providing attentive and courteous services, facilities and amenities to a traveller, meeting and greeting him at the door, providing efficient and caring service of food and beverage to him in the room i.e. providing "A Home away from Home", and making his visit a memorable and pleasant experience.

Reception, welcome and, in general, the treatment of a guest or a stranger in most friendly manner is Hospitality. In most of the countries all over the world a guest is received with a great amount of courtesy and warmth and is provided with entertainment. The basic concept of Hospitality is to make the guest feel that he has come amongst friends and that GUESTS ARE ALWAYS WELCOME. Although the basic concept of hospitality has remained the same, yet with the passage of time and development of technology and science, the needs and wants of travellers have changed greatly thus providing numerous services and facilities in terms of accommodation and other basic needs such as food and beverages. In olden days kings, lords, maharajas, landlords and sometimes the panchayats etc. used to provide food and shelter to travellers and their animals free of charges and it used to be a benevolent activity. But with the passage of time it has not only remained a benevolent activity but has become a flourishing business too.

A part of hospitality activity is being attentive, alert, and cordial with the guest without forcing yourself and your ideas on to him; at the same time being very polite and cooperative. All those working in hospitality industry have one common objective— "Creating an image of friendly reception and treatment" for guests and visitors.

As front office personnel, the hotel staff, in order to provide hospitality should make his guests feel at home and use pleasant tone of voice smilingly, offer his assistance wherever possibly can be provided. Don't ignore the guest, and don't be abrupt no matter how busy you are: anticipate his needs and wants and provide the same without his asking them.

As a hotelier, keep on checking the hospitality attitude of your organization. Make a check list and be sure that you and your staff are fulfilling each and every point of the check list. The check list may include areas such as front desk and lobby, etc. Make sure that the front desk is always kept clean, orderly and well lighted. Even the stationery used is so designed that it does not create confusion and clearly indicates how it is to be filled in, and is inviting. The lobby is kept clean and furniture kept at proper place. Lighting system is soft and appealing. The welcome spirit that the guest is looking for is there. Floor covering, pictures, furnishing etc. are appealing, attractive and aesthetically designed.

Further, the check list should include the intangibles such as training of the staff and willingness and positive attitude of the staff. The arriving guest is always greeted with a smile and proper salutation to show interest in his trip and his well being.

Historical Backdrop

Early travellers were either warriors or traders or people in search of knowledge and there were no hotels. Warriors and conquerors pitched their tents for accommodation while traders and persons travelling for knowledge placed a high value on hospitality and sometimes traded their merchandise for lodging.

Inn keeping can be said to be the first commercial enterprise and hospitality one of the first service for which money was exchanged. Inns of the Biblical times offered only a cot or a bench in the corner. Guests stayed in large communal rooms with no sanitation and privacy. The rates were, of course, reasonable. The company was rough. Travellers shared the same quarters with their horses and animals.

King James Version of Bible mentions that Mary and Joseph were turned away by a Bethlehem innkeeper, because there was "no room at the inn". According to Biblical scholars the innkeeper may have meant that the room was unsuitable for a woman about to give birth to a child. At that time, and probably for several centuries after that, men and women shared the same accommodation accompanied by their horses and livestock. The stable where Mary and Joseph spent the night was probably almost as comfortable as an inn and at the same time certainly more private than the inn itself.

In the 3rd century AD, the Roman Empire developed an extensive network of brick paved roads throughout Europe and Asia Minor, and a chain of roadside lodges was constructed along the major thoroughfare from Spain to Turkey.

Till the Industrial Revolution of the 1700s, no significant improvement was made in the inns and taverns and they were not very suitable for aristocrats. To accommodate wealthy travellers, luxurious structures were constructed with private rooms, individual sanitation and comforts of an European castle. These elegant new establishments adopted the French word for mansion—'Hotel'. Their rates were beyond the reach of an ordinary person.

In America early inns were modelled after European taverns with sleeping quarters shared by two or more guests.

Herman Melville in his novel *Moby Dick* has mentioned about a seaman who checked into a room of a nineteenth century inn and next morning woke up to find out that he was sharing the bed with a cannibal. Sharing beds was a very common practice in early American and European inns. Throughout the 1800s American innkeepers improved their services and continued to build larger and more amply equipped properties and most of these properties were located near seaport towns.

The tendency of Americans to travel more provided an inspiration to lodging operators. The nation's democratic spirit also led to the development of comfortable and sanitary lodging within the reach of an ordinary person.

Significant Service

Basically for all those who are away from their home, hospitality industry provides services. Hospitality industry consists of all those businesses and institutions that provide food and lodging—such as hotels, motels, lodges, inns, cruise ships and restaurants etc. To some extent it also includes the airlines industry. In a broad sense, any group engaged in tourism, entertainment, transportation and lodging are covered under hospitality.

Hospitality industry is a part of travel and tourism industry. Early travellers were mostly warriors, businessmen, scholars in search of knowledge or people in search of occupation. Mostly warriors would pitch their tents for accommodation while businessmen would look for a comfortable and safe place, and would often pay through their merchandise or cash to people providing them accommodation and food. The poor people travelling to far off places in search of job or occupation were provided the facilities of food and accommodation free of charges. As per some authentic sources, to facilitate travel throughout Western Europe a highway was constructed in 312 B.C. Travel could be done on this highway by chariots. Later in 117 AD this roadway was reconstructed and covered a distance of nearly 50,000 miles.

Hospitality business now is both profit making as well as non-profit making. For example, commercial hotels are profit making while canteens, cafeterias and religious catering outlets such as *langars* and *bhandaras* are non-profit making.

Hospitality industry provides services which are need oriented and the services vary with the needs. For example, the needs of a business executive shall be a business hotel while the needs of a student is generally a youth hostel.

Traditional ways of providing hospitality in our country varies from place to place. In Jammu and Kashmir, Kashmiri Pandits, who are very God-fearing people, consider guests as epitome of God almighty Himself and welcome the guest by a *rangoli* called *Vyog* patterned on their door-steps out of flowers and leaves. When the guests come, the host takes a glass of water and touch it on their forehead, so as to drive all evil spirits away from them. A special herb called *Isbandh* is also touched on the forehead and then burnt in the *Kangri.* The head of the Dogri family, another community of Jammu, goes to the door of the house to welcome the guest. The head female member of the family performs *aarti* of the guest and puts up a *tilak* on the forehead of the guest. Every day in the southern part of the country, ladies make *rangoli* of rice, flowers and flour etc. It is believed that by doing so they are inviting guests and giving a message that the house is open to welcome guests. Greeting guests with folded hands, touching their feet in respect, *aarti, puja,* garlanding, applying *tilak and* ringing of bells, are numerous other ways of providing warm reception and welcome—and hence hospitality—in various parts of our country. Beating of drums, *dhols,* blowing of trumpets, exotic dances and shows such as puppetry etc. are all different ways of expressing warm hospitality in our country.

In different parts of the world, traditional style hospitality is provided. For example, ladies decorated with flowers greet the guests in Honolulu. In some countries, local people gather to welcome visitors at airports. Providing shoeshine service for every guest in the morning in a hotel in Bangkok is a part of welcome to the guests. In one of the hotels in Mauritius, after the dinner service is over the staff collects in the dining area and sings local songs in the honour of the guests. Memorizing the names of the guests and addressing them by their names is another way of providing hospitality in one of the Traditional Style Hospitality for Visitors hotels in France. Singing melodious songs at the time of departure of a guest is done in one of the resorts in Fiji.

All the above mentioned examples along with many others reflect the concept of hospitality provided by highly trained and experienced staff. Through their sincere efforts every guest feels like a VIP and a welcome syndrome is generated.

The past, present and future of the hospitality industry are linked together. Comfortable and sanitary lodging was once considered the exclusive privilege of the wealthy only, but with the rise of industry and democracy, hospitality has now become available to common men also. Hospitality has both influenced and is being influenced by cultural, social and economical changes in society. Hospitality business tends to satisfy human needs and also play an important role in the satisfaction of social needs such as belongingness, longingness, love, esteem and status.

Hospitality Market : Hospitality has a very vast market. All those who have stayed in hotels or have plans to stay in hotels or any other lodging establishment can be put under hospitality market. Hence all travellers including tourists, visitors, businessmen, leisure travellers, pilgrims and company executives etc. can be the hospitality market. Depending upon the purpose of travel people can be classified under either *commercial hospitality market* or *leisure hospitality market*.

Hotel : Common Law states that a "Hotel is a place where all who conduct themselves properly, and who being able to pay and ready to pay for their entertainment, are received, if there be accommodation for them, and who without any stipulated engagement as to the duration of their stay or as to the rate of compensation, are while there, supplied at a reasonable cost with their meals, lodging and other services and attention as are necessarily incident to the use as a temporary home."

A hotel may be called as an establishment where primary business is to provide to the general public lodging facilities and which may also furnish one or more of the various services such as food, beverage, laundry, uniformed services etc. Hence, hotel can also be called as home multiplied by commercial activities.

As per the *Reader's Digest Dictionary* the term 'Hotel' refers to 'a house of entertainment of travellers'.

According to the *Encyclopaedia Britannica* the word 'Hotel' is of ancient origin, but its use in English for a house offering lodging and food for travellers is recent. The Hostlers of London took the name of Inn-keeping in 1473. The word 'Hostler' or 'Ostler' having come to mean an inn servant.

The term 'Hotel' was used in England in about 1760. Hotel or inn is defined by British law as a "place where a bonafide traveller can receive food and shelter, provided he is in a position to pay for and is in a fit condition to be received".

In legal terminology a hotel is an inn and is required under common law to offer to its visitors lodging, food and protection to their baggage. Hotel service is generally based on these three fundamental necessity of life. In addition to these a modern hotel provides its visitors many luxuries of modern urban city living, all under one roof.

Inns

Public houses in early times in England were called inns. Normally the term 'Inn' was meant for the finer establishments catering to nobilities and clergy. In France these were called 'Hoteleries'.

Taverns

The house frequented by common man were known as taverns. The less important establishments in France were called 'CABARETS'.

Hostel

Derived from the word 'Host' and was used very late. The head of the hostel was called 'HOSTELER' in French, while in England he was called 'Inn Keeper'.

Evolution and Development

Early history of accommodation for travellers can be traced back to the Greek word 'Xenia', which not only meant hospitality but also the protection given to a traveller from discomforts. The city was bound to offer hospitality. In Sparta city, although due to rigorous customs visitors were not encouraged, yet goddess Athena was considered as protector of strangers and hence her name was 'Xenia Athena'.

In this period travellers were mainly diplomats, philosophers, intellectuals and researchers. Guests were invited to stay with noblemen. In ancient Olympia, buildings constructed with the aim to accommodate strangers can be seen. They were called 'Leonidio' and were built in 4th century B.C. The concept of hospitality can also be drawn back to ancient times. Mention of it is found in 'Iliad' and 'The Odyssey' by Homer.

Hotel-keeping can also be traced back to many centuries and its evolution through the ages has been brought about by Britain's economical and industrial changes and developments.

During the seventh and eighth centuries, it was the monasteries that supplied hospitality to strangers and, as no charge was made for the accommodation, all travellers were expected to contribute according to their means to the Abbey funds. As more people began to travel they grouped themselves together, not only for company, but for mutual protection from highwaymen and robbers. Consequently, travellers arrived in groups at a monastery and it was often difficult to accommodate them all. To overcome this, separate lodging houses called 'Inns' (a Saxon word) were built. The word 'Inn' came to mean a 'Lodging House' and until the passing of the Hotel Proprietors Act in 1956, it was the legal term for 'Hotel' and hotel proprietors were legally referred to as 'Common Innkeepers'. 'Common' in this sense referred to Common Law.

In the thirteenth and fourteenth centuries, manor houses, being hospitable places, willingly gave accommodation to travellers. As no payment was expected, travellers tipped the servants as a 'thank you' for the generous hospitality received—thus the practice of tipping was born.

When high taxes crippled the generosity and hospitality of the owners of the manor houses, many became commercial inns. During Elizabeth the First's reign, posting houses were established and travellers, in addition to getting refreshment were able to change horses before continuing their journey.

The turn of the century saw an era that was called the 'Belle Epoch' when the grand and luxurious hotels flourished. A few hotels are still operating today. In London and some other cities attempts have been made to recapture some of the grandeur of the past era in the making of modern hotels, and bring back the memories the grand hotels of olden days.

The next stage in the cycle of evolution of the hotel industry was the coming of the motor car. It enabled people to visit those parts of the country not reached by railways. This gave birth to inland resorts and the hotel industry began to flourish.

International air travel has helped create the modern 'stop-over' hotel. With the increase in this form of travel, the number of hotels built close to airports has multiplied.

Another trend in Hotel-keeping is the motel which is the twentieth-century version of the old 'Coach Inn'. People travelling the country by car, stopping overnight here and there, require not only refreshment for themselves, but also safe parking for their cars. Post Houses, developed by the Trust Houses Forte Group are in fact the modern version of the old coaching inns.

An Account of the Development and Growth of Hotel Industry.

Hotel industry has followed the path of the traveller

- Travel by foot
- Travel by animal
- Rest for both (rest houses, monasteries and inns)

Inn-keeping

- An outgrowth of man's urge to travel. Roads used by merchants and couriers.
- Believed started 12,000 years ago.
- Concept of hospitality mentioned in writings dating back to Greece, ancient Rome and Biblical times.
- 6th century B.C. (Establishment of money)
- Rest stops were made near or accessible to water.

Rest Houses

- All along 'Roman Highway' (for troops, civilians and merchants).

- Later 'Coach Inns' were brought by stage coaches and travellers were put in 'Hostelries.'

In Florence (Italy) 1282

- It is believed a rest house was build here.

Paris (1312)

- It is believed a hotel in true classical sense was built in this year.

Early Inns

- Fairly clean.
- Self service unit (guest making their own bed).
- Small part of a self dwelling unit.
- Run by unreputed and unprogressive persons.
- Unheated rooms, straw beds for nobilities and stone beds for servants.
- Protection from robbers and pirates.

Pascal (1650)

- Cafe and coffee house were opened by him in Paris and London respectively.

Industrial Revolution (1750-1820)

- English inns—finest in the world.
- Development centered in and around London.

David Low (English Inn)

- English inn—was opened in London.

Hotel de Henri IV

- Built in Nantes in 1788 for a sum of £7500 (one of the first European hotels). It had 60 rooms.

Francis Tavern (1783)

- General George Washington gave farewell party to his top ranking officers here.

Colonial Inns

- Early inns were located at seaports and were established in their mother country style.

- Sleeping on floor, feet towards fire and head on rolled coat with a dozen or more people of both sexes sleeping together.
- Quick cold water bath in an outside basin.
- Use of communal towel.

Charlemagne Laws

- Free accommodation for travellers and free food bonus to travellers for 3 nights at one place in a continuous time period.

European Inns

- Formal atmosphere and patronized by aristocrats.
- Out of reach of common public.
- Mainly for aristocrats only.

American Inns

- U.S. assumed leadership after 1850. More progressive inns were used for gatherings, court of law, schools and town meetings etc. and the Massachusettes passed a law - "Penalty on towns that did not provide these facilities".
- Inns based on equalitarian enjoyment concept with 'informal' atmosphere.
- Informal atmosphere.
- Accommodation for all who could pay.
- Developed faster because of the
  - (i) Free and informal nature of Americans
  - (ii) Their Pioneering spirit and
  - (iii) Their Love of travelling

Growth of Organised Hotel Industry

- Switzerland and other emerging nations of Europe helped in more organized growth of hotel industry.
- Concept of small hotels and chalets started from Switzerland.
- Family hotels i.e. run by the family members and were called "Mom & Pop" in England.

Invention of Railways

- By the middle of 19th century brought in railway refreshment rooms.

Just before World War I

- Many fine hotels were made at resorts of France (Vichy and Evian), Germany (Baden-Baden) and Italy (Monte Catine) etc. and summer resorts of French and Italian Riviera. U.S. Became the leader in hotel industry.

First Building Created Specially for Hotel

- With 'City Hotel' (73 rooms) at 115 Broadway, New York in 1794 the U.S. became the leader in hotel industry.
- The hotel became obsolete within 15 years and was converted into an office.
- Later, hotels were made in Boston, Baltimore and Philadelphia.

Boston Tea Party

- The famous Boston Tea Party was planned in Green Dragon Tavern.

Tremont House

- A first class hotel was made in Boston in 1829.
- Provided private guest rooms. Doors with lock. A wash bowl with water pitcher. Free soap. Bell boy service.
- Closed after 20 years for renovations.

Thomas Cook (1860)

- Started railway coupons.

By the end of 19th Century

- Many elegant hotels such as 'Waldorf Astoria' in New York, Denvels Brown Palace, San Francisco Palace, Palmers House in Chicago, Planters House in St. Louis, etc. were made.

Cesar Ritz (1889)

- Introduced luxury hotels such as Savoy, Carlton and Hyde Park hotels in England.
- Started Gordon Hotels in London.

Sir George Reeves Smith

- Took over Savoy from Ritz and named it Savoy London.
- Also managed Metropole, London.

Berkley and Claridges

- Two famous chains emerged in England.

Sir Isador Salmon

- Chairman, J. Lyons & Company, started Cumberland, Strand and Regent Palace under Popular Hotel Company, London.

Fredrick Gordon (Former Solicitor)

- Built Holborn Restaurant

Sir Blundel Maple (Furniture Manufacturer)

- Fredrick Gordon and Sir Blundel Maple became partners and launched two companies.
- Gordon Hotels, 1890 and Fredrick Hotels Ltd., 1899.

Ellsworth, M. Statler

- Started a new chain and made his first hotel Buffalo Statler on 18th Jan. 1908.
- Gave the slogan, "Room and a bath for a dollar and a half. Free newspaper, circulating ice water and full length mirror were provided.

Conrad N. Hilton (Born in St. Antorio, Mexico)

- Purchased a hotel called Mobley in Cisco (Texas) somewhere around 1920.
- Opened a company Hilton Hotels Corp. in 1946.
- Purchased Statler chain in 1954.

1910-1920

- Period of relative inactivity.
- Then came N.Y. Pennsylvania (Largest hotel of that time).

1927

- Stevens Hotel (3000 Rooms). Now named Chicago Hilton, was made.

- Then came Pierre Hotel, N.Y., a very famous hotel of its time.

1930

- U.S. Depression. Affected hotel industry in particular and occupancy fell down to nearly 50%, and 85% hotels went into liquidation. This period was useful to hotel chains such as Hilton and Sheraton etc. who acquired properties from out of business hoteliers.

1940

- Situation improved and outbreak of World War II.

1950

- New concepts such as motels, boatels, floatels, rotels and loatels etc. developed.

Second World War

- Many trained staff joined army hence standards of service lowered. However occupancy improved with mass movement to approximately 90%.

1952

- Kemmons Wilson formed 'Holiday Inn' chain and first Holiday Inn was made in 1952 at Memphis-Tennesse.

1. *Motels:* Motels or motor hotels were born during this period. More and more American families travelled by their own automobiles. Moreover, habits, tastes and desires underwent a considerable change. A new mode of informality had come into the American way of life. Suddenly there was a way out to eliminate formal dress, tipping and parking problems. The rooms were well furnished in a modern way, wall-to-wall carpeting was provided, and T.V., a swimming pool and the convenience of one's own transportation was an added attraction.
2. *Boatels:* These are hotels on boats, sometimes named as houseboats.
3. *Floatels:* Hotels on ships giving the facilities and conveniences of a luxury hotel.
4. *Roatels:* These are hotels on wheels. A limited number of

rooms or cabins are there for couples. All conveniences of guests are looked into.

5. *Loatels:* Refers to 5-star de-luxe properties with the facility of helicopter landing on the terrace.

1960

- Development of Atrium Hotels of Hyatt.
- Many individual owners merged themselves with large chains such as Sheratons, Hiltons, Hyatt, Holiday Inns, Ramada Inns, etc. for franchise by paying a fee and then they could use the name, logo, reservation systems, national and international advertisement and operation manuals.
- Budget Hotel/Motels: In the later part of 1960s hostelries offered accommodation at prices significantly lower than the prevailing rates of first class motor-hotels by incorporating three important factors as follows.

Lower Initial Investment Cost (due to the following)

(i) *Smaller Guest Room :* 250 sq ft. as against 335 sq. ft. Less expenses on land (1.6 acre of land as compared to 2.5 acre for a 100 room hotel), decoration etc.

(ii) *Minimum Public Space:* Cutting down on large executive offices, large lobbies etc.

(iii) Simple and no frills designs.

Operating Efficiency

(i) *Compact Facilities :* Less time required to clean and maintain and less power consumed for heating and lighting.

(ii) *Fewer Guest Services :* Elimination of valet services etc.

High Volume

(i) *Price Location:* Reduction in price increases the business volume. Many budget hotels are situated next or adjacent to higher price hotels to attract price conscious travellers.

(ii) *Value:* The budget hotel provides clean, good quality guest room, comfortable bed, full baths, colour T.V., carpeting, standard furniture and fixtures, wall covering, bedspreads and cheerful drapes etc.

1970s Hotel Boom : Reminiscent of the 1920s boom, the hotel industry experienced the start of construction boom in the 1970s. Hilton, Sheraton and Westin Corp. opened convention oriented hotels. Airport hotels location also appeared in 1970s and also the Marriott location of major properties outside of central city area in the same year. Large amount of finances were made available by money lenders particularly by REIT (Real Estate Investment Trust).

Readily available franchise resulted in over building many poorly located and undercapitalized properties with inexperienced owners.

(i) Later there was energy crisis that curtailed travel.

(ii) Inflation caused construction cost and interest rate go very high.

(iii) Recession curtailed the business trips, conferences and conventions.

(iv) Marginal properties could not pay the mortgage amount and the lenders became owners. They either hired experienced hoteliers or contracted professional management companies to assume operational responsibilities. Since then a lot of changes in technological and management approach have taken place and today's hotel industry is progressing day by day. International business is rapidly developing and with this a lot of business executives are travelling out. Modern hotels are developing as per the needs and wants of the tourist and business class guests. Many international hotel chains such as Inter Continental, Sheraton, Park Royal, Hilton, Trust House Forte, Holiday Inn, Ramada Inns, Meridien, Sofitel, SRS Hotels, Utell International, Howard Jonsons, Wolfe International, Hyatt, Golden Tulip, Marriott, American International Hotel & Travelodge, Quality Inns, Accor, Imperial, Motel 6, CEDOK, Club Mediterranean, Red Roof Inns, Friendship Inn, Red Carpet Inn, Western International Hotel, United Inn, Super 8 Motels & Topeka Inns and a lot more have emerged from time to time.

Great Firsts in Hotel Industry

(Some of the important developments in U.S. Hotel Industry)

1846: Central heating

1859: Elevator

1881: Electric lights (2 years after patent)

1907: In-room telephones (31 years after invention)

1910: American Hotel Association (Now AHMA) began

1927: Radio in room (21 years after invention)

1940: Air cooling (Mostly in public areas)

1950: Electric elevator

1958: Free television

1964: Holiday Inn reservation system with centralized computer

1965: Message light on telephone

1965: Initial F.O. systems followed by room status

1970: Colour T.V. (Invented in 1954)

1970 (Early) : E.C.R. (Electronic Cash Register)

1970 (Mid) : POS. system and key less locks

1973 : Free in-room movies (Sheraton)

1983 : In-room personal computers

Landmarks in the Growth of Hotel Industry

1650 : Pascal opened a cafe in Paris and Coffee House in London.

1794 : City Hotel (73 rooms) at 115 Broadway, New York. First building specially made for a hotel.

1829 : Tremont House. Adam and Eve of modern hotel industry was opened at Boston (170 Rooms)

1889 : Cesar Ritz introduced luxury hotels such as Savoy, Carlton and Hyde Park hotels in England.

1890-1899 : Fredrick Gordon and Sir Blundel Maple launched Gordon Hotels and Fredrick Hotels Ltd.

Late 19th Century : Famous Waldorf Astoria in New York

18.1.1908 : Buffalo Statler by Ellsworth Statler in U.S. Considered to be the birth of commercial hotels.

1927 : Stevens Hotel in Chicago, later renamed as Hilton Hotel (3000 rooms) :

1950 : 2 new concepts (a) Motels and (b) International chain operations :

Hotel Rossia or : Moscow (Remained largest hotel of world for quite sometime) : Rossiya

West Inn Stanford : Singapore (Remained tallest building for quite sometime) :

1930 depression in : Decline in hotel industry world economy :

World War Period : Upsurge in hotels :

An example of Hotel Advertisement and Tariff Card in 19th Century England is given on the next page.

Growth in India

In India too the development of hotel industry is closely linked to travel. In India travel was mainly on animals (mule, horse and camel) and for rest during their travel at strategic points *Dharmashalas, Sarais, Chaupals* of *Panchayats, Chowltry* (in South India) and temples and religious places were provided by rich people such as Rajas, Kings, Zamindars etc. Usually free accommodation and food for travellers was given. During medieval period it was mandatory for the state authorities to provide food and shelter to the wayside traveller.

Musafir Khanas and Sarais : These developed during the Muslim period. Many famous and well known *musafir khanas* and *sarais* were made in the Sindh province during the Arab invasion, and also at Peshawar and Lahore. Muhammad Tughlak and Feroz Shah Tughlak made inns in the northern part of India. Later, Sher Shah Suri, Akbar, Jahangir and Shah Jahan made inns in different parts of India. Jahan Ara Begum built a very beautiful *sarai* at Sahibabad (Begamabad) and its beautiful garden is still there and is called Queens Garden or Azad Park. The fountain in the upper garden has the inscription *"Gar Firdaus Bar Rui Zaminast-Haminhastu, Haminhastu, Haminhastu"*.

Delhi has always been traditionally hospitable, and we find overwhelming evidence of this in the innumerable *sarais* and rest houses of this ancient city. Delhi has been built seven times in the area spanning from Mehrauli to Shahjahanabad. Delhi is believed to be the oldest living capital of the world. During their reigns rulers of Delhi built *sarais* throughout their kingdom for the comforts of travellers. The *sarais* afforded a *baoli* or a *talab* (a bathing tank), a stable, a *dargah* for prayer and sometimes a *bimarkhana*—a place for sick and ill travellers. A sufi or saint also lived often in the *sarai*. Many rulers such as Allauddin Khilji banned the selling, consumption and drinking of spirits in *sarais*. Most of the *sarais* in Delhi belong to the Slave Period. As per Shiab-ud-din Alumrai there were 2000 *Khangabs* and *sarais* in Delhi and its suburbs. Most of these have not survived. Some of the famous *sarais* are mentioned below:

1. *Qutub Sarai:* At the entrance of the tomb of Kamali Jamali, it had a 50 feet deep *baoli* in its courtyard.
2. *Ladha Sarai:* Also called as Baghi-Nazir, it is 300 yards south of the tomb of Jamali. It was built in 1748.
3. *Lado Sarai:* Also in the same vicinity, it was originally a caravan *sarai*.
4. *Sarban Sarai:* It is in Kamlapati Garden, very close to Delhi-Qutub Road.
5. *Daud Sarai:* It is situated about 500 yards south of the tomb of Maulana Qutub Quli Khan in Qutub area.
6. *Kallu Sarai:* Built during Tughlaq period, it is in the vicinity of Sarvpriya Vihar area. Its main feature, a rubble masonry building, is called as Bijay Mandal.
7. *Arab ki Sarai:* It was built in 1560-61 by Hamida Banu Begam, wife of Humayun, as a settlement of 300 Arabs (whom she had brought with her while returning from a pilgrimage to Mecca)
8. *Sheikh Sarai:* It was named after a popular saint Sheikh Allauddin who lived there and had his tomb during his own lifetime.

Some more popular *sarais* of Delhi are *Sarai Shahji* built in Mughal period, *Gur Ki Sarai* on the eastern side of Karnal Road with its mosque of Hyrewali, *Sarai Bangash* near Fatehpuri mosque, *Sarai Topkhana*, the *Darghah Shah Sabi Baksh* with its *musafir khana* on Faiz Bazar road, *Jai Sarai* on southeast of Hauzkhas village, *Katwaria Sarai* in the centre of the village, *Phus ki Sarai, Ghatu Sarai, Nepa Sarai* and the famous *Yusuf Sarai*, etc.

Journeys undertaken by some famous thinkers and philosophers in olden days in India: Fa Hien (Visited India in 402 AD), Hieun Tsang (626-643 AD), Marco Polo (1273).

These people have also mentioned of shelters for travellers in their accounts on India.

- *Sarais* started developing into inns and western style hotels with the coming of Britishers in important cities like Calcutta and Bombay.
- During this period boats were kept ready at ports. Agents took care of travellers and their luggage. Private carriage would take them to hotel on their arrival at the shore.
- As early as 18th century there were excellent inns (taverns) in India. Some famous inns were: Portuguese Georges, Parsee Georges and Paddy Georges.
- Some famous hotels of that time: Albion Hotel, Victory Hotel, Hope Hall (Rs.6 per day for room and meals).

Records are available showing that Philip Stanhope (1778), a traveller, stayed in a luxurious and excellent tavern in Bombay. David Prince, who visited India, stayed at Mac Farlanes Hotel.

A dinner to commemorate the capture of Shrirangapatnam was served at Maclean's Hotel in 1800 at Bombay. The same remained a resort for many years of Sans Souci Club which entertained Duke of Wellington, Lord Nelson and Sir Arthur Wellesley.

- Pallanjee Pestonjee (1840) started the first luxurious hotel in Bombay. It was famous for its excellent cuisine, beers and wines and its excellent management.

Later he opened another hotel at Fort in Bombay.

- Auckland Hotel (1843) was established in Calcutta.

Later it was renamed as Great Eastern Hotel in 1858 and later renovated for a sum of Rs. 10 lacs.

- Esplanade Hotel (1871) was built in Calcutta by John Wakson (Britisher), a silk drapery merchant (also believed to be an architect and builder). The hotel had 130 rooms.
- Later, some Swiss and other families also owned hotels in India. One such example was Hotel Fonseca in New Delhi which was later demolished and Hotel Taj Mahal at Mansingh Road was built, there.
- In 1903, JRD Tata constructed the Taj Mahal Hotel in Bombay. It was the first hotel of international standards and repute, built by an Indian for Indians.
- The Government realized the importance of tourism in 1962 when there was a drop in tourist arrivals from 1,39,804 to 1,34,360.
- Incentives were offered by the Department of Tourism (DOT).
- Hotel Corporation and Tourism Corporations were established.
- Ashoka Hotel Ltd. and Vigyan Bhawan were made in 1956 in a record time of one year.
- Later, the Union Ministry of Housing and Welfare constructed 3 hotels: Lodhi Hotel, Hotel Janpath and Ranjit Hotel.
- In 1963 an ad-hoc committee (Jha Committee) was set up by the Government of India to give recommendations about the development of Hotel & Tourism Industry and one of its major recommendations was that 'if adequate hotel accommodation of the right type for the kind of growth of tourism is to be provided, public sector will have to play a major role in this field'.
- Later, the Dewan Chaman Lall Committee was set up by the Government of India (Hotel Standard and Rate Structure Committee) to:

1. Lay down criteria for classification of hotels in view of international standard.

2. Suggest guidelines for the promotion of tourism to India and within India.
3. Suggest improvements on the existing arrangements and availability of sources for the promotion of national and international tourism.
4. Suggest a rate structure keeping in view the existing price structure in hotel industry. Till 1963 hotels were mainly run by private operators and only rest houses and tourist bungalows were run by the Department of Tourism. Hotels at Puri, Aurangabad and Ranchi were traditionally run by the Railways and State governments. Hotels at Brindaban-Mysore were also run by the State government.

- Formation of three corporations and ITDC

In 1964 three corporation were set up by Government of India, viz.

1. India Tourism & Hotel Corporation,
2. India Tourism Corporation Ltd., and
3. India Tourism & Transport Corporation.

On 24th September 1966, the Government of India decided to merge these corporations and issued "India Tourism Corporation Amalgamation Order 1966" and formed a new corporation—India Tourism Development Corporation (ITDC) with an authorized capital of Rs. 5 crores. Soon ITDC took over tourist bungalows at:

(i) Mahabalipuram, Tanjavur, Madurai and Tiruchirapalli (Tamil Nadu)

(ii) Bijapur and Hassan (Karnataka)

(iii) Khajuraho, Sanchi and Mandu (Madhya Pradesh)

(iv) Kullu and Manali (Himachal Pradesh)

(v) Bodhgaya (Bihar)

(vi) Bhubaneshwar (Orissa)

(vii) Kashi Nagar (Uttar Pradesh)

(viii) Ghana (Rajasthan)

Many small and big Indian hotel groups are operating in various parts of India. Some of them are given below. Apart from Indian, some international hotel chains such as Sheraton, Hilton,

Ramada, Sofitel, Meridien, Hyatt and Mariott are either operating or planning to operate in India on franchise basis.

Welcom Group : It is the hotel division of I.T.C. Ltd. ITC entered into hotel business in 1975 with the opening of Hotel Chola Madras.

The logo represents a traditional Indian welcome in the form of 'Namaste' in an open doorway with the slogan "Nobody gives you India like we do". The motto of Welcom Group is "We enjoy people".

Welcom Group has hotels in various cities in India such as Agra, Delhi, Aurangabad, Jaipur, Goa, Gwalior etc.

Oberoi Hotels : Rai Bahadur M.S. Oberoi started his hotel career as a clerk in 1922 at Faletti's Cecil Hotel in Simla. Later Mr. Ernest Clarke sold his share to Mr. M.S. Oberoi, who under the deed of dissolution dated August 14, 1934, became the sole, absolute, and exclusive owner of Clarke's Hotel, Simla and Delhi. Mr. Oberoi later took over the Grand Hotel at Calcutta on lease and by the end of World War II, the Grand Hotel became a byword for good service and elegant comfort in hotels. He established Oberoi Hotel Pvt. Ltd. in 1946 and later, on 26th May 1949, established East India Hotel Ltd. (EIHL) at Calcutta. Many hotels were added to EIHL during the period. Later two very important hotels were added—Oberoi Intercontinental in August 1965 in New Delhi and Oberoi Sheraton in 1973 in Bombay. EIHL is now one of the largest and one of the most reputed hotel chains of India with hotels not only in India but also abroad. Oberoi has a hotel training institute at Delhi and future plans of expansion.

Hotel Ambassador, New Delhi: One of the flagship hotels belonging to Lala Ram Parshad who is considered as one of the pioneers of the Hotel Industry in India (now managed by Taj Hotel in Delhi). In 1946, he purchased two hotels in Mussoorie, U.P. and operated one hotel in Bokaro. Lala Ram Parshad was appointed Technical Director of Hotel Ashok, New Delhi during its construction stage and was the first Asian to be elected as an executive member of International Hotel Association (I.H.A) in 1969. He was amongst the first few hoteliers to realize the importance of trained manpower in hotel industry and was associated with various Hotel Management Institutes and Food Craft Institute in India.

U.P. Hotels and Restaurants Ltd. : Famous as Clarke's Group of Hotels, it was established on 13th February, 1961. It started with its flagship hotel Clarke Shiraz Agra. Later hotels—Clarke's Awadh, Clarke's Amer, and Clarke's Varanasi at Lucknow, Jaipur and Varanasi, respectively, were added to this chain.

Ritz Chain : A chain belonging to R.N. Kapoor family with hotels at Mumbai, Hyderabad, Kolkata and Coonoor (in South India). Specialised in Italian cuisine.

Spencers : Started hotel business in 1912 in Calcutta. Purchased Connamera Hotel in Madras and opened West End in Bangalore, Malabar at Cochin and Trivandrum, Blue Mountains at Kotagiri in 1942 and Savoy in Ooty in 1943. Vegetarian hotels in Madras (Geetha, Ashoka and Ajanta) and Hotel Arakua in Bangalore.

Sinclairs : A chain of hotels operating in eastern part of the country with hotels at Darjeeling and Takdah.

Hotel Corporation of India (HCI) : A corporation set up in 1971. It started with its first hotel at Bombay in 1974. Later hotels in Delhi, Srinagar, Rajgir etc. were added to this group.

Leela Group : It has hotels at Mumbai and Goa.

Asian Hotels : The group has tied up with Hyatt chain and has two hotels in Delhi. It plans to have property in Jaipur and Agra.

Apeejay Surendra Group : (Park Hotel): It started with its first hotel Park Calcutta in 1967. Later a large hotel was added in Delhi and Resort hotel at Visakhapatnam was added to the group.

J.P. Hotels : The group has hotels in Delhi, Agra and Mussoorie.

Palace Hotels

1. Maharaja Hari Singh Palace was the first to be converted into Oberoi Hotel.
2. Maharaja of Jaipur converted his palace Ram Bagh to Hotel.
3. Maharaja of Udaipur was third in line (Taj) Lake Palace in Pichola Lake.

4. Later Jodhpur Palace (Oberoi), Jaisalmer Palace and Bikaner Palace were also converted into hotels.
5. Lakshmi Vilas Palace of Jaipur (of Maharaja Bhupal Singh).
6. Lalitha Mahal Palace of Mysore and Halcyon Castle of Travancore Maharaja.
7. Ushakiran Palace of Gwalior.
8. Hotel Jai Mahal Palace, Jal Mahal and Raj Mahal Palace in Jaipur are also converted or being converted to hotels.
9. Chamundi Hill Palace has also been converted to a hotel.
10. Bolghathy Palace near Cochin Port (Residence of former British Resident of Southern States) is also being converted into a hotel.

Hotel Business : Many economists have often described "Hotel Business" as unique and different from many other businesses. Hotel is selling both goods and services. It not only provides both tangible and intangible services, but one of its unusual characteristic is also that it is one of the very few places where production and consumption occur simultaneously; for example, ordering and subsequent preparation, services and consumption of food items. Both the products and services are offered on credit transaction. No other business allows the customer an immediate line of credit, for example, the moment he registers, his credit purchase starts with the room and a sequence of financial charges throughout the facilities without immediately paying for them at the "point of purchase". For example, purchase of food in restaurant, drinks in bar, valet services, etc. No other business offers as varied a range of services and products at the same place as hotel business. Customers choose one establishment from another for a variety of reasons. Some such factors are service standards, amenities, products, building location, economy and staff attitude etc. Factors like location and building are of course beyond the control of the hotel but factors such as decor, creation of atmosphere, service standard and attitude etc. can be adapted to suit the customer and hence give him satisfaction. A satisfied customer is one who is not only likely to come back but is also expected to speak good about the hotel to his friends and relatives, etc.

Each hotel must offer lodging, food and protection to their guest and assume a liability for guest property, provide a high standard of hygiene, cleanliness and sanitation and should confirm to the minimum requirements of the state regarding safe hotel construction such as height of the building, municipal by-laws, fire and safety standards, etc. Hotel managers must analyse the wishes and needs of their patrons regarding accommodation, services and facilities and should plan their operations to satisfy these wishes of the guests.

Hotel Services : The present day modern concept of the hotel is not just a place to provide accommodation, food and beverage, but is like a city within a city and offering to its guests every possible facility, accommodation, service and convenience, such as rooms, restaurants, bars, cocktail lounges, banqueting facilities, convention and conference facilities, telephones, radio and TV, laundry, valets, cigars, cigarettes, book shops, banking, parking, florists, chemists, gym, beauty parlours, travel agents, business centre, etc. Apart from these a vast shopping arcade providing various items like jewellery, men's wear, ladies' wear, toys, books, news stands and magazine, etc. are also provided. In addition to these, personal services like baby sitting, private detectives, planning of tour itineraries, railway/air booking and accommodation, booking in other hotels may also be provided. Further additional services as given below may also be given:

1. Fruits, flowers, and vegetable garden
2. Club and night club
3. Health club
4. Bank services (foreign exchange)
5. Swimming pool
6. Theatre
7. Hospital
8. Library
9. Service station
10. Post office
11. Poultry farms

12. Car rental and chauffeurs
13. Cinema ticket

All these facilities may occasionally be without additional charges to the guest but generally specifically charged.

Five Star deluxe hotels go all out to provide every conceivable service and amenities to their guests in the hotel and their rooms. Following is a list of all such services which are provided these days:

1. Airport greets and meets.
2. Limousine pick-up and enhanced limousine services and also drop by limousine.
   - Hot and cold towels
   - Cola and mineral water and chocolate service
   - General Managers' welcome address/audio cassette
   - Brochures/Magazines
3. On arrival at the hotel—welcome by name by the Lobby Hostess and escort to the lobby.
4. Express personalized sit down check-in and personalized in-suite check-in and express check-out and late check-out.
5. Tastefully furnished pre-assigned and pre-checked rooms with initialized linen, jacquise, tea/coffee dispenser, electronic safe (Elsafe).
6. Escort to room.
7. Champagne check-in.
8. Round the clock butler service.
   - Food and beverage service
   - Laundry service
   - Mini bar, shoe-shine, ice-bucket service and 24-hour room service
9. International newspaper—Times Fax, round-the-clock international news-scan.
10. Complimentary fruit basket and three tier amenity tray and cheese platter, etc.

11. Complimentary American breakfast.
12. Complimentary tea/coffee hour and also in-room tea/coffee maker.
13. Cocktail hour with hot snacks.
14. Personalized leather folder and stationery, welcome letter and personalized docket and designer toiletries.
15. Valet service—ironing of one or more dress or one or more suit complimentary once during guest stay.
16. Freshen-up service.
17. Usage of the exclusive club or any lounge in the hotel and library.
18. Stay linked amenities.
19. Use of board room.
20. Entry to exclusive health club and fitness centre.
21. Entry to the discotheque.
22. Flight reconfirmation service.
23. AT&T telephone exchange with electronic voice mail.
24. Well-equipped communication centre open round-the-clock.
25. Lounges at international/domestic airport.
26. CCTV/channel music and satellite television.
27. In-house laundry and dry-cleaning facilities.
28. International Subscribers Dialling.
29. Bank safe deposit and 24-hours money changes.
30. Take-away gifts.
31. Bon voyage complimentary at the airport lounge.

Various Departments in a Large Hotel

1. Sales
2. Personnel
3. Laundry
4. Housekeeping
5. Maintenance

6. Credit
7. Computer centre
8. Security
9. Purchases and receiving
10. Main stores
11. Horticulture
12. Accounts
13. Health club
14. Production
    (i) Main kitchen
    (ii) Satellite kitchens
    (iii) Bakery
15. Food and beverage service
    (i) Restaurants
    (ii) Banquets
    (iii) Coffee shop
    (iv) Room service
    (v) Bars
16. Front office
    (i) Reservation
    (ii) Reception
    (iii) Information
    (iv) Cash
    (v) Bell desk
    (vi) Telephone

Some Problems of the Hotel : Some common problems that a hotel faces are as follows:

Market : To determine whether there is demand for a hotel in the area where the site is located, certain very important factors must be considered such as:

(i) determine if the existing tourist capacity is adequate or not,

(ii) find out if the location of the hotel is a positive factor or a negative factor in creating demand,

(iii) find out if it is worthwhile to invest further in increasing the number of rooms over and above the existing number in the area,

(iv) determine if the present guest structure is future-oriented, and above all

(v) determine if the national and international economic situation allows to expand the business or not.

Labour Situation : Problem of labour is very important in hotel industry. For successfully developing new hotel projects it is the lack of adequate labour supply which creates problems rather than the problem from labour such as their demands etc. For this the two important points to study are union situation and the labour wage trend.

Sources of Financing : This is another very important factor and a big problem. Arranging of finances and control of credit line is a very serious problem confronting business today.

The Major Sources of Financing are:

(i) Long term mortgages.

(ii) Loans provided by government, semi-government and/or tourism promotion bodies.

(iii) Loans provided by financial institutions such as banks etc.

Hotel Guest

Hail Guest! We ask not what thou art:
If friend, we greet thee, hand and heart,
If stranger, such no longer be,
If foe, our love shall conquer thee.

—*ARTHUR GUITERMAN- Old Welsh Door Verse.*

As per Oxford Dictionary, a "Guest is a person who is invited to another person's house, on a visit or to dine together". The guest and the host hold a social relationship where a person is invited and entertained as a social obligation or with a motive. We extend warmth and welcome to our friends, relatives, near and dears in order to impress upon them our hospitality and good nature and make the experience as pleasant as possible. In India there is an old Sanskrit saying *"Atithi Devo Bhava "* meaning the guest is like God and as a person offers his best to God we shall also offer the best to our guest. There are numerous examples of the same in Hindu mythology and folklores.

A hotel customer/client is called a guest because the hotel offers homely and professional service to him, and establishes an immediate relationship with him. Thereafter it ensures satisfaction by providing nothing less than 'A Home Away From Home'. It is like projecting, 'what is an economic relationship as a personal relationship'. Unlike other business 'a guest-hotel transaction even when complete in all respect is futile, if the guest is not satisfied'. The hotel guest is the one who buys rooms, meeting space, food and beverage services and other services and amenities, etc. from the hotel. He is an important person to the hotel and is not just a cold statistics, but a thinking, feeling human being made of flesh and blood and has feeling and emotions like our own. He has certain needs and wants which he would like to fulfil. He is someone who, in his or her own mind, is always right, and is the reason for business, rather than an interruption to our work; a person who brings us his wants. It is our job to handle him profitably for him and for ourselves. He is a valued customer who is willing to pay fair price for a quality product and wants to be neither overcharged nor underserved. The guest is not dependent upon us; on the contrary, we are dependent on him. The guest is not someone to argue with or match wits with, nobody ever won an argument with a guest; even if you win, you and your hotel both loose.

Treat the guest in the hotel as you would treat a guest in your house. Make him feel welcome, and help him feel comfortable.

Hotel guests may be defined as "people who have, who are, or who will be availing the services of hotel, for a particular period in order to satisfy their demand for accommodation, food and beverage or entertainment, for which they are willing and able to pay."

The Guest's Name : As per the famous writer Dale Carnegie, "A man's name is to him the sweetest and most important sound." This also applies in full for every guest and all hotel employees must remember it and should not leave any opportunity to keep repeating the guest's name. The receptionist should concentrate on the name of the guest when he hears it by listening to the sound. Don't hesitate to ask if you miss the name in the first instance. Associate or link the person's name with his appearance, business or some other interest. Tie his name to his height, hair, mouth, attitude, clothes and shoes, etc. or to any other thing that strikes you. Repeat the guest's name during conversation as many times as possible, but make sure you don't make it very obvious.

Guest relation is an integral part of the hotel. It is a means for the management to reach out to the guest and convey to him the feeling of warmth and welcome.

Initially a guest/customer comes to a hotel for its good name and reputation about service and food, second time he comes to confirm his experiences and then further keeps on coming for its comfortable and emphatic atmosphere and becomes a regular customer, because by now he is pretty confident about the hotel.

As compared to other industries, hotel industry which is a service industry and a part of hospitality industry, requires greater personal touch and courtesy. A hotel guest is a customer and unlike a family or social guest, he pays for his stay, food and beverage consumption at the hotel. Why is he referred to as a guest instead of a customer? The idea behind referring to hotel customer or client as guest is offering homely as well as professional service in order to keep him happy and satisfied and make his experience as memorable as possible. The special treatment of allowing a line of credit for various services and products offered by hotel industry gives a special status to the guest of the hotel. Guest satisfaction is a very relative term. It basically means knowing and understanding guest needs and then providing them at least to that standard which he expects.

Guest Classification : Once a visitor or caller is identified as a prospective user of hotel services, he may be studied under different headings such as:

Guests on the Basis of Status: For example, (i) an expected guest, (ii) an in-house guest and (iii) check out guest.

Guests on the Basis of Recognition : Such as, (i) regular guest, (ii) V.I.P., special attention and distinguished guest and (iii) new guests, and

Guests on the Basis of Revenue: For example, (i) paying guests, and (ii) complimentary guests.

Types of Guests/Customers : Unlike other organizations and industries where the customers are very specific in nature, the customer profile in hotel business varies greatly. For example the facilities and services needed by a sportsman, a honeymoon couple, and a business executive staying at the hotel would be greatly different, and it is always useful to group customers as per their profile.

Tourist/Resort Hotel Guest: The guests will usually be on holiday and the objective of their visit will generally be relaxation and enjoyment. They would be looking for friendly, informal and relaxed services to suit their mood and leisure service and facilities such as swimming pool, health club, sports facilities like tennis, golf, water games, etc.

Transient Hotel Guest: Hotels where the guest does not need to sign a lease and can register for a day or even less. Generally fully equipped business centre, convention centres, conference and meeting rooms, audio and visual equipment etc. are essential. Mostly this group of hotels are situated downtown.

What Does the Guest Staying in a Hotel Expect : A guest coming to a hotel expects a unique and attractive property with friendly, courteous and competent service. He expects clean and well appointed rooms and public areas as per the standard, safe quality rood with personal touch and safety to him and his belongings. He also expects trained, skilled, and caring staff, good entertainment programmes, floor shows, etc. He expects TV, radio, and telephone etc. in the room. He appreciates hassles free and speedy check in and check out. Further, some added frills such as efficient room service, newspaper, wake call, shoe shine, laundry, valet services, car parking and video films etc., are expected by the guest.

The personality of the person coming in contact with the guest is very important. He should have friendly and positive attitude i.e. he should be tolerant, willing to accept the responsibility and should be people oriented. He should be helpful to the guests and should be in the business with his body and spirit. He should have neat appearance. He should be courteous and efficient.

Sometimes the guest may make special requests. Special requests of the guest can be classified into two groups.

Equipment Needs: Such as roll away beds, banquet table in the guest room, bed boards, additional blankets, pillows, iron and ironing boards, hair driers, hangers, special equipment for handicapped guest.

Procedural Requests : Such as split folio, wake calls, transportation arrangement, reservation in airlines, hotels and for entertainment shows, cinema and theatre, etc., special newspaper, etc.

Some important factors that the guest keeps in mind while returning back to a hotel are *price, cleanliness, good service, facilities, convenience/location, quiet and private accommodation.*

Guest Satisfaction : A hotel guest's significance can be seen from the fact that all activities and innovations in a hotel revolve around one term—*guest satisfaction*. Basically guest needs can be classified as follows:

Physiological Needs : Related to protection against heat, cold, rain etc. in the form of room and related to his appetite/thirst and special food requirement.

Economic Needs: Value for money i.e. is he getting returns worth the value of money spent by him? How much can he afford?

Social Needs : Attending functions and gatherings, to meet others, going out with friends.

Psychological Needs : Enhancement of self-pride, the need for variety.

Guest Dissatisfaction : This can be usually because of two reasons classified as follows:

Under the Control of the Hotel: Such as unhelpful staff, cramped conditions and lack of choice of product i.e. type of accommodation and other service available for offer to the guest.

Beyond the Control of the Front Office of the Hotel: Factors such as location, the weather, other customers and transport problems.

Guest satisfaction shall ensure repeat business, increased clientele and maximized revenue for the establishment.

Customer Relations : Better known as *Guest Relation* in hotel industry, it undoubtedly cannot be anything but providing hospitality to the guest of the hotel. It can be achieved by using procedures which will improve guest sales factor. It is important in this connection that we understand the basic principle that service is a two-sided coin and we must also understand the marketing concept which involves identification and satisfaction of guest needs.

Service is a Two-sided Coin : There are two sides to service:

(i) Operational side, and
(ii) People side.

Most of the hospitality operations do understand the importance of providing basic levels of physical services such as good food (food to be served hot, etc.), clean rooms and standard facilities etc.

But it is the 'people side' where the major shortfall tends to be. For a serious understanding of marketing concept and hence satisfaction to guest it may be said that the service provider (staff) is some kind of an amateur psychologist. Human needs can be arranged according to priorities. Needs like hunger and thirst come first and must be taken care of first, and other needs follow this. Coldness, rudeness or being ignored leaves some powerful human needs—the needs to be accepted, to belong to, feel secure, to have status, to have recognition, and to be wanted—unsatisfied.

Service of hospitality involves creating a feeling of well being and appreciation in the customer. This feeling can be brought in by good physical and operational delivery of service and at the same time good psychological delivery.

Delivery of Psychological Service : It requires understanding of:

(1) customer's need for recognition,
(2) importance of smile,
(3) a positive attitude,
(4) genuineness , and
(5) an understanding of the importance of customer's expectation

Recognition of Customer's Needs : It is vital to pay attention to customers and to demonstrate that you are paying attention. Aim at individualizing the customer, for example, by the use of the customer's name.

Smile: Smile is contagious like anger. No smile goes waste. No matter how bad you feel, you must keep smiling. Staff must be friendly. Hire right staff with right attitude for your customers.

Think positive: Make sure your staff has positive attitude. They take their lead from you. Treat your staff in a friendly and fair way. Don't tell your problems to your customers; it does not help in building a happy and successful image of your establishment.

Genuineness : Genuineness can't be preached and taught. It comes from within like positive attitude. Wherever possible address the guest by name. Use self-involvement techniques such as address the guest by name, etc. Genuineness means accepting the guest for what he is without judgment or censor.

Customer's Expectation : It is a very important point because normally a customer dissatisfaction is not related to the actual level of service provided but to the fact that the customer did not get what he expected and perceived.

The above points are very important in providing psychological service and hence maintaining good guest relation.

Often in large hotels there is a position called Guest Relations Officer. He/she is directly under either the Front Office Manager or the General Manager. It is a sales oriented position. His job is to create an image of credibility which will go a long way in building up business, specially repeat client etc. He is also expected to know the likes and dislikes as well as complaints etc. of the guest and to keep a record of these. As a part of the process of maintaining guest relation, the Guest Relations Officers should see that welcome drink and welcome activities such as *pooja, aarti,* and applying of *tika* and garlanding, etc. is done. Photographs of VIPs are to be taken and published in House Magazine. A personal check of the room of expected VIP arrivals should be done by the Guest Relations Officer. Frequent calls to check the comforts of the guest should be made. Complaints and enquiries and feed back are also very important.

Key Terms

Hospitality market	Guest needs
Chalets	Inns
Taverns	Hostel
Guest satisfaction	Choultry
V.F.M. (Value for Money)	Boatels
Motels	Roatels
Loatels	

3

The Categorisation

Since the hotel industry comprises of numerous hotels, and they provide numerous services, facilities and goods, the hotel industry lacks a single identity. Although the basic concept of hospitality, food and accommodation are same, yet hotels may have different characteristics and assets and each hotel would like to attempt to cash on its assets and develop its share of the particular market, and gain more and more recognition because of that asset. Placing a hotel into a particular group is not easy because of the diversity of services, facilities and amenities provided or not provided. Most of the hotels don't fit in any specific well-defined category. Nonetheless, several general classifications do exist.

Hotels are classified into several distinct categories to help the prospective guest in identifying the right type of hotel matching his standard and requirement. However, for the sake of convenience, we shall put them under four broad categories as given below.

1. On the basis of size.
2. On the basis of star system.
3. On the basis of ownership.
4. Other categories.

Size : Classification on the basis of size refers to the number of rooms (bed capacity) and should not be confused with the building height, or the area of the property, or the gross sales etc. The term number of rooms refers to the lettable rooms and does not include those rooms which are converted for other use such as for manager, house keeper, accounts etc. and rooms on the ground floor and basement which are generally used for offices, rentals, support services or other operational facilities leased for businesses and associations.

Usually the distribution is :

(i) a hotel of 25 rooms or less is called a *small hotel,*

(ii) one with 26 to 99 rooms is an *average hotel,*

(iii) from 100 to 299 it is called as *above average,* and

(iv) a hotel of more than 300 rooms is classified as a *large hotel.*

The Star Status

This system is one of the most commonly understood, accepted and recognised systems in India. This is also an official system of classification. In this system hotels are classified on the basis of facilities which the hotels have and the services which the hotels provide to the guests. Based on the number of services and facilities and their quality and standards, which may vary from a basic bedroom to a luxury room with modern fittings and equipment, the hotels are awarded stars ranging from one to five star deluxe.

Procedure : The classification of new and functioning hotels is done by the Ministry of Tourism. The department forms a committee called as Hotels and Restaurants Approval and Classification Committee (HRACC) which is headed by D.G. Tourism/ADG Tourism and comprises of members from hotel industry, Travel Agents Association of India, Department of Tourism and the Principal of Regional Institute of Hotel Management, Catering Technology and Applied Nutrition etc. This is a permanent committee to classify hotels into five categories i.e. from 1 to 5 star and also into a Five Star Deluxe category. The committee inspects once in three years the existing hotels which have been classified to confirm that the hotels are sticking to the standards.

A hotel applies on a prescribed application form to the Director General of Tourism, Transport Bhawan, Parliament Street, New Delhi (in case of 4 star, 5 star and 5 star deluxe category) and to the Regional Director of the concerned Govt. of India tourist office at Delhi/ Mumbai/Kolkata/Chennai, in case of 1, 2 and 3 star category giving basic details such as: 1. Name of the hotel, 2. Name of the promoter's, 3. Address, 4. Details of the site such as area, title, distance of hotel from railway station, distance from airport, distance from main shopping centre, 5. Details of hotel project such as category applied for, number of guest rooms and their area, their type with or without bathroom, details of public areas like lounge, lobby, restaurants, bars, shopping arcade, banquet/conference hall, health club, swimming pool and parking etc. 6. Details of air conditioning, 7. Approvals from government bodies such as Municipal or Corporation authorities, MRTP Act, Urban Land Ceiling Act, DGCA and any other concerned local authorities, 8. Proposed capital structure, 9. Want to avail of any or all of the following benefits of Income Tax Act-61 against each of the following provision — Section 80L, Section 80 H-H, Section 32 (i) (ii a), Section 32 (i) (v) and Section 33. The application fee which varies from 1 star to 5 star and 5 star deluxe is also sent along with the application. The hotel is supposed to fill up a questionnaire containing details of facilities, features, amenities and services and their standards in the form of questions which are divided into three categories—desirable, necessary and essential—and have marks allotted to them for a hotel to be considered for classification. All items marked under essential category must be there in the hotels, two items marked under necessary may be condoned while the items marked under desirable may or may not be there.

On a pre-notified date the HRACC team members visit the hotel personally and inspect the hotel, and finally on the basis of the report of the committee and the marks scored by the hotel, the hotel is either approved or rejected for the applied star category. Approved hotels become eligible for various fiscal reliefs and benefits. The department interacts on behalf of such hotels whenever necessary to ensure that their needs get priority consideration.

Eligibility for Star Classification : To be eligible to apply for classification, a functioning hotel must fulfil the following minimum basic requirements:

(i) The hotel must have at least 10 lettable bedrooms.

(ii) Carpet areas in respect of rooms and areas of bathrooms should by and large adhere to the following limits:

Category of Hotel	*Area Standard for Bedroom/ Bathroom*
5-Star/5-Star Deluxe Hotels	
Single	180 sq. ft.
Double	200 sq. ft.
Bathrooms	45 sq. ft.
4-Star and 3-Star Hotels	
Single A/C and Single Non A/C	120 sq. ft.
Double A/C and Double Non A/C	140 sq. ft. (Extra area may be provided if twin beds are to be provided)
Bathrooms	36 sq. ft.
2-Star and 1-Star Hotels	
Single A/C and Single Non A/C	100 sq. ft.
Double A/C and Double Non A/C	120 sq. ft. (All rooms should have proper ventilation and ceiling fans)
Bathrooms	30 sq. ft. or subject to local bylaws.

Failure to satisfy the above conditions will disqualify a hotel for consideration.

How to Apply for Star Classification : A classification fee (at the existing rate) is payable by the hotels applying for classification.

The classification fee is payable by means of a demand draft drawn in favour of the Pay and Accounts Officer, Department of Tourism, New Delhi. For reclassification, fee will be 50% of the fee payable at first time.

Application form for the particular star category applied for can be had from the Member Secretary, H.R.A.C.C, Department of Tourism, Government of India, 'Transport Bhawan', New Delhi.

The powers to classify hotels in 1 and 2 star categories have been delegated to the respective State Governments/Union Territories w.e.f. 1.1.1986. A hotel applying for 1 or 2 star category is, therefore, required to approach the concerned State Government/Union Territory.

Classification Criteria of Star Hotels : The general features, facilities and services expected of hotels in the different star categories, are broadly described below:

Five Star Deluxe Category : A hotel which applies for 5 star deluxe category has basically the same number of features as a five star hotel but is superior in quality of service, amenities and facilities etc. to a five star hotel's requirement.

Five Star Hotels

General Features : The facade, architectural features and general construction of the hotel building should have the distinctive qualities of a luxury hotel of this category. The locality including the immediate approach and environs should be of highest standards and of international standard and should be suitable for a luxury hotel of this category. There should be adequate parking space for cars. The hotel should have at least 25 lettable bedrooms, all with attached bathrooms with long baths or the most modern shower chambers. All public rooms and private rooms should be fully air-conditioned and should be well equipped with superior quality carpets, curtains, luxurious furniture of high standards, fittings, etc. in good taste. It would be advisable to employ the services of professionally qualified and experienced interior designers of repute for this purpose. There should be an adequate number of efficient lifts in buildings of more than two storeys (including the ground floor) with 24 hours service. There should be a well-appointed lobby and ladies' and gentlemen's cloakrooms equipped with fittings and furniture of the highest standard, adequate parking space and swimming pool.

Facilities : There should be a reception, cash and information counter attended by highly qualified, trained and experienced personnel and conference facilities in the form of one each or more of the conference rooms, banquet halls and private dining rooms. There should be a shopping arcade and bookstall, beauty parlour, barber shop, recognized travel agency, money change and safe deposit facilities, left luggage room, florist and a shop for toilet requisites and medicines on the premises. There should be a telephone in each room and telephone for the use of guests and visitors and provision for a radio or relayed music in each room. There should be a well-equipped, well-furnished and well-maintained dining room/restaurant on the premises and wherever permissible by law, there should be an elegant, well-equipped bar/ permit room. The pantry and cold storage should be professionally designed to ensure efficiency of operation and should be well equipped. There should be dancing facility and orchestra in dining hall.

Services : The hotel should offer both international and Indian cuisine and the food and beverage service should be of the highest standard. There should be professionally qualified, highly trained, experienced, efficient and courteous staff in smart, clean uniforms, and the staff coming in contact with guests should understand English. The supervisory and senior staff should possess good knowledge of English and staff knowing at least one continental language should be rotated on duty at all times. There should be 24 hours service for reception, information and telephones. There should be provision for reliable laundry and dry cleaning service, 24 hours housekeeping at the hotel should be of the highest possible standard and there should be a plentiful supply of linen, blankets, towels etc. which should be of the highest quality available. Each bedroom should be provided with good vacuum jug/thermos flask with ice cold, boiled drinking water except where centrally chilled purified drinking water is provided. There should be a special restaurant/dining room where facilities for dancing are also available.

Questionnaire For 5-star Category Hotel

Form 5-Star

Government of India
Ministry of Tourism, Department of Tourism
Hotel and Restaurant Approval and Classification Committee
(H.R.A.C.C.) Questionnaire for 5-Star Category Hotel

Name of the Hotel: ....

....

Questionnaire to be answered by hotels applying for 5-star category:

PART-I

Name and address of the Hotel:..

....

In order to be assessed for 5-star category, a hotel should have the following basic features and the absence of any one of these will disqualify it from consideration for the 5-star category:

1. The hotel should have at least 25 lettable bedrooms. Please state the number of guest rooms:
   (a) Single
   (b) Double
   (c) Suites Total

   Note: Please furnish a list showing carpet area of each bedroom and area of bathroom.

2. The locality including the immediate approach and environs should be suitable for a hotel of this category.

   Please indicate:
   (a) Distance from airport
   (b) Distance from railway station
   (c) Distance from main shopping areas
   (d) Please describe briefly the neighbourhood in which your hotel is located.

3. All public rooms and private rooms should be well appointed and fully air conditioned (except in hill stations where there should be heating arrangements). Please indicate:
   (a) Are all your public and private rooms air-conditioned?
   (b) Is your hotel centrally air-conditioned? If so, please give the tonnage and also the total floor area/cubic space.

4. All rooms must have well appointed attached bathroom with long baths or should be equipped with most modern

shower chambers. (In the case of cabana rooms, adequate shower facilities will be acceptable).

(a) Do all your rooms have attached bathrooms? If so, how many have long baths?

(b) How many are fitted with most modern shower chambers?

5. The kitchen, pantry and cold storage should be professionally designed to ensure efficiency of operation and should be well equipped. Please state who designed your kitchen, pantry and cold storage and when?

6. There should be ladies' and gentlemen's cloakrooms and the cloakrooms should be spotlessly clean and equipped with furniture and fittings of the highest standard available befitting a luxury hotel of this category.

   Do you have ladies' and gentlemen's cloakrooms attached to the public area? If so, how many?

PART-II

Maximum Marks *Marks awarded by the Committee*

1. Construction **10N**

The architectural features and general construction of the building should have the distinctive qualities of a luxury hotel of this category.

2. Maintenance **20N**

Maintenance of all sections of the hotel (i.e. building, walls, gardens, surroundings, etc.) should be of the highest standard.

3. Parking **5D**

There should be adequate parking space for car. Please state:

(a) How many cars can be parked in the parking space owned by your hotel?

(b) How many extra cars can be locally parked in the capacity of your hotel?

(c) How many cars can be parked by the guests/visitors of the hotel when such space is most required?

4. Swimming Pool **10N**

There should be well designed and properly equipped swimming pool (except in hill stations).

(a) Does your swimming pool have its own system for filtration, chlorination and changing of water?

(b) How often is the water changed?

(c) What arrangements does your hotel have for heating the pool in the winter?

5. Bathrooms **30E**

All bathrooms should be modern in design and should be equipped with fittings of the highest quality available befitting a luxury hotel of this category, with 24 hours service of hot and cold running water. The floors and walls should be covered with impervious material of elegant design and high quality workmanship. It is desirable that sockets for electric shaver should be provided.

(a) Do the bathrooms have sockets for electric shavers?

(b) Do the bathrooms have running hot and cold water for 24 hours?

6. Reception **15N**

There should be a reception, cash and information counter, attended by highly qualified, trained and experienced personnel.

Please state in detail the qualification, training and experience of the personnel employed at reception, cash and information counters. (Separate sheets provided at the end of the questionnaire may be used for answering this question).

7. Lobby **10N**

There should be a well-appointed lobby.

Please state the area of the lobby.

8. Conference Facilities **10N**

There should be one each or more of conference rooms/banquet halls and private dinning rooms.

Please give the number of conference rooms/banquet halls and private dining rooms with area of each.

9. Shopping Facilities **20N**

There should be bookstall, left luggage rooms, barber shop, recognized travel agency, beauty parlour, money changing and safe deposit facilities.

Note:

1. There should be a florist in a hotel of 100 rooms and above.
2. A store selling toilet requisites and medicines should be available in the premise.
   - (a) Is there a bookstall in your hotel? Yes/No
   - (b) Is there a left luggage room in your hotel? Yes/No
   - (c) Is there a barber shop in your hotel? Yes/No
   - (d) Is there a recognized travel agency in your hotel? Yes/No
   - (e) Is there a beauty parlour in your hotel? Yes/No
   - (f) Are there money changing facilities in your hotel? Yes/No
   - (g) Do you have safe deposit facilities for guests? Yes/No
   - (h) Is there a florist in your hotel? Yes/No
   - (i) Is there a store selling toilet requisites and medicines in your hotel? Yes/No

10. Lifts **10N**

There should be an adequate number of efficient lifts in buildings of more than two storeys including the ground floor, with 24 hours service.

- (a) How many floors are there in the building?
- (b) How many lifts are there in the building?
- (c) Please state their speed and capacity.
- (d) Are these available 24 hours?

11. Furnishing of Bedrooms **25E**

All guest rooms should be comfortable and spacious and well furnished with good quality, properly hung curtains, carpets etc. in good taste.

Note: New hotels are advised to employ the services of professionally qualified and experienced interior designers of repute in the designing and decoration of bedrooms.

12. Lighting **10N**

Lighting arrangements and fixtures in the rooms/bathrooms/ public rooms/corridors etc. should be so designed as to ensure aesthetic as well as functional excellence.

13. Telephones **10N**

There should a telephone in each room and telephone for the use of guests and visitors.

(a) Is there a telephone in each room?

(b) Is/are there a telephone(s) separately for the use of guests and visitors?

(c) How many telephone lines does your hotel have on the switchboard?

(d) What is the maximum number of operators on duty and for how many hours? Please use separate sheet provided at the end of the questionnaire for giving the educational background and training of the telephone operators, also stating their pay scales with allowances.

14. Radios **5D**

There should be provision for radio or relayed music in each room.

(a) Is there a radio in each room?

(b) Is there relayed music? If so, how many channels?

15. Vacuum Jugs/Flasks **5N**

There should be a vacuum jug or thermos flask with ice-cold boiled drinking water in each bedroom except where centrally chilled purified drinking water is provided.

16. Dining Room/Restaurant **15E**

There should be well-equipped, well-furnished and well-maintained dining room/ restaurant.

(a) How many restaurants are there in the hotel?

(b) Please give seating capacity of each.

17. Carpeting **15D**

All public and private rooms should have superior quality carpets/rags, which should be well kept at all times. If the floors are not completely covered, quality of the following will be assessed.

(a) Are all public and private rooms carpeted?

(b) Please state the areas which are not carpeted.

18. Linen/Blankets/Towels etc. **10N**

There should be a plentiful supply of all linen/blankets/ towels etc. which should be of the highest quality available and should be spotlessly clean. Bed linen and towels should be changed every day.

19. Crockery **10E**

Crockery, cutlery and glassware should be of the best quality available.

Note: No piece of crockery in use should be chipped, cracked or crazed. The silverware should be kept well-plated and polished at all times.

20. Bar **10N**

Wherever admissible by law, there should be elegant, well-equipped bar/permit room with an atmosphere of comfort and luxury.

21. Entertainment **10D**

There should be a special restaurant/dining room where facilities for dancing and provision of an orchestra are available. Hotels of this category should provide evidence that they have made a serious attempt to present specially choreographed Indian entertainment.

22. Cuisine **30N**

The hotel should offer both international and Indian cuisine. (The preparation, proper seasoning of dishes and presentation to customers will be assessed).

What are the various types of cuisine offered by your hotel?

23. Food and Beverage Service

(a) Restaurant Service **25N**

While assessing this item, the organization of the dining room/ restaurant, the waiters' knowledge of the menus whether in French or English, the correct laying of tables, the variety and appearance of buffet services and the methods used to keep hot dishes at the right temperature will be assessed.

(b) Room Service **20N**

The methods used to ensure speedy service and hot meals will be assessed.

(c) Beverage Service **15N**

The provision and service of alcoholic and non-alcoholic beverages including methods used to service hot and cold beverages at the correct temperature will be assessed.

24. Hygiene **20E**

The kitchen, pantry and cold storage should be clean and organized for orderliness and efficiency, scientific and hygienic methods should be used in working and for the washing of glass, crockery, cutlery etc.

(a) Is there a dishwashing machine in your hotel? If so, what is its capacity?

(b) What steps are taken to keep the place safe from all types of pests?

25. Other Services **10E**

(a) 24 hours' service should be provided for reception, information and telephones.

(b) There should be provision for reliable laundry and dry cleaning service.

(c) Does your hotel have its own dry cleaning and laundry?

(d) Does the hotel accept responsibility of the damage done in washing, dry cleaning or pressing?

26. Staff

There should be professionally qualified, highly trained, experienced, efficient and courteous staff. The overall component of trained staff will be assessed and marks given accordingly with a deduction in marks if the supervision is done by untrained staff.

(a) Manager **10N**

(b) **Executive staff** **10N**

(c) **Other staff** **20N**

(d) **The staff should be in smart and clean uniforms.** **10N**

(e) The staff coming into contact with guests should understand English and supervisory and senior staff should possess good knowledge of English. At least one member of the senior staff knowing at least one of the continental languages should be on duty at all times.

Note: In future classifications, knowledge of foreign language by some of the staff will be essential.

Please use separate sheets, provided at the end of the questionnaire for giving bio-data of directors directly concerned with the operation of the hotel, general manager, departmental manager, executive and supervisory staff including housekeeping, cooking and maintenance. The bio-data should include name, age, professional qualifications, on-the-job training and its duration and experience giving in detail the positions held and the duration of each and telephones.

27. Housekeeping **10N**

Housekeeping should be of the nicest possible standard.

28. Fire

I hereby solemnly declare that the information given above is correct to the best of my knowledge and belief. In the event of any of my statements found to be untrue, I fully understand that my application for approval/classification is liable to be rejected.

Signature of the Proprietor/
Managing Director/
General Manager
authorized to sign on behalf of the hotel

The Committee's Final Assessment:

Four Star Hotels

General Features : The facade, architectural features and general construction of the building should be distinctive and the locality including the immediate approach and the environs should be suitable for a hotel of this category. There should be adequate parking facilities for cars. The hotel should have at least 25 lettable bedrooms, all with attached bathrooms. At least 50% of the bathrooms must have long baths or the most modern shower chambers, with 24 hours service of hot and cold running water. All public rooms and private rooms should be fully air-conditioned and should be well furnished with carpets, curtains, furniture, fittings etc. in good taste. It would be advisable to employ the services of professionally qualified and experienced interior designers of repute for this purpose. There should be an adequate number of efficient lifts in buildings of more than two storeys (including the ground floor). There should be a well-appointed lobby and ladies' and gentlemen's cloakrooms equipped with fittings of standard befitting a hotel of this category.

Facilities : There should be a reception, cash and information counter attended by trained and experienced personnel. There should be a bookstall, recognized travel agency, money changing and safe deposit facilities and a left luggage room on the premises. There should be a telephone in each room and telephone for the use of guests and visitors and provision of a radio or relayed music in each room. There should be a well-equipped, well-furnished and well-maintained dining room/restaurant on the premises and wherever permissible by law, there should be an elegant, well-equipped bar/permit room. The kitchen, pantry, cold storage should be professionally designed to ensure efficiency of operation and should be well equipped.

Service : The hotel should offer both international and Indian cuisine and food and beverage service should be of the highest standards. There should be professionally qualified, highly trained, experienced and efficient and courteous staff in smart, clean uniform and the staff coming into contact with the guests should possess good knowledge of English. It will be desirable for some of the staff to possess knowledge of foreign language and staff knowing at least one continental language should be rotated on duty at all times. There should be 24 hours service for reception, information and telephones. There should be provision of reliable laundry and dry cleaning service. Housekeeping at the hotel should be a plentiful supply of linen, blankets, towels etc. which should be of the highest quality available. Similarly, the cutlery and glassware should be of the highest quality available. Each bedroom should be provided with vacuum jug/flask with ice cold, boiled drinking water. There should be a special restaurant/ dining room where facilities for dancing, orchestra are provided.

Three Star Hotels

General Features : The architectural features and general construction of the building should be of a very good standard and the locality, including the immediate approach and environs should be suitable for a very good hotel and there should be adequate parking facilities for cars. The hotel should have at least 20 lettable bedrooms, all with attached bathrooms with bathtubs and/or showers and should be modern in design and equipped with fittings of a good standard, with hot and cold running water. At least 50 per cent of the rooms should be air-conditioned and the furniture and furnishings such as carpets, curtains, etc. should be of a very good standard and design. There should be adequate number of lifts in buildings with more than two storeys (including the ground floor). There should be a well-appointed lounge and separate ladies' and gentlemen's cloakrooms equipped with fittings of a good standard.

Facilities : There should be a reception and information counter attended by qualified and experienced staff, and a bookstall, recognized travel agency, money changing and safe deposit facilities on the premises. There should be a telephone in each room (except in seasonal hotels where there should be a call bell in each room and a telephone on each floor for the use of hotel guests) and a telephone for the use of guests and visitors to the hotel. There should be a well-equipped and well-maintained air-conditioned dining room/ restaurant and wherever permissible by law, there should be a bar/permit room. The kitchen, pantry and cold storage should be clean and organized for orderliness and efficiency.

Service : The hotel should offer good quality cuisine both Indian as well as continental, and the food and beverage service should be of good standard. There should be qualified, trained, experienced, efficient and courteous staff in smart and clean uniforms and the supervisory staff coming in contact with the guests should understand English. The senior staff should possess good knowledge of English. There should be provision for laundry and dry cleaning service. Housekeeping at the hotel should be of very good standard and there should be adequate supply of the blankets, towels, etc. of good quality. Similarly, cutlery, crockery, glassware should be of good quality. Each bedroom should be provided with vacuum jug/ thermos flask with cold, boiled drinking water. The hotel should provide orchestra and hall room facilities and should attempt to present specially choreographed Indian dance.

Two Star Hotels

General Features : The building should be well constructed and the locality and environs including the approach should be suitable for a good hotel. The hotel should have at least 10 lettable bed rooms of which at least 75% should have attached bathrooms with showers and a bath room for every four of the remaining rooms and should be with modern sanitation and running cold water with adequate supply of hot water, soap and toilet papers. At least 25% of the rooms should be air-conditioned (where necessary there should be heating arrangements in all the rooms) and all rooms must be properly ventilated, clean and comfortable with all the necessary items of furniture. There should be a well-furnished lounge.

Facilities : There should be a reception counter with a telephone. There should be a telephone or call bell in each room and there should be a telephone on each floor unless each room has a separate telephone. There should be a well maintained and well equipped dining room/ restaurant serving good, clean, wholesome food and a clean, hygienic and well-equipped kitchen and pantry.

Service : There should be experienced, courteous and efficient staff in smart and clean uniforms. The supervisory staff coming in contact with guests should understand English. There should be provision for laundry and dry cleaning services. Housekeeping at the hotel should be of a good standard and clean and good quality.

One Star Hotels

General Features : The general construction of the building should be good and locality and environs including immediate approach should be suitable. The hotel should have at least 10 lettable bedrooms of which at least 25% should have attached bathrooms. Bathrooms should have western style W.C. All bathrooms should have modern sanitation and running cold water with adequate supply of hot water, soap and toilet paper. The rooms should be properly ventilated and should have clean and comfortable bed and furniture.

Facilities : There should be a reception counter with a telephone and a telephone for the use of guests and visitors. There should be a clean and moderately well equipped dining room/restaurant serving clean, wholesome food, and there should be a clean, well equipped kitchen and pantry.

Service : There should be experienced, courteous and efficient staff in smart and clean uniforms and the senior staff coming in contact with guests should possess working knowledge of English. Housekeeping at the hotel should be of a good standard and clean and good quality linen, blankets, towels etc. should be supplied. Similarly crockery, cutlery and glassware should be of good quality.

Heritage Hotel Category in Rajasthan : The Department of Tourism has introduced a new category of 'Heritage Hotels' in Rajasthan, which is proposed to be extended to other States in due course. It covers running hotels in palaces/castles/forts/havelies/residences of any size.

The guidelines for this additional new category in Rajasthan and application form for this particular star category (applied for Heritage Hotel category in Rajasthan) can be had from the Member Secretary, HRACC, Department of Tourism, Government of India.

Regulatory Conditions for Approval of Hotel Projects : All hotels approved by the Department of Tourism are required to furnish the following information.

1. The hotel will furnish documents relating to its legal status i.e.

   (a) If the company is incorporated under the Companies

Act, a copy of its Memorandum and Articles of Association.

(b) If it is a partnership firm a copy of the partnership deed and the certificate of registration under the partnership Act.

(c) If it is a proprietary concern, name and address of the proprietor etc.

2. The hotel will submit the following information to the Director General, Department of Tourism so as to reach on or before 31st May each year for the preceding financial years:

(a) A bank certificate in regard to foreign exchange deposited by the hotel.

(b) Total bed capacity offered by the hotel as under:

(i) Single rooms:

(ii) Double rooms:

(iii) Suites:

(c) Number of rooms occupied on a permanent/semi-permanent basis by residents/staff/ offices, etc.

(d) A specimen copy of the current tariff card.

(e) List of the names of the following officers with their designation, experience, etc. (department wise).

(i) Senior executives

(ii) Junior executives

(iii) Other staff

(f) Total number of persons employed, indicating separately the number of Indian and foreign staff.

(g) Annual report of the hotel and a statement showing the audited balance sheet and profit and loss account within 4 months of the close of the financial year.

(h) Statistical returns in regard to the number of guests, rooms, occupancy, income and employment on regular basis as prescribed by the Department of Tourism from time to time. Release of exchange, issue of import licences, grant of approval for fiscal benefits including income-tax relief etc. will be cleared only if the concerned hotel has submitted updated statistical returns.

3. The Regional Director/Director/Manager of the Government of India tourism offices of the region and the Director General, Department of Tourism should be kept informed from time to time of facilities introduced or withdrawn and of any additions or alterations made in regard to the bed capacity of the hotels.
4. The hotel tariff should be fixed in consultation with the Department of Tourism. Prior approval of the Department of Tourism should be obtained for any revision of hotel rates. The hotel tariff should be prominently displayed in each room. This card shall also indicate sales tax, service charges, etc.
5. Normally, no rooms will be let out for purposes other than residential. However, with the prior permission of the Department of Tourism not more than 10 percent of the rooms in a hotel can be let out to any person or company for residential or commercial purposes.
6. Any licence and/or approvals required from the local administration/police and or other concerned authorities for the construction/operation of the hotel should be obtained directly by the promoters from the concerned authorities. The approval by the Department will not in any way substitute for them. The Department's approval will be deemed to have been withdrawn in case of violation of this condition when brought to its notice.
7. In the event of the promoters making any changes in the plans of the project as submitted earlier, the approval of the Department will have to be applied for afresh.
8. In case the hotel is required to provide guides for tourists, only approved guides of the Department of Tourism should be employed.
9. The hotel should at all times adhere to the high standards of maintenance and services for which it has been recognized and in all dealings with its guests observe business practices worthy of an establishment of repute.

10. Officers of the Department of Tourism or any other officer deputed by the Department to inspect the hotel premises from time to time will be allowed free access with or without prior notice.
11. As a project which has been approved from the point of view of its suitability for foreign tourists, the promoters will be entitled to grant of loan from Central/State financial institutions and priority in the procurement of building material, telephone and telex connections etc. However, this approval should not in any way be construed as an assurance for the grant of these facilities since this would fall within the jurisdiction of the concerned authorities.

Form of Acceptance of Regulatory Conditions

To,

The Director General	The Regional Director
Department of Tourism	Govt. of India Tourist Office
Transport Bhavan	....
1, Parliament Street	....
New Delhi-110001	....

Subject: Acceptance of regulatory conditions

Dear Sir,

I have received a copy of the regulatory conditions prescribed by the Department of Tourism for hotels placed on its approved list, and wish to confirm that I have read and understood the same and hereby agree to abide by the same and such other conditions as may be laid down from time to time by the Department of Tourism for approved hotels.

Yours faithfully,
(Name in Block Letters)
Managing Director Partner/
Proprietor Name of Hotel.

Classification on the Basis of Ownership : Another way to classify hotels is to examine the ownership through which a hotel can be classed. The classification is as follows:

Independent Hotel : These hotels are on ownership basis and do not have any affiliation or contract through any other property. And also they do not have any tie up with any other hotels with regards to policy, procedures and financial obligations. The advantage in this type of hotel is that they need not maintain a particular image and they are not bound to maintain any set targets, but can independently adopt quickly to the changing trends.

Management Contractual Hotel : Another type of chain organization which operate properties owned by individuals or partners are management contract hotels. The contract is entered between the owner and the operator and usually as per the contract

- owner retains the legal and financial responsibilities.
- operator pays for the operating expenses and recovers from the owner.
- owner is responsible for paying taxes, insurance and debts.

Chains : There are many single owned hotels, yet more and more hotels and motels are now getting affiliated to each other. This gives them the advantage of a large central organization providing reservation system, management aids, financial strength, expertise, manpower specialities, merchandises and promotional help.

Affiliation

(i) Two or more operations belonging to some organizations; for example, Holiday Inns, Ramada, Sheraton Corp., Trusthouse Forte, Hilton Corp., Howard Johnson, Balkantourist, Day Inns, Travel Lodge, Intercontinental Hotels, Hyatt, Marriott Corp, etc. Within one chain the type of affiliation may vary.

(ii) A "Referral Chain" is made up of independently owned and operated hotel and motel and provides shared advertisement, joint reservation system and standardized quality. Virtually no shared managements or financial functions.

(iii) Another chain operation is "Multi-Unit Company" usually with a head office and several operations across the country and abroad.

The Concept of Franchise : Franchise is a system in which the franchise owner grants another the right or privilege to merchandise a product or service for a specified return.

Franchise Agreement : It is an agreement under which the owner operates as a member of the chain, utilizing the brand image, name, goodwill and obtaining for a certain fee some services of marketing and operating nature support from resources of a large organization, advertising, sales promotion, technical and financial help etc. Franchise can be described as the selling by the franchiser of the right to market a proven product. Hence major franchisers in hotel and motel business first established the quality of their product and their expertise in the field by operating company owned properties and only after demonstrating the success of their properties were they able to make their franchises marketable packages. Banks and lending institutions look with favour on the better known franchises, and are in fact reluctant to make time to potential investors, unless an affiliation with a referral organization has been established.

The most successful franchiser in the hotel industry is Holiday Inns. Other successful organizations in the field of franchise are Hilton, Marriott, Howard Johnson, Ramada Inns, etc.

Franchising must be looked at as a two-way benefit scheme. Franchiser provides certain services, and conveys certain rights to the franchisee and the franchisee has in turn certain obligations to the franchiser. For uniformity franchised units are generally standardized. Constituted to a specific standard of furniture and decor specification, fitting, fixture and equipment specification. Site selection and feasibility and appointment of architect.

Franchise Services : Franchiser provide services in 3 general categories:

(i) Methods and Systems,

(ii) Technical Assistance,

(iii) Marketing Methods.

Methods and Systems

(a) Proven systems and established operating procedures of a franchiser are provided to franchisee (operating manuals are given).

(b) Training programmes and sessions conducted by the franchiser to the employees of franchisee.

Technical Services : Franchiser provides various technical assistance in various forms such as assistance during development and construction phases, study of potential sites and its selection in obtaining finances by introducing the financers to the franchiser, making of capital budget, feasibility studies, architectural services, purchasing services (crockery, cutlery, furniture, equipment, linen, glass ware, and consumables etc.) These may be provided for a fee (which may be consolidated or separate for each service).

Marketing : Marketing techniques, name of the franchiser and its goodwill, logo, signs etc., reservation system marketing, advertisement programmes benefits (joint advertisement campaign) with franchiser, marketing packages, regional sales offices at strategic points.

Obligations of Franchisee : (i) *Definitive standard* (which define physical characteristics), for example, size of room, size of beds, type and number of furniture, T.V. etc. and also standard of swimming pool, F&B outlets, parking etc. (ii) *Operational quality standard* such as cleanliness, behaviour and attitude of staff, quality of service, tariff, frequency of changing of linen etc.

The franchisee is required to maintain both the above types of standards as per the franchiser's requirement.

Franchise Costs and Fees : (i) Payment of an initial fee which is non-refundable in the event of the termination of agreement due to the action or as a result of violation by franchisee. It is based on number of rooms. (ii) In addition to the initial fee a monthly fee is also payable to franchiser. (iii) Royalty based on room sales, advertising fees, reservation fees, training fees etc.

Methods of Computing

(i) Fixed monthly fee.

(ii) Fixed monthly fee plus an amount per reservation originating from reservation system.

(iii) Percentage of room sales.

(iv) Percentage of total sale.

(v) Fixed Rupee amount per available room.

(vi) Fixed Rupee amount per occupied room.

A combination of two or more of these is also possible.

Franchiser rent on a monthly basis the principal sign, identifying the hotel as a member of the chain rather than selling it outright.

Some Common Requirements for Franchise Membership

- Minimum number of rooms required
- Architectural design in conformation to hotel owner's requirement
- Scrutinization of location
- Certain services must be provided
- Centralized training programmes for management
- Highest calibre establishment in its category
- Certain standards regarding maintenance, operations, staffing and services.

Some Benefits of Franchise System

- Feasibility study
- Opening assistance
- OJT (on the job training) for staff
- Accounting services
- Advertising
- Central purchasing
- CRS benefits
- Financial assistance
- Discount on services and supplies
- Newsletters and brochures

Other Categories

1. On the basis of clientele: Hotels for aristocrats, sportsmen, doctors etc.
2. On the basis of location: Airport hotels, downtown hotels, suburban hotels, hotels situated on highways, motels,

motor hotels and motor lodges, hotels on hill stations etc., hotels on boat—boatels and floatels, etc.

3. On the basis of length of stay: Transit hotels, residential and semi-residential hotels, etc.
4. In Europe star classification by AA (Automobile Association) is often regarded as an accepted mark of quality like in India and stars five to one are awarded.

AA Rosette are also awarded in certain cases which depend upon specially recommended food. For example:

Single Rosette: Food standard higher than expected of the hotels of their standard. *Double Rosette:* Much higher food standard than expected of the hotels of that standard. *Three Rosette:* Outstanding standard food than expected of the hotels of that standard.

5. According to Guide Michelin symbols as follows are used—

Best hotels	2nd	3rd	4th	5th

XXXXX	XXXX	XXX	XX	X

6. In some of the European countries hotels are classified according to the standard as *deluxe, first class, second class, third class* and *fourth class* also. Another way of categorization in U.K. is as *deluxe* for *best, first class* for second grade, *middle class* for third grade and *moderate class* for fourth and fifth grade hotels.

Residential Hotels : Residential hotels are also called as apartment hotels or apartment house. Room in a residential hotel are sold on a monthly or yearly basis. Rooms may be furnished or unfurnished, single or *en suite.* Almost all residential hotels operate a restaurant, offer telephone service, laundry and valet service. Advance rents are usually collected while other charges are billed weekly. These type of hotels normally operate on European plan. Recent developments in this area include cooperative hotels and condominiums in which the tenants own the apartment and pay the management a fee for maintenance. When the rooms are not occupied by the owner the management often has the right to rent them on temporary basis, so that the hotel will contain both residential and transient guests. They are also called as *'en pension '*. Such establishments are very popular in U.S. and Europe. Long staying guests generally stay from months to year and rent may be paid per week or per month. Facilities are less then commercial hotels.

Semi Residential Hotels : These hotels provide accommodation to guests on weekly or monthly basis like residential hotels as well as on per day basis like transient hotels. Reduced rates are provided to long staying guests. Transient guests who want to take the advantage of reduced rates for longer stay also come to such establishments.

Transient/Transit Hotels : Hotel guests who fall under the category of transient guests are those who are *en route* guests i.e. who are in the process of moving from one destination to another and stop at the hotel for a short period of time as against a terminal guest who has reached his final destination. Hence hotels, which cater to a transient/transit guest are called transient hotels. They find their origin in olden days inns. Examples of transient hotels are motels, motor hotels, airport hotels etc. The rates of rooms are fixed on *"per diem "* basis. In large cities they operate on European plan generally while in small towns they may operate on American plan. The olden days establishments such as theatrical hotels popular in rural areas are also included under this heading. Transient hotels such as airport hotels attract its clientele from layover passengers and crew members of the airlines. Such hotels are situated generally near port of entry i.e. airport or seaport, or international bus terminal etc. Generally the length of stay is short i.e. few hours to few days. 10. Resort Hotels

Resort hotels are located at resort places such as islands, exotic locations, hill stations, beaches and health resorts and spas i.e. summer resorts, winter sports resorts and all season resorts etc. with breathtaking beauty. People go to these places for relaxation, to enjoy themselves, and to get away from the hectic city or for health reasons away from hectic city life or to pursue a specific interest/activity. Generally a guest stay is long such as a week or more and normally holidaymakers, sportsmen and patients who have been advised by doctors etc. go to the resort hotels. In resort hotels, such as hill resort hotels, business is dependent on season and they have off season and full season tariff. Resort hotels have homely and informal atmosphere. No dress code is required; more social contact with guests, lot of entertainment items such as beauty contest, floor shows, cabarets, fancy dress parties and stage shows etc. are popular. In addition recreational facilities like table tennis, badminton, golf, water games etc. can be there. Growth of resort hotels in U.S. took place due to vast highway construction programmes, as more people started travelling by cars. Many resort properties are at Florida, California, Arizona, Michigan, Wisconsin and Carolina etc. Resort hotels are not very popular in India because of various causes, the main reason being highways are not very well developed in India. Fuel for cars is very costly, automobile industry is not as developed as in Europe and America and, most important, people are not so rich and don't have spare and leisure time to enjoy.

Resort hotels have facilities like

(i) Extensive entertainment program
(ii) Tennis court, golf course with trainer
(iii) Saddled horses with trainer
(iv) Car parking and garaging and service facilities
(v) Mini golf course, squash, billiards, etc.

Commercial Hotels : Commercial hotels are situated in the heart of the city i.e. downtown busy commercial areas and urban areas. Mainly businessmen and commercial executives patronize these hotels. Generally duration of stay is a few days only and weekend business is slack. Best possible facilities of high standard are provided in commercial hotels. These days, business centre in a commercial hotel is a must. They must have services like facilities to meet the basic business demands, swimming pool, speciality restaurant, bar, disco, 24 hours room service, health club etc. Commercial hotels are sometimes also called *downtown hotels.*

Suburban Hotels : Suburban hotels are situated in suburbs, with quiet surroundings. They have moderate to low tariff and are generally patronized by budget guests.

Retirement Hotels : Hotels of this category are not popular these days. Such hotels cater to the needs of retired persons. They take care of their meals and lodging. They also offer some mild recreational activities to the senior citizens. Normally all the services are offered as inclusive package rate to the retired persons. Nowadays such establishments are called "Old Homes" and "Sandhya Houses" in India.

Green Hotels (Eco-friendly Hotels) : If we kill the environment we kill ourselves. Environment has always been a touchy subject vis-a-vis the hospitality industry. The spread of unplanned tourism and its allied evils hardly show any regard for the pristine beauty of the places identified for development and on grand plans. As a result, many rare flora and fauna that live on the thin red line of extinction are lost for ever as the sacrificial pigs of progress. Tourist activities are claimed to uproot the locals from their habitats, robbing them of their livelihood, eroding the quality of their life, disrupting their lifestyle, corrupting their value system, impinging on their socio-cultural ethos, polluting their soil, water and air and depleting natural resources and wreaking havoc on the region's flora and fauna.

Floating Hotels : This type of hotels are located on the surface of water such as sea, lake etc. Such hotels provide exclusive and exotic atmosphere. All the facilities of a first class hotel are there in this category of hotels. In many countries old luxury ships have been converted in to floating hotels. In India in Kashmir valley, houseboats are used as first class luxury hotels. They provide wonderful experience to a tourist.

International Hotels : These hotels are situated in metropolitan cities and provide modern western style luxury to their guests. They can also be called as full service hotels. Many such hotels are owned by big international chains. Such hotels find good market in commercial towns.

Motels : Motels, motor hotels and motor courts are designed to serve the needs of motorists. They must provide car parking, garage, accommodation, rest facilities and recreational facilities and hence motels are generally equipped with filling stations, motor garage, service stations, accessories, elevator service to automobile entrants, restaurants etc. The tariff is very low as compared to city hotels. They have easy access from highways, being located on highways or at road junctions. Motel accommodation is ranked with hotels in general in many countries.

Specific legislations laid down in some countries like France, Norway, Ireland, Iraq, Portugal and Turkey are regarding approval of plans, easy access for cars, minimum capacity, provision of restaurant, minimum standard of facilities and in Turkey provision of a petrol pump or service station.

In U.S.A. (original concept) motels/motor hotels/lodges originally provided simple accommodation with minimum service and formalities. Evolution of motor hotel stemmed from the need for more elaborate facilities. Rising cost of land in an around urban areas caused the development of motor hotels by substituting horizontal building with multistorey car parking centre, sophisticated restaurants, banqueting and convention facility like that of a hotel. In general motel classification standards are similar to hotels.

Budget Motels : These were developed in U.S.A. as low cost lodgings. The tariff was approximately $10 per night in 1974.

This includes prefabricated plumbing cases to which sanitary fittings can be easily connected, or complete bathroom units.

Motel accommodation may provide bedroom and bathroom facilities or include a large living area and a kitchenette. The latter is applicable to tourist area where longer staying guests require self- catering provisions and also for families relocated or temporary employees in that area, etc.

Casino Hotels : The focus in this type of hotels is on gambling and provision of casino. Casino hotels are not seen in India but are very popular in America, particularly in Las Vegas-Nevada. Top artistes come to the hotel and give their live performances and entertain the guests.

Condominiums : Condominium development involves a joint ownership of a complex. Each owner purchases and has full benefit of an unit such as a guestroom, suite, apartment or a villa and shares the cost common to the whole complex such as taxes, maintenance and upkeep of buildings and grounds, parks, tennis court, swimming pools, provision of services such as security, letting and management, etc. Each owner can occupy or sell his unit independently but is obliged under the terms of contract to contribute towards the pool of common facilities and services. Condominiums have many advantages over simply leased property. In a condominium the capital appreciates with rising value particularly on coast or lake sides. It relieves the owner of maintenance and upkeep worries. The owner can enjoy extensive recreational facilities exclusive to the complex. Condominium management look after the unit in the absence of the owner and if required, let it to provide income. In some instances letting or lease-back conditions may be written into the contract, particularly where the condominium unit in a complex may be used as a back up to a hotel operation, for example, to provide additional accommodation for conventions. It may be necessary for the developer to appoint an independent management agent in the initial stages and for subsequent control to be exercised by an association of owners. In some cases the developer may act as an estate agent and manager.

Apartotel : It is an apartment building also used as a residential hotel. Purchase of the apartment entitles full services of the hotel and during the period it is not occupied it can be added to the hotel pool for getting income. The concept was initially developed by Melia Coy of Spain in 1970.

Auberge, Gasthof, Herberge : It is the counterpart of inn in various countries. It represents a smaller unit which may have complimentary bar, restaurant and bedrooms for travellers. Here emphasis is given to eating and drinking facilities.

Boarding Houses : Boarding houses are establishments providing accommodation usually with meals and for a definite period of time—commonly for a week or longer. The facilities are generally restricted to use by resident guests. It can also be called a guesthouse, a private hotel, and is known in Europe as 'pension' or 'pension de famille'. Distinctions in these depend variously on length of stay, location, facilities and levels of sophistication of premises.

Holiday Villages : Providing extensive recreation and sporting facilities on an inclusive basis. In multiple units and provide self-catering (individual kitchen). In Spain located in areas where contact with nature and sporting activities is possible. Provision of green zones, playgrounds, and social amenities like library, nursery, television room etc. For social tourism based on family units providing a convertible living room, bedroom, bathroom, shower room and kitchen. Wide range in sports like riding, swimming, skating, golf etc. Design of building and landscaping highly sophisticated (Village Equastere de Pompadour, Club Mediterranee, Correze-France) retaining the village atmosphere. Typical size ranges between 500-800 beds, a 600 beds capacity being considered the optimum for efficient operations with a density of between 150-200 beds per hectare or 60-80 beds per acre.

Specific regulations may apply as in Spain, holiday villages are classified in 3 categories according to amenities and services.

In France, regulatory standards apply to commercial holiday villages and to non-commercial establishments like those of the association "Villages Vacances Families"— (v.v.f), which in 1973 was responsible for 70 villages and family lodges providing 33,000 beds.

Supplementary Accommodation : This group includes all forms of rented accommodation other than the above mentioned categories such as youth hostels, dak bungalows, forest lodges, travellers' lodges, recreational centre for children, dharamshalas, sanitaria and convalescent centres, camping grounds—these are sites demarcated with amenities for living in the open air in a tent, trailer or any other mobile provisional type of accommodation unit. Usually camping sites fall into four main groups, those for transit, weekend, holiday and tourist use.

Bed and Breakfast Inns : Also called as B & B Inns. These are lodging establishments that provide room with full breakfast. Usually they are converted residences or country estates. Main meals are not served. They are located along commercial and holiday routes and in rural and resort areas.

Time-share : This concept is also becoming popular these days. This is also known as 'vacation ownership' or 'holiday ownership' concept. The concept is that for a set period which may be one week or more each year and for a number of years the person gets the right to enjoy stay and other facilities and services in an apartment or any other type of lodging in a tourist complex. It is like advance purchase of time in holiday accommodation. Purchaser has to pay a one time capital sum and then an annual contribution towards the maintenance of the property. The fee usually covers services such as cleaning and maintenance of apartment and public areas, electricity, gas and water, insurance, operation of resort facilities e.g. swimming pool, local taxes and sinking funds for redecoration and replacement of equipment etc. Time-share concept started as early as 1960. Alexander Nelte, a German who was the manager of a hotel in Ticino developed this concept and created a company called Hapimag based in Switzerland. Further in 1967 another innovative developer introduced the concept at Superdevolur ski resort. The sales slogan was "Stop renting a room—buy the hotel—it's cheaper!" Although the time-share concept initially developed in Europe but was soon adopted by U.S. Soon the developer came to understand a serious drawback of the concept - lack of flexibility. In 1974 the solution to this drawback came with the development of the concept of exchange system RCI. In 1976 another company Interval International was formed with the same concept. Subsequently the idea trickled down to Mexico from U.S. and came back to Europe in 1980s and the British Holiday market in Canary Islands and the Costa Del Sol of Spain can be considered as the beginning of success story in Europe. The concept is also being appreciated in India and many companies such as Avelon Resorts and Sterling Holiday Resorts, Mahindra Holding, Nanda Tourist Corporation etc. are promoting this concept and the growth of time-shares at an annual rate of 15% since 1980 can be compared with that of travel and tourism overall of 4% and hotel accommodation 2% in the same period.

Boutique Hotels : A new concept in India. They are different from the hotels in that each room has a distinct personality. It is a small but very expensive hotel. Professional but at the same time very personal and intimate services by staff are prominent feature to give guest a richer experience; each restaurant of a boutique hotel has a different entertainment concept which include lighting that changes with the mood of the guest. For more personalized services and attention restaurant are kept small. They are each theme based and everything from decoration to food to service must be in tune with the theme. 'Guest needs understanding' is the highlight of this type of hotel.

Types Of Rooms : One of the most important knowledge that a salesman should have is the "Product knowledge". Similarly it is very important that all those involved in selling/booking of rooms such as reservation section staff and front desk staff and also the marketing and sales division staff has full and comprehensive knowledge of rooms which they are trying to sell and their availability and non-availability position. They should know what are the various types of rooms, their location and situation, and also the features of the rooms—can extra beds be provided in the rooms or not, facilities such as TV, mini bar, telephone, bedside lights etc. in the rooms. Also knowledge of the room rates and plans which the hotel is operating on is important. Given below are some typical rooms that the hotels have:

Single Room : The term refers to a room with a standard single bed to provide sleeping accommodation to one person. The room furnishing and fixtures as well as amenities and facilities standards would depend upon the standard of the hotel. The size of a single bed is generally 6' x 3'.

Double Room : Double room term refers to a room which has a double bed and provides sleeping comforts for two persons. A double bed is a large bed. The size of a double bed is generally 6' x 6'.

Twin Bedded Room : Twin bedded room is a room with two identical twin beds separated out by a small bed-side table. This room provides sleeping accommodation for two persons.

Interconnected Rooms : These are rooms which are connected to each other. They have a common wall and a door in the common wall to go from one room to another. They can be used for a family by opening the connecting door as well as can be given to two separate individual persons by closing the common door.

Triple Room : This room offers sleeping accommodation facilities to three persons and has either a double bed (or two twin beds) and an extra bed in it.

Quad : This room provides sleeping accommodation for 4 persons and accordingly has four beds.

Double-double : This type of room has two double beds in it and provides sleeping comforts for four persons, such as a family of husband, wife and two children. Also called a family or twin double room.

Suite : The term suite refers to a set of two rooms out of which one is a bedroom and the other is a sitting room or living room. For going from one room to another the use of corridor is not required. Suite is a costly room of the hotel. There are various types of suites such as:

Single Suite: It is a single room with a sitting room attached to it and meant for one person's sleeping comfort.

Double Suite: It is a double room with a sitting room attached to it.

Junior Suite: A large room with a partition separating the bedroom furnished from sitting area.

Duplex Suite: This type of suite has two rooms on two successive floors and is connected to each other with a common staircase. Generally the sitting room or living room is situated on a lower floor while the bedroom is on the next floor. This is one of the costliest accommodations of the hotel.

Penthouse Suite: Very luxurious suite of the hotel, and is situated on the terrace of the building. Mostly hired by top executives of companies, businessmen, famous writers, film personalities and sometimes by retired people who want peaceful life. These are away from the hustle and bustle of the hotel.

Luxury Suite or Deluxe Suite: These are the best possible suites that a hotel can have. May have more than one bedroom, along with a sitting room. Also sometimes these may have a small kitchenette and a small dining room, a changing room and an office room attached to them. The best possible furnishing and decoration are used in these rooms. The bathroom attached will also have the best possible sanitary fitments in it. These suites can be given exclusive names such as Presidential suite, Maharaja suite, etc. Additional facilities that may be provided are: (a) mini bar, (b) objects d'art, (c) valet service, etc.

Studio Rooms : These are rooms which are called multi-utility rooms also. They have utility furniture such as sofa-cum-bed, sofa convertible-bed, Murphy bed, closet bed or roll-away beds. The furniture is such which is used for sitting purposes during the daytime and for sleeping during the night time.

Cabana Rooms : This type of rooms are situated near the swimming pool of the hotel and are normally used by people who love water games and are fond of swimming. These rooms have twenty-four hours supply of hot and cold water, and a hard bed. Some hotels have beautiful rooms decorated with bamboos.

Lanai Rooms : This term is generally used by hotels which are situated on the hill stations for those rooms which have a view of waterfall or some water body or a garden from the balcony of the room.

Parlor : A living or sitting room not used as a bedroom. Also called Salon in some parts of Europe.

Efficiency : A sort of complete self-sufficient unit in itself. Containing a bedroom, living room, dining room, a small kitchen and bathroom. For example, cottages on hill stations and also on sea beaches.

Hospitality : A room used for entertaining (cocktail party etc.). Can also be called function-room. This room is not used for sleeping purpose.

Hollywood Living Room : A room with two single beds joined together and with a common head board.

Adjoining Rooms : Two or more rooms side by side without connecting door between them i.e. to say rooms can be adjoining without being connected.

Business-Club Type of Accommodation : Provided by some hotels. Sometimes one or two floors of the hotel are taken by a company and converted to provide accommodation to its top executives. They are equipped with all the facilities and needs of the top executives such as a bar, a lounge, business centre, and may be a library.

Changing Pattern of Accommodation Sector : The diversity and changing pattern of hotel use often make precise classification difficult. These days most of the hotels are deliberately designed to appeal to various market segments with the changing needs of market apart from traditional classification such as transit, residential and commercial etc. Many new forms of accommodation are being introduced such as sports hotel—as part of a sports hall complex, ski hotels—situated at ski resorts, boatels and floatels—associated with marine development, convention hotels—having one or more convention complex and allied services and facilities, motels, motor hotels and motor lodges and motor courts—designed to serve the needs of motorists and their vehicle i.e. car and should provide facilities for car parking, service and filling station and easy access from highway.

Hotels are also changing in character and operational style. More and more automation in services provided are taking place. Way back in 1971 Hotel SCHIPOL FROMMER in Holland was designed with self-operated room facilities and this helped in reducing the staff and guest ratio to 0.04:1

Another important point worth mentioning is that the age long distinction and difference between accommodation at hotels and hospitals is also getting blurred. Many modern private hospitals abroad and in India provide individual room facilities comparable and at times even better than a 5 star hotel room.

Another growing concept these days is of self-financed accommodation. With increasing affluence and improvements in travel and access facilities the trend in recent years has been towards the purchase of holiday accommodation such as apartments, chalets, villas, farmhouses etc. The development of high proportion of self-owned properties has certain disadvantages. Apart from low percentage of occupancy local employment and other benefits to the community are poor.

A New Trend

As an alternative to hotel accommodation which are becoming costly day by day, most visitors are looking for facilities that provide a home like ambience. A number of real estate developers and hospitality providers are coming up with new concept of service apartments— a growing segment of Indian hospitality sector. The concept which initially started from Mumbai and Bangalore is now becoming popular in Delhi with apartment like Avion, Silver Oaks, Vasant Apartments, Hill view and Residency USI. A service apartment is a fully furnished studio or two to three room unit with a small pantry with housekeeping maintenance services, utility charges, fridge, microwave, heater, telephone, airconditioner and other such facilities. Also provides valet service, a cook, a kitchen (for home-like food) and a chauffeur driven car. Usually they are rented on weekly/monthly basis. They make long staying guest feel at home. This is a niche sector and has tremendous potential. Since they are economical, service apartments are a home away from home for families and transients in city for a week or more. They help avoid tiresome transactions required to lease flats. Presently these service apartments are catering basically to NRI's, foreigners and corporate clientele. They usually provide larger living space at economical price. Apart from the above mentioned service apartments of Delhi some popular ones are Lake Side Chalet, Mumbai; Home Stead, Bangalore; Tara Niwas, Jaipur; Riviere Heights, Kochi and Sand Pebbles, Goa.

'SPA' development in India, Basic concept of SPA is a place of relaxation and rejuvenation for people, who are ill Evian is France is a very famous SPA. But with the change in time the SPA of today is a place for keeping the body fit and healthy not only though fitness centre but also supplemented by nutritionally balanced food. In this direction many SPA have come up. To mention few are Sanjay Khan a famous actor has built one on the outskirts of Bangalore. Hotel Crown Plaza Surya has launched a fitness and SPA at there health club Grand Hyatt's Oasis SPA has also began operation. A health SPA called' Anand' has been made in Rishikesh.

SPA prove essentially uses of therapeutic and physical properties of water therapy to relax tense bodies and minds, some of the centres in South India combine Ayurvedic massages with essential oils and also use aroma therapy.

Key Terms

Heritage hotels	Retirement hotels
Rosette classification	Franchise Boutique hotels
Holiday villages	Condominiums
Quad	Green hotels
Efficiency	Apartotel
Lanai	Murphy bed
Roll-away bed	Object d'art
Auberge	Gastoft
SPA	

4

Service Qualities

The essence of the long run success of any economically based enterprise is its ability to survive and prosper, which ultimately depends upon its net profitability. The main items provided by a hotel are rooms, food and beverages and services. The most important among this set is the service element, which determines the guest's attitude towards hotel, which ultimately affects the profitability. Hotel industry is very much a "people-industry" which produces intangibles. The service aspect particularly personalised services cannot be mechanised or automated. Quality, care, facilities are very vital than the quantity or numbers. The profitability of hoteliering firms largely impinge on the amenities and quality of its services, which is the crucial determinant of the volume of sales. If a hotel organisation aims to seek out a specific portion of the guest market and to maintain a high occupancy level, then it must pay close attentions to modifying the products and improves the quality of services it offers . In this chapter an attempt has been made to apply the service quality model in order to examine the gaps in services of the hoteliering establishments. It is tried to unravel the mysteries of why some firms are successful and others are not. Hopefully the issues raised here will stimulate the interest of both operators and researcher concerned in this type of tertiary activity.

The technology of most service organisations especially in hotel concerns, is conceived as "knowledge technology", as opposed to manufacturing technology where output quality is physically measured. In this regard service technologies tend to consist of the ideas, goals and rationale for the methods adopted. Furthermore services do not tend themselves to physical controls relating to quality factor and therefore should rely on intangible process of controlling In addition to produce the hotel services, the customers and the service worker must interact. This interaction process can be seen as a situation where workers not only produce the output but are simultaneously involved in delivering it as well.

The hospitality industry seems to be a relatively successful one, although in many developed countries the boom in tourism and the hotel business is over. Especially in the coming decades it will be necessary for the industry to emphasise quality not merely quantity. The hotel industry in developing countries should actively market its product. Marketing its product is simply attuning the hospitality offer to the wishes and expectations of the potential demanding consumer of hospitality. This marketing process can only be executed if one knows the needs and expectation of the guests and what can be offered. The principal factor that determines the guest's attitude towards a hotel is the quality of service received. Automation and mechanisation has helped in ruling out the human element in a number of industries but the human element is the determining element of the hotel business.

The architecture of a hotel, the decoration of the lobby the furnishings of a room are examples of hotel attributes that may be the reason behind a benefit, or tangible surrogates for intangible benefits, but they are not the benefits. The benefit is what they do for the consumer e.g. gives a sense of security, a sensation of prestige, or a feeling of comfort. And the credibility of these benefits tends to diminish rapidly if an expectation is not fulfilled. Decor is soon forgotten, if a room service takes an hour or so. A sense of security is not credible if slovenly characters are seen in the lobby or met on the elevator. It is this fulfilments of expectations, or lack of it, that creates the perception of deliverability for the consumer. The competing hotels may be seen as providing the same sense of security, grandeur, prestige and comfort. The tangible surrogates attributes their ability, to differentiate and at the same time, are no longer deterministic in the consumers choice of a hotel.

The definition and measurement of quality is no small matter for the growth and performance of hoteliering firms. These factors have been found to be particularly elusive with regard to services and almost undefinable at least in consistent terms, in regard to hotel services. If quality per se is 'elusive and indistinct' and often mistaken for impressive adjectives and not easily articulated by consumers then added intangibility of services certainly compounds the difficulty of definition and measurement. Yet as quality measurement and improvement has become so vital to managers and marketeers of the hotel services, and when, as has been pointed out, quality is the single most important consumer trend of the coming decades then it becomes imperative, both theoretically and empirically to analyse the factors and suggest measures to improve the quality of hotel services.

The search for quality trend has prompted some researchers to begin to develop various definitions of service quality models. A basic consistency and consensus seems apparent among these numerous studies. Essentially concerns rests on largely abstract dimensions, such as perception, expectations and satisfaction. This communality leaves apparent need, at least at this stage, to debate over such a framework. Rather it gives an opportunity to test these dimensions and to seek empirical confirmation.

Empirical verification of abstractions, however is no less elusive than the definition of quality itself. It seems, in fact, that the frustrating attempts at definition may be preventing, rather than facilitating, successful efforts towards empirical confirmation. But the difference between the abstractions can be measured. For example if quality is measured vis-a-vis expectations, and perception is the level of satisfaction derived, then it seems only logical that if the difference between the two can be measured then not a definition of quality, but a measurement of its existence or non-existence can be obtained. This measurement in fact may just, be a more significant marketing tool. It also has the advantage of being somewhat less of an abstraction, although not totally, to deal with, and this considerably eases the task. Many research investigators, have termed these differences between abstractions as gaps. Others have referred to the measurements of these differences as 'disparity analysis'. The analysis presented here is based on the service quality model. After a brief review of the conceptual foundations of the exercise, the findings from the present study of gap analysis in hotel services are presented.

The Quality

A concept called "missing service quality" was developed by Gronrops in his model. His model is based largely on the construct "image" which represents perceived service quality which in turn represents the 'gap' between 'expected services' and 'perceived services'. He explores the use of the term quality as if it were a variable itself rather than a function of a range of resources and activities. He argues that this range includes what customers are looking for, what they are evaluating, how service quality is perceived, and in what way service quality is influenced. 'Perceived quality' of service is dependent on two variables—expected service and perceived service. Service quality can have two dimensions:

(i) Technical quality

(ii) Functional quality

Technical quality lends itself to somewhat objective measurement by the consumer. It is what the consumer receives as a result of his interactions with a service firm. This could be a hotel, a room, a bed, a restaurant meal, or a doctors prescription. Functional quality on the contrary, represents the service process or the expressive performance of the service. This quality is perceived by the customer in a very subjective manner. Together, the technical quality and functional quality of the service represents a bundle of service dimensions and create an "image", a third quality dimension.

The "image" influence the consumer's expectations. In fact image is a quality dimension overriding substandard technical and functional quality delivery. It is interpreted to mean that the consumers may be satisfied in spite of some deficiency in technical and functional quality in the service. Conversely, the consumers may be satisfied inspite of their presence. It is very difficult to measure the 'image'. However, 'satisfaction of consumers' can be measured as a surrogate for 'image'. It is a reasonable assumption if there is a disparity between satisfaction and technical and functional delivery of services.

The Delivery

Thus it seems that, measuring service quality per se is not the purpose, but rather the quality in the delivery of the service is at least two and very possibly three dimensions described below. It appears at first glance to be a fine distinction but infact it is very important one because it eases the task considerably. The elusive quality now becomes a some what less elusive delivery, perhaps still intangible but less abstract.

Services in the hospitality industry are classified along three different dimensions.

(a) Person related services

(b) Product related services

(c) Information related services.

It is contended that although the hotel industry provides a number of product related services e.g. car parking, laundry etc., and information related services e.g. television and radio, more importantly it provides person-related services such as rooms and meals for individuals. Person-related services are geared towards the main objective of bringing about some change of state in the customer, or to maintain an existing state, which for one reason or other he is unable to do for himself or chooses not to maintain the existing state. Accordingly a hotel provides rest, recreation and refreshment. Consumption of persons related services generally involves four elements:

(i) direct consumption of physical goods (such as food, drinks etc.)

(ii) use of physical facilities (such as buildings and furnitures etc.)

(iii) interaction with persons providing the services.

(iv) information about the services.

The main characteristic is that the provider and consumer are inextricably involved in the process of delivering the services. Indeed the process is frequently as much a part of the service as its outcome.

There is a similar way of defining the quality of services. There are two meanings of the term "quality". The first relates to the particular attributes, which serve to define the nature of the service. The second usage refers to a qualifier in measuring such an attribute. The two meanings combined together gives a particular value or level of service characteristic. As an illustration it means that the menu is an attribute of a restaurant meal but the choice of menu is a qualifier, wider choice of menu is a service characteristic.

So service quality per se is so confounded in many cases that it is extremely difficult if not impossible to measure. The consumer of a particular service seeks to satisfy a somewhat hierarchical set of needs and wants partly related to the essential service and partly to subsidiary attributes. An essential purpose might be an overnight stay in a hotel. Subsidiary attributes may include accessibility, convenience of location, availability, timing and flexibility as well as interaction with those providing these service and with other customers. Customers always have the expectations as to now all these needs be met, which are in themselves rather hazy and imprecise. When presented with the actual offering of these multiple variables, the consumers from an impression which is almost immediately compared with expectations and the resultant level of satisfaction is determined. Each customer regards various service attributes as more or less important and various service characteristics as more or less desirable. All together the consumer obtains a service experienced comprised of multitude of service transactions which he selects from an offering. Each transaction contributes to the service experience and has characteristics relating to the whole set of transactions which is more than the sum of the individual elements, which creates an 'overall feeling' or 'image' about the firm.

Gaps in Hotel Services : There exists a considerable amount of difference in perceptions between customers and providers, usually which comes as a surprise to the management of the hotel concerned. There are various evidences that management perception of quality of service frequently differs from the perception of customers, colleagues and hotel staff even. This difference in perception is termed as 'service gap'. Here an attempt has been made to undertake an exploratory qualitative study investigate the concept of service quality. Four different categories are investigated to gain an insight into:

(i) What managers perceive to be the key attribute of service quality?

(ii) What customers perceive to be the key attributes?

(iii) Whether discrepancies exist between these two perception?

(iv) Whether these results can be utilised to establish a general model to more efficiently explain service quality from consumers' stand point?

The upper managerial personnel of 18 hoteliering firms, six hotels each from the High spending hotels, medium spending hotel and low spending hotels existing in the cities of Orissa are surveyed as to what they believe their customers expectations in selecting a hotel, their perception of their own hotels service delivery, what customers particularly like and dislike about their hotel and the overall fulfilments of expectations and satisfaction with their hotel in the view of customers who had spent nights there. The same questions are asked at 200 randomly selected customers staying in those hotels over a period of two weeks, during the month of January 1990. Out of 200 customers 93 were foreign tourists.

Both management and customers are asked to evaluate sixteen attributes on a 1-5 scale where 5 represents the highest rating. T - tests are used between each pair of attributes that represented a potential for service quality gaps. Mean score and significance levels are represented in data.

Four types of gaps are found as shown in the data. λ_1 (= $\alpha_1\alpha_4$) represents the gap between management's perception of consumers expectations (α_1) and consumers' expectations (α_4). λ (= $\alpha_3\alpha_4$) represents the gap between consumer's perceived service (α_3) and consumer's expectation (α_4). λ_3(= α_2 α_4) represents gap between management's perception of hotel service delivery (α_2) and consumer's perceived service (α_3).λ_4 (= $\alpha_2\alpha_4$) represents management's perception of hotel service delivery (α_2) and consumer's expectations (α_4). Lastly λ_5 ($\alpha_1\alpha_2$) represents the gap between management's perception of consumer's expectation (α_1) and management's perception of its service delivery (α_2). A service quality model has been developed here. The gaps leveled in these five propositions have definite impact on the consumers rating of service quality.

Service Gap (λ_1) : It is the gap between management perceptions of guest expectations and the expectation of the guests to determine if management actually knows what its guests expect. The survey reveals that for the most part management believes that guests expect more than the guests themselves expect. In the 10 cases where the gap is significant at < 0.10, guest expectations are higher than that of management only in 5 cases. Three of these five cases, however is considered extremely critical ones where management does not realise their importance: size of room (< 0.01), eating/drinking options (< 0.01) and shops in hotel (< 0.05). It is to be noted that all the five critical areas are clearly intangible functional qualities. These five areas also show up repeatedly in the survey as high in the list of features that travellers, particularly the foreign tourists look for in a hotel which encourage them to return. It should also be noted that many of the attributes which management perceives as eliciting higher consumer expectations are tangible technical qualities in character.

Service Gap (λ_2) : It is the gap between consumer expectations and their perceptions of services received effectually, i.e. what they actually get. In this case the respondents expectations exceed on 5 out of 9 attributes at a significance level <0.10. They are not exceeded, however on attribute 5, 8, and 14, all at < 0.05 significance. All these are critical attributes which primarily constitute the intangible functional qualities.

Service Gap (λ_3) : It measures the difference between consumers perception of delivery and what management believes they deliver i.e. managements success in carrying out what they perceive to be customer's expectation. It is not too surprising to learn that management perceives their service delivery as being more successful than customers perceive it to be in all cases, 9 out of 16 attributes at < 0.10 significance level. It implies therefore that the management of the high spending group and medium spending group hotels are very self-assured and complacent and very oblivious of their failings.

A subjective assessment of gap (X_3) is also done. Respondents of both the samples are asked open ended questions such as what do you (people) find particularly satisfying and dissatisfying about the hotel, where they stay. As multiple responses are permitted there is no significance test. However the most frequent responses and their percentages of total responses are shown in data. These findings show that the intangible are not as outstanding at the high spending group hotels as the management believes them to be. They also show that it is the intangibles at the HSG hotels which upset customers more and not the technical qualities which the management believes are upsetting.

Service Gap (λ_4) **:** It reflects a comparison of managements delivery to consumers expectations. The service gap pattern of A_3 prevails here. Management perceives their services delivery as lower than customers expectation in only three cases. In only two of these, cleanliness and food quality are the difference is significant at < 0.01 level. This clearly indicates a very high expectation of guests in these areas.

Service Gap (λ_5) **:** It measures an internal situation: Does management believe they deliver as much as they believe customers expect? In this case they clearly do believe it, with no significant exceptions.

The respondents of both the sample are asked to indicate on a 1-5 scale, whether the hotel experience is satisfying to them. Whether it meets their expectations. Customers, are asked to rate the hotel in terms of its overall 'image' or quality. The data shows that management once again believes that it is doing a better job of meeting customers expectations and satisfaction than the customers actually feel. It clearly indicates a major gap in service quality of sample hotels. The quality rating by the customers is good in case of H.S.G. hotels but in case of M.S.G. Hotels it is worse and it does indicate a real Jack of service quality. There is no reason for complacency from the management's point of view. The customers of HSG hotels are not really dissatisfied with its services they are less vulnerable to competition in the hotel industry of the state especially in the event of new constructions in a nearby location of the same city. On the contrary the customers are not really satisfied with the service quality of both MSG Hotels, LSG and which are highly susceptible to competitive threats of rival firms, operating in the same locality or cluster.

Quality of services itself largely depends upon the good and effective management. Management should not be centralised or departmentalised in the same way as other tertiary activities. It is supposed to be variable and flexible. It should relate to all activities and be undertaken at all levels of the organisation. It is essentially an integrating process. And hotel industry is very much a people-industry with humane elements. Many customers need to have direct access and interaction with the working staff. Their behaviour and attitude are an essential ingredient of the hospitality functions. They are the part of the finished product that the customer is paying for. An understanding of the pervasive influences, determining the attitude of workers within the establishment, which ultimately determines the quality of services, should therefore, form a central focus of the management. Customers satisfaction which affects the economic return of the hoteliering firm, is likely to be affected as much by the attitudes and behaviour of the staff as by the standard of accommodation and quality of food and other services.

Suggestions: GO System : The essential element in any hoteliering organisation's survival and growth is its ability to generate facilities and opportunities. With increased competition, evolving technologies and changing market needs, food service and lodging concepts are becoming gradually outdated or obsolete than ever before. Attempts to adapt to these changes have resulted in a wide variety of trends: menu diversification, fast food service, computerising the front desk, audio-visual entertainments, specialised conference halls, and ceremonial lounges. Unless the firm keeps abreast of the changes in the market place and manages to generate appropriate opportunities that satisfy consumer needs and anticipate their wants, it risks losing any competitive advantage it might have enjoyed or could attain.

There are many reasons why every department of a hotel should implement GO (generating opportunities) system. The reasons why the marketing function could benefit from a GO system are outlined here:

(a) The industry is fiercely competitive. The business that is constantly identifying, assessing and choosing appropriate market opportunities is likely to become a market leader. By GO system it is able to develop a unique selling proposition which results in a competitive advantage.

(b) The markets for hotel services are highly vulnerable to many factors. The firm has no special protection from competition, moreover shifts in technology, taste, fashion, travel, life-styles and even substitutes products or services can seriously erode a firms' market share.

(c) There is a constant need for novelty and excitement among many customers today. Those that succeed and grow in this business are those that identify what this need means and are able to generate viable opportunities that attracts clienteles.

(d) Market opportunities need not always focus on the new and different but on refinement and improvement of the critical factors. Constant attention on the aspects that ensures improved quality, reliability and care, helps make every guest feel important, welcome, comfortable, secure and safe.

(e) These establishments suffer from irregularities of demand which are difficult to control. By creating new products or services the level of demand of new segment of customers can be brought into a better balance. It raises the frequency of visits of a customer, amount spent per visit and length of his stay.

(f) All products and services offered by a firm, regardless of how novel or unique they once were become obsolete. So there is need to update or replace the concept and facilities when or before their popularity declines and sales fall off.

(g) An attempt to revive a moribund concept, menu or facility through revision, renovation or refurbishment and so forth can help to recycle the demand. It can endure, thrive or grow only if a stream of new products or services replaces those that have been saturated in the market or are of declining importance.

Thus in hotel operations it is necessary to combine the 'production' element of the speedy and efficient provision of accommodation and food and beverage with the people element of a high standard of service and an appropriate attitude and behaviour from its staff. This suggests the need for consultation and team work and for a participative style of managerial behaviour based on the effective integration of a high concern for production balanced with a high concern for customers. In order to realise the aims of the hoteliering firm, the well-trained manager is an essential asset: the professional who combines an understanding of the interlinking roles of marketing, finance and technology with a finely-tuned creative mind and service attitude. Creativity comes into play with the need for introducing services, which without increasing costs encourage guests to spend more within the hotel. The managers would discuss problems directly with the staff, allow them freedom of action within accepted terms of reference and handle difficulties in working relationships by attempting to find solutions agreed with them. A balance needs to be struck between the more easily identified financial costs and profitability and less obvious but equally important long term benefits which makes a positive contribution to the organisational effectiveness and the achievement of objectives.

5

Significance of Hotels

Accommodation facilities constitute the most important item in the package of facilities offered to the tourists. The success of tourism industry depends to a great extent on the availability and quality of accommodation facilities. Modern tourists are becoming progressively conscious of greater comforts and conveniences and as such comfortable accommodation is a deciding factor for growth of tourism. The Estimates Committee of the Lok Sabha in its report for 1975-76 has stated that "since the hotels constitute the most important and, in fact, a basic element of tourism infrastructure, the various measures taken and efforts made to tourism promotion will not produce the desired results if the hotel accommodation in the country lags behind." "Accommodation facilities are the places where tourists stop (cease to be) travellers and become guests. The level of guest satisfaction achieved by an area's accommodation facilities will, in a large measure, determine the total success of the tourism programme."

Various Types

Accommodation facilities can be of many types, viz., hotels, motels, inns, guest houses, private hotels, establishments with bed and breakfast only, holiday camps, holiday and conference centres, paying guest accommodations, choultries, youth hostels, etc. Among them hotels are the most important. Almost all foreign tourists stay in some hotel or the other. The other types of accommodation are mainly used by the domestic tourists in addition to hotels. An attempt was made during the enquiry to find out the relative importance of these different types of accommodation for the domestic tourists.

It could be seen from the table that out of 500 respondents, 323 (65%) used hotels, 134 (27%) choultries, 75 (15%) stayed with friends and relatives, and so on. Hotels being the most important type of accommodation, a large number of tourists use them. Next to hotels, come choultries because they are free or cheap. Till recently most of the pilgrim centres in India had only public choultries meant for the devotees. Now the situation has changed. The concerned authorities are providing fairly comfortable paid accommodation, which is mainly meant for the masses. A survey conducted by the Indian Statistical Institute in 1982-83 revealed that 76.8% of foreign tourists preferred hotels. The relevant figures for youth hostels, host family accommodation, rent-free places and other categories were 4.3%, 12.5%, 1.5% and 4.8%.

As majority of the foreign tourists and about 65% of the domestic tourists, as seen above, use hotels, this class of accommodation is studied in detail.

The Categories

With a view to maintaining standards and enforcing control, the Department of Tourism, Ministry of Tourism and Civil Aviation, Government of India, has a system of categorising the available accommodation as per certain criteria. Accordingly, the hotels could be either approved or unapproved. When a hotel comes in the approved list it presupposes that it is of international standard. Normally a foreign tourist would prefer only an approved hotel because it has the stamp of official recognition. This is an important aspect as far as a hotel is concerned because approval itself is sufficient advertisement. So though not at the initial stages, all the hotels above a particular standard try hard to get this recognition at least in due course. Most of the new hotels constructed as per standards stipulated by the Government automatically come in the approved list. The classification of hotels as per the above stipulations came into effect from 1963 and consequently data on hotels as per the classification are available from that year.

Approved Hotels : The number of approved hotels and the rooms therein are given for a period of time. It could be noted from the table that the number of approved hotels which stood at 186 in 1963 had come down to 166 in 1968 and to 152 in 1971 and steadily increased thereafter. It is not clear how the number of hotels could come down. The Hotel Review and Survey Committee, 1968, has also noted the reduction in the number of hotels but no explanation is given for the reduction. Perhaps it may be due to closure or sometimes due to derecognition. Yet another possible reason for the decrease could be that there might have been differences in the criteria adopted for approval over the years due to changing circumstances. However, there has been continuous increase in the number of hotel rooms. It has risen from 7,085 in 1963 to 29,332 in 1982 as seen from the table.

Over the period, the number of hotels has doubled and that of rooms more than trebled. This high rate of growth is certainly attributed to the patronage given by the Government in terms of some tax incentives and the creation of a Hotel Development Fund in 1968. During the recent years, 1978-1982, by and large the growth rates are lower, both in the number of hotels and in rooms in absolute terms. According to the Federation of Hotel and Restaurant Associations of India (FHRAI), this trend is attributed to reduced incentives. It may be added that during 1982-83 there has been considerable increase in hotel capacity particularly due to the construction of many large hotels on the eve of the Asiad.

Available and Required Hotel Capacity (Approved Category) : It would be ideal if the rate of growth in hotel capacity keeps pace with the rate of growth of tourist arrivals especially when the existing hotel infrastructure is not sufficient. Data reveals that during 1963-82, the increase in the number of hotels and rooms was about 100% and 300%. As against this, the increase in foreign tourist arrivals was 500% during the same period. This shows the wide gap between the demand for and supply of hotels.

It could be seen that throughout the period in question, there has been shortfall in hotel accommodation, which has been very acute since mid-1970s. However, by 1985, the gap between the demand for and supply of hotels, on the basis of projected room capacity and tourist arrivals is likely to be completely wiped out.

1. The foreign tourists stay in hotels for about 70% of the time of their stay in the country. (This percentage is worked out from 'statistical evidence that the average stay is 14 days, of which 10 are in hotels.') But, according to published evidence, the average stay of foreign tourists in India works out to 33 days in 1963, 20 days in 1968 and about 25 days each for the subsequent years. Hence, for the purpose of calculating the hotel requirement, the average stay is taken as 25 days throughout. With the assumed 70% stay in hotels the number of days of stay in hotels per tourist works out to 18 days.
2. The foreign tourist arrivals in a year is taken to be 1,000. Then the total visitor-days (foreign) for which hotel accommodation is needed works out to (1,000 x 18) 18,000.
3. It is estimated that 'the ratio of foreign to Indian guests in 5 star hotels is 73 : 27'. In respect of other approved hotels, this ratio is likely to be lower. The survey of tourists given in data would reveal that the ratio of foreign tourists to domestic tourists staying in luxury class and medium class hotels is 249 : 164—roughly 3 : 2. We have already seen the hotel requirement for the foreign tourists alone to be 18,000. Then the total requirement of hotel accommodation would be (18000 x 5/3) 30,000 visitor days. It would mean that when 18,000 beds are needed for 1,000 foreign tourists, another 12,000 beds have to be provided for the domestic tourists.
4. Normally the occupancy in approved hotels as would be seen later is 72%. If that is so, the total number of beds to be provided would be $\frac{30.000 \times 100}{72} = 41,660$ in a year.

   This works out to 114 beds per day.
5. From a sample of 50 hotels, the room-bed ratio is calcu-

lated for finding out the hotel room requirement for the 114 beds. The ratio works out to 1: 1.87. From this ratio it could be found that for 114 beds 60 rooms are required. Taking the foreign tourist arrivals for different years, the requirement of rooms is worked out for these years. The researcher is aware of the limitations in this calculation, namely, the room-bed ratio may not be truly representative for all the hotels and for all the years.

6. The estimate is conservative as we have assumed uniform demand pattern which is not very realistic.

The available figures in would give the impression that a large number of the tourists did not have any accommodation. But it is not so. Such of those who did not get accommodation in these (approved) hotels would have gone to the unapproved hotels which are not included in the above analysis. While analysing the occupancy ratio, it would be seen that some of the hotels have an occupancy ratio well exceeding the average and it is learnt that in some hotels, which are not covered in the survey, the occupancy ratio is over 100%. This indicates that some of the rooms would have been let out to more than one customer during the day depending on the time of checking out or in extraordinary cases extra beds would have been provided.

Unapproved Hotels : In addition to the approved hotels, there are a large number of unapproved hotels. There are as many as 324 such hotels (as per the *Hotel and Restaurant Guide: India,* 1983). Perhaps, the figure would be even more as the *Hotel and Restaurant Guide* includes only those hotels which are members of either the FHRAI or/and the regional hotel and restaurant associations. One would think that these hotels are substandard in terms of facilities and comfort. But they are not and in fact some of them are awaiting approval by the Department of Tourism. On enquiry it was found that their applications for recognition are pending with the Government. Their recognition is a question of administrative procedures and consequent delay and not one of quality of these hotels. "According to Government sources, applications for star classification from 171 hotels are still awaiting clearance with a room capacity of 14,003."

Even foreign tourists, who normally prefer approved hotels, stay in these hotels as "many of these hotels are clean and those who spend money from their own pockets naturally prefer inexpensive accommodation". ' That is to say, inexpensiveness coupled with comparatively good services and facilities makes these hotels suitable for the middle income and low income classes of tourists—foreign and domestic. As seen already, all along the shortfall in the approved category of hotels has been partly met by these unapproved hotels. Hence while taking an inventory of hotels, it would be realistic to include these hotels also.

Hotels under Construction : Many hotels are under construction or on expansion. "The Ministry of Tourism and Civil Aviation has approved another 205 hotel projects which are in various stages of completion with a room capacity of about 16,765". In Delhi alone 12 new hotels were under construction with an envisaged capacity of 4,358 rooms. Of these about 2,500 rooms were completed in 1982. The pace of construction is beset with many problems like lack of infrastructural facilities and essential inputs and inevitable bureaucracy.

Projection of Hotel Capacity : By the next year, when all on-going projects would be completed, there will be about 60,100 hotels rooms, calculated as under.

Approved hotel rooms	29,332
Unapproved hotel rooms (Awaiting classification)	14,003
Hotels under construction—expected to be ready by next year	16,765
Total	60,100

These projected 60,100 hotel rooms would be just sufficient to meet the demand, at the rate of 60 rooms per 1,000 tourists, for about one million expected foreign tourists. (As noted earlier, the projected demand for hotels include an appropriate fraction of the domestic sector also.)

Star-wise Classification of Hotels : "The criteria for classification have been set by the Department of Tourism and include everything from the size of the room to qualifications of the staff. Initially hotels are classified into 1 star, 2 star, 3 star, 4 star and 5 star. Recently yet another class, namely 5 star deluxe, is added. 1 and 2 star hotels may be referred to as economy class used by budget tourists. 3 and 4 star hotels are referred to as middle class hotels and 5 star and 5 star deluxe hotels obviously come under luxury class.

It could be seen that 2 star hotels outnumber the other hotels throughout. Next comes the 3 star hotels followed by 1 star. The number of 5 star and 5 star deluxe hotels lagged behind the 4 star hotels till 1979. From 1980 the same rose up. But in respect of growth, 1 star hotels have reduced in number, while the growth rate of 2 star hotels is not steady. Perhaps these could have been upgraded consequent on improved facilities. Regarding the rest, there has been significant growth though not uniform. During the 22 year period, the number of 5 star hotels has increased by 586%, 4 star hotel by 158% and 3 star hotels by 208%. The growth in hotel rooms as against the number of hotels would give a more realistic picture. It could be seen from the table that the number of rooms in 5 star hotels has increased faster than that of the other classes of hotels, followed by 3, 2 and 4 star hotels.

A considerable hotel capacity is in the unclassified category of hotels. In fact about 50% of the approved hotels and rooms during 1978-80 remained unclassified. It only signifies the inordinate delay in getting a hotel classified. A hotelier is anxious to get his hotel approved and classified as quickly as possible. It would be in the best interest of the hostelers, if this could be expedited. Things have started moving in this direction. The unclassified hotel capacity is reduced to 30% by 1984 from 50% in 1978-80.

User Pattern vis-a-vis Classes of Hotels : At this stage it would be of interest to study the user pattern of the different classes of hotels. It could be noted that fewer tourists use luxury class hotels compared to medium class and economy class hotels. Only 10% of the foreign tourists use luxury hotels while about 40 and 70% of them use medium and economy classes of hotels respectively. Out of the 500 domestic tourists interviewed, only 343 used hotels of one class or the other. Of these 343, only 17 used luxury class hotels, 157 medium class hotels and 310 economy class hotels. Evidently, it could be concluded from the above, that both foreign and domestic tourists mostly favour the medium and economy class hotels. Hence the need for more of these hotels. But presently over 30% of the hotel rooms are in the luxury hotels. However these luxury hotels are not mainly intended for the tourists. In fact their clientele are mostly from the business and Government.

Extent of Availability of Different Classes of Hotels : Supply of and demand for each class of hotels cannot be equated. Yet, the study of the extent of the tourists getting the class of hotels of their choice would indicate the gap. As, per data the availability of different types of hotels as stated by the foreign tourists is given. (This study is not extended to domestic tourists.)

Out of 48 tourists who used luxury class hotels, 42 (85%) could get this particular accommodation in most cases as indicated by a high percentage of availability, namely 60-100%. Similarly 75% of the tourists who used medium class hotels and 70% of the tourists who used the economy class hotels were able to get the particular class of hotels of their choice to the extent of 60-100%. Such of those who do not get hotels of their choice would naturally go in for other classes of hotels within their reach. From the table it could be seen that the demand for middle and economy classes of hotels is more than the supply, indicating the need for more of such hotels.

Regional Distribution of Hotels : The availability of hotel accommodation in terms of number of hotels or rooms is an important factor in the context of tourism development. Equally important is their geographical location/physical distribution. But there cannot be any hard and fast rule in this regard because normally hotels come up at places of demand and it is not realistic to expect equal distribution. However, it would be of some interest to study the existing position in India regarding the regional distribution and concentration of hotels in metropolitan cities.

The Federation of Hotel and Restaurant Associations of India (FHRAI) has divided the country into 4 regions geographically, viz., northern region covering Delhi, Uttar Pradesh, Rajasthan and all other northern States; Calcutta region covering Orissa, West Bengal, Bihar and other eastern States and eastern Union Territories including Andaman and Nicobar Islands; western region covering Maharashtra, Gujarat, Madhya Pradesh and Goa, Diu and Daman; and southern region covering Andhra Pradesh, Karnataka, Tamil Nadu and Kerala, and the Union Territory of Pondicherry.

The more conspicuous aspects seen from the table may be highlighted here. The regional distribution of the approved hotels is lopsided with 119 hotels in the southern region, 111 in the northern region, 99 in the western region and 41 in the Calcutta region. This would give the impression that Calcutta region is very much lagging behind compared to other regions. This is so because most of the areas included in the Calcutta region, particularly Assam, Tripura, etc., are not conducive for development of infrastructural facilities. Besides there would not be enough demand for accommodation in these areas due to non-accessibility. Even basic transport facilities are being developed only now. Such developments supplemented by the extension of Vayudoot services to this region would improve the tourist flow into the region.

The southern and northern regions are better placed than the other regions in regard to hotel infrastructure. This incidentally reflects the relatively more and increased tourist traffic in these regions. The situation with reference to the northern region would be slightly better when the 12 large new hotels constructed in connection with the Asiad are also taken into account. The position is not much different with reference to the unapproved hotels.

As regards the star-wise distribution of hotels, the northern region stands first in terms of number of all categories of star hotels. With respect to 1, 2 and 3 star hotels, the northern region is followed by the southern region, western region and Calcutta region. On the other hand, the relative position of the regions is different in respect of 4, 5 and 5 star deluxe hotels. Here the northern region is followed by the western region, southern region and Calcutta region.

It is of interest to note that the southern region with the largest number of approved hotels occupies 2nd place with regard to 1,

2 and 3 star hotels and 3rd place in respect of the other star hotels. This is partially explained by the fact that almost 50% of the approved hotels in the region are yet to be classified. Similar is the situation with regard to the Calcutta and western regions also. Perhaps when the classification process is complete, the star-wise distribution of hotels would be different. It also emerges from the study that there is a case for speedier classification of hotels, once they are approved. In respect of unapproved hotels the pattern of distribution is the same.

The distribution of approved hotels in the major 4 metro cities, namely, Delhi, Calcutta, Bombay and Madras, reveals that out of a total of 128, 37 are in Delhi, 12 in Calcutta, 50 in Bombay and 29 in Madras. The relative position of the 4 cities with reference to the unapproved hotels is more or less the same. A casual look at the distribution of hotels in these four cities vis-a-vis their respective regions reveals that 33% of the approved hotels and 30% of the unapproved hotels in the northern region are in Delhi alone. The corresponding figures for Calcutta work out to 29% for both approved and unapproved hotels. Bombay accounts for 50% of approved hotels and 53% of the unapproved hotels of the western region. In the case of the southern region 29% of approved hotels and 9% of unapproved hotels are in Madras. These figures speak of the degree of concentration of hotels in these four cities. This situation should not be explained away by saying that these cities are predominant. The point of interest is that there are other cities in the different regions, but they have not grown as big as the metro cities though most of them have fairly known for the tourist attractions. So a case may be made for extra effort to decentralise the hotels in the less developed cities in the respective regions.

It is of significance to study the position of Tamil Nadu in this context. From the table it could be seen that there are 48 approved hotels, including 23 star hotels and 25 unclassified ones. In other words, 13% of the approved hotels in India and 40% of the approved hotels in the southern region are in Tamil Nadu. These figures are quite encouraging as far as Tamil Nadu is concerned. This is partly due to locational advantage as the major city in the southern region, *viz.*, Madras, is in Tamil Nadu. This natural advantage is supplemented by the more encouraging steps taken by the Government to develop tourism.

The study is further extended with reference to total number of rooms in the four major cities to give yet another dimension to the analysis. It could be seen from data that in respect of the rooms in approved hotels, Bombay stands first with 4,054, followed by Delhi with 3,875, Madras with 2,032 and Calcutta with 1,135 rooms. It may be noted that over 50% of the rooms in the approved hotels are in these four cities, though in terms of number of hotels, these four cities together account for only about 35% of the total number of approved hotels.

It is not intended here to make out a case for equitable distribution of hotels in the different regions/cities or creation of hotels standardised capacity. The differences are bound to exist. This pattern of distribution of hotels would change in due course with the changing emphasis and with the development of new and more tourism centres.

Ownership Pattern of Hotels : It is of academic interest to know the ownership pattern of hotels. This is studied with reference to 364 hotels, both approved and unapproved, taken at random from 16 cities/tourist centres with eight or more approved hotels each according to the *Hotel and Restaurant Guide,* 1983. The data are presented data.

It could be noted from the table that out of 210 approved hotels with 19,801 rooms, 24 hotels with 941 rooms are owned by sole trading concerns, 40 hotels with 2,221 rooms by partnership concerns, 80 hotels with 5,444 rooms by private limited companies and 60 hotels with 10,678 rooms by public limited companies.

It is of significance to note that a large number of luxury hotels are owned by corporate undertakings while a few such hotels are owned by the non-corporate sector. In the case of 3 star and the luxury class hotels the corporate sector owns 60 while the non-corporate sector owns only 16. Out of the 12 one star hotels 3 each are owned by partnership and sole-tradership concerns, 5 by private limited companies and 1 by public limited company. The non-corporate sector owns 20 two star hotels while the corporate sector owns only 11 such hotels.

In terms of rooms, out of 25,325 (approved and unapproved taken together) 10,768 are owned by public limited companies, 6,170 by private limited companies, 5,165 by partnership and 2,123 by sole tradership. In a nutshell, in respect of approved hotels corporate sector claims a major share. In the case of unapproved hotels the non-corporate sector predominates.

This position is not due to any special treatment to the corporate sector in the matter of granting approval, but due to the fact that the corporate sector by and large are financially well off, construct hotels according to standards and stipulations for the grant of approval, while the hotels in the non-corporate sector usually are not of international standards, perhaps due to less favourable financial position.

Size of Hotels : Number of rooms per hotel is taken as the measure of size. Size of hotel depends on a host of factors such as location, class and ownership of the hotel and so on. A hotel in a metropolitan city would normally be big. Similarly higher the 'star' of the hotel, bigger is the size. Further, eventually hotels owned by corporate undertakings tend to be big while those owned by non-corporate undertakings tend to be small as mentioned earlier.

The average size of hotels in Bombay, Calcutta, Delhi and Madras and the all-India average are given. It could be seen that the average size of hotels in these four cities is comfortably higher than the all-India average. The table (last column) also gives the average size of hotels, star-wise. It could be seen that the average size of 5 star hotels works out to 240 rooms, 4 star hotels to 81 rooms, 3 star hotels to 52 rooms, 2 star hotels to 42 rooms and 1 star hotels to 33 rooms. Average size of unclassified hotels works out to 55 rooms. The Hotel Review and Survey Committee reported that the average size of hotels star-wise was 170, 72, 46, 36 and 31 rooms for 5, 4, 3, 2 and 1 star hotels respectively in 1968. Over the years there has been significant growth in the average size of 5 star hotels, i.e., from 170 rooms in 1968 to 240 rooms in October 1982. In the case of other classes of hotels also the size has increased but only marginally.

It could be seen that by and large, hotels owned by soletraderships are small in size compared to others. The average size of approved hotels owned by sole tradership is the lowest with 39 rooms per hotel and is the highest for those owned by public limited companies with 178 rooms. In the case of partnership and private limited companies the average size works out to 55 and 68 rooms respectively.

The average size of hotels, all hotels approved and unapproved taken together, given in the last column reveals that the hotels owned by the public limited companies are the biggest with an average of 174 rooms per hotel. This figure is roughly 3 times, 4 times and 5 times the average size of hotels owned by private limited companies, partnership and soletradership.

***Hotel Room Tariff* :** Fixing the hotel tariff is just like pricing any product or service. It is beset with many problems. The price should be affordable to the public and remunerative to the owners. In the case of hotel industry, the problem of price fixation is more pronounced because of the highly perishable nature of its service, seasonal spurt and slag in the demand and unadjustability of supply to demand in the short run. Further, the cost of construction, operating cost, locational factors, the degree of competition, etc., are also to be considered.

It is said that room tariff normally is not determined by market forces of supply and demand. It is true that tariff quoted by the hotels concerned has to be approved by the Department of Tourism. "But practically every year early in September hoteliers represent to the Department of Tourism for a 10 to 15% increase in their room tariff. Their applications are rubber stamped by the Department and hotel charges go up annually in early October." Why should this be approved? The Department cannot act otherwise. The hoteliers have a better bargaining power because of sellers market prevailing in this industry due to the heavy shortage in hotel capacity.

But, if the market conditions change the pricing mechanism also would change. What has been happening in New Delhi since the Asiad is an example in question. To meet the anticipated short-term increase in demand on account of the Asiad, as many as 12 new and large hotels were constructed. But the anticipated increase in demand did not materialise. The sudden increase in the hotel capacity has changed the market condition from sellers market to buyers market. Many hotels are now selling rooms at cut rates. "Some of them like Samrat of the ITDC Chain have officially announced off-season discounts of 30% but others are doing so under the counter. Two of Delhi's posh hotels are selling rooms to single occupants for as little as Rs. 300 against the listed tariff of Rs. 750 or Rs. 775." This may be an isolated instance but it certainly proves the point that market forces have a definite say in price fixation, apart from regulatory measures by the Government.

Check-Out Time : The room tariff quoted by the different hotels are normally for a day. Some hotels take 24 hours' stay as a day while in others there is a particular check-out time, usually 12.00 noon. The latter practice is certainly against the interests of the inmates. The hoteliers may have their own good reasons. However, it may be suggested that the Government would do well if it tries to maintain uniform and standardised procedure in all hotels. Incidentally this would create a better goodwill among the tourists. It may be added that the hoteliers are seized of this matter and have made a beginning in this direction.

Tariff Plan : The room tariff are of three types, namely, the American, plan, Modified American plan and European plan. "American plan includes three full meals and room. Modified American plan includes the price of the room, breakfast and dinner. No meals are included in room rates under the European plan." The European plan is adopted in most of the unapproved hotels in India. In the case of a sample of 50 approved hotels, 20 offer all the three plans, 15 offer European plan only and the rest either the American plan and/or the Modified American plan.

These different plans are good as far as they go but in passing it may be mentioned that it would be better if the tourists are given the freedom to eat anywhere they like. The American plan and the Modified American plan give the impression that there is an element of compulsion attached to them. This should be avoided. However, in practice almost all the tourists eat from where they stay unless they are on the move. It is important to give the freedom to the tourists because invariably most of them will be on the move on sightseeing during day time and it would be too much to expect them to come back for their noon-meal and sometimes even for the supper. Perhaps there would be some valid reasons from the point of view of the hoteliers, because they should have an assured demand to justify their investment in the restaurant section of the hotel which is not usually frequented by the general public as much as in the case of economy class hotels.

Room Rates in India vis-a-vis in Certain Asian Countries : A comparison of room rates in India with those in other countries shall help in assessing the competitiveness of Indian hotels. In the case of deluxe hotels, Indian rates are the lowest. In the case of 1st class hotels Indian rates are the second lowest, the lowest being that of Colombo. Again ours are the lowest in respect of standard hotel rates and of the economy class. This is confirmed from the survey. It was found that 385 out of 500 tourists have opined that Indian tariff is relatively lower their own countries. About 80 have stated that the tariff is equal to theirs while about 35 stated that the tariff is higher than theirs. It could be concluded from the above that Indian hotel tariff, by and large, is lower. This is a favourable factor and could be effectively used as a promotional incentive. But care must be taken to see that we are not underquoting ourselves. In our eagerness to earn foreign exchange, are we in effect attracting and subsidising the middle and low income foreign tourists at the expense of our own people? It may be suggested that there should be a more pragmatic and realistic approach to the tariff policy.

There may be a temptation to quote lower rates thinking that it will attract more custom but in all probability it will create a psychological feeling among the international tourists that Indian hotels are of a lower standard. They may not appreciate a lower rate for better comforts and services and so as a matter of caution it is necessary to keep a watch on the tariff movements elsewhere and try to keep pace with them. It may be added that the above line of argument/suggestion has been made with respect to tariff prevailing in hotels which are frequented by foreign tourists, who are mostly relatively affluent. As regards the tariff in hotels frequented by domestic tourists, especially the middle and low income group, the need for lower and cheaper rates can rarely be overemphasised.

Sundry Levies : Apart from the listed tariff, some hotels charge sales tax, luxury tax, service charge, etc. There is no uniform code or procedure. These charges and taxes also vary from hotel to hotel. It is officially stated that in hotels which charge service charges, tipping is prohibited. But in practice how effectively this prohibition is done is anybody's guess. In this context, it is suggested that efforts should be made to standardise the procedure and practice with respect to these sundry charges. With the practice there is a psychological inhibition in the minds of the tourists that they are fleeced. An all-inclusive rate would certainly create better goodwill and confidence.

Psychology in Rate Fixing : The user psychology and behaviour should always be kept in mind in tariff fixation. There are tourists who are extremely sensitive to price levels and for them reduced rates would be a stimulant. Yet reduction in tariff must be very cautiously done so that it does not lead to customer suspecting the quality of the hotel. Another category of tourists are willing to pay for quality though price remains the important factor. The third category is the luxury group tourists. "Service has traditionally been a distinguishing, often famous, feature of the hotel. Customers from high income brackets are attracted by the comfort and status of such establishments. Price must be used to reinforce this image rather as a competitive device. These are 'status symbols' for their guests; then they have to ensure that they remain one of the most 'expensive' hotels." That is to say that high tariff sometimes will be a stimulant for the luxury class tourists as much as low tariff will be for budget class tourists. This is an important point to be borne in mind in making tariff policy decisions.

In passing it may be highlighted that there is need for providing enough physical comforts and services commensurate with the tariff. It is seen from the survey that out of 235 foreign tourists staying in star hotels, 152 have stated that the tariff is commensurate with the services rendered. The rest felt that though there are enough physical comforts, the services provided are not satisfactory. This certainly points out that there is greater need for trained personnel at various counters.

Occupancy Ratio : By occupancy ratio is meant the ratio between 'sold rooms' and 'installed rooms'. It means the extent of utilisation of hotel capacity. Hence higher occupancy ratios would mean greater utilisation and *vice-versa.* An unduly high occupancy ratio would indicate a short supply of rooms. Hotel industry on the whole with its 'perishable product' and diverse demand pattern due to time and locational factors cannot hope for 100% occupancy of all its units at all times. There are bound to be differences in occupancy ratios of different hotels for obvious reasons. Hence a study of the occupancy ratio for different types of hotels would help in ascertaining the extent of utilisation of hotel infrastructure and also in deciding upon the priority to be adopted in the development of different classes of hotels.

***Occupancy Ratio for Different Classes of Hotels*:** The all-India average occupancy ratios for different categories of approved hotels are recorded for five years for which complete data are available. It could be seen from the table that the occupancy ratios over the years have come down for almost all classes of hotels, with the exception of 2 star hotels. (No satisfactory explanation can be ascribed to the increase in the occupancy ratio of 2 star hotels. It may be quite accidental.) The average occupancy ratio for all hotels taken together has decreased from 75.8% in 1978 to 70.2% in 1982 and to 64.2% in 1983 and 65.5% in 1984. The decrease could be attributed to increase in total capacity without corresponding increase in demand. In the four-year period the increase in foreign tourist arrivals is only 15% while the number of rooms in approved hotels has increased by 34%. Category-wise the occupancy ratio for 5 star hotels has come down from 87.3% in 1978 to 79% in 1982 and to 66.6% in 1984. The decrease in occupancy ratio of the 5 star hotels is the steepest. This could be due to substantial increase in the number of rooms, to the tune of about 170%. Considering this increased capacity, the decrease in occupancy ratio is only marginal. Similar trend is found in other classes of hotels too. In respect of unclassified hotels there is decrease in both the number of rooms and in occupancy ratio, the latter decreasing steeply. One possible reason for this steep decrease could be that most of such hotels when compared to the star hotels are in places other than the 4 major metropolitan cities where the demand for hotels is comparatively less. It could be seen that out of the 28 unclassified hotels in the northern region only

2 are in Delhi, of the 19 in Calcutta region only 5 are in Calcutta, of the 45 in western region only 17 are in Bombay and of the 59 in southern region only 10 are in Madras.

Now certain questions pose themselves. Whether the present occupancy ratio is normal or otherwise? Whether new hotels should be commissioned or not? If yes, what class(es) hotels are to be commissioned?

Whether the present occupancy ratio is normal or not is a matter of opinion. All approved hotels in India fix room rates according to the modified Hubbert formula. Accordingly, the excess of their operating expenses over income from other sources (restaurant, etc.) has to be recovered from room income, at 60% occupancy ratio. Normally a hotel with 60% occupancy ratio would break even. The approved hotels have 65% occupancy ratio which is certainly very encouraging.

Since the demand for hotel rooms has always been on the increase, more hotels are to be developed. In doing so it should be remembered that foreign tourists prefer medium class hotels and domestic tourists prefer economy class hotels. That means emphasis should be laid on 3, 2, and 1 star hotels and economy hotels like the Janata hotels.

Accessibility of Hotels : Accessibility refers to the relative location of a hotel with respect to the nearest city proper, railway station, bus stand, airport, etc. Normally, except the airport, all other important places including trade centres, bus stand and railway station, are within the city. Till very recently it was thought that hotels should necessarily be within the city proper or as near as possible to the places of activity. That is why almost all the hotels, except the new ones, are located within the city proper. On an analysis of the physical location of 100 hotels, both approved and unapproved. It was found that 94 hotels were within a distance of 10 km from the downtown area, 89 hotels were within 10 km from the nearest railway station and 91 hotels were within 40 km from the nearest airport. 10 km to the railway station/downtown or 40 km to the airport should be considered normal. Now it is clear that the already established hotels are very much within the city complex. Some of them are located even in the most congested and uncomfortable places.

Of late the trend is changing, perhaps not out of choice but out of necessity. Sufficient and convenient land for a new hotel within a city is almost a luxury today. From the tourists point of view, perhaps they will like to have sprawling hotel complex far away from the polluted, noisy and sometimes maddening atmosphere. They will like to have a comfortable hotel with clean and fresh air, extensive gardens, lawns, natural setting, etc. All these could be relatively easily provided if new hotels are located away from the already congested cities. This would initially appear to be an unwise proposition with respect to 'sales'. But with the improved transport and communication facilities and established 'brand image' proximity of hotels to the heart of the city has only limited significance.

The latest thinking on this aspect is the establishment of hotels in semi-urban and rural pockets. "Land is fairly cheap in non-metropolitan areas, so hotels can be built out; they don't have to be built up. Natural light, ventilation and renewable sources of energy can be tapped far more effectively out in the country than they can be in towns. Further such settings lend themselves to the village-hamlet atmosphere, thus attracting domestic tourism from the cities. So if these complexes are effectively planned, they can have a built-in flexibility, responding to quick changing tourist patterns, catering to a wide cross-section of travellers." Such a hotel is referred to as condominium hotel or shortly 'contel.'

Experts consider that there is enough and more scope for 'contels' in India. But the practitioners must be convinced about the new concept. A beginning in this respect is already on the anvil. It is held that with the introduction of travel circuits to develop tourism in a most integrated manner, major hotel chains are thinking in terms of setting up their units at strategic halts so that the groups travelling under their sponsorship could be easily accommodated in their own 'net.' In this regard, the Tamil Nadu Tourism Development Corporation has a place of pride, in the sense that most of its hotels are located *en route* of its weekly conducted coach tours, providing accommodation to its clientele under one roof and at the same time getting an assured business. Thus the 'contel' concept is basically a strategic marketing technic. It is held that 'contel' could rectify the imbalances in hotel industry like too much concentration, too many luxury class hotels, too many large-sized hotels, etc.

Provision of Facilities

Hotels provide a vast range of services and facilities. Though originally conceived as a place where a temporary sojourn is provided, over the years the basic feature of a hotel has changed very much. With the emergence of status-symbol consciousness, hoteliers started playing to the expectations of the public by providing a variety of facilities, some of which are highly sophisticated. The facilities provided by the chosen approved and unapproved hotels are given.

It could be seen from the table that as many as 35 distinctive facilities are provided by hotels apart from accommodation. To ensure competitiveness and to meet the user demands, hoteliers have added a host of services to the 'basket' they sell.

Most of the approved hotels offer varieties of facilities compared to the unapproved hotels. Precisely that is why these hotels come under the approved category. However, in certain respects the hotels have to gear up their services such as own transport facilities, tour arrangements, etc., for the benefit of the tourists. To meet the increasing demand of the business tourists, secretarial and similar services need to be extensively provided.

Normally one would think that this is the way it should be, but there are strong views against this kind of tendency of providing a host of ancillary services. The travel writers, Hugh and Collen Ganzter, opine that "A hotel is a hotel. It is not a restaurant... not a shopping arcade... not a health club, beauty parlour, office centre or convention hall. In other words, we must return to the concept of a hotel as an inn, a hostel and a lodge... Hotels have been forced to engage numerous specialist organisations under their umbrella because their status-conscious guests wanted to be cossetted. That age is passing fast."

However, from what we see around us with respect to the nature and varieties of facilities provided by most of the modern hotels and also the attitude of the so-called elite tourists, it is doubtful whether such change would set in so sooner what is important is the attitude of the tourists and guests and not that of the hoteliers. The possible extent of change in the attitude of the tourists is anybody's guess. After all money increases the craze for luxury. Businessman would cash such human nature.

Complaints : It is but natural that in the case of industries dealing directly with people, there would certainly be complaints by the users as to the quality, range and price of facilities and services rendered. The industry should welcome users' complaints and suggestions and try to do the maximum to eliminate their recurrence.

An attempt was made to ascertain the broad areas of users' (foreign tourists) complaints about hotels in the country. It could be seen that poor maintenance of even available facilities was the major complaint followed by poor sanitation, lack of sufficient physical facilities and the like.

Most of these complaints are real. A day's stay in a hotel would reveal how poorly the installed facilities are maintained. The shortcomings of Hotel. The hoteliers would do well to bestow more attention to the areas of major complaints.

6

Housekeeping Department

The Housekeeping Department in a hotel is responsible for the cleanliness, maintenance and aesthetic upkeep of the hotel. Just as the nomenclature signifies, the role of housekeeping is to keep a clean, comfortable and safe house. It is an extension of basic house-keeping multiplied into commercial proportions. Therefore, just as we enjoy keeping a 'sparkling' home for ourselves and guests who visit us at home, the housekeeping department takes pride in keeping the hotel clean and comfortable, so as to create a 'home away from home'. In the home, it is the lady of the house on whom the responsibility of housekeeping falls. It is not surprising that this tradition extends to hotels as well where the housekeeper is, in most cases, a woman.

The concept of housekeeping is simplistic but when one considers maintaining a 'house' of several hundred rooms and numerous public areas, the task becomes gigantic. It takes a well organised approach and technical understanding to enable housekeeping to cope with the volume of work.

A hotel survives on the sale of rooms, food and beverage and other minor operating services such as the laundry, health clubs etc. Of these, the sale of rooms constitutes a minimum of 50 per cent. In other words, a hotel's largest margin of profit comes from room sales because a room, once made, can be sold over and over again. A good hotel operation ensures optimal room sales to being in the maximum profit.

The room sale is dependent on, apart from several other things, the quality of room decor, room facilities, cleanliness of the room and how safe it is. The criteria by which each guest decides whether a room is good or bad is strictly personal. Since their choice is varied, the task of appealing to all kinds of guests becomes overwhelming. To make a room appealing to a guest is the task of housekeeping which has to ensure the basic human needs of comfort and security. Thus the personal effort the housekeeping department makes in giving a guest a desirable room has a direct bearing on the guests experience in a hotel.

This manual attempts to give readers that technical and human approach to housekeeping which will make their hotel the most sought after.

The Plan

There is no ideal or universal model for the layout of a Housekeeping Department. The layout differs from hotel to hotel and is dependent upon its size and physical space limitation. However, if the housekeeper is involved in the facility planning stage, she must be told the number of function rooms and the volume of business anticipated so as to estimate the amount of linen required as also the types and sizes of table clothes to cater to a variety of tables. She must also determine whether the management intends to contract out horticulture, tailoring, maintenance, upholstery, etc. to include or preclude space for such activities. It is important not to ask for space more than is actually required because space is limited and entails cost. It is necessary to estimate carefully the traffic flows and size of equipment, trolleys, etc. that need to be moved around so that there is no cluttering and congestion. As a rule of thumb, the following spaces would have to be provided for the essential activities of the department.

Main Office

This is the main administration centre for the department. It must be an independent cabin to provide the Housekeeper with silence to plan out her work. It will also provide her the privacy to counsel her staff or hold departmental meetings. It should preferably be a glass panelled office so as to give her a view of what is happening outside her office. The office should be preceded by a cabin for the secretary who would control movement into the Housekeeper's Office.

Desk Control Room : This is the main communication centre of housekeeping. It is from here that all information is sent out and received concerning the department. It is the nerve centre for coordination with the front office, banquets, etc. The Desk Control Room should have a desk and a chair with preferably more than one telephone. It should have a large notice board to pin up staff schedules, day-to-day instructions, etc. The Desk Control Room is the point where all staff report for duty and check out at the duty end. It would normally adjoin the Housekeeper's Office.

Linen Room : This is the room where current linen is stored for issue and receipt. The room should be large, airy and free from heat and humidity. It should have adequate shelves, easily accessible, to stock all linen. It should be secure and offer no possibilities of pilferage. (Linen is expensive and the linen room stores linen worth several thousands of rupees.) The linen room should have a counter across which the exchange of linen takes place. The room should preferably be adjoining the laundry (if the hotel has one) so that the supply of linen to and from laundry is quick and smooth. Only authorised personnel working in the linen room should be permitted to enter it.

Linen Uniform Store : This room stores the stocks of new linen cloth materials for uniforms, etc. The stock maintained should be enough to replenish the whole hotel once over. However, these stocks are only touched when the current linen in circulation falls short due to damage or loss. The room should be cool and dry. It should be provided with shelves and racks to store all linen and uniforms. Larger hotels may have enough space for an independent Uniform Store in addition to a Linen Store.

Uniform Room : This room stocks the uniforms in current use. It is possible that smaller hotels may choose to combine the Uniform Room with the Linen Room. A separate Uniform Room really depends on the volume of uniforms in circulation. The only difference would be that the uniform room would have adequate hanging facilities as many uniforms are best maintained when hung.

Tailors Room : This room is kept for house tailors who attend to the stitching and mending work of linen and uniforms. If the house policy is to contract out all tailoring and mending work, the tailors room could be avoided.

Lost and Found Section : This should be a small space away from the thoroughfare, secure, cool and dry with a cupboard to store all guest articles that are lost and may be claimed later.

Flower Room : This should be an air-conditioned room to keep fresh flowers for such flower arrangements as the hotel may require. The room should have work tables a sink and water supply.

Floor Pantries : Each guest floor must have a floor pantry to keep a supply of linen, guest supplies sand cleaning supplies for the floor. It is the housekeeping nerve centre for the floor. The floor pantry should keep one complete set of linen for that floor over and above what is in circulation in the rooms. The pantry should be away from guest view and situated at the service landing near the service elevators. It should have shelves and cupboards to stack all linen and supplies.

Heavy Equipment Stores : This will be a room to store bulky items such as vacuum cleaners, shampoo machines, ladders for chandelier or window cleaning, etc. The room should be clean and dry. It should also be securely locked to avoid stealing or pilferage by other departments.

Green House : As horticulture comes under housekeeping normally, a green house to foster specialised plants is necessary in the garden areas. The green house should have wooden racks to store pots. etc.

Horticulture Equipment Store : There are a number of garden equipments such as lawn movers, spades, rakes, pots. etc. that are essential to gardening operations. These need to be stored safely. A store close to the gardening operations must be provided. The larger the landscapes to be tended, the larger will be the storage measurements.

Organisation of a Housekeeping Department : The scope of housekeeping embraces the entire hotel Naturally the largest work force of the hotel belongs to the Housekeeping Department. It would be appropriate at this stage to ascertain as to who comprise Housekeeping Department and what their roles are in brief.

Executive Housekeeper : Responsible and accountable for the total cleanliness, maintenance and aesthetic upkeep of the hotel. This is achieved with the resources available to her of manpower, materials, machines, money, space and time.

Assistant Housekeeper : May be one for each shift of a large hotel. She may be the housekeeper of a small hotel or the only deputy to the Executive Housekeeper of a medium-sized hotel. She manages the resources given by the Executive Housekeeper to achieve the common objectives of cleanliness, maintenance and attractiveness in a given shift. Her accountability normally ends on the completion of her shift.

Uniform Room Supervisor : A non-management person solely responsible for providing clean serviceable uniforms to the staff of the hotel. As the hotel staff are all practically in uniforms her task is gigantic as she has to keep an inventory control on various uniforms at various stages of use, such as, when sorted ones are handed over, or those which are being washed or drycleaned in the laundry, or those on the person of the staff, or those in store for issue.

She would set the systems of control as also the budget for the procurement of additional material for room uniforms.

Uniform Room Attendants : The Uniform Supervisor is assisted by Attendants who actually do the issue of uniforms while receiving soiled ones for onward transmission to the laundry. These attendants are in actual contact with the staff.

Helpers : They are to be found both in Uniforms and Linen Rooms and do the physical work of transporting, counting and bundling of uniforms and linen

Linen Room Supervisor : A non-management person soley responsible for the acquisition, storage, issue and cleanliness of linen in its various forms. Types of linen are many, some of which are bed sheets, towels, table clothes, table napkins, etc. Hers is a mammoth task to keep track of all linen as they would number in thousands.

Linen Room Attendant : Assists the Supervisor by actually issuing linen and filling such records as necessary.

Floor Supervisor : Responsible for the cleanliness, maintenance and attractiveness of the guest floors attached to her in a shift. Her scope encompasses guest rooms, corridors, staircases, floor pantries of the allotted floor.

Public Area Supervisor : Responsible for cleanliness, maintenance and attractiveness of all public areas which include restaurants, bars, banquets, gardens, administrative offices, shopping arcade, health club, swimming pool, main entrances and car park areas.

Room Attendants : Known also as chamber maids or room boys. They do the actual cleaning of guest rooms and bathrooms allotted to them. They are not responsible for the cleanliness of corridors, guest elevators or floor pantries.

Housemen : Usually handy men who do the heavy physical cleaning required in guest rooms and public areas. Their job would include heavy duty vacuuming, shifting of furniture, cleaning of window panes, mopping, brassoing, sweeping, etc.

Head Houseman : Supervises the work allotted to Housemen, especially those in public areas. He would deputise on behalf of the Public Area Supervisor especially at night if state laws prohibit women working at night. In medium-sized hotels he could be the person in charge of housekeeping on night shifts.

Desk Control Supervisor : Is the hub of information dissemination in housekeeping and is thus the critical person in housekeeping operations. The Housekeeping Desk must be manned 24 hours as guests and staff will contact this desk to transmit or receive information concerning housekeeping. It is the Desk Control Supervisor who coordinates with the Front Office for information on departure rooms and handing over cleared rooms. The Desk also receives complaints on maintenance from Housekeeping Supervisors spread all over the hotel.

Cloak Room Attendants : Cloak room attendants are persons, male or female, responsible for the cleanliness, maintenance and service in public area guest toilets. Their responsibility would include ensuring the supply of clean dry towels, soaps and perfumeries, if prescribed by the management.

Hat-checkers : This is a service provided by superior hotels in cold climates. A hat-check room is where hat and heavy overcoats are deposited by guests as soon as they enter the hotel lobby so as to spare them from the inconvenience of carrying them around in the hotel. The hat-checker would carefully label these guest articles and hang and store them correctly so as to return them to the guests when they are leaving the hotel.

Night Supervisor : Is special in a manner that would require him or her to be able to handle any aspect of housekeeping at night including desk control operations, issue of linen and uniform in an emergency, etc. Her area of activity extends over guest rooms, public areas as also linen and uniform rooms. She is solely responsible and accountable at night for smooth housekeeping through her night brigade and has larger decision-making authority than other supervisors as she is the housekeeper for the night.

Horticulturist : Many hotels may contract horticultural work to an outside agency. However, a large number of large hotels have horticulturists who maintain the gardens of the hotel as well as supply flowers from the gardens for interior arrangement. Flowers are used largely by Housekeeping to enhance aesthetically various parts of the hotel. They are used in banquet functions, guest rooms, restaurants, lobbies, offices, etc. The horticulturist would have to ensure smooth supply of flowers as well as assist the Housekeeper in flower arrangements.

Head Gardener : Supervises the brigade of gardeners in maintaining hotel gardens and keeping them contemporary each season.

Gardeners : Does the actual digging, planting, watering, etc. of gardens on a day-to-day basis.

The following pages give detailed job descriptions of the above job positions. The list of duties and responsibilities may vary a little from hotel to hotel but the basic gist as mentioned above would remain the same. Job specifications have also been provided to aid in recruitment and selection.

Job Descriptions of Housekeeping Personnel : A job description, by its very nomenclature is a written description of the job to be performed in a job position. It specifies the parameters within which a job is done. It is thus a realistic guide to any employee recruited for a particular job. These parameters not only include duties and responsibilities but reporting relationships, authority and control, coordination with other departments, status within the departmental hierarchy, etc. Professional organisations would normally hand over a job description to all new recruits. This offers several advantages.

1. The new recruit knows exactly what his or her job entails. This in itself is a vital part of induction.
2. A job description acts as a basic foundation to set standards of performance. This induces and informs the exact standards expected of them.
3. The job description ensures that both the superior and subordinate view the job required to be performed in commonality, otherwise this could lead to misperception of the job and thus friction.
4. It acts as a legal document for any disputes arising out of lack of role clarification.
5. It protects an employee from an unreasonable superior who may like to overburden an employee through unnecessary role deviations.

In addition to job descriptions are job specifications. A job specification stipulates the type of person required to do a particular job as defined by a job description. Figure below is a typical format for a job specification as also points that explain it.

Executive Housekeeper : This is one of the most important positions in the hotel since it carries responsibility for the cleanliness, maintenance and aesthetic appeal of facilities in order that they are sanitary, desirable and in saleable condition. The good housekeeper, because of the need to cooperate with many other department heads, must possess a high degree of tact as well as good organising ability. To achieve an understanding of the total scope of the job, given below is a typical job description.

Job Description

Title of position:	Executive Housekeeper.
Reports to:	Hotel General Manager.
Supervises:	All Housekeeping employees.
Coordinates with:	Food and Beverage Manager, Chief Engineer, Front Office Manager, Night Manager, and Laundry Manager.

Scope of Job

1. Supervise and be responsible for cleanliness, order and appearance of the hotel rooms and public areas, annexes, cottages, employees, facilities, service corridors, linen and uniform rooms and shopping arcades.
2. Schedule, recruit, train, recommend hiring, discharging and discipline of all department employees through management and in accordance with labour regulations.
3. Prepare reports as required.
4. Participate in all department head meetings.
5. Supervise preparation of maintenance requisitions and maintain follow-up file to ensure that all public areas and guest accommodations do not deteriorate from standard.
6. Train all employees to perform the standard procedures as applicable to their job positions.
7. Develop and recommend standard procedures for new tasks or changed conditions.

8. Inspect personally, and supervise inspections by Assistants of all areas in a frequent and unvarying schedule.
9. Pay particular attention on inspection to the presence of odours and pests.
10. Work closely with the General Manager on day-to-day Housekeeping requirements.
11. Supervise all linens and recommend the maintenance of adequate quantities of cleaning equipments and cleaning supplies with due regard to delivery requirements and import restrictions.
12. Develop and supervise the maintenance of the lost and found procedure including the disbursement of unclaimed articles to employees.
13. Prepare the annual housekeeping budget for submission to the General Manager.
14. Identify reliable suppliers of housekeeping materials including carpets, linen, etc. and recommend them to the Purchase Department.
15. Develop housekeeping systems and procedures and see that they are followed.
16. Plan, control and supervise horticultural requirements and commitments.

Among the Executive Housekeeper's duties, the following should never be overlooked:

1. Daily inspection of public spaces and employees' locker rooms.

2. The issuance of orders to housemen, window washers, upholstery and furniture yard employees and cleaners. Daily breefing of Housekeeping Supervisors, Room Attendants, Uniform Room and Linen Room Supervisors.
3. Daily checks on the quality of house cleaning in guest rooms with particular attention to suites.
4. Checking incoming order of supplies.
5. Immediate attention to complaints.
6. Inspection trips of shops, linen room and guest rooms and the issuance of instructions for correction.
7. Coordinating the preventive maintenance schedules of rooms with the Maintenance Department.
8. Daily review of the reports of Deputy Housekeepers/ Supervisors and/or Head House man.
9. Immediate attention to requests from guests and to orders and requisitions involving replacement or change of room equipment.
10. Frequent contact with the Interior Decorating Services covering proposed work, work-in-progress and finished work.

Job Specification

Job Title:	Executive Housekeeper.
Category:	Management.
Educational Qualifications:	Minimum graduate, preferably in Home Science or a Diploma in Hotel Management.
Age Limits:	30-45 years. Higher ages will be considered on individual merits.
Equipment Skills:	Knowledge of all housekeeping equipment.
Physical Qualification:	Healthy and Sturdy. Should be able to prepare a budget.
Mental Qualification:	Must display leadership skills.
Personality Consideration:	Written and spoken English and/or Hindi and the local language.

Language Skills:	Minimum five years as a Deputy Housekeeper or Incharge of hospital, or college hostels.
Previous Experience Desired:	Should be good at managing resources of money, materials, space, time, men and equipment.
Special Requirements:	Should have training skills and an eye for detail.

Housekeeping Supervisor : This position should be occupied by a competent, personable individual who knows her employees well and is, above all, able to meet the public. This latter requirement is important since supervisors are actually representatives of the Executive Housekeeper in the areas assigned to them.

Job Description

Title of Position:	Housekeeping Supervisor.
Reports to:	Assistant Housekeeper.
Supervises:	Housekeeping employees allotted to her area of activity.
Coordinates with:	Front Office, Engineering, Laundry, Room Service.
Scope of Job:	*Public Area*

1. Check all public areas against area check-lists and see that they meet the standards of cleanliness stipulated.
2. Remove furniture, curtains and other fixtures, which require repairs, mending, spotting, washing, etc.
3. Maintain a regular and complete advance scheduled programme for renovating public areas after receiving the final concurrence of the Executive Housekeeper.
4. Prepare schedule for the chandelier cleaning crew.

5. Prepare schedule for the carpet shampoo crew.
6. Inspect staff turnout.
7. Train new recruits.
8. Submit performance appraisals of staff working under her control.
9. Clean safety and security systems in public areas, e.g. locks, shutters, etc.
10. Account for furniture movements, if any.
11. Initiate and follow-up maintenance orders for public areas/ service area under her control.
12. Check and control equipment like hoovers, floor washing machines, floor polishing machines, carpet shampoo and beating machines and ensure that they are used correctly.
13. Undertake daily rostering of staff when required.

Floors

1. Assign duties to the Floor Housemen and Room Attendants.
2. Inspect staff turnout.
3. Inspect each room completed by Room Attendants according to specified room checklist and ensure they meet the standards of the establishment in terms of cleanliness, functional and aesthetic value.
4. Check par stocks of linen and guest supplies and cleaning supplies on floors and ensure timely delivery of soiled linen to laundry and requisition fresh linen from linen room, guest supplies/cleaning supplies from the stores.

5. Train Room Attendants and Housemen for maximum productivity and standards of efficiency.
6. Submit performance appraisals periodically for each staff under her control.
7. Check all safety systems on the allotted floors.
8. Liaise with security on security aspects on guest floors.
9. Account for movement of linen from her floor.
10. Prepare housekeeping occupancy lists for Front Office.
11. Check all maid's carts to ensure it is well stocked with linen and supplies and as per standard layout.
12. Follow up on maintenance orders sent to Engineering. Sign for work completed.
13. Liaise with Housekeeping Desk for list of rooms that need to be cleared for sale.
14. Call room service for the clearance of soiled trays from guest rooms.
15. Check on the serviceability of all housekeeping equipment on the floor.
16. Undertake daily staff scheduling when required.
17. Record "lost and found" items as per laid down norms.

Job Specification

Job Title:	Housekeeping Supervisor.
Educational Qualification:	Minimum graduate, preferably in Home Science. Senior room attendants may also

	be considered provided they have six years experience and a craft course in Housekeeping.
Age Limits:	26-35 years.
Equipment Skills:	Must be able to handle vacuum cleaner.
Physical Qualification:	Healthy and sturdy.
Mental Qualification:	Ability to do simple calculations.
Personality Consideration:	Should display leadership skill.
Language Skills:	English, Hindi and preferably the local language.
Previous Experience:	Three years in a similar capacity.
Special Requirement:	Must have an eye for detail. Social skills to meet guests.

Uniform/Linen Room Supervisor : His/her basic role is to issue uniforms and linen to staff according to systems and procedures laid down by management. Also to control the movement of soiled and fresh linen and uniforms to and from the linen/uniform room.

Job Description

Title of Position:	Uniform/Linen Room Supervisor.
Reports to:	Assistant Housekeeper.
Supervises:	Linen room attendants and helpers.
Coordinates with:	Laundry essentially but all other departments' personnel.

Scope of Job:

1. Schedule linen/uniform room staff.
2. Check periodically the condition of uniform and hotel linen.
3. Assign daily work to tailors.
4. Devise and maintain an effective control system to issue clean linen and uniforms.

5. Coordinate closely with the Laundry department to ensure timely supply of fresh uniforms and linen.
6. Conduct periodic inventories of linen and uniforms.
7. Ensure that all linen, uniforms needing stitching, mending are immediately attended to before being sent to the Laundry department.
8. Ensure that the Linen Room is kept neat and clean.
9. Ensure that all linen, uniforms, materials are neatly and systematically stacked and arranged.
10. Train the staff to perform their duties effectively and, efficiently.
11. Maintain all relevant records in respect of material, uniforms/linen—their storage and movement.

Job Specification

Job Title:	Uniform/Linen Room Supervisor.
Category:	Non-Management—Skilled.
Education Qualificational:	Same as Housekeeping Supervisor.
Age Limits:	21-35 years.
Equipment Skills:	Basic handling of sewing machine.
Physical Qualification:	Healthy and sturdy.
Mental Qualification:	Ability to do quick calculations.
Personality Consideration:	Should display administrative qualities.
Language Skills:	English, Hindi: preference local language.
Previous Experience:	Five years in a Linen/Uniform Room.
Special Requirements:	Well organised.

Night Supervisor **:** Supervises all night force engaged in cleaning public areas and guest rooms of the hotel.

Job Description

Title of Position:	Night Supervisor.
Reports to:	Assistant Housekeeper
Directly Supervises/ Controls:	All staff working at night in the Housekeeping Department.
Limits of Authority:	Report on the performance of night crew.
Coordinates with:	Engineering—for maintenance follow-up.
	Front office—for receiving, departure rooms and cleaning them for sale.
	Security—on security aspects.
	Lobby Manager—for receiving any managerial decisions.
	Room service—for clearance of trolleys from guest floors.
	For placing complimentary VIP baskets and bars.
Scope of Job:	Same as given for a Floor Supervisor and Public Area Supervisor.

Job Specification

Job Title:	Night Supervisor.
Category:	Non-Management.
Minimum Educational Qualifications:	Graduate in Home Science preferably with a three-year diploma in Hotel Management or one-year craft course in housekeeping.
Age Limits:	21-35 years.
Equipment Skills:	Knowledge of all housekeeping equipments.
Physical Qualification:	Healthy and sturdy.
Mental Qualification:	Should know simple calculations.
Personality Consideration:	Should display administrative and leadership skills.

Language Skills: English, Hindi and preferably the local language.

Special Requirements: Should be a mature career-minded woman with an eye for detail.

Room Attendant : This position is perhaps one of the most critical in a hotel as it comes under every resident guest's scrutiny. His efforts in keeping the rooms clean and safe directly contributes to the guest experience.

Job Description

Title of Position: Room Attendant.

Reports to: Floor Supervisor.

Supervises: Housemen and Trainees.

Coordinates with: Housekeeping Control Desk, Laundry, Room Service, Engineering.

Scope of Job:

1. Clean guest bathrooms and replenish supplies.
2. Clean guest bedroom and replenish supplies as per room checklist.
3. Report missing or broken hotel property to the Floor Supervisor.
4. Maintain a polite, dignified and helpful attitude towards the guests.
5. Attend daily briefings and give attendance.
6. Receive allocation of floor and rooms.
7. Replenish maid cart with guest supplies, detergents and linen.
8. Count soiled linen handed over to floor linen room.
9. Handover lost and found articles to Supervisor.
10. Make physical check of rooms for preparing the Housekeeping Occupancy List.

11. Check that all bulbs and switches are working, in case of defect or fuse, report the same to the Floor Supervisor.
12. Change the water glasses daily and fill the water flasks.
13. Turn down beds in the evening and draw the curtains.
14. Remove and dispose off refuse and rubbish at the assigned area.
15. Return keys to the Housekeeping Department before going off duty.
16. Ensure that Housemen polish guest shoes and assist the Bell Boys in carrying luggage when required.
17. Prepare room checklist.

Job Specification

Jop Title:	Room Attendant or Chamber-maid.
Category:	Non-Management—skilled.
Educational Qualifications:	High School, preferably with a craft certificate in Housekeeping.
Age Limits:	21-35 years.
Physical Qualifications:	Healthy and sturdy.
Mental Qualifications:	Should do simple counting.
Personality Considerations:	Personable and well-groomed.
Language Skills:	Should understand English and be able to communicate in basic English.
Previous Experience:	One year preferred.
Special Requirements:	Must have high personal standards of hygiene and cleanliness. Should have no hesitation to clean rooms and bathrooms.

***Uniform Linen Room Attendant*:** The role of this position is to issue uniforms and linen to staff according to systems and procedures laid down by the management. Also control movement of soiled and fresh linen and uniforms.

Job Description

Job Title: Uniform/Linen Room Attendant.

Reports to: Uniform/Linen Room Supervisor.

Scope of Job:
1. Issue uniforms to all hotel employees on a one-to-one basis.
2. Count soiled uniforms/linen received and deliver the same to the Laundry department.
3. Maintain records of linen and uniforms movement.
4. Store uniform and linen according to prescribed methods.
5. Check for damages when receiving dirty uniforms.
6. Check for fitness of uniforms as per norms laid down before issuing.

Coordinates with:
1. Upholsterers and tailors; Linen and Uniforms Room Supervisor, Floor Boys, and Maids.
2. Laundry for sending soiled linen and uniforms and receiving fresh ones.

Job Specification

Job Title: Uniform/Linen Room Attendant.

Category: Non-Management—Semi-skilled.

Minimum Educational

Qualifications: Matriculate.

Age Limits: 21-35 years.

Physical Qualification: Sturdy.

Equipment Skills: Nil.

Mental Qualification:	Should be able to do basic counting.
Personality Consideration:	Nil.
Language Skills:	Local Language, Hindi.
Experience required:	None.
Special Requirements:	One month departmental training.
	1. Females would be preferred at this job.
	2. Emotional stability understress essential.

Cloak Room Attendant : The role of this position is to maintain high sanitation standards in cloak rooms in public areas and to ensure the safety of hotel property in the assigned area:

Job Description

Title of position:	Cloak Room Attendant.
Reports to:	Public Area Supervisor.
Supervises:	Junior Housemen/Sanitors.
Coordinates with:	None.
Scope of job:	1. Take soiled hand towels to the linen room for replacement.
	2. Maintain adequate stocks of soap, detergents and hand towels to meet demands at peak level.
	3. Maintain shoe-shine kit and clean guest shoes if required.
	4. Maintain all cupboards and fixtures installed in the cloak room.
	5. Maintain a polite, dignified and helpful attitude to guests.
	6. Report any plumbing deficiencies to Public Area Supervisor.
	7. See that cloak rooms are emaculately clean. Faucets should be sparkling,

wash basins dry and the environment free of unpleasant odour.

8. Supply the guests with towels, soap, comb, brush and powder.
9. Sweep, wash and scrub the floors.
10. Clear the soiled linen periodically from the baskets and keep in Janitor's Room provided.
11. Brush the guest's jacket if required.

Job Specification

Job Title:	Cloak Room Attendant.
Category:	Non-Management—Unskilled.
Educational Qualifications:	Matriculate.
Age Limits	21-35 years.
Equipment skills:	Nil.
Physical Qualifications:	Sturdy.
Mental Qualifications:	Nil.
Personality Consideration:	Well-groomed.
Languages	Should understand English.
Previous Experience	Nil.
Special Consideration	Should have personal standards of hygiene and cleanliness.
	Should be willing to work in bathrooms.

Tailor/Upholsterer : This job position entails stitching and mending linen and upholstery as assigned and replenishing all upholstery which requires replacement.

Job Description

Job Title:	Tailor/Upholsterer.
Reports to:	Linen Room Supervisor.
	Assistant Housekeeper.

Work Performed

1. Mend all damaged linen.
2. Mend all damaged uniforms.
3. Refurnish all damaged upholstery which is given by the Supervisor.
4. Estimate the requirement of material and request the Linen Room Supervisor to requisition it from stores.
5. Withdraw material from the stores and take to the work area assigned.
6. Pre-shrink all materials which have a tendency to shrink.
7. Cut the material as per requirement of each particular item.
8. Check the quality of springs, foam and replace, if necessary under directions of the Linen Room Supervisor.
9. Fasten springs properly with strings and place the foam in position.
10. Keep the work area assigned neat and tidy.
11. Keep systematically all items, i.e. needles, thread, etc. and requisition and render accounts of the same.
12. Render account of material consumed and balance left over should be handed back to stores.

Directly Supervises/ Controls : Sewing machines.

Coordinates with : Linen Room Supervisor.

Job Specification

Job Title: Tailor/Upholsterer.

Category: Non-Management—Skilled.

Minimum Educational

Qualification: Matriculation.

Age Limits: No limits but within superannuation age.

Equipment Skills: Adept at using sewing machines.

Physical Qualification: Healthy and sturdy.

Personality Considerations: Nil.

Language Skills: Hindi.

Experience Required: Five years experience in tailoring of linen and upholstery.

Special Requirements: Nil.

Head Gardener **:** This job position is required to maintain landscaped area and gardens in a hotel as prescribed keeping in mind cleanliness, aesthetic appeal and freshness all the year round through a well motivated team of gardeners.

Job Description

Job Title: Head Gardener.

Reports to: Horticulturist/Executive Housekeeper.

Work Performed:

1. Ensure that the prescribed landscaping in terms of gardens, rockeries, waterways, etc. are maintained as per original concept.
2. Brief, schedule and allot duties to gardeners to meet daily exigencies.
3. Dig-up landscaped areas for fresh planting.
4. Procure seeds from reliable sources at least cost.
5. Be knowledgeable about seasonally of plants and their maintenance conditions.
6. Procure, control and supervise the usage of manure and fertilisers.

7. Ensure that seeds planted are done so with consideration for ultimate aesthetic appeal and survival.
8. Ensure that gardeners follow the watering schedules, reporting any water shortage problems and suggesting alternatives.
9. Cut, prune, trim hedges, bushes, flowers to enhance aesthetic appeal.
10. Maintain nursery up to prescribed conditions and ensure steady supply of saplings.
11. Provide the hotel with flowers, garlands, wreaths, bouquets as required. Also prepare, provide and maintain indoor plants for the hotel.
12. Ensure that lawns are well mown and kept clean at all times.
13. Train and motivate gardeners.
14 Ensure that gardeners handle garden tools and machines correctly and carefully.

Directly Supervises/ Controls : All gardeners.

Coordinates with:
1. Fertiliser supplier—for supply of acceptable fertiliser.
2. Nurseries and seed markets—for purchase of good quality saplings seeds.
3 Housekeeping—for maintenance of indoor plants.
4. Flower shop—for supply of flowers (if applicable).

Job Specification

Job Title: Head Gardener.

Category: Non-Management—Skilled.

Minimum Educational Qualification: Matriculate.

Age Limits: Nil, but below prescribed superannuation age.

Equipment Skills: Should handle lawn mowers.

Physical Considerations: Sturdy.

Mental Qualification: Simple counting.

Personality Considerations: Nil.

Language Skills: Hindi.

Minimum Experience Required: Eight years as gardener in a reputed nursery, garden, etc.

Other Qualification:

1. Ability to work under varying weather conditions.
2. Thorough knowledge of types of plants and their conditions.

Houseman : The Houseman's job is to do heavy physical work as assigned such as hoovering carpets, cleaning large window panes, carrying heavy furniture, washing of public areas and garbage clearance as also complement the work of room attendants on guest floors.

Job Description

Job Title: Houseman.

Reports to: Floor Supervisor/Public Area Supervisor. Asst. Housekeeper.

Works Performed

1. Hoover carpets.
2. Shift beds, chairs, heavy furniture for cleaning carpets beneath them.
3. Beat carpets and shift from one area to another.
4. Clean swimming pool when assigned.

5. Clean all surfaces including garden paths, etc.
6. Polish all brassware.
7. Clean all windows, doors and ventilators.
8. Clean and replenish linen from floor and pool area.
9. Do all heavy cleaning like shaft cleaning, terrace cleaning.

Directly Supervises/ Controls : None, only the equipment used.

Coordinates with: The area assigned.

Job Specification

Job Title: Houseman.

Category: Management—Semi-skilled.

Minimum Educational Qualifications: Matriculation.

Age Limits: 18 to 40 years.

Equipment Skills: Should handle vacuum cleaners, carpet beaters, shampoo machines.

Physical Considerations: Strong and sturdy.

Mental Qualification: Able to do simple counting.

Personality Considerations: Well-groomed.

Language Skills: Should understand English and communicate in basic English.

Experience Required: Nil.

Special Requirement: Nil.

Gardeners (Malis) : The gardener keep landscaped areas and gardens clean, aesthetically beautiful and fresh through daily schedules as assigned.

Job Description

Job Title:	Gardener.
Reports to:	Head gardener. Horticulturist.
Work Performed:	1. Take daily briefing from Head Gardener. 2. Dig landscaped area to keep to concept as also for fresh planting. 3. Plant seeds and saplings as per conditions and concept prescribed. 4. Lay manure and fertilisers economically ensuring proper coverage. 5. Water all gardened areas as per daily schedule and routine. 6. Maintain the nursery as instructed. 7. Cut, trim, prune hedges, bushes, flowers to enhance aesthetic appeal. 8. Prepare such flowers, potted plants, wreath, bouquets, etc. as required by the hotel. 9. Maintain indoor plants as per schedule when assigned. 10. Utilise garden tools correctly. 11. Be punctual and regular.
Directly Supervises Controls:	None.
Coordinates with	Housekeeping—to maintain indoor plants.

Job Specification

Job Title:	Gardener.
Category:	Non-Management—Semi-skilled.

Minimum Educational Qualification:	Matriculate.
Age Limits:	18 and above but below superannuation level.
Equipment Skills:	Should be able to use basic garden tools, lawn mowers.
Physical Qualification.	Sturdy.
Mental Qualification:	Nil.
Personality Consideration:	Nil.
Language Skill:	Hindi.
Minimum Experience Required:	Two years as gardener in a reputed nursery, garden, etc.
Other Qualifications:	1. Ability to work under varying weather conditions.
	2. Thorough knowledge of types of plants and their conditions.

Departments that Housekeeping Coordinates with

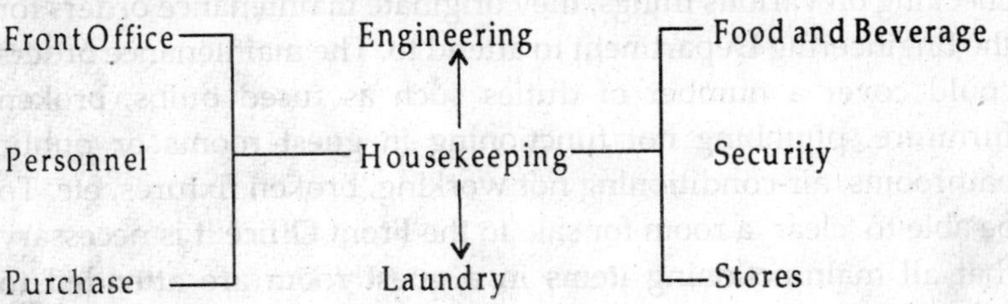

Front Office

Coordination with the front office is one of the critical features of housekeeping operations. As soon as there are guest departures the Front Office rings the Housekeeping Desk and reports the room numbers of rooms vacated so that Housekeeping can take them over to clean and prepare for sale. Once a room is clean, the Housekeeping Floor Supervisor rings the Front Office directly or through the Housekeeping Desk and hands over the room to front office for sale. Rooms received by Housekeeping for cleaning are called "departure room" while cleaned rooms handed to the Front Office for sale are called "clear rooms." The precision with which the above duty is done enables the Front Office to have rooms to sell to a waiting customer. This is especially critical in hotels with high occupancies.

Personnel : Housekeeping coordinates with the Personnel Department for the recruitment of housekeeping staff, salary administration, indiscipline, grievance procedures, identity cards for staff, induction, locker facilities, transfers, promotions and exit formalities.

Purchase : The Purchase Department procures out-of-stock items for Housekeeping such as guest supplies kept in rooms, stationery, linen of various types, detergents, etc.

Engineering : One of the most important functions of Housekeeping is the maintenance aspect of the hotel for the purpose of keeping furniture, fixtures and facilities in working order, contemporary and safe for guests. Hence a close coordination is necessary with Engineering which actually carries out the task of fixing out-of-order furniture and fixtures. As Housekeeping personnel are constantly spread throughout the entire hotel, checking on various things, they originate maintenance orders for the Engineering Department to attend to. The maintenance orders could cover a number of duties such as fused bulbs, broken furniture, plumbing not functioning in guest rooms or public bathrooms, air-conditioning not working, broken fixtures, etc. To be able to 'clear' a room for sale to the Front Office it is necessary that all malfunctioning items in a guest room are attended to promptly by Engineering. Hence close coordination/cooperation is necessary. Housekeeping would also hand over rooms to Engineering for major repairs or renovation.

Laundry : This is a department that can either enhance or mar the quality of housekeeping services. The responsibility of laundry to housekeeping is two-fold:

(a) To wash and dry-clean linen and staff uniforms to a very high standard of cleanliness.

(b) To supply clean uniforms and linen to Housekeeping on time.

Housekeeping has to ensure that clean linen is issued to guest rooms, restaurants, health clubs, etc. as this directly reflects the quality and image of the establishment. If these are not received on time from the laundry, rooms would not be ready or restaurants would not open, etc.

The coordination becomes critical in view of the large volume of linen and uniforms that is involved.

Food and Beverage : The restaurants and banquets constantly require clean table clothes, napkins, etc. Their staff, as well as those in the kitchen, require clean uniforms—the former because they are in guest contact and the latter due to strict standards of hygiene required in kitchens by most governments.

Security : The guest room is the most private place and a hotel goes to great lengths to ensure guest privacy and security. However, a guest can take advantage of this privacy by gambling, smuggling, etc. Housekeeping has to be alert to these goings-on, and seek the Security Department's intervention if necessary.

Stores : Larger hotels have a Housekeeping Store that stocks housekeeping linen and supplies independently. Smaller hotels may stock them in the general store except for linen which should be issued to the Housekeeping Department. The coordination with the Stores would ensure the availability of day-to-day requirements of Housekeeping.

Manning, Recruitment and Selection : Having decided on the physical layout and facilities in the Housekeeping Department, the next task for the Housekeeper is to decide how many people should comprise her work force. This is a critical factor as ad hoc recruitment could result in excess work force and high wage bills. The number of people would depend upon the structure of the hotel, i.e. block construction or clusters of rooms, etc. number of floors and rooms per floor, number of public areas, size of landscape, etc. However, as a guide for Housekeepers, given below are certain common norms to aid in determining the manning strength.

Executive Housekeeper	1	Only for a hotel over 300 rooms.
Asst. Housekeeper	2	To cover two shifts while the Executive Housekeeper covers one general shift. This level of housekeeper could be the No. 1 Housekeeper of a medium-sized hotel, i.e. 100 to 299 rooms.
Floor Supervisor	1 :30 rooms	For a morning shift.
	1: 60 rooms	For an evening shift.
Public Area Supervisor	1/shift	The Night Supervisor would oversee public area work.
Linen/Uniform Room Supervisor	1	Even if the two areas are separately located.
Linen/Uniform room helper	1 /shift	
Room Attendant	1:14 rooms	This is subject to floor layouts and physical location of rooms.
Linen Attendant	1 /shift	Additional attendants may be had depending upon size and complexity of linen operations.
Houseman	1 : 60 rooms/shift	
Desk Attendant	1/shift	
Tailor	Subject to load	This service is usually contracted out.
Upholsterer	1	This service is usually contracted out.
Horticulturist	1	Only if the hotel as large landscaped spaces. Otherwise this service can be contracted out.
Head Gardener	1/20 gardeners	
Gardeners	1/4500 sq. ft. of landscaped area	

Recruitment and Selection : The processes involved in recruitment and selection are:

1. Tapping the right source.
2. Developing man-specifications.
3. Applications for the job.

4. The interviewing process.
5. The selection process.

The sources of supply for housekeeping manpower are:

Executive Housekeepers

(a) Local hotels.

(b) Asst. Housekeeper in the hotel.

(c) One developed from in-house housekeeping management programmes.

Asst. Housekeepers

(a) Housekeepers of medium-sized hotels.

(b) Promotion of Housekeeping Supervisors within the hotel.

(c) One developed from in-house housekeeping management programmes.

Supervisors

(a) Local hotel management schools with six months induction in the hotel.

(b) Promotion of deserving room attendants within the hotel.

(c) Floor Supervisors from competitive hotels.

(d) War Widows Association.

(e) Employment bureaus.

(f) Housekeepers of hospitals and school/college hostels.

(g) Home science colleges.

(h) Local craft institutes.

Room Attendants	(a) Local craft institutes
Linen Attendants	(b) Local schools and colleges
Cloak Room Attendants	(c) Employment bureaus.
	(d) Local domestic science schools.
	(e) Hotel's personnel departmental active files.
Houseman	(a) Employment bureaus.
	(b) Hotel Personnel Department's recruitment file.

Tailors	(a) Local tailor shops.
Upholsterer	(a) Local furniture marts.
Gardeners	(a) Horticultural departments.
	(b) Local nurseries.

Job specifications or man-specifications give a description of the person for particular job. In recruitment, the job specifications must be clearly identified so as to make correct selections.

***Pre-interview Activity*:** Prior to interviews, the following needs to be ensured:

1. All candidates should apply on the prescribed hotel application form. This ensures standardisation of records as well as receiving the kind of information that the hotel would like to know.
2. Coordinate with members of the interview panel for the date, time and venue of the interviews. In determining the venue, ensure that there are two secluded spaces: (a) one in which candidates will wait, and (b) the other where the interview board will sit. The venue should be easily accessible to the interviewees and should ensure that operational areas do not get crowded.
3. Communicate to prospective candidates the date, time, venue and the person to be contacted.
4. On the day of the interview ensure there are enough chairs, sofas in the waiting room to seat candidates. Literature on the hotel and drinking water should also be provided. In the interview room a large desk should be installed with chairs to seat the inter view board on one side and a chair for the interviewee on the other. Copies of the application form for the list of candidates, duly filled, interview rating forms, pads and pencils should also be provided.

The Interview

1. Interviews must commence on time. Remember the candidate is evaluating the organisation on the basis of his/her experience during the interview process.

2. The candidates must know the sequence in which they will enter for interview.
3. One of the basic principles in the interview process is to let the candidate talk. One of the faults that arises is that the Board speaks more than the candidate.
4. Stick to the requirements as specified in the job description and job specification.
5. Put the candidate at ease to bring out the full potential of the candidate.
6. Note down comments in the interview rating sheet.
7. Ask such questions that would illicit information over and above what is given in the application form. Questions on information in the application form may be asked for further clarification only.
8. Remember to ask for salary slips in support of salary details given by a candidate employed in another organisation. Ask for references to later establish the genuineness of a candidate.
9. Give an opportunity to the candidate to ask for details of the organisation, its benefits and the job involved.

Selection : The following matters need to be kept in mind when making a selection.

1. The physical condition of the candidate. Housekeeping employees must be sturdy and healthy. Reject obese/fat people as they could be prone to blood pressure and heart problems.
2. Read the application form closely to ascertain why a candidate has left his previous employment.
3. Check the type of reference given.
4. Check the length of service in previous organisations—a chronic job-hopper is not desirable.
5. Check that the candidate meets the job specification in terms of education, experience, age, etc. Avoid selecting over-educated people because they could be unhappy in a job that will not challenge or stimulate them over a period of time.

6. Select strictly against vacancies.
7. There are a number of tests available to determine a candidates proficiency in language, dexterity, conceptual skills numeracy, etc. Check with the hotel's Personnel Department for such tests.
8. Inform all candidates, whether selected or not, about their status as a consequence of the interview.

Qualities of Housekeeping Staff : For the purpose of recruitment, induction, training and self-development it is essential to know the qualities that Housekeeping staff must possess. These are as important as the skills they possess because of the nature of business that hotels are in. Being a service industry, personal projection of staff enhances the image of the hotel as well as the quality of personalisation that only humans can give.

Grooming : Most essential especially for Floor and Public Area Supervisors, Room Attendants and Housemen who are in guest contact. Such staff would be normally uniformed, hence each staff member must ensure that his/her uniform crisp, clean and well pressed. Lady staff must wear light make-up and restrict their jewellery to the minimum such as wedding bands and ear tops. A light cologne is preferred to heavy perfume. Hair must be tied in a bun or worn short. Most hotels have a maid's cap for chamber maids. It keeps the hair in place as well as ensures hygiene. Shoes worn must be low heeled and sturdy as housekeeping staff work long hours on their feet.

Personal Hygiene : A guest would be quite revolted if he sees that the people who service his bed and room, (which he perceives as personal) are dirty and unhygienic. Housekeeping staff must have clean hair, manicured fingernails, clean hands and feet and must take steps to ensure that no body or mouth odour is present. Staff must report to the doctor in case of infections, cuts or bruises as this could effect personal and guest safety.

Honesty : This is a very essential attribute for housekeeping staff, especially Room Attendants, who have access to all guest rooms. Guest belongings, sometimes invaluable are often found lying around in the room. The temptations to thieve are great—it is only the personal quality of discipline and integrity that checks these temptations. "Lost and found" again gives housekeeping staff a chance to smuggle out of the hotel guest belongings that are lost inadvertently. Honesty ensures that the procedure laid down for such cases is followed strictly.

Courtesy : Room Attendants, Floor and Public Area Supervisors are always in contact with guests. It is often that a guest requests some housekeeping service or the other. It is essential that while talking to guests in such moments, it should be done with utmost politeness and charm. Guests will certainly remember pleasant staff as this adds to his or her positive experience.

Tact and Diplomacy : Often guests may request comforts and services that are outside the management policy. It takes a lot of tact and diplomacy to decline-without hurting a guest's feelings. Occasionally, room attendants are confronted with embarrassing situations both for the guests and the staff member. It is tact alone that can diffuse such a situation.

Eye for Detail : It is one of the greatest qualities that housekeeping staff must have. It is with this quality that the finer aspects of housekeeping are taken care of and it is what determines a good service from an average one. This quality enables housekeeping staff to take into consideration the minutest details.

Physical Fitness : Most work in housekeeping is manual. A housekeeping member when on duty is on his/her feet almost continuously. It would require a sturdy physical constitution to cope with the demands of housekeeping work. This quality is essential and must be stressed at the time of recruitment of housekeeping staff. This can be ascertained through the personal medical history of candidates as well as by medical examination by the Company doctor. This quality may also be observed during the probationary period of the employee.

Cooperativeness : Housekeeping staff need to be cooperative to achieve efficiency in the hotel. For example, if they are not willing to clear rooms for sale in the stipulated time, the Front Office will be unable to sell a room to earn more revenue or may be faced with an irate customer who has a confirmed reservation but is waiting to be allotted a room because it is being attended to by the housekeeping department.

7

Housekeeping Know-how

Laundry Services

The relationship between Housekeeping and Laundry is very significant for the smooth functioning of housekeeping services. The importance of Laundry is inevitable as it processes soiled linen and uniforms and supplies Housekeeping with clean stocks on a daily basis to maintain high standards of housekeeping. It is thus important for housekeeping personnel to know something of the operations of the laundry to fully understand its importance and contribution.

Valet Service : One of the primary roles of the laundry is to provide valet services to house guests. A valet is one who, on call, fetches soiled clothes from guest rooms and returns them either washed or dry-cleaned as per the guest demands. In hotels that do not have an in-house laundry, it is the Housekeeping Department that provides the valet service. The Housekeeping Control Desk phone number in such a case is listed in the guest room directory of services. It is essential for housekeeping personnel to know that in a guest room there are two laundry slips distinguished by their different colours—one signifying dry-cleaning requirements while the other washing requirements. Both forms have similar listings of various common garments that gents and ladies wear. The guest is required to fill the appropriate form and submit it along with the soiled clothes in laundry bags provided. Sometimes the valet is required to fill the form in the presence of the guest. What must be noted is the guest's name, room number, signature and most important when the laundry is required. For 'same day' service the hotel levies an additional charge. If the hotel is unable to provide a 'same day' service the valet must inform the guest accordingly. The valet must inspect each soiled garment of the guest and bring to his notice any tears, stains, etc. that he may like to have attended to. This is also a precaution lest the guest sues the hotel for damages. There are times when a guest leaves his laundry bag in the room without informing the laundry when he goes out. It is then the room attendant's responsibility to call Laundry and deliver the laundry to the valet.

Hotel X Y Z Ltd.

Name .... Room No .... Date ....

To be Returned ❑ Today ❑ Tomorrow ❑ Express Service

Required on ❑ Hanger ❑ Folded

Gentlemen Count	Guest Count	Hotel Rs.	Price Rs.	Amount
Shirt			15.00	
Suit			40.00	
Safari Suit			40.00	
Coat			20.00	
Trouser			20.00	
Vest			5.00	
Underwear			5.00	
Socks			4.00	
Handkerchief			2.00	
Pyjama Suit			25.00	
Pyjama/Loongi			15.00	
Shorts			10.00	
Ladies				
Dress			35.00	
Blouse/Ladies Shirt			15.00	
Petticoat			15.00	
Bra			5.00	
Panty			5.00	
Skirt			20.00	
Pyjama Suit			25.00	
Pants			20.00	
Nighty			16.00	
Stocking			8.00	
Saree			25.00	
Salwar Kameez			28.00	
Children				
Shirt			10.00	
Shorts			6.00	
Dress			15.00	
Pyjama Suit			15.00	
Trousers/Jeans			15.00	
Total:				

Please tick the desired service √

Services and Charges:

Normal Service:

Laundry collected before 10 a.m. will be returned on the same day after 6 p.m. at no additional charge. Sundays and Holidays normal service on 25% extra charge.

Urgent Service:

Laundry received between 10 a.m. and 1.00 p.m. for same day return will be charged 50% extra.

Express Service:

Laundry given between 8 a.m, and 8 p.m. to be returned within 3 hours, will be charged double.

General:

In case of any discrepancy or an undeclared defect the order will be executed only after further clarification.

In case of any loss or damage the hotel will be responsible for a sum not exceeding 5 times the cleaning charges of the garment.

In case of any special laundry jobs required please contact our Laundry Manager who will be glad to help.

Please do not pay cash. The amount will be debited to your room bill.

Kindly check pockets before sending laundry.

Guests are requested not to leave the laundry outside their rooms. Our valet will be happy to assist. Dial.

V. No: Guest Signature

Name	Room No.	Date
Pieces	Voucher No.	Amount

Hotel X Y Z Ltd

Name .... Room No .... Date ....

To be Returned ❑ Today ❑ Tomorrow ❑ Express Service

Required on ❑ Hanger ❑ Folded

Gentlemen Dry Cleaning	Guest Count	Hotel Count	Price Rs.	Am Rs.
Suit (2 Pcs)			50.00	
Coat			30.00	
Trouser			20.00	
Waistcoat			15.00	
Safari Suit			40.00	
Tie			10.00	
Overcoat			55.00	
Pullover			20.00	
Shirt			18.00	
Pressing				
Suit (2 Pcs)			27.00	
Coat			15.00	
Trouser			12.00	
Waistcoat			10.00	
Tie			5.00	
Shirt			8.00	
Ladies Dry-Cleaning				
Costumes (2 Pcs)			50.00	
Salwar Kameez			35.00	
Dress			45.00	
Saree			30.00	
Blouse/Shirt			18.00	
Skirt			25.00	
Pants			25.00	
Shawl			25.00	
Cardigans			20.00	
Pressing				
Costumes (2 Pcs)			25.00	
Salwar Kameez			25.00	
Dress			15.00	
Saree			15.00	
Blouse/Shirt			8.00	
Skirt			15.00	
Pants				
Total:				

Please tick the desired service √

Services and Charges:

Normal Service:
Laundry collected before 10 a.m. will be returned on the same day after 6 p.m. at no additional charge. Sundays and Holidays normal service on 25% extra charge.

Urgent Service:
Laundry received between 10 a.m. and 1.00 p.m. for same day return will be charged 50% extra

Express Service:
Laundry given between 8 a.m and 8 p.m. to be returned within 3 hours, will be charged double.

General
In case of any discrepancy or an undeclared defe the order will be executed only after further clarification.
In case of any loss or damage the hotel will be responsible for a sum not exceeding 5 times the cleaning charges of the garment.
In case of any special laundry jobs required please contact our Laundry Manager who will be glad to help.
Please do not pay cash. The amount will be debited to your room bill.
Kindly check pockets before sending laundry.
Guests are requested not to leave the laundry outside their rooms. Our valet will be happy to assist. Dial 7.

V. No: Guest Signature

Name	Room No.	
Pieces	Voucher No.	Amount

Exchange of Soiled and Fresh Linen/Uniforms with Laundry : The procedure for receiving soiled linen and uniforms by the Linen Room has already been explained in Ch. 6. The linen and uniforms are sorted out in the Linen Room, counted in the presence of a representative of the laundry and handed over in bundles. When fresh linen is received, this is checked against the Linen Exchange Form.

Process of Laundry

Sorting and Marking : When soiled linen, uniforms and guest garments are received by laundry they are sorted out according to those requiring dry-cleaning and those requiring washing. They are further sorted into degrees of soilage, type of fabric, so that the concentration of detergents can be applied accordingly. Guest garments are marked by indelible ink on tags that are stitched onto the garments.

Washing/Dry-Cleaning **:** Sorted garments or linen are washed or dry-cleaned in batches in the machines provided.

Hydro-Extraction/Tumbler **:** Washed linen or garments contain water twice their weight. The water is squeezed out in hydro-extractors. The clothes are removed when the cloth has approximately 25 per cent water left. This is recommended for effective ironing. Articles like towels, bath mats, etc. which have a woolly texture are dried in tumblers to retain their fluffiness.

Ironing **:** Larges cloths like bedsheets, table cloths, pillow cases, etc. are ironed with a flat iron also called a calender machine. It works by passing cloth through two cylinders retaining steam with felt covering that gives heat. The cloth is fed by laundry staff called feeders and received at the other end by folders who fold the linen as prescribed by the Housekeeping Department.

Uniforms and guest garments are ironed by means of various types of presses:

Hot head press—

where two flat surfaces press the garments. Both surfaces are hot.

Steam press—

same principle as the hot head press except that the surfaces have perforations through which steam passes.

Shirt press—

special press to give gents' shirts their proper contours and creases—specially sleeves, shoulders and collars.

Hand press—

common domestic press used for light garments and linen.

Other Information on Laundry : Laundering has for many generations been carried out mainly by rule of thumb and it is only in recent times, that research and investigation of different methods have been made. Research has shown that laundering is a very complex and difficult procedure. In brief, laundering procedure can be divided into three parts:

(a) What has to be laundered, i.e. textile fibres.

(b) What is used in laundering, i.e. water, soaps, detergents and alkalis.

(c) How laundering is carried out, i.e. washing processes, starch and associated treatments.

What has to be Laundered : The textile fibres may be classified in three categories:

1. Vegetable fibres, animal fibres, synthetic or man-made fibres:
   - (i) Vegetable fibres—which have their origin in some form of plant life. These are cotton, linen, jute.
   - (ii) Animal fibres—which have their origin from animal life. These include wool, silk.
   - (iii) Synthetic or man-made fibres—such as nylon, Dacron, terylene. Except for vegetable fibres, animal and synthetic fibres safely respond to dry-cleaning procedure. But in case they are top dirty, they too can stand a mild wet cleaning treatment.

What is Used in Laundering

Water : It is the most important material used in laundering, not only because of the large amount required but also because the success or failure of the washing process depends upon the suitability of water supply.

One source of water is rain which, as it falls, comes in contact with compounds of the atmosphere and is able to absorb some of them. It thus becomes slightly acidic in nature. This acid rain may dissolve some minerals from the earth. Water from springs and wells carries many compounds dissolved in it.

The most important impurities in water from the laundering

point of view are the compounds of calcium and magnesium and in certain cases, iron.

When a soap is added to hard water, the calcium and magnesium compounds react with soap to form insoluble 'lime soaps' which are precipitated in the form of a sticky paste that traps dirt and redeposits it on the fabric. Thus instead of becoming white, fabric becomes dull and greyish.

The hardness of water (power to kill the soap) again can be divided into two parts:

Temporary hardness (bicarbonates of calcium and magnesium) which can be removed by boiling (changed into carbonates).

Permanent hardness (sulphates of calcium and magnesium) which can be removed by chemical treatment known as water softening.

Soap and Detergents : Soap has been known to man from earliest times, when it was customary to mix the ashes of wood fire under the cooking pot with rancid fats from the cooking pot itself. Today soap is made by the contribution of fatty acid and alkalis at different temperatures.

A good soap in laundering should have the following properties:

(i) Good washing power (detergency)

(ii) Ease of rinsing

(iii) Easy solubility and purity

Synthetic Detergents : The main disadvantage of using soap in laundering is that it is killed by hard water. It is sensitive to acids and to salts. Careful attention in rinsing is required in order that no traces of soap are retained in the fabric. Detergents give more efficient performance in hard water, are easily soluble and are easily rinsed from fabric. They can be used with the builders or alkalis. In general, they are not as efficient soil removers as soap/alkali solutions. It is at the oil suspension stage that the synthetic detergents appear to be weaker and inferior to soap/alkali solution. Because of this, redeposition of soil may take place.

The use of CMC (carboxymethyl cellulose) in synthetic detergent/alkali solution brings about a great improvement as the redeposition of the suspended soiling matters is resisted and with better whiteness results.

Alkalis : They are used in laundering for a variety of reasons. The main reason is that the cleaning effect, when they are used in conjunction with soap or other detergents is greater than with soap or detergent alone. They are also known as builders. At times they are used to soften water before addition of soap. Acids and alkalis are measured according to a scale of values known as the pH scale. The pH scale has fourteen main divisions from 1-14. Pure water has a pH value of 7 and is a natural point.

An alkaline solution has a pH value more than 7, the farther away from 7, the stronger is the alkaline solution. A solution which is acid has a pH value below 7. The farther away from 7 the stronger the acid. pH value denotes the nature of alkali and not the amount of alkali present in the solution.

A strong alkali can only be used on cotton whereas a mild alkali on wool and silk.

The following are the lists of alkali used in the Laundering Department: (a) sodium meta-silicate, (b) trisedium phosphate: also known as (soda ash) and sodium carbonate and (c) sodium silicate also known as water glass and borax.

Sodium metasilicate is preferred for three reasons in laundering (where the hardness of water is not more than 4 degrees), otherwise soda ash.

A 0.2 per cent solution of metasilicate has the right amount of active alkalinity to convert the acid soap to soap rapidly and effectively. Active alkalinity is measured according to the pH scale. A 0.2 per cent solution of metasilicate has a pH value of 11.2.

Also, sodium metasilicate does not set stains and thereby has the power to suspend dirt.

Washing Processes : In any washing process, there are four stages. These stages are of equal importance and failure of any one of these will cause a fault in the final result. They are as follows:

(i) Wetting out

(ii) Soil removal

(iii) Soil suspension

(iv) Removal of soil from machine

Wetting Out : In this stage the load must be thoroughly and evenly penetrated by washing liquors. Without this thorough wetting, no washing process can be efficient. Although this holds good for all processes, it is especially important in the case of wool washing. Wool is naturally water-proof and resists wetting, and because of this, special attention must be paid to the wetting out stage.

Soil Removal : The separation of soil matters from the fabric is the main object of the washing or cleaning process. The best conditions for soil removal have been the subject of intense research, and it has been found that these conditions differ according to the type of article washed. It must be obvious that failure at this stage means failure of the whole process.

Soil Suspension : Precaution against redeposition of soil on the fabric can be taken by holding the soil in suspension in the washing liquors. It is not generally realised that this part of the process is the most difficult, and that the slightest departure from the correct conditions means a lowering of the standard of washing. The difficulty arises from the fact that the soiling matters appear to have a powerful attraction for fabrics and are readily redeposited. When the redeposition is spread evenly, the result is generally greyness. Sometimes the redeposition is uneven when it may take the form of black specks, known as scum.

Removal of Soil from Machine : The rinsing stage is of no less importance than the other stages. It should be understood that, in the first place, rinsing is a continuation of the soil suspension stage, and that all the conditions for soil suspension must be maintained until all soiling matter have been removed. Only when there is no longer danger of redeposition of soil can the detergent liquors be removed entirely. The main object of rinsing is the gradual dilution of the detergent liquors and gradual reduction of temperature in the machine.

Bleaching : Bleaching with sodium hypochlorite has no dirt removing power. It is impossible to bleach dirty work and make it white. Bleach may improve the colour of white work after all the soiling matter has been removed. But this is not a good practice. It is better to produce a good colour by correct washing methods. Control of bleaching procedure should be rigid, especially the amount of bleach and the temperature.

There are five conditions for the use of a laundry bleach: (i) Know the strength of the bleach purchased. (ii) The maximum strength of bleach in a machine should never exceed 5 g available chlorine per gallon of detergent liquor or 3 g available chlorine per pound of load. (iii) Highest temperature should be 140°F. (iv) The required amount of bleach should be diluted with water before adding to the washing machine. (v) The diluted solution should be added as the machine rotates downwards, so that the bleach is carried in the washing liquor immediately and not sprinkled over the work, as would be the case, if the machine were rotating upwards.

Blueing : It is very difficult to retain the whiteness of white linen and washed linen. Eventually it becomes yellow white. This yellowness can be corrected by applying a film of blue in the linen which gives it the appearance of a better white.

It is not possible to make a dirty fabric look white by blueing. The effect of blue would be to make the colour farther away from white, since the blue is used to correct yellowness.

Fire Prevention : In dealing with this subject it is necessary to realise that it falls into two separate categories— Fire prevention and Fire Fighting.

One of the most important requirements for fire prevention is good house-keeping—house-keeping of the kind that fall under the jurisdiction of the Maintenance Department rather than the Housekeeping Department. This kind of good housekeeping automatically, through orderliness and the elimination of hazards, helps to prevent fires.

The Chief Engineer is normally responsible for fighting fires in each hotel. He is responsible for instructing every employee in his department on organising and supervising fire drills and for the maintenance of a well trained group which acts as a fire patrol as well as fire fighters.

The instruction given to maintenance employees should enable them to be able to classify types of fires and to be familiar with the proper methods of extinguishing them. Some fires call for a wetting and cooling method below the ignition point, others require a blanketing effect which either excludes or dilutes oxygen to a point where it will not support combustion.

Classification of Fires : For all practical purposes, there are three general classes of fires:

Class A : Fires occurring in ordinary dry combustible materials such as wood, textiles, papers, rubbish, etc. In these fires the quenching and cooling effect of quantities of water or solutions containing a high percentage of water are of first importance.

Class B : Fires in inflammable liquids such as oils, grease, etc. In these fires a blanketing effect is essential.

Class C : Fires in electrical equipment where the use of non-conductive agents are required for extinguishing them.

Types of Extinguishers : For Class A fires the soda acid extinguishers, which eject water under gaseous pressure when they are inverted, are effective. Their use is limited, however, to small fires since they contain only two and a half gallons of water. Direct application of water from hoses must be used when fires are beyond the capacity of these small extinguishers.

For Class B fires carbon dioxide (fog or foam) extinguishers are required.

For Class C fires carbon dioxide fog is the extinguishing agent of choice since it is non-conductive. Care must be exercised in using carbon dioxide extinguishers. The nozzle should never be touched with bare hands when the extinguisher is in operation.

Regardless of the type of fire, carbon tetrachloride or mixtures containing carbon tetra-chlorkit; should not be used.

Distribution of Extinguishers : As a guide to the adequacy of protection, given below are some tips:

Class One: In light hazard occupancy, such as offices, or

public areas, there should be one fire extinguisher for every 5,000 square feet so located that an individual will not be required to travel more than 100 feet to reach the nearest extinguisher.

Class Two: Ordinary combustible occupancy, where fires of broader extent may be anticipated, such as kitchens boiler rooms, etc. Locations of this nature should have an extinguisher for every 2,500 square feet so located that an individual will not be required to travel more than 50 feet from any point to reach the nearest extinguisher.

Class Three: Hazardous occupancy, such as woodworking shops, upholstery shops, paint shops, etc. This class should be protected with one extinguisher for every 2,500 square feet so located that an individual will not be required to travel more than 50 feet from any point to reach the nearest extinguisher, plus special extinguishers in confined areas for special hazards. It is to be understood that fire hose racks connected to standpipes or emergency water supplies are included in the extinguishers mentioned above.

The Suggestions

The following is the chronological sequence of procedure to assist hotels in developing their own individual fire fighting method. Circumstances may not always permit adherence to all of the points in this line of approach but it should prove advantageous.

1. Close windows and doors of the room in which the fire has started. If in a general area close doors to all surrounding rooms.
2. Ascertain the extent and seriousness of the fire.
3. Ring fire alarm box or call switchboard operator for internal assistance. Remember that it is advantageous to avoid the hysteria which accompanies a general fire alarm.
4. In informing the telephone operator give a quick accurate description of the location and extent of the fire. This will avoid loss of time through misdirection of the Maintenance Department or the outside Fire Department.

5. Employees of the Maintenance Department should proceed to the location of the fire with extinguishers from their department as rapidly as possible. A fire cart is recommended.
6. Employees of the Maintenance Department should consider it their duty to remove all combustible or volatile material away from the fire area.
7. The first consideration must always be for the safety and peace of mind of the guest. Personnel having contact with guests must maintain an attitude of calm and reassurance.
8. If the fire is in a guest's room, the guest should be evacuated immediately into the corridor and the corridor doors and adjoining room doors should be closed.
9. It is recommended that the emergency stairs are used for evacuating guests.

First Stairs : In most hotels the stairwell known as the service stairways are also the fire stairways. Stairways are hazardous even under the most favourable conditions. As a result the problem of keeping treads clean and free of oily or other slippery substances, as well as steps and railings in structurally safe conditions, is important. These passageways should always be kept well lit clean and free of obstruction and debris. Keeping stair shaft areas clean and bright with suitable light coloured paints lends a great deal to promoting general safety. At the same time these procedures induce cooperation towards general cleanliness and sanitation.

Care of Fire Extinguishers : Fire extinguishers may be rarely or never used, however, when they are needed, they are needed in a hurry and must always be in working order. All fire apparatus, should be in working order. All fire apparatus, extinguishers, hose, valves and sprinkler systems should be inspected semi-annually and carry tags indicating the date of inspection and the initials of the inspector. This work may be done by trained Maintenance Department employees or by an outside contractor. Used extinguishers and hoses should never be replaced until they have been properly serviced.

In the case of a woven fire hose, the procedure involves stretching the hose flat and drying in thoroughly before replacing.

If this procedure is not followed weak spots will develop which rupture the first subsequent time that water pressure is applied.

Tank type (soda acid, fog and foam) extinguishers must be recharged. This work should be done by experienced professional people.

In addition to the periodic inspection described above, it is necessary that soda acid extinguishers be tested at least every two years to ensure the solidity of the outside container and to ascertain the condition of the discharge hose and nozzle. These tests will avoid the possibility of explosions which can occur where tank bodies are weakened by corrosion or nozzles plugged.

Both Housekeeping and Maintenance Department employees should constantly be on the alert to ensure that fire extinguisher stations are not used to store or serve as temporary resting places for room service trays or cleaning materials.

Fire Regulations : In following the suggested procedure outlined above, each hotel should develop a set of fire regulations. These regulations should be printed, framed and posted adjacent to every extinguisher and in service landings and personnel locker rooms.

Fire Alarm Systems : The fire alarm system and its coding should be thoroughly understood by every Maintenance Department employee. Printed copies of the code should be displayed in the Maintenance Department, all shops and service stairways.

Fire alarm systems should be tested monthly. These tests might well be conducted in concert with employee fire drills. If an alarm has been pulled it should be re-set and the glass replaced immediately following the fire. This is a responsibility of the Chief Engineer.

The Chief Engineer should ensure that the fire alarm system has an uninterrupted supply of electric power. He is responsible for ensuring that the system is connected to the emergency generator or, in the absence of such a generator, an alternate supply of power, such as a bank of storage batteries, which are properly connected and in working order.

Fire Doors : Like other fire equipment, when the need arises their proper functioning is very important. Therefore, they should be under constant observation and care. Fusible links and door closers should be inspected semi-annually and fire doors must never be blocked.

Fire Drills : The hotel management and the Maintenance Department should cooperate in organising fire brigades around a cadre of Maintenance Department employees. This brigade should, at the time an alarm is called, be so organised that it can arrive at the scene of the alarm properly equipped in less than two minutes.

Employees of other departments, such as Housemen, Maids and Waiters can be organised to assist in such tasks as removing furniture, directing guests, etc. Properly organised drills held on a monthly or bi-monthly basis can serve as a very effective weapon in campaigning against a potential emergency.

Fire Protection Checklist : The manager of each hotel should either personally supervise the use of the checklist or delegate the responsibility for examining the checklist after the Engineering Department has made the survey. Any items that are shown as effective as a result of the review should be promptly entered in a log book for correction. The management should follow up and insist that appropriate action be taken on every open item in the log book until the deficiency is corrected. A notation should be made in the log book when the defect has been eliminated.

Note: Draw a line through any item listed below that is not pertinent to your hotel. The following items should be checked on a monthly basis:

	Date Checked	*Log, Page No.*
1. Check all exits and exit lights.	( )	....
2. Stairways on fire escapes unobstructed.	( )	....
3. Clean air-conditioning filters.	( )	....
4. Check filters, kitchen hoods.	( )	....
5. Test fire alarm system.	( )	....
6. Check floor lamps for long or worn cords.	( )	....
7. All sprinkler control valves open.	( )	....

8. Check fire pump operation. ( ) ....
9. Check fire supply lines and tanks. ( ) ....
10. Check watchman's time charts. ( ) ....
11. See that all house fire alarm boxes and hose outlets are unobstructed. ( ) ....
12. Clear rubbish at shaft bottoms. ( ) ....
13. Check fire doors, shutter, for defects. ( ) ....
14. Are any extinguishers missing? ( ) ....
15. Are stair doors kept closed? ( ) ....
16. Remove waste behind stoves, ranges, refrigerators in kitchen. ( ) ....
17. Are there clean housekeeping conditions? ( ) ....
18. Check "No Smoking" signs in restricted areas. ( ) ....
19. Check fire hazards, paint shop. ( ) ....
20. Check fire hazards, carpenter shop. ( ) ....
21. Check fire hazards, upholstery shop. ( ) ....
22. Check fire hazards, cellars, ballrooms and other public rooms. ( ) ....
23. Exits obstructed—signs and lights? ( ) ....
24. Fire appliances visible for use? ( ) ....
25. Plentiful supply of ash receivers? ( ) ....
26. Electrical outlets overloaded? ( ) ....
27. Rubbish or waste in ante-rooms? ( ) ....
28. Check hazards in sample rooms. ( ) ....
29. Flameproof decorations used? ( ) ....
30. Emergency lighting system? ( ) ....
31. Check laundry ducts and hoods.

The following items should be checked on a semi-annual basis:

32. Hold fire brigade drill. ( ) ....
33. Check fuse boxes for improper fuses. ( ) ....
34. Are vital records safely protected? ( ) ....
35. Clean all electric motors. ( ) ....
36. Examine and check space heaters. ( ) ....
37. Test kitchen range extinguishing systems. ( ) ....

38. Do window screens open easily? ( ) ....

39. Clean ail vent ducts. ( ) ....

40. Is exit information posted in guest rooms? ( ) ....

41. Are more ash trays needed? ( ) ....

Textiles : There are four major methods by which cloth is produced:

1. Weaving 2. Knitting

3. Braiding 4. Melting of loose fibres.

1. Weaving is a method of fabric construction in which two sets of yarns are interlaced at right angles. The manner in which the sets of yarns are interlaced determines the characteristic of the fabric and variety.
2. Knitting is the construction of a fabric by forming the yarn into loops which hang one upon the other. This fabric may be constructed from a single yarn that runs across the fabric from a single group of yarns that run lengthwise, the work may be done by machinery or by hand.
3. Braiding is the method in which yarns from a single source are crossed diagonally and lengthwise; this form of interlacing is used not only with every type of textile fibre but also with a wide range of materials such as straw, leather or any flexible material which can be made into a continuous length.
4. Melting of loose fibres is called felting. The fibres are laid in thick layers and a treatment with chemicals is given by which fibres are beaten up to form a fabric. Wool is the most common fibre used for making felt.

Making of a Fabric : If we take a piece of fabric and try to open it up, we find that the fabric is made up of strands, while the yarn is made up of little particles which we call fibres. In order to understand fabrics we have to know what makes a fabric.

Fibres collected together and sorted out, when twisted together from a yarn; these yarns when interlaced together form a fabric. There are two kinds of fibres: natural fibres and man-made fibres (from natural resources.)

Natural fibres include animal and vegetable fibres.

Animal fibres: Wool, hair and silk.

Vegetable fibres:

1. Seed fibres: Cotton.
2. Stem fibres: Jute, sunn and raine.
3. Leed fibres: Pineapple banana and cacti.
4. Fruit fibres: Coconut.
5. Mineral fibres: Asbestos, gold and silver.

Man-made fibres: Rayon and nylon.

Wool : Wool is derived from sheep and is of two qualities. The long fibres are made into worsted yarns and the small fibres are made into woollen yarns.

All finer quality of fabrics are made of worsted yarns.

Knitting yarns, carpets, blankets and felts are made of woollen yarns.

Process of Making the Fibres into Yarns: The fibres are sheared off and sorted out, washed and dried, then oil applied and the fibres are combed so that they lie parallel to each other. From here the yarns are spun.

Silk : Silk is derived from insects like caterpillars. These worms form a cocoon or nest around themselves with the saliva from their mouths. They lie in the cocoon and change into moths, break the cocoon, lay the eggs on leaves and die.

Silk is also divided into two kinds—Cultivated silk and Wild or Tussar silk. Cultivated silk is where the moths are killed inside the cocoon and after degunning the cocoon the yarns are reached out. This is the only fibre in nature which comes in the yarn form with 200 metres to 400 metres length. The wild silk is from broken cocoons and yarn is 2″ to 21" long.

All finer qualities of fabric are produced from the cultivated silk and the thicker ones from wild silk.

Cotton : Cotton is derived from plants which are 3 to 5 feet tall. The flowers of cotton are in pods. These pods are cracked and opened. The cotton fibres are removed and further cleaned. The seeds are removed, then these fibres are combed to lie parallel to each other and from this the yarns are spun. As earlier mentioned all long fibres make finer and thinner yarns and hence the quality of the fabric depends on the quality of fibres used in the yarns.

Jute : These plants are very much like bamboo but of thinner quality. These are cut and collected, put into water to rot, then the green layer is removed and fibres are collected and spun in yarns. They are used for sacks, furniture, etc. Raine and sunn are similar to jute except that they are more coarse.

Coconut Fibres : These are well known. Hair is the husk of the coconut. The coconut is steeped in water and the fibres are removed and spun into yarns. These are used for door mats and ropes, etc.

Asbestos is derived from rocks and these fibres are mixed with other textile fibres and made into a yarn. These are used for firemen's garments and to form iron mats as they are poor conductors of heat.

Silver and gold are made into a filament form and spun with other yarns.

Synthetic or Man-made Fibres : These are of two kinds—the rayon group made from cotton or the bark of wood; and the nylon group made of coal gas or mineral gas.

Yarns : In order to have a standard quality of yarn all over the world a number is given to the yarn. This number determines the thickness and thinness of the yarn which in turn is known as *count* in the textile world.

In order to explain what a count is the procedure is as follows:

> One pound of cotton fibres is taken out of which a yarn is spun which is 840 yards long. The thickness achieved out of this is called a 1' single yarn. If from 1 lb 1680 yards are spun the count will be 2's single. If four times it will be 4's single. The thinness of the yarn goes up to 120's.

In order to get stronger yarns the yarns are doubled or trebled. There are termed as ply yarns.

If two 3's single yarns are taken together and spun the count will be 2/3's. 2 denotes the number of yarns and 3 denotes the count.

When we buy fabrics we notice the printing or markings of manufacturers. Ply yarns are stronger than the single yarns and this denotes the quality of the fabric. A fabric will mention the count of the yearns and the width of the fabric.

Weaving : As mentioned earlier two sets of yarns interlaced together form a fabric. These two yarns are termed as the warp and weft.

Warp: These are sets of yarns on looms. These have to be smooth and strong and they go through the tension of being lifted up and passed through needles.

Weft: These can be any yarns or material as they are merely passed through warp yarns.

Basic weaves: There are three basic weaves:

(a) Plain weave

(b) Twill weave

(c) Satin weave

All other weaves are either variations of the above or mixtures of the three basic weaves.

Plain Weave: Two sets of yarns are alternatively picked up and the weft passed through; this process is done alternatively.

Twill Weave: Four sets of yarns are picked up in the following order:

1 and 2, 2 and 3, 3 and 4 and repeated.

Satin Weave: Eight sets of yarns picked up in the following order:

8, 7, 6, 5, 4, 3, 2,1.

The more the sets of yarns the more intricate is the design. Therefore, there are three types of looms where the following kinds of fabrics are woven.

Plain Loom: Two to four sets of yarns are woven. The fabrics are plain woven fabrics.

Dobby Loom: From 4 sets to 32 sets of yarns are woven.

This gives a geometrical pattern and most of the furnishing fabrics are woven by this method.

Jacquard Loom: From 32 sets to 600 sets of yarns. The designs are versatile.

Plain Loom Woven Fabrics

1. Asbestos cloth
2. Billiard cloth
3. Blazer cloth
4. Buckram
5. Calico, DCM, Tatas, Bombay Dyeing fabrics
6. Casement cloth, muslin, long cloth, mercerised cloth, organdie, piece, dyed cloth, poplin, printed fabrics. voile, cambric.
7. Taffeta
8. Chiffon
9. Chintz
10. Denim
11. Flannel
12. Glass cloth
13. Home spun fabrics
14. Rugs
15. Shirtings
16. Ticking (fabric for mattresses)
17. Waterproof fabrics
18. Woollen cloths
19. Worsted cloths
20. Khadi
21. Silks

Dobby Loom Woven Fabrics

1. Applique fabrics
2. Corduroy

3. Blanket range
4. Braided fabrics
5. Gents shirtings/suitings
6. Crepe
7. Double cloth
8. Satin fabrics
9. Gaberdine
10. Gauze and lene fabrics
11. Curtain fabrics
12. Reversible fabrics
13. Towel materials
14. Velvet
15. Woollen and worsted fabrics with geometrical patterns and motifs only
16. Khadi
17. Silks
18. Bed covers

Jacquard Loom Woven Fabrics

1. Brocade
2. Tapestries
3. Damask
4. Lace fabrics
5. Lappet fabrics
6. Furnishing fabrics (upholstery)
7. Quilts
8. Shadow effects with patterns
9. Intricate woollen patterns
10. Silks with patterns

Dyed and Printed Fabrics : All fabrics are given some kind of ornamentation.

Dyeing : There are two kinds of treatment given to fabrics in dyeing:

(a) The yarns are dyed according to the shade and colour required.

(b) The fabrics after weaving are dyed and called piece dyed.

Yarn dyed fabrics are better as the fastness of the colour and durability is greater and they fade less when exposed to sunlight. Piece dyed fabrics fade easily.

To find out the fastness of the dyes on a fabric there are three methods—the chemical test, washing test and rubbing test.

Chemical Test: The material is immersed in a test tube containing a solution of Knights Primrose Soap (a neutral salt) and this is placed in a bath of hot water for half an hour at a temperature of 50°C. The liquid from the tube is poured into a, white porcelain dish and examined for discolouration.

Washing Test: Leave the fabric in water for 12 hr. Wash with soap. Examine the water for discolouration.

Rubbing Test: A piece of white cotton material is moistened and rubbed across the material. If the dye is loose it will show on the white piece of material. All fabrics which are exposed to sunlight tend to fade, so all curtains facing the sunlight are usually lined with another fabric or dry light curtains are used with the other curtains.

Types of Dyes Used

Cotton Fabrics: Vegetable dyes, Coal tar dyes, dyes from mineral sources like iron, chromium, tin or copper.

Silk Fabrics: Vegetable dyes and acid dyes.

Woollen Fabrics: Acid dyes, vat dyes.

Jute Fabrics: Similar to cotton dyes.

Synthetic Fabrics: Acid and mordant dyes. Ornamental dyed fabrics are Resist Dyes (Batik) and tie and dye fabrics.

Printed Fabrics : There are three types of printed fabrics:

1. Block printed
2. Screen printed
3. Roller printed

Chart Identification of Yarns, Fibres and Fabrics

Fibres	*Touch Method*	*Chemical Method*	*Microscopic Method*	*Burning Test*
Cotton	It looks dull and does not reflect light	Cotton when dipped in concentrated sulphuric acid will dissolve	Under the microscope cotton appears as a flat, ribbon-like fibre with a number of twists	Cotton when burnt gives a smell of burnt paper
Silk	It is soft and silky to handle	Concentrated hydrochloric acid dissolves silk	Silk looks like a filament but with lumps here and there	It burns quickly and melts to a beed-like form which is washable and smells of burnt hair
Wool	Wool is soft and lustrous and the fibre can be felt	A weak solution of caustic soda will dissolve wool	Wool has scales like bamboo at intervals	Wool burns slowly with little or no flame and gives a smell of burnt feathers
Synthetic fibres	Synthetic fibres are silky to handle and have a stay lustre	A concentrated solution of mineral acids will dissolve synthetics	They have a rod-like effect with no variation	They burn quickly and smell like burnt paper

Block Printing: These fabrics are very traditional and have the advantage of having as many colours as possible.

Screen Printing: This method is a low cost method as it can do the printing bulk but loses its beauty of colour application as it is exact and harsh.

Roller Printing: It is a very common method because the printing is done very fast. This is the bulk printing technique.

Identification of Yarns, Fibres and Fabrics : There are three methods of identifying fibres. However, as synthetic fibres today are being mixed with natural fibres it has become more essential to know how to identify the fibres before punching them.

Floral Art : Decorating flowers is a creative and stimulating art which often carries a message or theme and expresses the mood or emotions of the arranger.

The basic principles which any visual art must comply with are:

1. Proportion or scale
2. Balance—symmetrical and asymmetrical
3. Dominance or emphasis
4. Rhythm
5. Transition
6. Repetition
7. Variation
8. Contrast

Proportion: This relates to the height of plant material, size of container, its shape, size of room, wall or table or other interior decor.

Balance: (i) Symmetrical; (ii) Asymmetrical

(i) The Western Style—Europe and America.

(ii) The Eastern Arrangement—started in Japan. This is made to appear balanced by adopting a self-balancing shape like S; placing arrangement on one side of container so that the void in the design is towards the vacant side of the container or table or by keeping an accessory on the empty side. These help produce a visual weight, which can be increased by tall height, compactness, stronger darker colours or greater distance from the central axis.

An asymmetrical design can be viewed from the front only while a symmetrical design is free standing and is usually a mass arrangement.

Central Interest: Also known as the Focal Point. It is characterized by converging of lines or flowers, presence of largest and most interesting flower stronger and darker colours and greater density.

Besides this, there may also be a dominant theme:

Movement	Texture
Direction	Colour
Line	Flower
Mass	

Rhythm: Rhythm is related movement in respect to line, form, pattern or colour. The eye should move smoothly and freely without any distraction.

Repetition: It must be restrained to avoid monotony.

Variety and Contrast: These aspects especially in relation shape, texture, colour and foliage impart interest and strength to the design.

General Rules

1. Material is usually 1½ times as tall as height and width of container.
2. Use only three kinds of flowers and foliage.
3. Not more than five kinds of material.
4. Design or lines can be circular, crescent, oval, oblong, triangular or pyramidal.
5. Three dimensional effect or depth can be created by placing material in graded planes that is, at different distances from the central axis.

Themes : Vertical lines depicting stately and bold character:

Horizontal lines appear restful and calm.

Circular patterns denote satisfaction or completeness.

Diagonal suggests movement or force.

Radiating lines symbolise alertness and activity.

Cascading or hanging lines stand for depressive moods.

Colour schemes may be *monochromatic or polychromatic.*

Red	Love and bravery
Blue	Serenity
Yellow	Cheerfulness, youthfulness
Orange	Courage, energy and hope
Magenta	Richness and luxury
Black	Mysticism and drama
White	Purity and delicateness
Grey	Mildness and restraint

Training : No Housekeeper's role is complete unless she is committed to and involved in the training of her staff. This section is intended to help a Housekeeper evolve a simple training scheme that will ensure the achievement of desired levels of performance.

What is Training? Training is the process of changing a given behaviour up to a desired behaviour.

Why is Training Important?

1. Trained manpower is not easily available in the market.
2. Training costs money, time and effort.
3. Training condenses the experiences that others have gained over several years.
4. Training helps to equip a person to do a job in the shortest possible time.
5. Training connotes self-development to staff, thus presenting the possibility of better assignments and better pay packets.
6. Training removes the anxiety of workers as to whether they can do the job successfully.
7. Training helps the management to have a well coordinated team.

What must Training Include : A balanced training programme develops:

(a) Knowledge—All learning through senses of sight, hearing, touch, smell and taste.

(b) Skills—The use of hands and limbs in coordination with the mind.

(c) Attitude—A positive mind to use knowledge and skills profitably and successfully.

Knowledge : Knowledge inputs may be procured from a training manual. Each lesson is concise and to the point to make learning easy. Knowledge acts as an effective backdrop to any skill functions. It is important to teach the common housekeeping terms as a lack of this could lead to communication breakdowns. Do not overburden the trainee with too much knowledge.

Skills : Skills are very important especially in an industry like hotels, for it is the skills that contribute to a guest experience. The most effective way to impart skills training is through on the job exposure. What the Housekeeper needs to do is look at the job description of each job position study the scope of job performed in each job description as it is this that an incumbent needs to do. Amongst the list of activities there are some that an incumbent needs to know immediately and others that he or she needs to know later. One of the ways to determine what an individual should know immediately is to pick out those activities that have a direct and immediate impact on the guest. For example, in a room attendants job description what she needs to know immediately is how to clean a room, how to make a bed and how to clean a bathroom. These tasks have a direct bearing on guest experience. Similarly, descriptions should include such activities that make an impact on a guest. These activities need to be taught first before the incumbent comes in contact with the guest. Such items will be few though most important. The other items can be taught in due course. The best methodology is to demonstrate the activity and get the trainee to practice it upto standards. At no cost should a trainee be permitted to learn through trial and error in an actual situation as this could lead to guest complaints and disruption in operations. Remember that all trainees are not the same. Each one has his or her individual capacity to learn. Some are quick to learn but others are slow.

Attitudes : Attitudes govern the success of performance. It is important for the Housekeeper to constantly counsel the trainee especially if she is new. Encouragement, during practice for work well done helps in developing an incumbent's self-confidence. Criticise with the intention of developing. Criticism should be aimed at the task and not the individual. Give ample opportunities to receive and give feedback. This keeps communication channels open and lets both the trainer and trainee know exactly where they stand in relation to each other.

First Aid : It is important for all housekeeping personnel to know about first aid as they could be the first ones on the spot to give immediate attention to a guest and also an employee. Many hotels organise training classes by the Red Cross for their housekeeping staff who are awarded certificates in recognition of having completed a first aid programme. This shows the importance hotels give to skills of first aid as inherent to housekeeping personnels' jobs.

The first step is to have a first aid cupboard or box in a central location. This cupboard could be located at the Desk Control Room due to its easy accessibility. The cupboard should contain the following items:

1. Clinical thermometer
2. Cotton wool
3. Bandage roll ½", 1" and 2"
4. Adhesive dressings (band-aids, etc.)
5. Sterilised gauze
6. Tweezers
7. Bed pan and urine bottle
8. Rubber sheeting
9. Safety pins

Medicines

Tincture Iodine
Tincture Benzoine
Junction violate solution
Dettol
Burnol or Furacin
Crocin tablets
Aspirins
Mercurochrome
Fruit salts
Antiseptic creams

The cupboard should be cool and dry and clearly captioned for easy identification. Following are some immediate steps that can be taken towards first aid:

Burns and Scalds

1. Apply Burnol liberally.
2. Place burnt area under cold running water or ice.
3. If burns are serious, apply sterile dressing and send to hospital Immediately

Bleeding

1. Clean wound with cotton dipped in dettol.
2. Put dry antiseptic dressing or tincture iodine for bigger wounds.
3. Put pressure on wound by placing a gauze on it and bandaging the area tightly.

Clothes on Fire

1. Prevent person from running.
2. Smother flames by wrapping patient with heavy material, e.g. curtain, blanket, heavy coat.
3. Treat burns as given above.

Fainting

1. Loosen clothing.
2. Lay patient flat on back with feet raised or place in chair bending the head forward between the knees.
3. Apply warmth to lower limbs and rub limbs upwards.
4. Give hot, sweet tea to drink when the patient is able to take it.

Fracture

1. Immobilise the limb by tying both legs or the arms across body respectively.
2. An alternative is to get two boards and tie leg/arm between them.
3. Send for a doctor.

Heart Attack

1. Call for a doctor immediately.
2. Do not move person from the room.
3. Clear all other people.
4. If critical, try artificial respiration by mouth-to-mouth method.

Insect Sting : Apply soda-bicarbonate soaked in solution or paste over the inflamed area.

Object in Eye

1. Do not let the eye be rubbed.
2. Use eye bath with warm water to rinse out the eye.
3. If no improvement check eye against the light and locate foreign matter. Remove it with the corner of a clean hand kerchief.
4. If foreign matter is embedded in the eye-ball do not get it out. Drop two drops of castor oil in the eye, cover eye with soft pad, bandage lightly and take to a doctor.

Sprain

1. Apply dry bandage firmly wrapped round the affected part and soak with cold water.
2. Rest the limb.

Shock

1. Rest the patient by laying him or her on the coach.
2. Loosen clothing.
3. Give warmth by hot beverage and hot water bottle.
4. Keep the surrounding area silent.

8

Housekeeping Practices

Budgeting

One of the prime roles of any Executive Housekeeper is to prepare her departmental budget prior to every financial year. This is solely her responsibility which requires experience and knowledge because the funds available to her to run the departments depend on her financial budget and her experience in preparing it.

What is a budget?	A budget is a statement of intended expenditure for a given period.
Importance of budgeting :	(i) It sets out the parameters of how much of expenditure is permitted for various items of cost.
	(ii) The efficiency of a department is reflected in the extent to which it stays within a budget.
	(iii) It helps in focusing on priorities of expenditure.
	(iv) It acts as an in-built control on activities.

Types of Budgets : The Housekeeping Department has two types of budgets.

Capital Budget : Intended expenditure on assets that have a longer life and are thus more expensive, e.g. vacuum cleaners, carpets, furniture, curtains, linen etc.

Operational Budget : Intended expenditure on items of daily or short-term consumption, e.g. guest supplies, cleaning supplies, salaries, wages, etc.

Capital Budget : Capital expenditure involves larger sums on such investments that have a long-term impact. It is thus natural that decisions on these items are critical and should be made by a group involving the General Manager, Financial Controller and the Executive Housekeeper. Decisions to incur capital expenditure in Housekeeping arise from:

(a) Renovation of rooms or public areas.

(b) Addition of rooms or public areas.

(c) Replacement of equipment, furnishings, carpets, etc.

(d) Introduction of automation in the department.

How to Prepare a Capital Budget : A capital budget should be prepared with great care as it involves large sums of money. Having received a decision from management on capital expenditure the Housekeeper should observe the following steps:

Supplier Identification : While the Purchase Department keeps a track of reliable suppliers, it is the Executive Housekeeper who does the field work in identifying suppliers. The following considerations have to be kept in mind.

(i) Reliability of suppliers operation.

(ii) Quality of product. This can be ensured through in factory inspection and performance history in other organisations.

(iii) Cost factors of product, transportation and handling charges.

(iv) Whether suppliers meet time parameters of supply.

(v) Whether suppliers meet your special specifications.

Receiving Competitive Quotations : It is prudent to identify several suppliers because the hotel can then have the advantage of competitive prices. Quotations should be called for after informing suppliers of the hotel's exact quantity and quality requirements.

Selection of a Supplier : While a supplier with the lowest quotation would normally be the apparent choice, care must be taken on the points given above in making a choice. It may be wise to pay a little more if the probability of these various factors is higher. The decision should be a joint one with the involvement of the General Manager.

Making a Budget : Armed with quotations the capital budget can be broken into:

(i) Product

(ii) Freight, Transport

(iii) Handling charges.

Operational Budget : The various heads of expenditure that are normally reflected in a Housekeeping budget are:

Cleaning Supplies :	Detergents, brasso, duster cloths.
Guest Supplies :	Guest stationery, soaps, tissues, sewing kits, hangers, etc.
Office Stationery and Postage:	Memo pads, writing implements, formats, stamps, etc.
	Tailor Shop Expenses Thread, needles, buttons, lace, etc.
Cleaning Equipment :	Brooms, mops, buckets, etc.
Salaries and Wages :	Includes in addition retirement benefits, bonus, allowances, etc.
Heat, Light and Power :	Air-conditioning/heating, electricity consumption in the department.
Repair and Maintenance :	Expenses on maintenance of furnitures, fixtures and equipment.
Local Travel :	Expenses on visits to suppliers, staff transportation.

Horticultural Expenses :	(a) Landscaping—seeds, manure, saplings, nursery pots.
	(b) Florist—flowers, flower holders and vases.
Pest Control :	Insecticides and pesticides.
Laundry :	Washing materials.

Information on expenditure should be largely based on aggregate consumption in the last three years. Information can be got from stores consumption records for cleaning supplies, guest supplies, stationery, tailor shop expenses. The Purchase Department could give the expenditure on cleaning equipments, horticultural expenses that are issued directly to the Housekeeping Department. The Personnel Department also keeps a record of salaries and wage costs for the past year. The Financial Controller would be in a position to give expenses, that he would have received from the Engineering Department on heat, light and power, repair and maintenance. The Security Department which normally controls transportation would be in a position to give the annual costs of local transportation of the Housekeeping Department. If pest control and horticulture are on a contracted basis, the annual contract figure is known. Care must be taken on whether the contract will expire in the year that is being budgeted for.

Even after taking into consideration past trends it is prudent to add a 10 per cent mark-up to account for the inflation factor. Additional cost-factors are added on for any special circumstances planned for the coming year such as conferences, increased occupancies, etc. which have a bearing on the housekeeping budget.

Lost and Found Procedure : "Lost and found" in Housekeeping parlance refers to those articles inadvertently left or lost by a guest in the hotel. Such articles can range from jewellery, costly electronic goods to simple garments, etc. However, the hotel considers it its duty to protect such articles till such time that they are claimed by the guest.

Procedure

1. When an article is found the finder should immediately report this to the Housekeeper.

2. The Housekeeper immediately fills a Lost and Found Slip in duplicate giving the date, time, room number/location, guest's name if found in a room, name of the finder.

Valuable/Non Valuable

Date............................

Finder's Name ....

Location/Room No .... Description of Article ....
(where found)

Time :............................ Hours ....

Name of the Guest ....

Address : ....

....

....

....

....

....

Signature of Depositor Signature of Receiver

A B C

DISPOSITION Address/Telephone No.

A. Recd. property by owner

Sig. .... Date .... Name ....

B. Postal Receipt No.................... Date ....

Sig. of despatcher :.. ....

C. Recd. property by finder ....

Sig. : ....Date ....

Gate Pass No. : .... Date Tel No ....

Property handed over by ....

.... cc : Article

Sig. : .... Finder

Security

File

Lost and Found Slip

3. The first copy is attached to the article and stored in a theft-free lost and found cup board especially for the purpose.
4. The duplicate copy is kept in a Lost and Found Register which again records details as given above including the description of the article.
5. The Housekeeper then obtains the forwarding address of the guest from the Front- Office who would have the information in the registration card. If the guest's name is not known then Housekeeping would have to wait for the guest to claim it.
6. The Housekeeper may write to the guest to either claim it or give further instructions. If no reply is received from the guest a reminder may be given.
7. If the guest returns to claim it he would have to furnish the details of the article before it is handed to him. His signature in acknowledgement of receipt would be taken on the slip and register.
8. If it has to be mailed to the forwarding address as instructed by the guest the same should be done under registered post with the charges made known to the guest and claimed from him.
9. If the guest does not claim the article in spite of reminders, the article is kept for a specific period as prescribed by the management (usually six months) and either gifted to the finder or auctioned to housekeeping staff.

Often guests present gifts to employees. This is discouraged; however, some guests are offended if the gift is not taken and hence the employee is permitted to receive it. Such items would not be classified as "lost and found". In such cases a letter from the guest acknowledging his act of gifting the item must be received by the employee. The employee would have to declare this to the Housekeeper and Security Officer. A gate pass would have to be made by Security authorising the employee to take out the item from the hotel premises.

Name ....

Deptt. ....

Contents of Article ....

Permit to remove from hotel premises approved by Deptt. Head

Signature ....

(If gift from guest) signature verified from Front Office by Lobby Manager

Signature ....

Time .... Date......................................

1st Copy Security Guard

2nd Copy Security Office

3rd Copy File

Employee Gate Pass

Cleaning Methods : Cleaning is the main role of housekeeping, hence, over the years, various methods have been tried and tested to give housekeepers clear tips on how to clean various surfaces. The subsequent pages bring together the experiences and knowledge of experts in cleaning methods Cleaning basically involves the removal of dust and other foreign matter from surfaces. The choice of a cleaning method depends on various factors as listed below:

1. The nature of soiling.
2. The nature of surface soiled.
3. The properties of cleaning agents suitable for the surface.
4. The best way to clean without dispersing dust to other areas.
5. The process should be cost effective in terms of the cleaning agent and labour time
6. The method should restore the surface to its original sheen and colour.

While the methods used have to be viewed individually, depending upon the surface, there are some general principles that can be applied to all cleaning:

1. All loose dust and litter should be removed before dealing with any stubborn stains/dirt.
2. Use lighter cleaning methods first before attempting stronger methods.
3. Before any implements or cloth are used, they should be made clean and dry.
4. When in doubt choose the simplest methods.
5. Abrasives should be used as a last resort as they can damage the surface.
6. Use an agent that is least offensive in smell if alternatives are available.
7. When cleaning a surface, be cautious of marring the surrounding area, e.g. finger prints on walls, grazing other articles, etc.
8. Use methods that are least inconvenient to guests. Disturbance can be caused by noise or obstacles placed in public areas.
9. Be sure that during the process of cleaning areas do not become accident-prone, e.g wet, slippery floors, etc.
10. Cleaning should be carefully planned so as to ensure the least time.
11. Cleaning should be periodic to ensure a sparkling house.
12. All staff must be properly trained in cleaning methods and the use of cleaning agents. One of the basic methods used is cleaning with water. The role of water is as follows;

10. (a) To hold the dirt and remove it away as in rinsing.
    (b) To react with the dirt and grease, break it down and hold it in suspension. This is done with the aid of detergents.
    (c) To emulsify and hold grease in suspension together with the dirt so that it can be re moved. The use of alkalis helps in the process.

Chart above gives a summary of the cleaning of surfaces.

Carpet Upholstery Care and Maintenance

Carpets : Carpets are an expensive asset to hotels. They feature in capital budgets. Great care is taken in the selection and laying of carpets in rooms and public areas. The décision to purchase carpets is done by a senior committee including the General Manager and investor. Decisions on carpets have a long-standing impact hence it is important that such decisions are correct ones. Being valuable assets, their care and maintenance have to be regular and follow the correct procedure. Basically there are four categories:

1. Woollen carpets have the largest piles. Their colour is faster and they have a luxurious feeling, are easy to maintain but the most expensive. They are not highly inflammable. Absorb sound well.
2. Cotton carpets are not as resistant as woollen carpets. Their colour fades faster. They are inexpensive hence do not portray a luxurious look. They do not absorb sound well. This type is not recommended for superior hotels.
3. Synthetic-carpets are highly inflammable. They do not last very long and do not have resistance. Their colour is fast and they can be dyed well. They absorb sound.
4. Silk carpets are very expensive and delicate hence their usage is limited to special rooms. They do not last long but are luxurious looking. They have fast colours and absorb sound well have less resistance as the piles are smaller than those of woollen carpets.

Laying of a Carpet : This activity is a specialised job entrusted to carpet specialists. When laying a carpet, scrub, wash and dry the floor to be carpeted. Spray the floor particularly skirtings and corners with pesticide. Mop up the excess pesticide till the floor is completely dry. Roll out the underlay which is of rubberised coir and cut and fit corners and skirtings. The underlay should be 1/2" thick in rooms and 1 /4" thick in corridors.

Carpets should be pre-measured/pre-cut to size, rolled out with carpet grippers to avoid puckering and fitted well into the desired area. Raw edges are blanket stitched to give a neat appearance as well as to avoid fraying.

Daily Cleaning of a Carpet : Cleaning can be done by two methods:

(a) Electrical method, e.g. vacuum cleaners.
(b) Manual method, e.g. carpet brush, boxer, etc.

Chart Cleaning of Surfaces

Cleaning of Flooring

Type of flooring	Special Remarks	Daily Clean	Special Clean
Bitumastic	Avoid use of white spirit and paraffin. Surface can be painted.	Sweep, wash mop or use electric scrubber with hot water and tenopol-Vim solution.	As daily clean.
Ceramic tiles		As above.	As above.
Marble			Remove stubborn marks with steel wool or fine scouring powder.
Cork/Wood	Avoid use of excess water and alkalis. Should be sealed and/or polished as it is very absorbent. Can be sanded down. *Sealed:* Reseal as required. May be polished using a water-based polish. Remove build-up as necessary, using hot water and a special removal agent. *Unsealed:* Polish with a spirit-based polish. Remove build-up as necessary, using white spirit and fine steel wool or a nylon web pad Rinse and re-wax. Can be sanded.	*Sealed:* Sweep, damp mop or vacuum clean. *Unsealed and polished:* Sweep mop or vacuum clean. Buff with electric polisher.	*Sealed:* If polished, re-polish spray buff or spray clean. *Unsealed and polished:* Re-wax using little polish and much buffing.

Contd...

Type of flooring	*Special Remarks*	*Daily Clean*	*Special Clean*
Granolithic	Can be brought to a smooth finish by machine, to improve its appearance.	As bitumastic.	As bitumastic.
Linoleum	Avoid scrubbing, coarse abrasives and alkalis. *Sealed:* Re-seal as required. *Sealed and Unsealed:* Polish using water-based polish. Remove build-up as necessary, using hot water and special removal agent.	Sweep, mop or vacuum clean.	Wash by hand or mop with hot water (used sparingly) and detergent. If polished, re-polish, spray buff or spray clean.
Magnesite	Avoid use of water, alkalis, acids and coarse abrasives.	Sweep, mop or vacuum clean.	
Resin seamless	As ceramic tiles.	As daily clean.	
Rubber/ Thermoplastic/ Vinyl	Avoid use of alkalis, spirits and coarse abrasives. Use water-based polish as linoleum.	Sweep or damp mop.	As linoleum.
Terrazzo	Avoid use of acids and strong alkalis.	As bitumastic	As daily clean. Remove stubborn marks with fine scouring powder.

Daily Cleaning Of White Metals

Metal	*Apparatus Required*	*Stain Remover*	*Method of Cleaning*	*Rubbing up*	*Notes*
1. Aluminium	Hot soapy water. Clean hot water. Saucepan brush, or saucepan scourer, or steel wool. Net cloth.	Nylon soft brush	(i) If greasy, steep in very hot water, otherwise steep in cold water. (ii) Wash with hot soapy water, using a saucepan brush, or a saucepan scourer, or a piece of steel wool. (iii) Remove stains by using a nylon soft brush. (iv) Rinse thoroughly in clean hot water. (v) Dry with the net cloth.	The scouring with nylon soft brush brightens the surface a little but cannot be considered as polishing.	Soda must never be used in the cleaning of aluminium.
2. Chromium-plate	Warm soapy water. Warm clean water. Flannelette or net cloth. Linen cloth. Two soft clean dusters.		(i) If dirty, wash with warm soapy water. (ii) Rinse with clean warm water. (iii) Dry with the linen cloth.	Rub hard whilst dusting.	

Metal	Apparatus Required	Stain Remover	Method of Cleaning	Rubbing up	Notes
3. Galvanized Iron	Bucket of hot soapy water. Soda. Net cloth, or floor cloth. Bucket of clean hot water. Paraffin. Newspaper.	Nylon soft brush	(i) Wash in hot soapy water. (ii) If greasy, add soda. (iii) Remove stains with : (a) powdered bath-brick; or (b) silver sand/nylon brush. (iv) Use a net cloth or a floor cloth, according to the type of article being cleaned. (v) Rinse thoroughly with clean hot water. (vi) Dry with the net cloth or the floor cloth. *Another Method:* (i) Clean with paraffin, using a pad of newspaper. (ii) Rinse thoroughly with clean, hot water, using a floor cloth. (iii) Dry with the cloth.	None	

Metal	*Apparatus Required*	*Stain Remover*	*Method of Cleaning*	*Rubbing up*	*Notes*
4. Iron			Clean according to the protective coating.		Never use except with a protective coating of (a) paint (b) tin, (c) zinc, (d) enamel, (e) black lead.
5. Lead	As for chromium-plate.		As for chromiumplate.	As for chromium plate.	For stayed marks use nylon soft brush.
6. Monel Metal			(i) Wash with hot soapy water, using a net or flannelette cloth. (ii) Rinse with clean hot water. (iii) Dry with thc nct or flannelette cloth, and finish with the linen cloth.	None	
7. Oxidized Silver	As for chromium-plate.		As for chromium plate.	As for chromium plate.	
8. Pewter	As for chromium-plate.		As for chromium plate.	As for chromium plate.	
9. *Stainless Steel* :					
(i) Cooking	As for aluminium.	None	As for aluminium.	As for aluminium.	Soda does not react with stainless steel. May therefore be used for cleaning greasy pans.

Metal	Apparatus Required	Stain Remover	Method of Cleaning	Rubbing up	Notes
(ii) Cutlery	As for ordinary steel knives.	None	As for ordinary steel knives.	None	
(iii) Ornamental	As for chromium plate.	None	As for chromiumplate.	As for chromium plate.	
10. Staybrite mentals	As for chromium plate.		As for choromium-plate.	As for chromium-plate.	
11. Steel:					
(i) Cooking utensils	As for aluminium.	As for aluminium.	As for aluminium.	As for aluminium	Soda can be used for cleaning.
(ii) cutlery	*For Cleaning* Jam jar of hot soda water, newspaper, very hot soapy water, cotton mop, soda, knife cloth. *For polishing* Duster or selvyt duster, knife polish, knife board, cork or piece of potato, knife machine, duster.	Cleaning powder	(i) Remove grease by wiping the knives with newspaper. (ii) Steep the blades in the jam jar containing hot soda water. (iii) Wash in hot soapy soda water, using the cotton mop. (iv) Remove stains. (v) Rinse off the stain remover. (vi) Dry with a knife cloth. (vii) Rub with the clean dry duster.	*A. On a knife board* (i) Place the rounded end of the knife board to the left of the worker. (ii) Hold the knife flat on the board and rub firmly. (iii) Use only a small quantity of knife polish. (iv) Attend to the back and shoulders of the knife. (v) Obstinate stains can be removed by rubbing with a cork or a piece of potato.	The handles of knives must never be allowed to get wet, otherwise the cement holding the blade in position will be softened and the blade becomes loose. Polishing has to be done daily.

Metal	*Apparatus Required*	*Stain Remover*	*Method of Cleaning*	*Rubbing up*	*Notes*
				B. By means of a knife machine (i) Place the knives in position. (ii) Turn the handle until the knives are well polished. (iii) The shoulders and backs may have to be polished on a knife board. (iv) Dust thoroughly with a duster.	
(iii) Ornamental	Two duster.	Dust thoroughly to remove surface dust.		(i) Rub with dry steel wool; or (ii) with emery paper.	The amount of daily rubbing up varies according to weather conditions.
12. Silver (i) Solid (Ornamental) (iii) Table	As for chromium plate. Bowl of very hot soapy water. Bowl of very hot clean water. *Note:* A double sink can be used instead of the bowls. Cotton mop Two enamel trays (a) to hold dirty silver (b) to hold clean silver	Kitchen salt to remove egg stains	As for chromium plate. (i) Separate the spoons from the forks. (ii) Put all the spoons (or the forks) into the hot soapy water. (iii) Wash thoroughly, using the cotton mop. (iv) Rinse in very hot, clean water, or rinse in boiling water, having first placed the sheet of aluminium and soda in the rinsing basket.	As for chromium plate. (i) Rub hard whilst drying. (ii) Rub daily with: (a) chamois leather, or (b) selvyt duster, or (c) impregnated cloth. (iii) Use the chemical solution, method for rinsing, e.g. aluminium soda, and boiling water.	Silver saltcellars should always be fitted with glass liners to prevent the silver surface getting 'pitted' by the salt. Silver salt-spoons must always be removed from the salt for the same reason.

Metal	Apparatus Required	Stain Remover	Method of Cleaning	Rubbing up	Notes
			(v) Lift out the rinsing basket and allow the silver to drain (vi) Dry whilst still hot with a clean dry linen cloth.		
3. Zinc	As for galvanized iron.		As for galvanized iron.	As for galvanized iron.	
14. Tin:					
(i) Polished	Hot soapy water Soda Net cloth	Sand or commercial cleaning powder.	(i) If very dirty steep in hot soapy water. (ii) Wash in hot soapy water, using a net cloth. (iii) If greasy, soda can be added to the washing water. (iv) Remove stains by using a nylon soft brush. (v) Rinse in clean hot water. (vi) Dry with the net cloth. (vii) Finish drying in a warm place.	None	
(ii) Unpolished	As for polished tin	As for polished tin.	As for polished tin.		

Cleaning of Furniture

Furniture	Apparatus Required	Daily Cleaning and Polishing	Weekly Cleaning and Polishing	Spring or Periodic Cleaning and Polishing	Notes
1	2	3	4	5	6
1. Cane	*For daily and weekly cleaning and polishing* Two cleansoft dusters, or soft dusting bruсh. *For spring or periodic cleaning and polishing.* Two clean soft dusters, or soft dusting brush. Bowl of tepid salt water. Bowl of cold salt water. Flannelette cloth. Linen cloth.	Dust or brush thoroughly.	As for daily cleaning and polishing.	(i) Dust or brush thoroughly. (ii) Wash with tepid salt water using a flannelette cloth. Allow one tablespoonful of salt to one quart of water. (iii) Rinse with cold salt water, using the same proportions of salt to water. (iv) Dry with a soft linen cloth. (v) Finish drying in the open air if possible, or by or by an open window. *Note:* If very dirty, tepid soapy water may be used for washing, but should be avoided unless absolutely necessary as it softens the cane and helps to discolour it.	Salt helps to stiffen, bleach, and remove stains from cane. *To tighten limp cane chairs.* (i) Dust thoroughly. (ii) Dab the cane with boiling soda water. Allow 1 oz. soda to 1 qt. of water, use a net or flannelette cloth. (iii) Dry with a linen cloth, and finish drying in the open air. (iv) Do not allow the strong soda water solution to touch the framework of the chair or the polished surface will be damaged. (v) Always hold a cloth under the cane to prevent sagging, and to encourage shrinkage. *Note:* If possible do this work outdoors.

Furniture	*Apparatus Required*	*Daily Cleaning and Polishing*	*Weekly Cleaning and Polishing*	*Spring or Periodic Cleaning and Polishing*	*Notes*
1	2	3	4	5	6
2. Leather	*For daily and weekly cleaning and polishing* Two clean soft dusters. *For spring or periodic cleaning and polishing* Two clean soft dusters, or electric vacuum cleaner, warm soapy water, or vinegar and oil flannelette cloth, linen cloth.	Dust thoroughly to remove surface dust paying particular attention to folds around buttons.	As for daily cleaning	(i) Remove surface dust by using dusters, or an electric vacuum cleaner. (ii) If very slightly soiled wipe the surface with a cloth wrung out of warm soapy water. (iii) If dirty, rub with a mixture of oil and vinegar. (iv) If very dirty wash with warm soapy water. Use a flannelette or net cloth. (v) Rinse thoroughly and dry. (vi) Polish, using a little good furniture polish or cream or a white shoe cream with spirit.	Furniture polish cream supplies the leather with wax oil, which keeps the material supple and prevents cracking.
3. Polished wood	*For daily cleaning and polishing* Two clean soft dusters or dusting brush. *For weekly cleaning and polishing* Two clean soft dusters, or dusting brush. Bowl of warm vinegar and water. Flannelette, or chamois leather. Linen cloth. Suitable furniture polish. Reg. Two dusters.	(i) Dust thoroughly to remove surface dust. For very carved surfaces use a small dusting brush. (ii) Whilst dusting rub the surface thoroughly to brighten it.	(i)Dust or brush thoroughly to remove surface dust. (ii) If sticky wash with vinegar and warm water, used in equal quantities Use a flannelette cloth or a chamois leather. (iii)Dry with a clean linen cloth.		*Removal of stains hotplate marks* Rub with one of the following: (i) Linseed oil. (ii) Spirits of camphor. (iii) Dark furniture polish. *Marks made by scent of perfume :* (i) Wipe up immediately. (ii) Rub with paraffin and leave for twenty four hours.

Furniture	Apparatus Required	Daily Cleaning and Polishing	Weekly Cleaning and Polishing	Spring or Periodic Cleaning and Polishing	Notes
1	2	3	4	5	6
			(iv)Polish with a suitable furniture polish applied with a rag, and rubbed in thoroughly. (v) Finish polishing with two clean soft dusters. *Note:* Discretion must be used as to the application of polish. It is unwise to use it too often.		(iii) Polish with furniture polish. *Scratches:* (i) Paint over the scratch with iodine, or rub with a mixture of equal parts of camphorated oil and turpentine. (ii) Leave for 24 hours. (iii) Polish with furniture polish.
4. Leather Cloths.	As for leather.	As for leather.	As for leather.	As for leather.	When washing avoid making the surface too wet.
5. Upholstered Furniture.	*For daily and weekly cleaning and polishing* Two clean soft dusters, or soft dusting brush. *For spring or periodic cleaning and polishing.* Upholstery brush, or cane beater, or vacuum cleaner. Bowl of warm soapy water, ammonia, vinegar, salt, flannelette cloth, or linen cloth, linen cloth for drying.	(i) Brush gently to remove surface dust. (ii) If very light-coloured or of very delicate material, it should be dusted with a clean soft duster.	As for daily cleaning and polishing.	(i) Remove the surface dust by: (a) brushing thoroughly or (b) beating thoroughly. (This should be done outside), or (c) using a vacuum cleaner, (ii) Wash the surface with warm soapy water, with the addition of ammonia, allowing ½ teaspoonful of ammonia, to one quart of water.	

Furniture	*Apparatus Required*	*Daily Cleaning and Polishing*	*Weekly Cleaning and Polishing*	*Spring or Periodic Cleaning and Polishing*	*Notes*
1	2	3	4	5	6
				Use a soft clean cloth and work over a small portion of the surface at a excess use of ammonia results in discolouring material; avoid using on pink, green and turquoise. (iv) Give a final rinsing with cold water, vinegar, and salt use enough vinegar to colour the water, and one tablespoonful of salt to one quart of water. (v)Dry with a soft cloth. (vi) Finish drying in the open air, by a wide-open window, or near a fire. *Alternative methods of cleaning* 1. *Warm bran.* Rub the surface with bran previously warmed in a hot oven. Leave for about an hour and then brush thoroughly. 2. *Bread crumbs mixed to a paste with* (a) petrol, or (b) methylated spirit rubbed over the surface. Leave for an hour and then brush off.	

Furniture	Apparatus Required	Daily Cleaning and Polishing	Weekly Cleaning and Polishing	Spring or Periodic Cleaning and Polishing	Notes
1	2	3	4	5	6
6. Wicker (i) Brown	*For daily and weekly cleaning and polishing* As for cane. *For spring or periodic cleaning and polishing* Two clean soft dusters. or soft dusting brush. Bowl of warm soapy water. Flannelette or net cloth. Soft nail cloth. Clean dry linen cloth. Liquid furniture polish. Rag. Two dusters.	As for cane.	As for cane.	(i)Remove all cushions. (ii) Dust or brush thoroughly to remove surface dust. (iii) Use vacuum cleaner's attachment. (iv) Wash with warm soapy water, using a flannelette or net cloth. If very dirty a soft nail brush can be used. (v) Rinse thoroughly and dry. (vi) Finish drying in the open air of possible. (vii) Polish with a liquid furniture polish.	(a) If soapy water tends to remove the brown stain, use paraffin for washing the wicker. (b) Avoid the use of furniture cream as it is difficult to remove form crevices. (c) Avoid making the wicker too wet, as this tends to make it creak and crack. (d) Never dry wicker in front of a fire, as it will cause the wicker to creak.
(ii) White	*Fore daily and weekly cleaning and polishing* As for cane. *For spring or periodic cleaning and polishing* Two clean soft dusters, or soft dusting brush. Bowl of warm, salted water. Bowl of cold water. Flanelette or net cloth. White furniture polish. Reg. Two clean soft dusters.	As for cane.	As for daily cleaning and polishing.	(i) Remove all cushions. (ii) Dust or brush thoroughly to remove surface dust. (iii) Wash with warm salted water, using a flannelette or net cloth. If very dirty a soft nail brush can be used. Allow one tablespoonful of salt to one quart of water. (iv) Rainse thoroughly with cold water. (v) Dry with a soft cloth. (vi) Finish drying in the open air if possible. (vii) Poigh with white furniture polish.	

Electrical method: The vacuum cleaner is the principal machine in this category. It has the advantage of sucking dust from between piles. It also lifts piles, smoothens in one movement and removes dust completely. Some modern vacuum cleaners have a "combination floor nozzle" that provides the advantage of cleaning floors as well as carpets at the drop of a switch. Whenever using the nozzle move against the pile first and then along with the pile to remove hidden soil built inside the carpet piles. Use smooth brisk movements with downward pressure for smoothening and positioning the piles. Care must be taken to empty out the vacuum cleaner dust-bag everytime a few rooms are done as congestion in the bag would stop the suction.

Manual method: The common method is with a carpet brush and dust pan. Brush against the piles and make them stand. Use brisk movements between piles to scoop out dust. Relaying the piles back is time consuming and could be done the next day. Collect the dirt in the dust-pan and empty out pan in the garbage bag after every room. Carpet brushing is useful when the noise of vacuum cleaners would disturb sleeping guests especially in the mornings.

Special Points for Carpet Cleaning

1. Ensure the power points are functioning properly when using a vacuum cleaner.
2. When cleaning carpets pay attention to corners and under edges of carpets as dust normally collects there.
3. Any pins, needles or glass pieces must be removed with a brush and dustpan first before vacuum cleaning as these could puncture the bag.
4. Any large objects are also to be removed from the floor as they could damage the suction process.
5. Keep suction nozzle away facing downwards when on, as other articles like fine garments, jewellery, etc. could be sucked in.

Carpet Shampooing Procedure

1. Remove carpet from the room and spread out upside down on an open concrete surface.

2. With a carpet beater, beat out dust in slow motions to cover each area at least three times.
3. Roll the carpet and remove loose dust from surface underneath with a soft broom.
4. Roll out carpet with the correct side up.
5. With shampoo machine apply shampoo in circular motions slowly. Ready-made shampoos are available in the market. The carpet specialist will prescribe the mixture.
6. The extra foam of the shampoo is removed by the carpet brush.
7. The carpet is left in the sun to dry.

Note: Some hotels prefer to have the carpet shampooed in the room itself.

This is a job for specialised agencies. However, the above method is recommended as it provides opportunity to clean below under-lays.

Storage of Carpets : It is recommended that carpets should not be stored. However, due to renovation, change of carpets, etc. a housekeeper is faced with the problem of storing carpets. The following procedure may be followed:

1. The room must be properly pest controlled every third day. It should be a dry place.
2. Carpets being stored for long durations must be opened out on a flat surface. Pests do not get a chance to cut into a flat surface.
3. However, if due to shortage of space, carpets have to be rolled, they should be opened every second day to air them as well as permit the piles to have them natural flow.
4. Rolled carpets may be covered with discarded linen or polythene sheets.

Removing Spots and Stains from Carpets

Oily Materials:

Stains	*Cleaning Procedure*
Butter	1. Remove excess material.

Grease	2. Apply perchloroethylene.
Oil	3. Dry the carpet.
Cream	4. Repeat with the chemical if necessary.
Ball Point Pen Ink	5. Brush the pile.

Food Stuffs and Animal Matters:

Tea	
Coffee	
Milk	1. Remove excess material.
Gravy	2. Absorb fluid and/or scrape off solids.
Sauces	3. Apply Detergent/Vinegar/water solution.
Salad Dressing	4. Dry the carpet
Ice Creams	5. Apply perchloroethylene.
Chocolate	6. Dry and brush the pile.
Egg	
Blood and Vomit	

Starchy Food Stains and Others:

Candy	
Sweets	
Beverages	1. Absorb fluid and/or scrape off solids.
Fruits	2. Apply Detergent, vinegar, water solution.
Ink (Washable)	3. Dry and re-apply if necessary.
Urine	4. Brush the carpet pile.
Excrement	

Grease and Gums:

Paint	
Tar	1. Remove excess material.
Lipstick	2. Apply perchloroethylene.

Nail Polish	3. Dry and apply detergent, vinegar, water solution.
Heavy Grease	4. Re-apply perchloroethylene.
Crayon Shoe Polish	5. Dry and brush the carpet pile.

Upholstery **:** Upholstery is a special fabric used for covering furniture. These fabrics are thicker and come in various designs and colours to lend an aesthetic appeal to furniture. Since upholstery material is purchased and used in bulk, it features in capital budgets, as the costs then become high.

Upholstery can be cleaned daily with a vacuum cleaner which has a special attachment called an upholstery brush; or with a manual upholstery brush.

To clean upholstery it is necessary to remove the cushions and back, rests to get to crevices and corners where dust collects. It also enables reaching out to areas which are hard to reach.

To give a fresh look to upholstery and to remove general stains, solvent oil can be used.

The upholstery hand brush has soft bristles to avoid damage to the fabric. Brushing should be done in brisk movements to bring out the dust effectively.

Stains **:** Stains are one of the greatest challenges to a housekeeper. Stains are inevitable in any operation and a housekeeper's expertise is judged by her ability to remove stains of varying types. The process of removing stains is called "spotting".

Good spotting equipment can be obtained at quite a moderate outlay and it will amply repay its cost in speeding up spotting operations of stains in addition to creating an excellent standard of work.

The advent of the steam gun and steam spotting table has done much to simplify the spotter's task. The steam gun has proved to be an excellent piece of equipment for the removal of the majority of food stains, especially those of a sugary nature. The steam gun also accomplishes the removal of quite a large number of stains without resort to chemicals.

The steam gun must be very carefully chosen as its design greatly influences the class of work which it will handle. The nozzle should be of the fish-tail type, as this is not so prone to blowing holes in fabrics. The handle should, if possible, be of the air insulated type, as a handle which becomes hot during spotting slows down the work. In using the steam gun the spotter should remember to spray with a continuous circular motion, holding the nozzle at an angle of 45° in relation to the fabric. Brushes play an important part in spotting a stain. Brushes with white bristles are ideal for this purpose for use on white fabric, as should any soiling matter be picked up it is easily detected and the brush can be cleaned before a garment becomes soiled.

Brushes used for woollens should be large—about 11 inches.

Silk spotting brushes are usually smaller about 1¼ inches in length.

The bristles are longer so as to avoid chafing of fabrics.

All brushes must have a face which is perfectly flat as uneven bristles give a rough surface and damage the fabric. Brushes should be well rinsed and left for drying each evening.

For the purpose of absorbing excessive water there is nothing finer than good chamois which should be large and thick. This should be rinsed in clean water and spread to dry. This will lengthen the life of the leather and prevent it from going old. Always use the chamois with a tamping action.

It is necessary during spotting operations to use an absorbent pad under stains which are being spotted, to soak up chemicals and solvents and the dissolved matter which they carry out, and so prevent spreading of the stains.

A drying cabinet is ideal to dry garments after spotting operations.

A magnifying glass is most useful in spotting stains which are difficult to recognise with the naked eye.

Classification of Stain : All stains fall under three categories:

Absorbed stains: These are caused by staining agents which are thin in consistency and penetrate the fabric easily. Such stains are soft and pliable, except where fair amounts of sugars and syrups are present, when some stiffening will be noticed. Beverages of all types, i.e. beer, tea, coffee, coca cola, and medicines such as cough mixtures are few of the causes of this type of stain.

Built-up stains: These are caused by liquids which fail to penetrate the fabric and lie on the fabric surface. Stains of this nature are diverse such as paint, distemper, tar, sealing wax, lacquers, glues and resinous compounds.

Compound stains: These are a combination of the previous two types as they both penetrate the fabric and leave a built-up residue on the surface of the material. Such stains are found to be of medium stiffness and never quite hard or soft and pliable. Blood stains are a good example on this type of stain. For identification of stains the following are useful guides:

Sight: By this method classification will be quickly observed, i.e. absorbed, built-up or compound.

Odour: By the small emitted especially if the stain is given a light steaming, perfumes, disinfectants and other aromatic stains can be recognised.

Colour: A few of the colour stains which help in identification are bright yellow which is often a sign of medicinal stains.

Reds can be associated with inks, paints and dye-stuffs; blues with paints, inks and dye-stuffs; black for tar, inks, paints, heavy red oil; and green for ink, paints or dye-stuffs.

Feel: It is of considerable help in establishing the origin of stains, as stiffness denotes the presence of oxidised oils, varnish, sugars and starches. Sugar and starch turn white when subjected to the treatment of scratching the stains.

Location: This helps to pinpoint the cause of the trouble. Perfume stains will usually be located on the lapels of garments and some cases under the arms.

Stain Removal : Chart below gives some hints as to what methods are available for the removal of different stains on various fabrics.

Chart Stain Removal

Condition	*Fabric*	*Method of Removal*
Tea, coffee, cocoa		
(a) Fresh		
(b) Dry	White cotton and linen.	Pour boiling water through at once. Wash and boil.
	All other fabrics.	Steep immediately in warm water. Wash.
	White cotton and linen	1. Steep in glycerine overnight. 2. Spread borax on stain and pour boiling water through. 3. Bleach with household bleach.
	Unbleached and coloured cotton and linen.	1. Steep in glycerine overnight. 2. Steep in hot solution of borax. 3. Fast dyed fabrics may be treated care fully with diluted household bleach.
	Other fabrics.	1. Steep in a warm solution of borax. 2. Steep in warm hydrogen peroxide or sodium perborate solution.
Fruit and wine stain		
(a) Fresh	White cotton and linen	Cover stain with salt. Pour boiling water through. Wash boil.
	All other fabrics.	Steep in warm water.
(b) Dry	White cotton and linen	1. Spread borax on stain and pour boiling water through. 2. Treat with liquid household bleach.
	All other fabrics	1. Steep in warm hydrogen peroxide solution. 2. Steep in warm solution of sodium perborate.
Mildew. This is formed by the growth of a fungus on damp fabric.		
	White cotton and linen	1. Bleach by sunlight. 2. Treat with liquid household bleach.
	All other fabrics	1. Bleach with hydrogen peroxide.
Grass stain	All fabrics.	1. Steep in glycerine. 2. Steep in surgical methylated spirit to remove all the green colouring (chlorophyll).
Blood and all protein stains	All washable fabrics.	1. Steep in enzyme stain remover. 2. Steep in cold water and salt. Proportion: 1 tablespoonful to 1 quart.

	Unwashable fabrics	Cover stain with paste of starch and cold water.
Perspiration	White cotton and linen.	1. Steep in enzyme stain remover. 2. Bleach in sunlight. 3. Treat with liquid household bleach.
	All other fabrics.	1. Steep in enzyme stain remover. 2. Wash. 3. Bleach according to fabric.

Iron rust: This is caused by the formation of ferric oxide on the fabric. It is removed by the action of an acid which forms a soluble iron salt with the oxide. Iron-rust stains should be removed before the fabric is wetted as dampness spreads the stain. Liquid household bleach fixes the stain so must never be used.

Iron rust stain

	White cotton and linen.	1. Spread salts of lemon over the stain, pour boiling water through. 2. Use commercial rust remover, following instructions carefully.
	All other fabrics.	1. Steep in warm solution of salts of lemon. 2. Use commercial rust remover.

Ink: Writing ink generally contains a metal and a dye, hence two treatments are necessary: treatment with acid to act on the iron and with an alkaline solution to neutralise the acid and remove the dye. (Black Ink)

(a) Fresh	White cotton and linen.	Wash out as much as possible. 1. Spread salts or lemon over the stain, pour boiling water through wash. 2. Treat with borax if washing is not to be done immediately. 3. Treat with commercial ink remover followed by borax solution.
All other fabrics.		1. Wash out as much as possible. 2. Spread tomato juice over stain. Leave one hour. Rinse and wash. 3. Cover the stain with salt and steep for one hour in lemon juice.
(a) Dry	All fabrics.	1. Treat with alternate solutions of lemon juice and borax. 2. Treat with commercial ink remover.

Red Ink This stain washes out unless made with a persistent dye.

	All fabrics.	1. Steep in borax solution. 2. Steep in ammonia solution. 3. Bleach according to fabric.

Marketing Ink This stain is difficult to remove and should be treated when fresh.

Stain	Fabric	Treatment
	All fabrics.	1. Steep in iodine solution followed by steeping in a solution of sodium thiosulphate. 2. Bleach according to fabric.
Ball Pen Ink	All fabrics.	Saturate a pad of cotton wool with surgical spirit or with grease solvent. Work with pad over the stain to absorb the ink into the pad.
Iodine	All fabrics.	1. Steep in ethyl alcohol. 2. Steep in sodium thiosulphate solution.
Medicine	All fabrics.	Steep in ethyl alcohol or surgical spirit.
Laundry blue	All fabrics.	Steep in a warm solution of acetic acid or vinegar. Proportion: 1 tablespoonful to 1 pint.
Dye	All fabrics.	Bleach according to fabric. Reducing bleaches are often most effective.
Paints	All fabrics.	1. Paints made with linseed oil should be steeped in turpentine. 2. Cellulose paints should be steeped in a grease solvent. 3. Varnish lacquer paints will dissolve in methylated spirits. 4. Some paints have a special point remover.

Chewing gum: As this has a rubber base it is very difficult to remove.

		A benzene-based grease remover may have some effect. Otherwise treat with turpentine

Scorch: The fibres of the material are burned in this case but a mild scorch stain may be reduced by bleaching.

	All fabrics.	Sunlight bleach. Bleach according to fabric.
Grease stains		
(a) Solid	All fabrics.	1. Scrape off as much as possible. Place stain over absorbent paper. Place a moderately hot iron on top. Work from outside of stain to centre. Continue until paper has absorbed the stain.
(b) Liquid	Cottons and linens	Wash with hot water and a detergent.
(including fish oils)	Other fabrics.	When hot water cannot be used the stain should be treated with grease solvent before washing.

	Unwashable fabrics.	1. Cover the stain with French chalk, leave for some time to absorb grease. 2. Treat with a safe grease solvent.
Lipstick, grease-paints	All fabrics.	Treat fabric with a grease solvent. Remove remaining stain with bleach suitable for the fabric.
Nail varnish: This usually contains acetone or amylacetate.		
	Cotton and linen and all fabrics except acetate and triacetate.	Remove with varnish remover. Acetone and amyl acetate are both injurious to acetates so must not be used on these fabrics.
Furniture polish	All fabrics	1. Wash 2. Treat with grease solvent or drycleaning spray.

Cleaning of Chandeliers : Chandeliers are expensive lighting provided in special suites, banquet halls and lobbies. They cost large sums of money, are delicate and add aesthetic appeal and stature to a room. Their cleanliness and maintenance is a laborious job and must be carefully handled as parts of chandeliers may be not easy to replace if broken. Chandelier cleaning schedules spread over a year depending on the number of chandeliers in a hotel.

Chandeliers should be dismantled piece-by-piece and dipped into warm soapy water solution. Each individual piece is to be gently cleaned and rinsed out in clean water. A second rinsing should be given in water in which ammonia has been mixed in the ratio of one teaspoonful of ammonia to two and a half litres of water. This will give a sparkle to the pieces.

A modern method has been devised by Marvin Glenn whereby chandeliers are cleaned much quicker than with conventional methods. This involves a "catch basin" made of paint cloth with a plastic back and hung below the chandelier to catch dirt. Tall thin glasses, preferably plastic are placed over electric light bulbs to protect them from the ensuing moisture. An upholstery shampoo machine sprays detergent solution through a fine nozzle with enough pressure to clean each prism of glass. Liquid runs off through the tube at the bottom of the plastic and into a bucket.

Cleaning Agents : Cleaning agents are perhaps the most critical aids to housekeeping staff in keeping a sparkling house. Basically the cleaning process is to remove dust and grit. While normal dusting with a cloth or vacuum cleaner removes dust in its loose particle state, cleaning agents would be required when dust becomes grit and is stubborn to remove.

Some of the Common Agents used these days are:

Water — Is probably the most common and widely used agent as it is freely available. However, it might be useful in all circumstances. It is useful for rinsing and finishing of cleaning processes. Precaution must be taken to change the water if it gets dirty because it could leave a film of dirt instead of removing it. Warm water dissolves soap more readily than cold water, hence it must be used to remove dirty soap lather. Caution must be taken that the water is 'soft' as no detergent is effective with hard water. Moreover, hard water does not wet the surface well as a precondition for good cleaning action.

Liquid Cleaning Agents — While in modern days we have one or two multipurpose cleaning agents it is useful to know some traditional liquid cleaning agents. Liquid cleaning agents can be either diluted in a little water or used directly with a dry cloth.

Ammonia is an alkali which softens water and emulsifies grease.

Methylated spirits are effective against grease stains.

Paraffin is also a grease solvent.

Turpentine is a grease and paint solvent.

Vinegar is a mild acid unaffected by hard water and useful in removing light stains in baths.

Hydrochloric acid is useful in removing stubborn stains in bathrooms but care must be taken in its use as it is damaging to the skin and destroys fabrics and light bathroom fittings.

Carbon tetrachloride is also an excellent grease solvent. Care must be exercised there, too, as the fumes are harmful.

Washing Soda — This agent is vastly outdated due to the advent of domestic detergents like vim, etc. However, it is particularly useful for emulsifying grease on drain pipes, gutters or stone surfaces. In a strong concentration it could be injurious to skin, fabrics brushes, wood and paint. Washing soda is useful as a water softener.

Soda—bars, Powders, Flakes — Today soaps have been replaced by excellent synthetic soapless detergents which are unaffected by hard water. In this case rinsing is not important as these products suspend dirt and grit most effectively without leaving a smear. However, some housekeepers may not have access to these detergents and may have to rely on soaps.

Powders and flakes are useful in getting instant lather but are expensive. When used, care should be taken that they are thoroughly dissolved. Being expensive, one should know exactly how much powder or flake is dissolved to get an optimum benefit as also how long the resultant solution is effective. Good bar soaps are still most economical but much more strenuous than modern methodologies. They should be stored on open shelves in a dry store.

Abrasives — Again an outmoded agent as they could leave scratches on surfaces. However, they are still used in cases of very stubborn stains on various surfaces.

Silver, sand, steel wool, glass paper may be used for removing stains on plain wood, stone or cement floors.

Emery powder or *paper* is suitable for removing rust from steel.

Pumice powder is used for removing stains from sinks and bath tubs.

Whiting is a mild abrasive for cleaning white paint.

Nylon scourers are made today to have an abrasive effect and yet prove less damaging to surfaces.

Polishes

Polishes fall into three types—liquid polishes, pastes and creams. These fall primarily into three broad categories—spirit base, oil base and water base. Spirit-based—Used for metal mirrors, window panes and bakelite. Oil based—Used for stained, wax polished or painted wood, linoleum and synthetic floorings with an oil or resinous base, cork or wood waste, leather and leather substitutes, tiles enamelled and lacquered metals. Water based—Used on sealed floors, thermoplastic floors and rubber flooring. There are some basic principles applied in using polishes. They are:

1. Polish should be used only after dirt and dust on surfaces are thoroughly removed.
2. Polish must be used in small quantities as excessive polish could smear surfaces.
3. Polish should only be used as a last resort.
4. Polish should be rubbed off thoroughly as surfaces could then become sticky or greasy and thus show finger marks when touched.
5. Surfaces provided with permanent or semi-permanent polish sheens must be polished very carefully as the original sheen could be destroyed. Examples are:
   (i) Wax polish must not be applied to french polished surfaces.
   (ii) Wax polish must not be applied to a

floor treated with a shellac dressing (which is a semi-permanent polish).

(iii) Metal polish must not be applied to chromium-plated or lacquered metals.

6. Polishes are expensive, therefore they must be stored correctly and controlled in use.
7. Polishing of floors is more economically done by polishing machines.

Selection of Cleaning Agents—General Principles

1. Use mild rather than strong agents as they are less injurious to surfaces.
2. Purity of sample is also important. There are cheap substitutes that might show immediate results but on the long run may damage surfaces as they are likely to contain strong chemicals and abrasives.
3. Buy polishes in manageable containers as bulk purchases could cause congestion in stores. The containers must have reliable lids, corks, etc. as defective ones could result in wastage due to evaporation and drying.
4. Multipurpose polishes could save managing too many polishes which requires more supervision.
5. Strong smelling agents (e.g. paraffin) must be avoided due to the offensive smells they lend to the environment.

Cleaning Equipment and Standards

Selection of Equipment : As equipments are expensive their selection is of utmost importance. The correct choice and quality of equipment could save costs due to breakdowns, reduce fatigue and thereby demands on labour as also ensure efficiency in overall operations. In determining the purchase of equipments, the following need to be kept in mind.

1. Quality of equipment by usage history in other organisations.
2. Reliability of supplier to meet time deadlines.
3. Transportation on time to replenish stocks.

4. Equipment should be light, well balanced and easy to manipulate.
5. Availability of future stocks.
6. Sturdiness in terms of usage.
7. Cost factors.

Rules for Storage of Equipment

1. The store should be dry and well ventilated as dampness causes rust of metal parts or mildew leading to degeneration of equipments.
2. The store should provide enough space for easy access to shelves and to facilitate proper cleaning.
3. There should be adequate racks and cupboards properly labelled for easy identification.
4. Stock records should be maintained showing:
   (a) Date of purchase
   (b) Kind of stock and quantity
   (c) Name of supplier
   (d) Cost per unit
   (e) Date of issue into service
   (f) Remarks on suitability and durability
5. Certain rules must be maintained for the issue of stocks:
   (a) A definite time should be specified for issue.
   (b) Issue should be done strictly against worn out equipment.
   (c) Equipment should be clearly marked as to the floor or public area.
6. Storage rooms should be subject to regular inspection.
7. Expensive equipment like vacuum cleaners should be covered with polythene sheets and kept air-tight.

Cleaning Equipments : Cleaning equipments can be broken into six categories:

Mechanical Equipment

(a) Electric vacuum cleaners with a full range of nozzles and attachments for all types of surfaces.

(b) Electric polishers and scrubbers.

(c) Shampoo machines.

Containers

Buckets and pails	—plastic or galvanized metal
Basins and bowls	—plastic
Dust pans	—plastic or galvanized metal
House maids box	—plastic
Room maids cart	
Refuse bins	—plastic or brown paper sacks
Wastepaper baskets	—plastic or galvanized metal

Brushes

Toilet brush
Sink brush
Scrubbing brush
Carpet hand brush
Tapestry brush
Cane chair brush
Soft hand brush
Wall brush
Feather brush

Mops and Brooms:

Firm carpet broom
Yard broom
Mops—large and small
Soft sweeping broom
Squeegee—windows/floors

Cleaning Cloths

Cloth dusters
Rags for applying polish
Flannelette cloth for polishing
Chamois leather
Glass cloth
Floor dusters

Sundry Equipment and Protective Cloth

1. Step ladders or stool steps
2. Cleaning rubber gloves
3. Equipment racks for holding brushes, dustpans, etc.
4. Airing rack for dry cleaning cloths
5. Discarded linen for covering
6. Adjustable ladders for public areas

Mechanical Equipment—Use and Maintenance : Vacuum cleaners photograph 4 are recommended where there is a large amount of carpeted area in the hotel. There are many types of vacuum cleaners. The upright models work on a combined suction and beating process; and the floor models, cylindrical or spherical operate solely on suction. The value of the vacuum cleaner is that it is quicker, less laborious and raises no dust which gets deposited elsewhere in the room. When using the vacuum cleaner it must be checked for functionality. When using it over carpets it should be done crossways over the carpet to ensure that suction has time to draw out the dust and grit. A regular movement is most effective and can be judged by feeling the "pull" against the carpet. The wire connected to the power socket should be straight as the coiling of the wire could lead to unmanageable knots which may even fall under the suction, small objects, particularly if they are sharp, such as pins, needles, etc. should be picked up by hand otherwise the nozzle or suction tube could get damaged and the suction effectiveness reduced. The dust bags of vacuum cleaners should be cleaned daily or more often depending upon the use. A vacuum cleaner with an empty bag provides greater suction than the one whose bag is full of dust. The bag may be emptied out into a newspaper of paper sack and kept with the rubbish. All brush attachments should be kept free from dust, bits of cotton and hair that are picked up in the course of cleaning.

A dustette is a small, light vacuum cleaner used for cleaning curtains, upholstery and mattresses. It cleans by brushing and suction and is very easy to handle.

Mechanical scrubbers are used on large uncarpeted floors after they are washed with water and detergent. Scrubbers are used to clean any sticky grit on floors.

Mechanical polishers are used on large polished wood or vinyl floor surfaces. The floor must first be swept clear of dust and mud marks. Polish is lightly rubbed into the floor surface for the best results.

Containers—Use and Maintenance : Most containers are made of plastic these days for aesthetic appeal, lightness and easy maintenance. Containers must be cleaned every day by gently rinsing them inside out. These must be dried before stacking. Buckets may be piled upside down.

Brushes—Use and Maintenance : Brushes are manufactured to fulfil a number of objectives. Brushes with soft fibre or nylon bristles are designed to brush dust carpets, cane, etc.

Scrub brushes have short coarse bristles designed for use on surfaces which have become ingrained with dirt and stains.

Brushes must be freed of fluff, hair and dust each day. Periodic washing is also recommended. Natural bristles tend to lose some of their stiffness if washed frequently but by giving brushes a final rinse in salted cold water, the bristles regain their natural stiffness. Nylon brushes wash more easily and dry quickly. In general, brushes must be washed by working the bristles up and down in warm water and soap lather and rinsed clean with cold water and sunned.

Mops and Brooms—Use and Maintenance : In principle, soft-bristled brooms are used on smooth floors while coarse-bristled ones are used on coarse surfaces especially outside. Brooms are maintained in the same manner as brushes. Mops must be washed in hot soapy water or detergent (never both together). The use of a soapless detergent will prevent the formation of scum. The mop should be worked up and down in at least two changes of clean hot water. The addition of a soapless detergent to the rinsing water will again prevent the formation of scum. The mop should be tightly squeezed out by hand, shaken well in the open air and left to dry.

Coarse cotton mops are used for large stone or cement floors. It takes less time to clean than hand washing but cannot ensure a good standard of cleanliness.

Cleaning Equipment Standards : Good cleaning, sanitation and maintenance are dependent upon high quality tools efficiently used. In order to assist housekeeping personnel in securing proper tools for the various cleaning procedures, listed below are standards and specifications of most tools and equipment which they will require. These specifications will also assist in making purchase orders for these items since the qualities and descriptions may be produced by several manufacturers. If a particular piece of equipment is not included in the list it is because it is an item which is subject to substantial change from year to year. Standards and specifications for such pieces of equipment will be maintained by the Purchasing Department on a current basis. Vacuum cleaners and polishing machines fall into this category.

Bottle Detergent : Eight ounce polythene container approx 3-3/4" x 6" with threaded 3/4" opening and plastic screw cap. Graduated in 1/4" oz. on two sides. Graduations clearly legible.

Brooms—Corn : All selected corn, free from seed and twins, all strands of full even length; triple wire bound to straight hardwood handle, unpainted. Corn-shaped with firm shoulders, stitched with six rows of soluble waxed cotton twine. To weigh 36-38 lb per dozen.

Brooms—Whisk : All selected whisk corn 8" or 9" long excluding handle, firm shoulders, evenly trimmed, wire bound to hard woodcore; stitched three rows of double waxed cotton twine. Ball or crimped metal top; metal to twin hanger.

Brushes—Dust : All plastic, nylon or equal, bristles firmly set in polished hardwood block; length 9" exclusive of handle. Handle 5", bristles, minimum 2-1/4'.

Brushes—Floor : All plastic nylon or equal, bristles staple set in a polished hardwood block; detachable straight grain polished hardwood handle. Brush length 16" or 24", bristle length minimum 3".

Brushes—Pick-up : All plastic, nylon or equal, bristles staple set in 8" polished hardwood block. Detachable straight grain polished hardwood handle 36" long. Minimum bristle length 2-1/8".

Brushes—Scrub : All bassine fibre bristles firmly set in a polished hardwood block, round or pointed ends. Size 10½" x 2-3/4". Bristles $1\frac{1}{8}$ out of block, evenly trimmed.

Brushes—Window : 100 per cent sterilized black horsehair bristles firmly set in 10" polished hardwood block; detachable straight grain polished hardwood handle. Minimum trimmed length of bristles $2\frac{1}{8}$", handles 60".

Carpet Sweepers : Heavy gauge enamelled steel body with pressed steel ends, moulded plastic wheels, nylon bristle brushes, spring action separately employing pans; rubber bumper all around; detachable sectional handle.

Chamois : Full oil tanned, free of thin areas, hard or rough spots. Size 20" x 32".

Dust Pans : Twenty gauge steel, one piece with integral handle. Smooth straight leading edge, 1" bevelled; no seams or open edges. Black enamel finish, size 8½" x 12".

Dust Pans—Lobby : Twenty gauge brass; one piece bottom and half-cover with smooth straight leading edge bevelled 1/2" sides crimp beaded, full bottom and half-cover. Reinforced handle holes. Straight hardwood or brass handle with heavy weight spring wire clips for attachment. Plan 7½" x 12½ x 2½"; handle 30".

Dusters—Wall : Four ply cotton yarn double stitched to 6 oz. pre-shrunk canvas shaped to fit a 3" x 12" frame; centre opening reinforced with heavy twill binding tape. Same tape used as ties over frame; rustproof 1/16" spring wire two position frame attached by adjustable joint to straight grain hardwood handle.

Mop Handles : $1\frac{1}{8}$ polished hardwood heads at least 6" wide, rust-proof malleable iron or cadmium-plated steel; lengths 34" and 63". Screws or bolts and nuts, cadmium-plate steel or brass.

Mop Heads : Ten ply long staple fully combed and bleached cotton yarn 18" long, bound in 10 oz. canvas 6" wide, double lines of double stitching both ends and centre. Weight 24 oz.

Mopping Outfit—Large : Sixteen gauge galvanized steel sheet two compartment tank, capacity 12½ gallons each side; cast bronze draw-offs mounted on 6" plate type, ballbearing rubber tired casters; 1" vinyl or rubber bumper all around. Equipped with standard roller tank mop wringer with hinged handle.

Mopping Outfit—Small : Two 16 qt. heavy duty pails, one downward pressure black malleable iron mop wringer all mounted on a 1¼" x 1/8" rust-proof angle iron chassis with 3" soft rubber tired ball-bearing steel disk casters. Rubber bumpers both ends; tubular rust-proof detachable and adjustable steel handle one end. Pails to standard specification.

Mops—Sanitary : 100% six ply acranial yarn double looped and stainless steel wire bound to a 16" hardwood handle. Minimum length of yarn 4" below binding.

Pails : Twenty gauge hot dip galvanized steel, double locked seamed concave bottom, with rolled reinforced rim 1/4" below bottom. Heavy fail handle attached by double riveted ears perpendicular to body of pail. Smooth rolled top edge, single side seam. Capacity 10 qt.

Sponges—Cellulose : 100 per cent foamed cellulose size 2¼ x 4½ x 7¼" equal to Dupont 10 A.

Spray Detergent : 32 oz. polyethylene or copper container, 1½" threaded opening for attachment of pistol type spray nozzle. Nozzle all brass, exterior plated; brass filter on intake. Equal to MacCarl Fogmaker.

Squeegee—Floor : Black angle iron head with malleable iron handle stock and removable iron front from blade fastened with brass screws. Width 18" to take single rubber strip 5/16 x 2½". Handle straight-grain polished hardwood.

Squeegee—Window : Cast brass with removable brass bar screws; double rubber strips full length 1/16" thick. Size 8" and 12". Handles straight-grain hardwood, detachable.

Pest Control : The most effective method of control is, of course, the employment of well-qualified professional exterminators on a contract basis. However, these exterminators cannot be expected to maintain the premises absolutely insect-free without the supplemental support and assistance of hotel personnel. For this reason it is recommended that all maids carry insecticide sprays on their carts and use them routinely when cleaning guest rooms and terraces. Recommended insecticides are harmless to human beings and animals but should be kept away from foodstuffs. These insecticides do not have a residual life and are, therefore, effective against a great many crawling insects, cockroaches in particular, on direct contact.

The residual insecticides necessary for a successful campaign against these insects are relatively toxic and must be handled with great care. It is recommended that they be used only by professional exterminators unless the hotel has in its employment an individual who can be trained in their use.

Cleanliness and constant vigilance, particularly in handling food, refuse and garbage, is the best defence against rodents. All containers of these items should be clean and tightly covered and should preferably be in metal. Wire enclosures should be used for dry foodstuffs in cartons or bags. This procedure plus periodic campaigns by the contract exterminators should keep the hotel free of rats and mice.

Control of Odours : There is no area of hotel housekeeping and maintenance more important than the control of odours. Where surface soil or disorder might offend the eye in a particular locality, odours permeate the air and can be offensive to guests at locations far removed from the source of the odour. Odour control depends on cleanliness, which is a housekeeping function, and on ventilation, which is a Maintenance Department function.

Smoke, kitchen and bar odours must be controlled by adequate ventilation to secure optimum results. The Maintenance Department must constantly attend to the cleanliness and good operation of ducts and fans. Filters must be changed frequently. Air handling grills and louvres must be kept clean and unobstructed.

Housekeeping staff should be supplied with prescribed air-refresheners which counter musty and stale odours in a room.

However, this is only complementary to actual housekeeping practices such as:

(a) allowing fresh air into a room by opening windows and allowing it to breathe;

(b) drying wet carpets by sunning them;

(c) following accepted cleaning methodology especially in bathrooms;

(d) throwing away residual food (coordination with Room Service for the clearance of trays, etc. is essential as deteriorating food could lend a stink to the immediate environs);

(e) taking particular care in the cleaning of nooks and crannies and under furniture for it is here that debris can lie for days).

9

Front Office

The Front Office in a hotel is the department responsible for the sale of hotel rooms through systematic methods of reservation, followed by registration and assigning rooms to customers. The term 'sale of rooms' may appear misleading to those unfamiliar with the industry. 'Sale' here means the use of hotel rooms at a price. A room is termed 'sold' for the day when a guest leases the room for stay in the hotel. "Room tariff" i.e. rate charged per room is computed for a "revenue day" which begins at noon of a particular day and ends at 12.00 hrs. the next day. In other words room charges are levied for a revenue day which is between noon and noon. Of course, a room may be sold for half-a-day as well, for which special rates are applicable. Such rates are referred to as "half-day" rates.

The front office in a hotel holds prime importance in view of the basic nature of business of a hotel, i.e. to sell rooms. Revenue collected from the sale of rooms contributes to more than 50 per cent of total hotel sales. The profit percentage from sales of rooms is very high. It has a complementary role of image-building, which is the first and last point of contact of every guest. If one looks at each component of a front office role, one could have a better perception of this department. While the title Front Office is a generic term to include a number of activities, smaller hotels are satisfied to call it simply Hotel Reception. Thus the role of the front office is thus to reserve, receive, register, assign rooms to guests and act as a continuous source of information to guests during their stay at the hotel.

To Reserve : A section of the front office is called the Reservation. This section is the hub of the department. Requests for reservation of rooms from various sources are received and the information is processed, properly documented, stored and retrieved at the appropriate time to ensure a guest his room upon arrival. Room, the chief product of a hotel, being a highly perishable commodity (as its sale is linked with a time element) the reservation department ensures that rooms are not allowed to "perish".

To Receive Register and Assign : This activity is handled by the section called Reception. The personnel in this section actually welcome and receive the guests and assign them a room after a few registration formalities.

Source of Information

The Information section is vital to front office operation. It controls the room keys, mail and messages. It is also equipped with all the information of the Hotel facilities and the city.

Though the major functions of the Front Office may seem simple, the actual mechanics to execute them successfully is complicated. The various systems and procedures on which the front office hinges shall be explained in detail later.

Qualities of Front Office Staff

As the front office is a critical department in a hotel in view of its revenue generating capacity and influence in image-building, the staff working in it assume a special importance.

Great care is taken in the selection of front office staff as they play a key role as:

Salesmen : They motivate the guest to spend more on the various hotel facilities.

Problem Solvers : Guests invariably approach the front office for help in case they have a problem or complaint. The staff have to be diplomatic and resourceful to solve the problem at the shortest possible time.

A Reference Point : Guests who want information or want to pass on information use them for this purpose.

Coordinators : Since they are a reference point, the front office staff are required to coordinate with other departments, airlines, travel agencies and city tour offices to give the guest personalised service.

Image-builders : As an extension to their salesman's role, front office staff can certainly generate a good image for the establishment in their manner of dress, communication, personal conduct and efficiency.

Essential Attributes : In view of the important role they play, the front office staff must have the following essential attributes:

A High Sense of Personal Grooming: Uniforms must be clean and neatly pressed. Hair should be groomed well. It is preferable for ladies to tie their hair up in a bun. Nails should be manicured. A soft cologne is preferable insted of heavy perfumes. Jewellery should be restricted to one ring and a necklace for ladies. In short, the front office staff must be seem at their best at all times.

Personal Hygiene: This is imperative to front office personnel. As they are constantly exposed to hotel guests, a clean appearance helps to project a good image not only of themselves but of the establishment as well.

Self Confidence: This is necessary as front office personnel meet guests of different countries, statuses and cultures. They should be comfortable and feel at ease in dealing with these people.

Communication must be Correct and Clear: It is preferable that front office staff know more than one language. It helps in communicating with guests who cannot speak English or the local language.

Diplomacy is the Greatest Attribute Required: Very often there are situations when a guest is irate over something; a diplomatic dealing helps in diffusing the explosive moment. It is quite common for a busy hotel to have no room to offer a guest who has come with a confirmed booking. A diplomatic approach is the only way by which the guest can be pacified.

Calmness to take the busy Demands of a Front Office's Operations: Being the nerve centre of the hotel, the front office is constantly in touch with guests and therefore invariably comes under tremendous pressure. The guests always expect personalised, priority treatment and the pressure of demand never ceases. Coupled with this are difficult guests who can unnerve a person. The front office staff should thus have a high degree of tolerance for pressure of work and be calm and composed at all times.

Ability to Remember Names and Faces: This single attribute distinguishes the good from the average amongst the front office staff. Every individual has an ego and his/ her name is most precious and personal to him. If the front office staff can call most guests by their names, this immediately flatters them and personalises the guest experience. The guest begins to feel he is welcome as people recognise him by name.

Good Manners: As the hotel is a meeting place of social elites all the grace and etiquette associated with good society comes into play. Guests of all statuses come to stay in the hotel and they are used to good manners and politeness. Wishing a guest the time of the day and saying "Thank you" are basic etiquettes shown.

Ready Smile: This is very becoming to front office operation. Guests like to be handled by a cheerful staff at the desk. Their smile exudes cheer to the guests and puts them at ease.

Physical Fitness: Front office operations require the staff to stand for long hours at a stretch. The staff must be sturdy, agile and active.

Quick Decision Making Ability: Guests often approach the Front Desk with problems and requests. Front office staff must be able to decide quickly a course of action that satisfies the guest, at the same time keeping the interests of the organisation alive.

Possessed with the attributes mentioned above, the front office staff could make a fine team that is an asset to the hotel. Figure below suggests an organisational hierarchy for a typical large metropolitan hotel.

Front Office Organisational Hierarchy of a Large Hotel

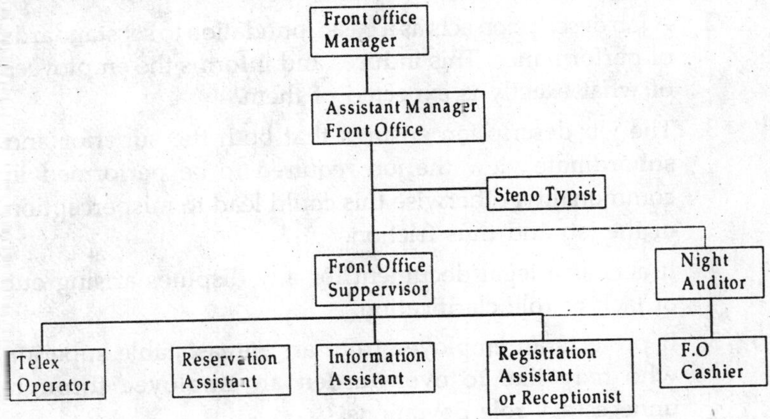

Note: Dotted line indicates operational control relationship as opposed to administrative control relationship.

The figure below suggests hierarchy of a small hotel.

Front Office Organisational Hierarchy of a Small Hotel

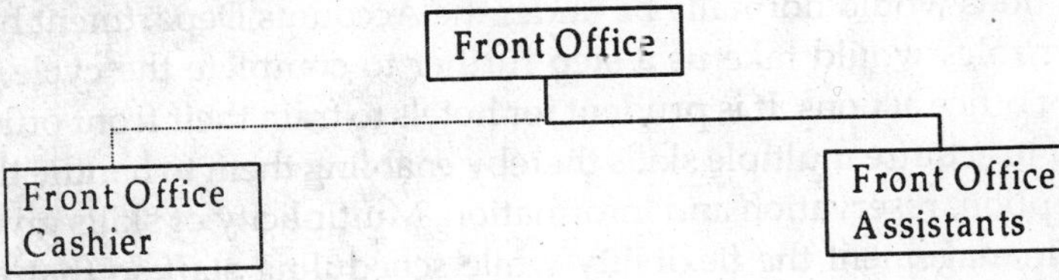

Front Office Assistant

A Job Description, by its very nomenclature is a written description of the job to be performed in a job position. It specifies the parameters within which a job is done. It is thus a realistic guide to any employee recruited for a particular job. These parameters not only include the duties and responsibilities of the job position but also the working hours, reporting relationships, authority, equipment handled, coordinational specifications with other departments and job positions, status within the departmental hierarchy, etc. Professional organisations would normally hand over a job description to all new recruits. This offers several advantages:

1. The new recruit knows exactly what his job entails. This in itself is a vital part of induction.
2. A job description acts as a basic foundation to set standards of performance. This induces and informs the employees of what exactly is expected of them.
3. The job description ensures that both the superior and subordinate view the job required to be performed in commonality, otherwise this could lead to misperception of the job and thus friction.
4. It acts as a legal document for any disputes arising out of lack of role clarification.
5. It protects an employee from an unreasonable superior who may like to over-burden an employee through unnecessary role deviations.

To enable readers of this book to appreciate the full significance of subsequent chapters, the following pages elucidate typical job descriptions of front office personnel. In order to comprehensively cover the front office operations the job descriptions of the Front Office Cashier and Night Auditor, have been included. These two positions would normally be under the Accounts Department but their roles would take us a step further to complete the cycle of front office actions. It is prudent for hotels to train their front office staff to acquire multiple skills thereby enabling them to handle the reception, reservation and information. Multiplicity of skills gives the management the flexibility while scheduling staff so that all positions are manned in spite of absenteeism, leave, staff turnover, etc. the front office employee reciprocally views his job as enriched and is saved from the monotony of doing one job only. The job description offered for front office basic staff is common, with subsections provided for the unique activity offered in various job positions in the departments. We have found it important to give the front office cashier and night auditor separate job descriptions in view of their specialised tasks though front office staff in smaller hotels are adept at these roles also.

Job Description of Front Office Assistants

Job Position : Front Office Assistants

Category : Non-Supervisory

Reports to : 1. Front Office Supervisor
2. Front Office Manager

Job Definition : Reserve, register and assign rooms to guests and be a continuous source of information during their stay in the hotel.

Directly Controls/Supervises : Room racks, Arrival-departure register, Guest racks, Reservation racks, Guest room keys, Guest mail.

Assigned Area of Activity : Front Office: Information, Reception and Reservation Desks.

Hours of Operation : One shift in 24 hours for 8 hours or as per policy of the Management.

Authority : Refuse reservations; give discounts as per policy; assign rooms and deal with guests as found fit; can refuse divulging guest informations to others.

Work Performed : Reservation

1. Promptly and courteously handle all reservation requests.
2. Update regularly the reservation chart and rack.
3. Keep all reservations correspondence up-to-date.
4. Keep room availability status board up-to-date.
5. Handle amendments and cancellations of reservations.

Reception

1. Promptly and courteously register guests and assign them rooms.
2. Update the room rack continuously.
3. Calculate room availability position and advise reservation.
4. Issue VIP amenities voucher.
5. Complete pre-registration formalities for VIPs, invalids, old people, groups and airline crews.
6. Execute government formalities regarding foreigners.
7. Coordinate closely with Housekeeping for clearance of rooms to sell
8 Prepare room-reports and occupancy statistics.

Information

1. Maintain guestroom keys safely and accurately.
2. Provide up-to-date information on the hotel and city to guests.
3. Receive and disburse guest mail.
4. Continuously update the guest rack.
5. Receive messages of guests and forward them correctly and promptly.
6. Liase with lobby to page guests.

Bell Captain

Job Title : Bell Captain

Category: Supervisory

Reports to

1. Sr. Bell Captain
2. Lobby Manager

Job Definition : To supervise and provide all porter services with efficiency and politeness.

Directly Controls : Bell-boys

Assigned Area of Activity : Principally the lobby area but is authorised to work in any part of the hotel depending upon the errand demanded.

Hours of Operation : One shift of 8 hours in 24 hours, or as per policy of the management.

Authority : To check bell boys in their daily operations.

To appraise their performance.

Work Performed

1. Brief all bell boys at the beginning of a shift.
2. Ensure that bell boys in their shifts are well groomed and uniformed.
3. Control the movement of all bell boys.
4. Assign errands to bell boys.
5. Ensure that the bell desk is well stocked with postage.

6. Initiate action again "scanty baggage" guests.
7. Organise paging services in the lobby.
8. Execute formalities regarding "left luggage".
9. Assist in security vigilance functions.
10. Assist in crew and group wake call procedure.
11. Perform any other duties that are required by management front time to time.

Bell Boy

Job Title : Bell Boy

Category : Non-Supervisory

Reports to :

1. Bell Captain
2. Sr. Bell Captain
3. Lobby Manager

Job Definition : To handle guest baggage at the time of arrival and departure and to do errands as required.

Directly Controls : Guest baggage during transit in the hotel.

Assigned Area of Activity : Principally the lobby area boy is authorised to work in any part of the hotel depending upon the errand demanded.

Hours of Operation : One shift of 8 hours in 24 hours, or as per the policy of the management.

Authority : None

Work Performed

1. Carry guest baggage at the time of guest arrival.
2. Carry guest baggage into the guest room and explain all controls in the room to the guest.
3. Issue postage against cash to guests.
4. Deliver guest baggage to "left luggage" room if required.
5. Check the guest room at the time of guest departure.
6. Carry baggage at the time of guest departure.
7. Check guest rooms to validate the Discrepancy Report.

8. Page guests in the lobby area if required.
9. Report "scanty baggage" guests to Bell Captain.
10. Perform any errands as required by guests and management.

Coordinates with

Front office: for the arrival and departure of guests to validate Room Discrepancy Report.

Security: for reporting and assisting in dealing with undesirable elements in the lobby.

Control of Bell Boys

As is evident from the job description of the Bell Captain, one of his primary functions is to control bell boys. This control is necessary as bell boys are subject to many errands that take them to all corners of the hotel and even outside. To be able to optimise the productivity of the team within a given shift the Lobby Control Sheet is constituted. The purpose of this sheet is to keep a record of and check on the movement of bell boys.

HOTEL XYZ LTD.

LOBBY CONTROL SHEET

Captain.. Sheet No..........................
Date ....198.................. Shift- from .... To ....

Room No.	Attendant No.	Arr	Dep.	Room	Service Change To	Call	Time		Comments
							From	To	

The control sheet above is sell-explanatory. The bell boys are given code numbers to easily record their activities. Alternatively, the bell boys names may be also used. For an arrival, the room number is filled in after the front office has intimated the same. The "room changed to" column would indicate the number of the new room a guest has been allotted. His old room number is mentioned in the first column.

Through this sheet the work-load per bell boy is ascertained and the bell captain is able to distribute work-load uniformly. He gets a chance to find out who the lethargic members of the team are through the time control. Of course, the bell boy should know in advance a reasonable time that an errand would take to fill his remarks in the last column.

Front Office Salesmanship

The difference between a successful hotel and an unsuccessful one is the ability of the staff to get a guest to spend an extra rupee and get the value for it. Very often a guest may enter a hotel without an exact idea of how he is going to utilise his free time. A gentle suggestion by an employee at the right time can stimulate a guest to utilise a service and pay for it. The front office staff have a key role to play in hotel selling.

Knowledge of the Products : This is one of the most important factors for salesmanship. Here is a checklist of things that front office personnel should be knowledgeable about:

Room : Location, view it commands, size, type, room rate, decor, guest facilities in the room such as hot/cold water, channel music, telephone, refrigerator, television, weather controls, etc.

Restaurant and Bars : Number of outlets, locations, types of cuisine, entertainment, timings, buffet or a'la carte, menu, table reservation procedures.

Arcade : Service offered by travel agency, bank, post and telegraph office, health club, swimming pool, barber shop, pastry shop, shoe-shine, beauty saloon, drugstore and shopping.

Other Supporting Services : Telephones, party arrangements, baby sitter services, valet and laundry service, reservations for other hotels of the chain, telex, typist facility, doctor service.

City Information : City tour facilities, church timings, theatre timings, maps and locations of shopping centres, historical, business and cultural places of interest, railway timings, airline schedule, inter-state bus terminals, nearest location of a 24-hour chemist shop and nearest hospital.

There are many more items of information that front office staff are equipped with to make them living encyclopaedias. The important point to remember is that only with a knowledge of the product can one actually sell it.

Sales Promotion : Front office staff must be aware that the guest attaches value to the service sold and will be prepared to spend for it. For example, if a room has a maximum, moderate and minimum rate attached to it, the maximum must be quoted but the value of this rate must be sold. The room may be overlooking the swimming pool, or be away from the noisy elevator foyer, or have soft decor to please a guest on a hot day. Whatever it be, each proposition must be given a value.

After the room is allotted the front office assistant may recommend a suana bath and massage at the health club especially after the guest has returned from a long journey. The assistant may volunteer to reserve his table at one of the restaurants and bars.

The good front office assistant must always give the guest a choice so that he feels that the final decision was his. While offering a room two locations should be given. When recommending a restaurant two are offered to choose from (provided the establishment has more than one dining place).

Guest Needs : As individuals have varying needs, a guest may stay in a hotel for comfort, address value, entertainment, convenience of location, standards of facilities offered, etc. It is important to identify the needs of each guest and try to appeal to those needs. Another important aspect of a guest is that he has left his home and would like a home away from home. It is a question of emotional adjustments to unfamiliar surroundings. An employee should try and make him feel at home and anticipate his needs for home comforts through personalised service. By appealing to a guests' needs one can stimulate sales.

Desire to Help : This trait could be the cornerstone to successful salesmanship in the hospitability industry—it is essential to be genuine in all communications with guests. The more genuine the front office staff are in their approach, the greater is the desire to be helpful. A guest is sensitive and can see through a "put on" act as against sincerity in words and deeds. Unless an employee enjoys being hospitable, genuine concern becomes act. A simple way of bringing out this genuine concern is to display empathy. Empathy is energised by asking oneself, "what would I expect of the hotel if I were a guest".

Communication : How one speaks is important to all sales efforts. Brusque language is bound to put guests on the defensive and a sale can never be energised. Here are some typical phrases to use:

"May I help you".

"May I suggest (or recommend).........."

"I beg your pardon"

"May I request you to.........."

"One moment please..........."

"Would you kindly............."

It is highly recommended that one should avoid the use of slang or abbreviation. Always refer to male guests as gentlemen and female guests as ladies or young ladies. Normally the establishment would select those candidates for the post of front office assistant who have a clear, mellow and proper mode of speech.

10

Coordinating Departments

Lobby

Arrival : The bell boy escorts guests from the main door with their luggage to the front office. After the guest has been registered the front office informs the bell boy of the room number so that the guest may be escorted to his room and his luggage placed in the room.

Departure : In most hotels, a guest wishing to check out of the hotel calls the bell desk for a porter to carry his luggage down. The bell desk informs the front office of the intentions of the guest so that the cashier can prepare his bill. It is only after the front office is satisfied regarding the payment of bills and retrieval of room key will they allow the bell boy to remove the luggage outside the premise of the hotel.

Shifting : Often, a guest requests the front office for a change of room. The front office intimates the bell desk to send bell boys to help in the shifting of luggage.

Scanty Baggage : "Skippers" are those guests who leave the hotel without paying their bills. This is made possible because the "skipper" comes with little luggage to avoid bringing the attention of the bell boys to his "secret" check out. Alternatively, if he has just a briefcase, he may leave the hotel under the pretext of a business call. The bell boys have to be alert to notify the front office about guests with scanty baggage so that a necessary advance is taken from them and a close watch is kept on them.

Message : The information section of front office alerts the bell boys to deliver messages received by them for guests in the hotel.

Paging : "Paging" is the system of displaying the name of a guest on a small board with a long handle. The board is held above the head of the bell boy and has small bells which are rung to draw the attention of customers to the board. When a phone call is received for a guest in a specified location, this paging system is used to contact guests. The bell boy does the paging in most public areas especially the lobby.

Housekeeping Room Report : To keep a tight control on rooms, the housekeeping and front office have to closely coordinate. One way is through the room report whereby the housekeeping staff checks each room on every floor and advises their status through a report.

HOTEL XYZ LTD

Discrepancy Report

Room	Per Room Asstt.		Per House Keeper		Investigation Remarks
					Asstt. Manager

Discrepancy Report : A discrepancy report is prepared by the front desk on receiving the Room Report from the Housekeeping. The front office compares it with the Room Rack for reconciliation of room status. Discrepancies noticed between room rack and housekeeping room report are noted down on a separate report called the "discrepancy report" which is then handed over to a bell boy for physical check and reporting back of the room under discrepancy. After a physical check of the room the bell boy notes down the correct status which is accepted by the front office and room rack and reconciled accordingly.

Room Clearance Arrangement : When a guest checks out, the front office has to immediately inform the housekeeping desk (which is the central point of information for housekeeping) or the floors, to clean the room so that it is ready for sale again. This information is controlled on a Departure Intimation control sheet. Housekeeping in return would have to inform the front office immediately after a room has been cleaned and prepared for sale to a guest. In technical parlance when the front desk informs the housekeeping desk about a check out room, it is referred to as giving a "departure room" to housekeeping and when housekeeping informs the front office about rooms which are ready for sale, it is known as "cleared rooms".

HOTEL XYZ LTD.

DEPARTURE INTIMATION CONTROL SHEET

Dale ______________ RECEPTION

ROOM NO.	NAME OF GUEST	NAME OF PERSON INFORMED AT			TIME	BY
		House keeping	Telephone Dept.	Room Service		

NIGHT ROOM REPORT

FIRST FLOOR				SECOND FLOOR				THIRD FLOOR				FOURTH FLOOR				AUDITOR'S ADJUSTMENTS	
Room No.	Code	Guests	Rate	Room No	Code	Guests	Rate	Room No	Code	Guests	Rate	Room No	Code	Guests	Rate		
102				202				302				402					
103				203				303				403					
104				204				304				404					CODE
105				205				305				405					Travel Agents :—
								306				406					Airlines —
				207				307				407					Walk-ins —
				209				309									
				210				310				410					
111				211				311				411					
112				212				312				412					
115				215				315				415					
120				220				320				420				TOTAL	
										GROUPS							
									Name		Rate						
																Recapitulation	
																Floor No. Guests Amount	
																1st	
																2nd	
																3rd	
																4th	
TOTAL				TOTAL				TOTAL				TOTAL					GRAND TOTAL

Occupancy Statistics : After reconciling the "Room Rack" with the Housekeeping Room Report, the Front Office Reception compile data on the "occupancy" position of the hotel for the day in the form of a report for the purpose of management information. This compilation and analysis of occupancy data is referred to as "night room report" and is invariably prepared by the night receptionist.

Special Arrangement for Groups and VIPs : The front office informs housekeeping to be alert to attend to rooms occupied by groups or VIPs. Service has to be quicker and efficient. Housekeeping provides "flowers" for VIPs in the room on receipt of the Amenities Voucher issued by the Front Desk.

Day Date

- Please Send Complimentary
- Flowers
- Full—Single ( )—Double ( )—Special ( )
- ....

To .... Arriving ....

Room No. ....

....

Authorised by ....

Copy of Auditor MAURYA—FO—021

Accounts

Front Office Cashier : The front office cashier receives payments for a guest's stay in the hotel. This is the point where all the charge vouchers (bills) generated by the guest are received, to be included in the overall bill. Close liaison between the lobby staff and cashier is imperative. The Bell Captain must inform the cashier about the intended check out of a guest so that the guest's bills are updated and kept ready for presentation. Also, the cashier is informed of a new arrival by the Reception by opening and forwarding a new folio in the guest's name giving room number and time of check in, with defined billing instructions which the cashier places in the bill tray against the appropriate room.

Night Auditor : The Night Auditor audits all guest bills received by the front office cashier and prepares and proves for the calendar day.

City Ledger : This is the credit section which receives bills from front office that has extended credit as per previous arrangement between the hotel and the guest. This department follows up with the individual or company for the payment of the bills.

Room Service

Arrivals and Departures : The Room Service is kept closely intimated on arrivals and departures of guests. It is this department that provides food and beverage services to the room and must be informed as to the occupant in order to raise bills accordingly.

VIP Procedures : The front office informs room service through the Amenities Voucher and a List of the VIPs' expected to arrive in the hotel so that special service is extended. Also the room service provides a complimentary basket of fruit, liquor, cakes and pastries or whatever gesture the establishment wishes to extend to a VIP as per the policy.

Telephones

Arrivals and Departures : This is another department that is informed immediately of the arrival and departure of a guest so that when calls come for a particular guest it is fully knowledgeable about his/her presence in the hotel so that calls may be connected to him/her. Also calls made by the guest are recorded or metered.

Engineering : The engineering department is responsible for any maintenance of furniture, fixtures and equipment and for rectifying faults in the services provided, like air conditioning, plumbing, etc. Sometimes when guest keys are lost, the workshop of the engineering department makes duplicate keys from key blanks, besides changing the location of the lever by altering the lock and key plan of the hotel.

Stores : The stores are responsible for supplies of relevant forms, formats and stationery.

Sales : There is very close coordination between the front office and sales especially in soliciting their help in improving room sales on lean occupancy days. The front office also informs sales whenever an important guest, who influences the business of the hotel 'checks in', so that special attention can be given to him/her. Sales keeps the front office updated with the new agreements made with travel agents and airline crews and viable accounts.

Guest Arrival/Departure Procedure

Arrival Procedure

Step 1 : When a guest arrives, the doorman buzzes the Bell Captain Desk for a bell Boy.

Step 2 : The bell boy should wish the guest and collect his baggage and bring it into the lobby via the baggage entrance and place baggage at the bell desk which is located normally opposite the Reception counter. The bell boy should wait for the guest to register at the front office. If the hotel has tags to identify baggage these should be attached to the baggage. Inform scanty baggage to the lobby manager or front office.

Step 3 : The Information counter at the front office will indicate that the guest has been allotted a room by handing over the errand card which mentions the room number. The room key is also handed over with the errand card. Bring to the guest's attention any baggage damaged to protect the hotel from blame.

Errand Card

Guest Arrival Errand Card

Bell Boy No.			Date	
Room No.		Name		
Suit Case	Brief Case	Hand Bag	Packets	Others
Remarks				

Bell Boy Sig. Capt's Sig.

Step 4 : Lead the guest to his room along with his baggage. Some hotels have separate baggage elevators.

Step 5 : The bell boy should open the door of the guestroom and let the guest enter first. After positioning the baggage at the allotted rack in the room, the guest must be told where the floor-lights are located, channel music, air-conditioning/central heating thermostat control, internal locking system, etc. are located.

Step 6 : Offer any other help and if not required, wish the guest a pleasant stay. Do not solicit for tips.

Step 7 : Report back to the bell desk.

Note: A hotel may have different coloured errand cards for arrival and departure of guests.

Departure Procedure

Step 1 : The bell desk will receive a phone call from the guest about his intention to check out. Write the room number carefully on the errand card, a stack of which is kept at the bell desk itself. Inform the Bell Captain and proceed to the room.

Step 2 : Knock on the guest's door and announce yourself. Look around the room for any guest articles left, any damaged hotel property and switch off the airconditioning/ heating, lights, etc. Collect the room key and depart from the room letting the guest lead the way. Ensure that the guest room is locked. If the guest wants to carry the room key himself, permit him to do so.

Step 3 : Place the baggage at the bell desk. Stick on any hotel stickers or publicity tags. Hand over the room key to the Information counter and errand card to the Front Office Cashier. Wait for the guest to pay the bill.

Step 4 : The bell boy will receive an authorisation to take the baggage out of the hotel only after the Front Office cashier has signed that the guest has paid his bills, and the Receptionist that the room key has been received.

Step 5 : Take the baggage to the car porch and load it to the transport.

Step 6 : Report back to the bell desk and hand over the errand card with the authorisation signatures.

11

Practices and Procedures

Briefing and Scheduling

Briefing : Briefing is that process at the beginning of a work shift which is provided by management to facilitate a two-way communication between management and staff. It is the one time during a shift that all housekeeping staff are together to share information and feelings before they disperse to their work areas. Briefing is normally undertaken where all employees have to report on duty at the beginning of the shift. This is after the employees have formally clocked into the hotel at the time office and have already received their fresh uniforms which they change into in their respective locker rooms. All employees must report for briefing properly attired and at the scheduled commencement of the shift or earlier. In Housekeeping briefing is conducted at a prescribed common Housekeeping Lounge or at the Housekeeping Control Room. Ideally, the Executive Housekeeper must conduct the briefing; however, due to odd shift timings she may delegate this responsibility to her deputy. Here are some issues that should normally be covered in a briefing that should last no longer than 15 minutes.

Dress Turnout : Housekeeping staff are mostly in guest visibility and contact areas. It is thus important that they are well-groomed and clean. While grooming projects the image and quality of the hotel, a guest also likes to feel that the people who clean his room are themselves very clean. It is thus important for the Housekeeper to ensure the following:

1. Personal cleanliness—fingernails should be clean and cut short; men should have shaved and should emit no body odour.
2. Hair should be clean and neatly combed/arranged. Hair nets are suggested but not essential.
3. Little or no make-up.
4. Careful use of lipsticks for maids.
5. No necklaces or bracelets—earrings, if worn, must be small and unobtrusive.
6. Uniforms must be clean and well pressed. They must be of the proper size and well fastened.
7. Stockings (if required) should be clean, of a permitted colour and free of holes.
8. Shoes should be dark in colour, low-heeled and clean.

Policies and Procedure : Any new policies and procedures introduced by management must be made out and explained to the staff.

VIPs in the House : The names, room numbers and the importance of each VIP staying in the hotel must be communicated to all staff, especially those assigned to their floors.

Allotment of Duties : At a briefing the duties of each staff member and the areas of accountability are explained. This would mean that maids are assigned a floor and allotted their number of rooms. The housemen, likewise, are told which floors or public areas they are assigned to for cleaning. They are also told which supervisor would be in charge.

Feedback of Staff : The Executive Housekeeper must receive any professional or personal grievances of staff. It would help productivity if problems are resolved or at least heard with the intention of resolving them. This can also be an opportunity to test out whether policies and procedures already explained have been understood and implemented.

Training : Briefing is a time which can be used as a training opportunity. Simple tasks may be demonstrated so that they can be practiced under supervision at their work place.

Standards of Performance : An Executive Housekeeper must constantly remind housekeeping staff of the standards expected by management. Standards could be the number of rooms to be completed by a maid in her shift or the time taken to complete a departure room etc. At a briefing, the housekeeping staff should get a first hand feedback on whether they are maintaining the required standards.

Recognition and Praise : Since all housekeeping staff on a given shift assemble for a briefing, it is the ideal time to give a word of praise or recognition to deserving candidates.

Other Information : It is important to give information of a general nature, especially of the going-on in the hotel to staff. One normally shrugs off general information as it does not concern staff—but all information is knowledge and brings in a feeling of pride and a team spirit to the totality of hotel operations. Information like the gala functions in the hotel, the re-assignment of people in the hotel, promotions, increments, etc. must be shared.

Knowledge of Rooms : The sale of rooms constitute approximately 50 per cent or more of the total hotel revenue. A 'sale' of room would mean the leasing of the room for occupation for 24 hours at a predetermined cost. A room not sold on a particular day has lost its opportunity to earn revenue for that day. Hence rooms are referred to as highly perishable commodities. The loss of an opportunity to sell a room can also be due to inefficiency of housekeeping in having a room ready when required. What does a room mean to a guest?

It means Comfort : Hence, hotels spend efforts in ensuring the quality of beds, mattresses; weather, control, channel music, hot and cold water, attached baths, etc. The comforts must be regularly maintained and functioning. It is Housekeeping's responsibility to ensure this.

It means Security : The primary security devise that hotels provide is to restrict entrance to the room/suite through only one door; a double locking system from inside; strict control on room keys and master keys; chain locking the door from within to further augment the door locking system; precautions in the room to ensure all electrical wiring is concealed and no equipment in the room is faulty; fire exit layout in the room, etc.

It means Privacy : Room windows are provided with curtains. Superior hotels would have daylight curtains and heavy night curtains. Windows would normally overlook good scenic views, away from the prying eyes of others in the hotel or the outside public. The entrance into a room procedure is well defined to ensure guest privacy. Attached baths are also a measure towards privacy.

It means Convenience : A guest is provided entertainment, food and beverage services, telephone services, etc. in his or her room. The guest is thus free to spend all the time towards fulfilling the purpose of his visit—be it a holiday or business. The House keeping Department should ensure such literature in the room as to enable a guest to know how to reach such conveniences and avail of them.

It means Cleanliness and Hygiene : The Housekeeping Department has a pivotal role to play in this aspect.

Above all, the Room is Very Personal to a Guest : Hence he demands the highest standards in everything that the room stands for.

In addition to the above, it is important for all housekeeping personnel to know the different types of rooms that hotels provide.

Single Room	Meant for a single occupancy. The room has one normal sized bed.
Double Room	Meant for double occupancy and has one large bed meant for two.
Twin Room	Meant for double occupancy. The room provides two single beds. Hotels may reserve the flexibility to sell it on single occupancy as well.
Studio Room	Meant for single or double occupancy. It has one normal bed and a sofa-cum-bed which

	acts as a sofa during the day and can be pulled out into a bed for the night.
Single Suite	Meant for single occupancy. A suite is a two-room set—one room furnished with drawing-cum-dining facilities and the other as a bedroom with a normal bed.
Double Suite	It is the same as a single suite in concept, except that the bedroom has a large double bed, or two normal sized beds to facilitate double occupancy.
Cabana	Rooms attached to the pool-side for changing or resting. The room has one sofa-cum-bed.
Duplex Suite	Room built on two floors with an inter-connecting staircase. Such suites normally have two bedrooms.
Triple Room	Provided mostly for families. It has twin beds with an extra cot.

All the above rooms may be furnished with extra roll-away cots on the demand of the guest at an extra charge. All rooms normally have attached bathrooms. Exceptions would be in hostel where common bathrooms per floor is more economical for the guest and management for the low charges they levy on rooms.

Rules on a Guest Floor : Prior to commencing work, all housekeeping staff, especially room attendants, must follow some floor rules that lend an air of efficiency and least inconvenience to guests. The floor and rooms are most private and personal to guests who are concerned by the people who frequent them. They lay a large trust in the management of the hotel through the room attendants who are privy to their rooms and belongings. To uphold this trust the following rules must be strictly observed:

1. Speech amongst the floor staff must be restricted to a minimum. In case communication is necessary, this must be done in low tones even when guests are not in sight.
2. Unnecessary movements like running or jumping must be avoided.

3. The passageway must be kept free of equipment, trays or trollies.
4. The floor telephones must be attended to promptly.
5. Room attendants must greet all guests according to the time of the day.
6. Staff must be helpful and readily give required information. Misleading a guest through misinformation must be avoided.
7. Alertness to guest movements is necessary so as to report anything suspicious.
8. Remember the guest is always right. Arguing with a guest is prohibited. If a guest is being unreasonable refer him/her to the next superior.
9. It is prohibited to enter rooms which display a "Do not disturb" sign outside. If a DND sign is on for a long time, this may be reported to the floor supervisor.
10. The door of the room in which the attendant is cleaning should always be kept wide open.
11. If the guest returns when the room is being cleaned the room attendant may ask the guest if she can continue or come later.
12. In spite of following the procedure for entering a room, if the guest is inside either sleeping or awake, quickly withdraw, apologising if required and shut the door softly.
13. Always follow the procedure of entering a room even if the room is seemingly vacant.

The Maids Cart : The maids cart is a trolley meant to stock a given number of linen item, supplies and equipment to service an allotted number of rooms. Each maid, after receiving her room assignment, should check her supplies against a standard list to avoid needless trips. The maid is responsible for the condition, cleanliness and appearance of her cart.

The lower shelf of the cart is used to carry heavier items like mattresses, protectors and bed sheets and night spreads. The middle and top shelf stock pillow slips and bath linen. Linen will include:

Night spreads	1 for each bed
Sheets	2 for each bed
Pillow cases	2 for each bed
Bath towels	1 for each guest
Face towels	1 for each guest
Hand towels	1 for/each guest
Bath mats	1 for each bathroom
Mattress protectors	few to replace as necessary

These terms should be arranged in neat stacks, the heavier items below and the lighter ones on top.

The top tray should be neatly arranged with the following guest room supplies and cleaning agents:

Room	Bathroom
Water tumblers	Gargle tumblers
Service directory	Shoe mitts
'Do not disturb' cards	Soaps/soap dish
Guest stationery	Toilet rolls
Ball point pens	Toilet tissues
Telegraph forms	Blade dispensers
Bibles/Gita	Shower caps
Ash trays	Soap suds
Match boxes	Shampoo bottles
Laundry forms	Disposal bags
Laundry bags	
Clothes hangers	
Candle stands	
Scribbling pads	
Guest house rules	
Guest comment forms	
Sewing kits	
Breakfast knob cards	
Plastic shirt bags	
"Polish my shoe" card	

In addition, there should be supplies of such promotional material as the management of the hotel may from time to time prescribe. In any event, this material should include:

Room service menu.

Room service beverage list.

Tent cards for special promotion.

In addition, the cart may carry cleaning equipment such as feather brush, dustpan, mops, sponges, dusters, carpet brush or vacuum cleaner, clean scrub bucket, scrub brush on the same end of the maids cart as the trash bag. The exact location is below the trash bag.

The cleaning material will include:

Disinfectants: dettol, deodorizer.

Cleaning agents: Vim, sanitizer (sanifresh), liquid soap (teenopol), naphthealene balls, room freshner and anol.

Polishing material: Brasso, wax polish.

After securing all the supplies and equipment outlined above, each maid should proceed to her duty station and begin the cleaning procedure on the assigned number of rooms with room checklists.

Maid carts are to be placed along the corridor wall on the same side of the corridor where rooms are being serviced. The cart should be so positioned as to service a minimum of two rooms without much movement of the room attendant to minimise trips to the cart and thereby reduce the fatigue factor.

When designing maid carts consideration must be given to the fact that the cart should be lightweight to ensure easy mobility by the maid. Heavy carts also pucker corridor carpets. The wheels of the cart must be of a good standard and well oiled periodically to ensure smooth movement.

Room No.	*Name of Article*	*Room No.*	*Name of Article*	*Remarks*
1.	Room number	2.	Door	
3.	Lock Operation	4.	Threshold	
5.	Peephole	6.	DND-Make my room card	

Room No.	*Name of Article*	*Room No.*	*Name of Article*	*Remarks*
	7. Lights -md switches		8. Wardrobe door	
	9. Micro light		10. Hangers	
	11. Extra Pillows		12. Laundry bags	
	13. A.C. Operation		14. Luggage chest	
	15. Lining paper		16. Shoe shine card	
	17. Wall paper		18. Vestibule ceiling	
	19. Dresser and stool		20. Ash tray	
	21. Matches		22. Candle and candle stand	
	23. Tent card		24. Portfolio	
	25. Guest house rule		26. Writing material	
	27. Telegraph form		28. Guest comment form	
	29. Room service menu		30. Breakfast knobs	
	31. Laundry and Valet list		32. Sewing kit	
	33. Plastic bags		34. Waste paper basket	
	35. TV and TV programme		36. TV Comments form	
	37. Mirrors		38. Chairs and tables	
	39. Heavy curtain		40. Sheer curtain	
	41. Window operation		42. Window Cleaning	
	43. Safety		44. Safety bar	
	45. Headrest		46. Bed and mattress	
	47. Bed cover		48. Studio bed	
	49. Wall plaques		50. Bedside table	
	51. Bedside lamp		52. Lamp shade	
	53. Telephone		54. Message pad	
	55. Service directory		56. Pen	
	57. Thermos flask		58. High ball glasses	
	59. Telephone		60. Gita	
	61. Bible		62. Light switch	

Room No.	*Name of Article*	*Room No.*	*Name of Article*	*Remarks*
63.	A.C. switch	64.	Message light	
65.	Music operation	66.	Carpet	
67.	Skirting	68.	Walls & Ceiling	
69.	Cobweb chicking	70.	Toilet door	
71.	Toilet door latch	72.	Bolt	
73.	Robe hook	74.	Bottle opener	
75.	Washbasin and counter	76.	Mirror	
77.	Mirror screw caps	78.	Tissue & blade box	
79.	Soap & soap dish	80.	Ash tray	
81.	Toilet tumblers	82.	Shower cap	
83.	Shoe shine strip	84.	Soap suds	
85.	Toilet rolls	86.	Spindle	
87.	Tissue	88.	Waste paper basket	
89.	Disposal bag	90.	WC	
91.	WC Band	92.	Flush	
93.	Drain & C.P. grating	94.	Bath tub/Bath tub stopper	
95.	Bath tub nuts, bolts & caps	96.	Tap & shower operation	
97.	Shower curtain	98.	Clothes line	
99.	Bath mug	100.	Towel rack-Towels-Bath mat	
101.	Chrome fittings	102.	Tiles & Ceiling	
103.	Toilet marble	104.	Light fixture	
105.	Prismatic cover	106.	Tidy Guestclothes & belongings	

Code G : Good 1 : Needs Improvement P : Poor N : not done

Fig. Room Checklist

Cleaning a Room

How to Enter : Prior to reporting on a floor the room attendant already knows the status of a room in her given lot of rooms. The room attendant can prioritise rooms to be attended to first on the basis of immediate needs; however, the normal practice is to attend to vacant rooms first, then departure rooms, "Clean my rooms," and finally occupied rooms. For occupied rooms look whether the room has a "Do not disturb" card on the door knob. If it does, then go to a room which does not. Knock at the door firmly with the index finger knuckle announcing clearly "Housekeeping." When there is no answer, repeat the knock after 10 seconds announcing yourself as before. If there is still no answer open the door with the floor master-key. Push the door again, knock announcing inside the room "Housekeeping." When there is no reply and one is relatively sure that there is no one in, open the door wide and keep it that way till the entire cleaning cycle in the room is complete.

Room Cleaning Procedure

1. Switch off the room air-conditioner or heating. Draw all curtains and open the windows for airing the room.
2. Remove soiled linen from beds and bath. Shake out the linen to ensure that no guest articles are lost in the folds of linen. Put the soiled linen in the linen hamper provided in the maids cart.
3. Check for maintenance requirements and report the same to the control desk and enter in room check-list.
4. Check for lost and found in departure rooms and report to supervisor desk.
5. Contact Room Service to remove used trays.
6. Turn the mattress side-to-side on succeeding days followed by end-to-end turning. Smooth out mattress to air it.
7. If a vacuum cleaner is not available, brush the carpet first to enable the dust to settle while doing the next task.
8. Clean bathroom.
9. Empty all ash trays into the waste paper basket in the room. Collect other loose trash on tables and floors and throw them in the waste paper basket.
10. Pick up guest clothes and hang in closet or place in dresser.
11. Collect all loose papers or magazines and stack them neatly on the desk.
12. Clean all the surfaces in single circular motions with a dry

cloth. Use a hand dust pan to collect any unwanted matter on the surfaces without lifting dust in the air. Ensure that all surfaces are spotlessly clean. Pay special attention to nooks and corners especially those points that may not obviously be visible to the guest eye.

13. Use a stiff upholstery brush or vacuum cleaner (with the appropriate attachment) on upholstered furniture arms, backs and seats.
14. Replace, if necessary, stationery as prescribed by management. The number of items must exactly be as per standard.
15. Dust and replace each item on dressers, bureaus and desks. Special attention must be given to the display of publicity material as prescribed by the management.
16. Clean lamp shades with a clean dry duster. Lift lamps and clean under the base. Replace lamp and adjust the shade.
17. Disinfect telephone mouthpiece with dettol. Wipe balance of the telephone with a damp cloth. Check phone for the dial tone.
18. Clean mirror with a dry cloth first and then with a damp newspaper to make it sparkling.
19. Dust closet, shelves, hangers and rods. Brush the closet floor. Supply new laundry bags and replace missing hangers and drawers/shelf with plastic or paper liners.
20. Dust both sides of all room doors, baseboards, window sills, inside and out, bottom and centre sashes or windows, sash rails and tops of radiators and air-conditioning units.
21. Close windows.
22. If a vacuum cleaner is available then vacuuming of carpet should be done at this stage as against brushing the carpet.
23. Arrange furniture if necessary.
24. Switch on the air-conditioning or heating on the minimum temperature for a departure room and at the same temperature the guest has left it for an occupied room.
25. Have a last look at the room referring to the checklist for completion of work.

Making a Bed

1. Remove soiled sheets and pillow cases and shake out individually.
2. Turn out mattress as previously described.
3. Shake out mattress protector and re-lay it on the mattress. Change the protector if soiled or smelling.
4. Open out fresh lower sheet evenly and tuck it securely at the head, foot and sides.
5. Open out fresh top sheet and distribute it evenly over the lower bedsheet. Ensure that the laundry crease is in the same line as the inner sheet for even distribution. The sheet hem should be evenly pulled up to the headboard. Tuck this sheet at the foot.
6. Open out blanket and distribute it evenly on the top sheet using the crease as described earlier for even distribution. Ensure that the blanket labels are at the foot. Pull the blanket four inches from the headboard.
7. Fold top sheet, at the head of the bed, over the blanket and fold the sheet and blanket once again.
8. The blanket and top sheet are together tucked uniformly on both sides while the corners at the foot of the old are mitred.
9. Cover pillows with fresh pillow slips. Fluff the pillow and even out pillow slips to look neat and tidy. Since pillow slips are larger than the pillow the excess slip should be neatly folded downward. The side of the pillow which has the fold should be away from guest view.
10. Cover completed bed with the bed spread ensuring it is right side up and falling evenly all around the bed. Keep extra bed spread towards the head board to crease in between the pillows so as to make the bed look appealing. The bed spread corners should be aesthetically done.
11. Put spare blankets in plastic bags in the uppermost or lowermost shelf in the guest closet. Blankets are folded in such a manner that the hotel insignia appears on the top.

Certain areas in the room or bathroom elude the maid's

attention and tend to accumulate dust. Such areas are normally hidden from a guest's eye. However, its cleanliness reflects the standard of cleaning of the hotel. Experience shows that the following areas are overlooked and appropriately called the "dirty dozen."

Dirty Dozen

1. Top of door edges and ceiling.
2. Air-conditioning ducts and diffuser grills.
3. Under bathroom counters.
4. Beneath the grab-bar and dresser table.
5. Behind the WC bowl—the Strap.
6. In the toilet roll niche.
7. Faucet nozzle filter.
8. Toilet vents.
9. Top of picture frames.
10. Area above pillow racks.
11. Rear surface of doors.
12. Interior surfaces of drawers.

Cleaning a Bathroom : Basic principles:

(a) Cleaning activity starts from the ceiling downwards to the floor.

(b) Floors are cleaned from the wall farthest to the door to the exit.

1. Open all windows and exhaust vents.
2. Shake out all soiled bathroom linen, e.g. towels, bothroom mats. etc. and deposit in the linen hamper of the maids cart.
3. Collect all trash in bathroom waste basket and deposit in trash hamper of the maids cart.
4. Clean the ceiling and air-conditioning vents for cobwebs.
5. Wipe off light bulbs and shades with a dry cloth. Check that all bulbs are working.
6. Wipe down the walls using a sponge or damp cloth. Follow with a dry cloth ensuring that tiles are free of water marks.

7. Clean mirror first with dry cloth, then with damp newspaper and finally with dry cloth. Ensure that the mirror is smudge and scar-free. Clean the medicine cabinet.
8. Wipe dry the shower curtain with a sponge.
9. Scrub dry the area next to the wash basin.
10. Scrub and clean dry the bath tub ensuring that the water faucets and shower are sparkling and in working condition.
11. Scrub the toilet bowl and bidet using the special brush or mop and the prescribed sanitizer. The inner rim should be cleaned. Ensure it is dry and spotless inside. Clean the WC from the outside with a sponge till it is sparkling and dry. Clean the lid and toilet seat of the toilet bowl dry and close them by placing the disinfectant label.
12. Replenish fresh bath linen and guest supplies as per the number of persons in the room at the following number per person.

Linen	*Supplies*
One bath towel	2 toilet rolls
One face towel	1 bathroom tumbler per person
One hand towel	1 soap dish
One bath mat	2 soaps per guest (25 g each)
	1 candle stand with candle
	1 ash tray with a match box
	1 shoe mit
	1 soap sud satchel per person
	1 shower cap per person
	2 disposal bags
	1 blade dispenser
	1 face tissue box
	1 waste basket

Place advertising material as prescribed.

13. Scrub the floor with the prescribed mop and ensure it is dry.
14. Finally close the windows, shut all lights and close the bathroom doors.

Note: In occupied rooms, when cleaning the counter around the wash basin, collect all guest be longings onto one side and clean the other. Shift the belongings to the other side to clean the surface they were occupying. Finally replace all belongings as the guest had left them.

Room Maintenance Procedure : As Housekeeping has contact with all rooms and public areas practically in every shift, it is they who detect, report and ensure the completion of all maintenance work. This requires close coordination with the Engineering Department. It is important for housekeeping personnel to know the exact discipline under Engineering that various maintenances come. Given below are some suggestions.

Electrical Work : Air-conditioning or heating, fused bulbs, lights and lamps not working, defective plugs and plug points, short circuiting of any kind, faulty geysers and refrigerators.

Boiler Work : For supply of hot water to guest bathrooms.

Mechanical Work : Faulty equipment of any kind would come under this category, e.g. vacuum cleaners, ice cube machines.

Plumbing : Faulty taps, showers, drainage systems, water closets, etc.

Civil Works : Any masonry work.

Carpentry : Broken or shaky furniture, mirrors, woodwork, cupboards, etc.

In addition to the above the locksmith is a specialist who attends to locks and keys of any kind.

The moment a housekeeping member detects a maintenance requirement he or she must call the Housekeeping Desk and lodge the complaint, clearly stating the nature of complaint, the kind of assistance required and the exact location of the complaint. The attendant at the Housekeeping Desk will then prepare a "Maintenance Order" which is handed over to the Engineering

Control Room. The Engineering Control Room, classifies the complaints and gives "work orders" to the concerned mechanic, carpenter, plumber, etc. who would go on his round of attending to such complaints.

The room attendants role is to open the guest room where maintenance is required and under his/her supervision ensure that the maintenance work is complete in all respects. Only when housekeeping is satisfied will they sign the "work order" slip in acknowledgement that the work is complete.

From : Housekeeping Dept. To : Engineering Dept.

Please do the Following.

Room .... Date ....

Time ....

Electrical

Dresser Lamp	Passage Light / W.robe Light	Bath room Light	Long mirror Light	Shaver Socket	Switch Plates	Fan coil	Room Status Light socket	Fire alarm sensor

Plumbing

Shower rose	Tub stopper	Tub mixer	Hot water tap	Basin waster	Cold water tap	Flush valve	Floor drain c.p. gr.	

Carpentry/Misc.

Curt: railing	Ward robe	

Others (Specify)

Music/T.V./ Locks/Mirrors/Shade

Fig. Maintenance Order

Job completed by...................... date............................ time.

HOTEL ABC

Work Order

From : Housekeeping Dept. To : Engineering Dept.

Please do the Following.

Room .... Date ....

Time ....

Electrical

Dresser Lamp	Passage Light / W.robe Light	Bath room Light N E	Long mirror Light	Shaver Socket	Switch Plates	Fan coil	Room Status Light socket	Fire alarm sensor

Plumbing

Shower rose	Tub stopper	Tub mixer	Hot water tap	Basin waster	Cold water tap	Flush valve	Floor drain c.p. gr.	

Carpentry/Misc.

Curt: railing	Ward robe	

Others (Specify)

Music/T.V./ Locks/Mirrors/Shade

Job completed by................................ date............................ time.

Fig. Work Order

Evening Service : In hotels, normally the bulk of room cleaning should have been done in the morning shift. The exception would be rooms with the "Do not disturb" sign. Such rooms are normally occupied by late night/early morning arrivals by international flights. All rooms, however, require an evening service mostly to prepare the room for the night. This service should be done prior to the guest retiring for the night. Following is the procedure:

1. Knock at the door and enter the room as per the procedure mentioned earlier.
2. Put floor lights switch on mainly to ensure that all lamp bulbs are functioning.
3. Draw the heavy curtains.
4. Hang guest clothes if lying around.
5. Take off bed cover, fold neatly and store in the room cupboard, either in the topmost or lowermost shelf.
6. Fold one corner of the blanket to enable a guest to slide into bed.
7. Place the breakfast knob order card along with posette/chocolate/sweet as prescribed on the pillow.
8. Remove soiled glasses and bottles if any. Replenish fresh glasses and fill the water flask with drinking water.
9. Empty and clean ash trays and waste basket.
10. Replace soiled towels.
11. Replenish missing toiletries and other supplies.
12. Set climate control as directed.
13. Turn out all lights except the passage lamp/night lamp as prescribed.
14. Lock the door properly.

Second Service : This is a service provided on the specific request of a guest. This normally happens when a guest has/had a party or meeting in his room and would like his room to be put in order as a consequence. The following matters would normally be attended to:

1. Remove soiled dishes, bottles and glasses.
2. Remove room service trays, if any.
3. Wash the room where necessary.
4. Replace used guest supplies.
5. Empty and clean ash trays and waste basket.
6. Arrange the bed properly.
7. Replace soiled bothroom linen.

8. Flush the toilet bowl and dry the area around the sink.
9. Use air-refresher if necessary.
10. Replace water-tumblers and fill water flasks with fresh water.

Reportable Matters List : One of the important qualities of a room attendant is an eye for detail. The management reinforces this quality through training as well as providing a room checklist to ensure that all matters in a room cleaning are covered. Such matters can be handled by the room attendant directly. However, there are certain other matters that a room attendant must report as per rules and regulations of the department in most cases. This lesson attempts to aid the room attendant in reviewing matters that are required to be reported.

Housekeeping Room Report: Preparing room report.

No Baggage: This refers to occupied rooms without luggage. While the housekeeping report would reflect this it is important to immediately report this matter to the Floor Supervisor. A room with this status would either mean an unauthorised occupancy or a person who could slip out of the hotel without paying his bill. The luggage of a guest is normally the only security the hotel has in the event of a guest not being able to- pay his bill. A guest without luggage is therefore of concern to the hotel management.

Scanty Baggage: This is a room which has small light luggage that could be carried by hand without indicating an obvious departure should a guest walk out with it. Scanty baggage is of the same concern to management as no baggage.

Overnight Damage or Articles Missing: An alert room attendant would know her allotted rooms very well. It is thus easy to detect any damage by guests to hotel property or property missing in a room. Reporting this immediately especially in the case of "departure rooms" could enable the hotel management to levy a charge on the guest or take any security actions.

Changes in Guest Occupancy: A room attendant would know the status of how many people are occupying a room. An obvious way is by the number of beds used in a twin or double room or by clothes and bath linen used. It is quite possible that a room sold as single occupancy shows double occupancy. This must be reported as routine. The guest may legitimately have someone join him or her and is paying for it. But the management is concerned if the guest is paying for single occupancy and the room shows double occupancy.

Birds or Animals: Hotels as a policy normally do not permit guests to keep pets in the rooms as they disturb other guests. For this hotels have arrangement for kennels for housepets. There are some guests who may smuggle a pet into the room. The room attendant should report this immediately.

Suspicious or Unusual Guest Conduct: Room attendants would recognise by and large the occupants of rooms in their charge and should be able to decipher who a genuine visitor is as against someone suspicious. The room attendant must alert the Floor Super visor even if she has the slightest suspicion. The same would go for guests misbehaving with staff or other guests or creating noise that disturbs other guests.

Guests Who are Ill: It is obvious that guests who are unwell require immediate medical attention.

"Do not Disturb": The room attendant must report a DND sign outside a room for an unusually long time. It is possible that a guest is seriously ill or up to something not permitted by the hotel.

Change of Rooms: A guest may request for a change of room. This must be reported immediately so that the occupancy status can be rectified both by Housekeeping and the Front Office.

Expressions of Guests: There are guests who will offer praise or criticism on the standard of his room or stay. This must be reported so as to recognise the person or department or rectify a mistake where applicable.

Presence of Vermin: This is important as it could effect the sanitation standards of the hotel. An immediate effort towards pest control could redeem a lost situation.

Arms and Ammunition: These could be a potential hazard.

In addition to the above, the room attendant should report as part of her duties, lost and found articles, maintenance requirements and room service trays left in the room to the appropriate department to ensure a clean, safe and efficient room.

Weekly Cleaning Procedure : In addition to her daily cleaning routine, a room attendant normally has some cleaning chores that are of a time-consuming nature. Such items may sometimes be beyond her physical capacity and need the assistance of the Houseman. Such tasks are:

1. Polishing brassware.
2. Scrubbing of bathroom tiles.
3. Pest control.
4. Laundering of lace curtains.
5. Scrubbing of shower curtains.
6. Cleaning of window panes.
7. Scrubbing of balconies/terraces.
8. Vacuuming of carpets under heavy furniture.
9. Changing paper underliners in guest closets, and drawers.
10. Cycling potted plants with the nursery.

The weekly schedule is set out by the Floor Supervisor who controls this activity through a register in a format as shown in Fig. below.

Week Beginning

Room No.	Brasso	Bathroom Tiles	Window Panes	Balcony	Pest Centrol
101 102 103	Date done	Date done			

Fig. Weekly Cleaning Register

Under Repair Room : The management may stipulate a preventive maintenance cycle for all rooms or a room may be taken over by the Maintenance Department for a major maintenance job like painting or masonry work. In such cases there is a procedure to be followed:

1. Inform the Housekeeping Desk and/or Front Office that the room has been taken for repair and should not be sold.
2. Call the tailor and have the curtains removed and sent to the linen room.

3. Send lamp shades, bed covers, skirtings, linen, guest supplies, etc. to the floor pantry or linen room.
4. Cover the telephone with polythene or disconnect it.
5. Seal taps of sinks and water closet.
6. Disconnect the radio/music system and cover them with polythene bags if not portable. Otherwise remove to the floor pantry or music room.
7. Furniture that has upholstery is sent to the upholstery yard for shampooing or mending. Other furniture is sent to the floor linen room and covered with discarded linen.
8. All carpets are rolled up by Housemen and sent for shampooing.
9. Potted plants are given back to the nursery.
10. All drawers should be removed and stored.

Note: All articles should be labelled so as to indicate which room they have been withdrawn from.

Room Report

Room Report (Fig.) is prepared in triplicate by the Housekeeping Department, each shift as an independent check on occupancy. This report is prepared by the Floor Supervisor or a designated room attendant and is sent to the Housekeeping Desk who make a consolidated report of all floors or directly to the Front Office who tally the report with their room rack as a check on unauthorised occupancies or inadvertent mistakes in recording a room occupancy. In case of discrepancies the Front Office should make a physical check of the room to establish the correct occupancy status. Of the three copies, the original is sent to Front Office, the first copy to Accounts and the second copy is kept by Housekeeping as a record.

The Room Report is basically a list of room numbers against which the Housekeeping Supervisor indicates, by a prescribed code, the status of a particular room. The codes may vary from hotel to hotel but the basic information and intention is the same. Typical codes are:

Floor Room No.	No. of Guests	Code	Room No.	No. of Guests	Code
01			26		
02			27		
03			28		
04			29		
05			30		
06			31		
07			32		
08			33		
09			34		
10			35		
11			36		
12			37		
13			38		
14			39		
15			40		
16			41		
17			42		
18			43		
19			44		
20			45		
22			46		
23			47		
24			48		
25			50		

O—Occupied
V—Vacant

L—Luggage Bed Unused
N—Occupied No-Luggage
R—Repairs

Day	Month

Hour	AM PM

Room Assistant ....

Fig. Room Report

Code	*Status*
O	Occupied
V	Vacant
DND	"Do not Disturb" sign on
L	Luggage in Room but Bed Unused

UR	Under Repair
N	Occupied but no Luggage
SB	Scanty Baggage
OOO	Out of Order
DL	Double Lock
NC	Not Cleared Though Departure has Taken Place

Linen and Uniform Room

Linen Room : The Linen Room usually serves as the base of operations for most housekeeping departments and is usually under the control of a supervisor who has the responsibility for issues and control of all linen. Usually affiliated with the Linen Room are sub-departments for uniforms and linen repair.

Linen rooms are of two types depending upon the size and complexity of the individual hotel. Type "A" represents centralised distribution in which all issues are made from the Linen Room and complete control is vested in the Linen Room Supervisor who may issue on a par basis for the number of rooms assigned to each maid or who may issue on an exchange basis holding the maid responsible for returning to the Linen Room the exact number of pieces both clean and soiled as the original issue of clean linen. This system is highly satisfactory and should be used where potential pilferage presents a problem. Type "B" linen rooms are decentralised. The main Linen Room in this kind of situation stocks clean linen for replenishing floor pantries or for handling unusual occupancy situations or laundry breakdowns. Floor linen pantries carry par stocks and linen sufficient to serve a number of rooms which the closet is designed for. Floor linen closets are replenished up to par by the Linen Supervisor.

Figures below give typical layouts of a Linen and Uniform Room respectively. Smaller hotels who find the volume of linen and Uniforms manageable may have a single room. In all cases there are storage conditions to be fulfilled.

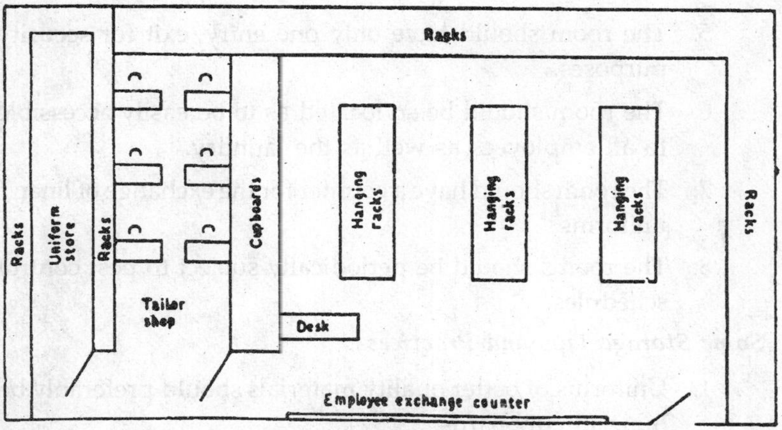

Fig.

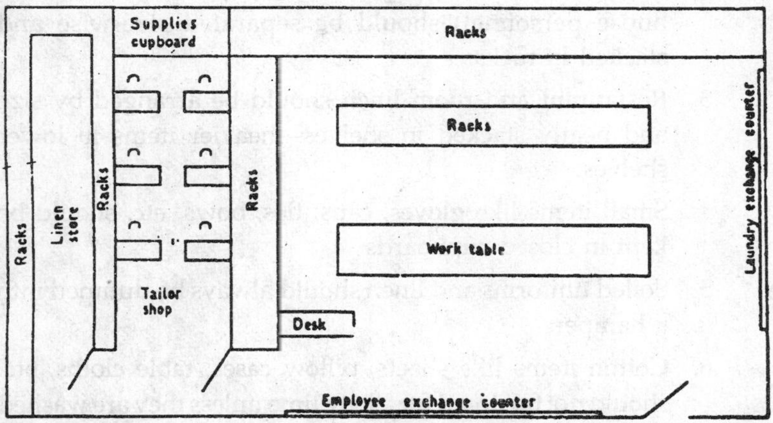

Fig.

Storage Conditions

1. The rooms must be so constructed as to eliminate the possibility of damage by insects:
2. The room must be well-ventilated, cool and dry.
3. Hot water or steam pipes should not run through the linen and uniform rooms. The rooms should also be protected against dampness, sunlight and chemical fumes.
4. Properly designed racks should be used so that rust and white ants do not get to the materials. The last shelf of the rack should be at least six inches above the floor.

5. The room should have only one entry/exit for security purposes.
6. The room should be so located as to be easily accessible to all employees as well as the laundry.
7. The room should have a counter for the exchange of linen/uniforms.
8. The rooms should be periodically subject to pest control schedules.

Some Storage Tips and Practices

1. Uniforms of better quality materials should preferably be hung in cupboards.
2. Uniforms made of cheaper materials (used by back of the house personnel) should be separated size-wise and stacked in racks.
3. Restaurant and room linen should be arranged by size and neatly stacked in shelves—heavier items in lower shelves.
4. Small items like gloves, caps, ties, bows, etc. should be kept in closed cupboards.
5. Soiled uniforms and linen should always be dumped into a hamper.
6. Cotton items like sheets, pillow cases, table cloths, etc. should not be stored for a long time unless they are washed to remove starch. Starch or finishing chemicals attract insects and make fabric dry and brittle which may have a tendency to turn pink.
7. Coloured bonnaza embroidery or indelible inks should be laundered before storing to avoid discolouration.
8. For long-term storage, wrap items in plastic foils or pack in paperlined cartons after washing. Dark paper is preferred to preserve colour. Wrap loosely to permit air to circulate in fabric.
9. Woollen items must be washed before storage. They should be wrapped and sealed in air-tight plastic foil.

Equipment and Accessories for Linen and Uniform Rooms

1.	Trollies	For transporting linen/uniforms to and from the laundry.
2.	Ladders	For reaching higher shelves of racks and cupboards.
3.	Cupboards	For storing high quality linen/uniforms.
4.	Racks	For storing common linen and uniforms.
5.	Mobile Uniform Stand	For transporting uniforms that are hung on hangers.
6.	Sewing Machines	For mending of linen and uniforms.
7.	Hanging Racks	To hand uniforms that cannot be folded and stored.
8.	Hangers	For hanging uniforms.
9.	Coat Brushes	Used for brushing dust off uniforms.
10.	Hampers	For dumping soiled uniforms and linen till the time they are sent to the laundry.
11.	Linen Bags	For separating linen/uniform item-wise till they are given to the laundry.
12.	Plastic and Paper Bags	For packing unused linen and uniforms.
13.	Folding Tables	For folding uniforms and linen.

Types of Uniforms Used

Aprons	For cooks and utility workers
Blouses	For Housekeeping, Front Office, lady staff and Hostesses.
Belt	For parking attendant, doorman and lady captain.
Bell Bottoms	For room attendant, Health club and lady staff.
Bush Shirts	For health Club, laundry and pool area staff.
Bows	For managers—black.
Dungarees	For engineering technicians and housemen.

Caps	For parking attendants, drivers, utility workers and cooks.
Coats	For stewards, cooks, utility workers, captains, receptionists, gardeners and housemen.
Churidars	For doormen.
Gloves	For stewards.
Gumboots	For Kitchen steward ing, Laundry, Horticulture and Engineering staff.
Jackets	For bell captains and restaurant captains.
Rubber Slippers	For the silver polisher.
Kameez/Kurta	For room attendants and health club masseusers.
Ladies Shoes	For room attendants.
Long Coats	For the cashier, laundry supervisor, house doctor and kitchen stewards.
Woollen Overcoat	For security personnel.
Pullover	For security and horticulture personnel.
Raincoat	For doormen, parking attendants and security personnel.
Scarf	For cooks.
Saree	For hostess, housekeeping supervisors and front office staff.
Salwaars	For room attendants.
Shoes—Leather	For doormen and parking attendants.
—Loafers	For markers, housemen, security guards, kitchen personnel, engineering technicians.
Trousers	For cooks, utility workers, stewards, captains, receptionists lobby staff.
Turbans	For the doorman.
Turras	For the doorman.

Ties	For managers and front of the house personnel.
Umbrellas	For security personnel, parking attendants and doormen.

Types of Linen Used

Bath Rug	24" x 42"
Bath Towels	25" x 45"
Blanket	72'x108'
Bed Spread	72'x 108"
Dusters	22' x 22'
Hand Towels	6" x 74'
Face Cloth	9½"x 10½"
Moultan	72" x 104'
Mattress Protector	64" x 96" (single)
Table Napkins	21" x 21", Tea, 12" x 12"
Pillow Slips	24" x 32"
Pool Towel	36" x 80"
Staff Towel	36" x 62"
Bed Sheets	72" x 108"
Table Cloths	90" x 90", 45"x45", 54"x54", 58"x62" 64"x64", 72"x78", 72" x 104", 72" x 240" 45" x 45"
Tray Cloth	16" x 27"
Tea Cosy Cover	As per size of the cosy
Waiter's Cloth	18" x 27"

Par Stocks

Definition : Par stock is the minimum linen and uniforms required to meet the daily demands so as to ensure smooth operations.

Importance of Par Stock

1. To make correct and efficient investment of capital.
2. To prevent overstocking and thereby avoid chances of spoilage during storage, storage space problems, etc.
3. To ensure proper supply at all times.
4. To help in effective budgeting.
5. To simplify inventory taking.
6. To bring about manageable control.

How to Establish Par Stock

Linen — Determine the requirement of each guest room and restaurant per shift. This is multiplied four times as per cycle mentioned below:

One change in circulation.

One change in the housekeeping stores.

One change in the laundry.

One change in the linen room.

Uniforms — The par stock of uniforms is decided on the basis of :

(a) cloth material;

(b) job position and the nature of jobs.

Four changes are kept for uniforms changed daily such as steward's coats, utility workers' uniforms, etc. on the following basis;

One change in circulation.

One change in the laundry.

One change in the Uniform Room.

One change in the Housekeeping Store.

Three changes are kept for uniforms changed on every alternate day. Terry cotton and woollen uniforms have two changes kept as par stocks.

Inventory Control : Since uniforms and linen are heavy investments it is necessary to keep a close control on this very important asset. Effective control is possible through the following practices:

(a) Control on misuse, shortages and mix-ups.

(b) Proper storage.

(c) Regular stock-taking.

(d) Spot checks.

(e) Proper supervision.

To prevent damage of linen and uniforms the following tips need to be kept in mind.

1. Check for faulty linen chutes, carts, baskets, washers, etc. which might tear linen and uniforms.
2. Losses of small pieces of linen can be avoided by keeping mesh bags at strategic points for passing employees.
3. Put restrictions on the misuse of linen by employees by inspecting employee locker rooms or fining them for misuse.
4. Laundry should be careful not to put excessive amount of bleach powder. The usual amount is 1% bleach per 100 lb of linen. Also bleach powder could be damaging at washing temperatures higher than 150°F.
5. Linen should be exchanged strictly on a one to one basis.
6. Damp white linen/uniforms should not lie on concrete or iron. Concrete stains are almost impossible to remove. Iron rust may cause holes at the point of contact after washing.
7. Employees must not wipe spilled medicines or other spillage with white linen. They should use dusters specifically provided for the purpose.
8. Laundry should load washing machines properly. Underloading could 'beat up' the linen. Hydro-extractors on high speed operation could tear fabrics. Laundry tumblers should be checked regularly for pins, paper clips, etc. that could prick holes into fabric. Proper pressure and heat must be kept on all irons as it could cause burn stains.

Stock-taking

Definition : Stock-taking is the physical verification by counting of stocks of all items in the cycle at periodic intervals or at the time of closing of books for valuation purposes or for the accuracy of recording entries in books, so that the overages or shortages can be found out by a variance in physical balances and the accounts inventory ledger balance.

Methods and Principles Involved

1. Physical counting is done after every three months and is also known as quarterly inventory.
2. All items are segregated and grouped (including discards).
3. Counting of items in circulation and in store is separately done and added together.
4. Discards are stamped "condemned" kept aside.
5. Counted total should tally with last inventory figures plus issues received after that.
6. Inventory must be conducted in the presence of the Housekeeper, Accounts Kardex Clerk and the auditor.
7. Stock-taking is taken as per three groupings each on a separate day:

   (i) Uniforms (ii) Room linen (iii) Restaurant linen

Figure gives the Room Linen Inventory Form in which stock figures are taken.

Floor No					Floor Supervisor....................					
Room Nos	Sheets	Pillow Slips	Night Bed Spreads	Mattress Protectors	Bath Towels	Wash/Face Cloth	Hand Towels	Bath Mats	Bath Rugs	Blankets
101										
102										
103										
104										
105										
106										
107										
108										
109										
110										

Fig. Room Linen Inventory Form

Exchange of Linen and Uniforms : This is a critical function of Linen/Uniform Room. To make the exchange more orderly specific timings are given to each department. Also linen/uniform are exchanged strictly on a one to one basis. Following is the procedure for exchange:

Exchange Procedure

1. Room linen is either directly received by the laundry or by the linen room.

2. In either case, the Floor Supervisor physically counts each soiled item on the floor and enters the figures into the Room Linen contract sheet.
3. Two copies of the room linen control sheet are sent with the hamper of soiled linen to the laundry or Linen Room.
4. The Laundry Supervisor or Linen Supervisor, whoever is responsible, recounts the soiled linen brought down and verifies with the Room Linen Control Sheet. The concerned supervisor then stamps "Received" after the tally and returns one copy while the third copy is retained by him/her. If the Laundry Supervisor is directly receiving the laundry he/she then sends the second copy to the Linen Supervisor while retaining the third copy himself.
5. Against the Room Linen Control Sheet the Linen Supervisor issues fresh linen on a one-to-one basis. In case the Linen Room is short of fresh linen at the point of time then he/she enters the balance due on the Room Linen Control Sheet and issues the shortfall in the next lot.

Floor No.................. Time .... Date................				
Articles	Sent by Floor	Received by Laundry	Sent to Floor	Balance
Sheets Pillow Slips Bath Towels Face Towels Bath Mats Face Cloths Night Spreads Mattress Protectors Bed Spreads Sofa Covers Shower Curtains Blankets Bath Rugs Dusters				
	Signature	Signature	Signature	Signature ....

Fig. Room Linen Control Form

Uniform Exchange Procedure

1. In the case of a new employee, uniforms are issued against a specific authorisation letter received from the Personnel Department.
2. For regular employees ensure that they have arrived at the stipulated time.
3. Check uniforms for damages.
4. Issue fresh uniforms strictly on a one to one basis ensuring the uniform is of the correct size and name if the uniform is specially tailored for a person.

Note: If the soiled uniform received is damaged and can be mended warn the employee. If the uniform cannot be mended report the matter to the supervisor. If the employee is a chronic offender the amount can be charged to his personal account.

Restaurant
Time............................ Date ....

Description	Par Stock	Soiled Linen	Fresh Linen	Difference to be Rectified
Table Cloths White				
240x72				
90x90				
64x64				
72x104				
72x78				
58x62 Orange				
Table Cloths Coloured				
90x90 Gold				
72x78 Gold				
72x78 Orange				
72x104 Pink				
64x64 Pink				
60x76 Check				
Table Cover				
54x54 Gold				
45x45 Gold				
45x45 Orange				
54x54 Pink				
Napkins				
21 x 21 Crested				
21x21 Pink				
21 x21 Orange				
21x21 Gold				
21x21 Check				
12x12 Tea				
Tea Cosy Covers				

Fig. Food and Beverage Linen Exchange Form

Restaurant Linen Exchange Procedure

1. Make sure that the person exchanging linen has come in the stipulated time.
2. Check soiled linen received for damages.
3. Count every item, verify with the Food and Beverage Linen Exchange Form.
4. Enter the figures into a Linen Exchange Register especially kept for food and beverage outlets.
5. Give the same number of fresh items in exchange and enter the figures in the Linen Exchange Register.
6. Forward the soiled linen to Laundry for washing by physically counting each item in front of the Laundry Supervisor.

Exchange of Linen/Uniforms with Laundry

Sending Soiled Uniform/Linen : The uniforms/linen are sorted/separated as per size, department, quality, kind and physically counted in the presence of the Laundry Supervisor and handed over. Uniforms for dry cleaning are submitted against a Daily Delivery of Uniforms Form; room linen against the Linen Control Sheet and restaurant linen against the Soiled Linen Exchange Register. In all cases the Laundry Supervisor's signature is taken.

Receiving Fresh Linen:

1. Room linen is received from the laundry on the basis of figures shown in the copy of the Room Linen Control Sheet received and stamped by the Laundry Supervisor.
2. Restaurant linen is received on the basis of figures in the Linen Exchange Register earlier filled in when exchanging with the restaurant staff.
3. Uniforms for dry cleaning are received with the help of figures shown in the Daily Delivery of Uniforms Form filled in earlier when giving uniforms for dry cleaning.
4. Linen is received from the Laundry in lots as and when it is ready. Each type of linen is totalled and filled in the Inventory of Room Linen Form. The difference in items due from the Laundry is established by comparing the

Items	Total Balance B.F.	To Laundry	From Laundry	Balance	To Laundry	From Laundry	Balance	To Laundry	From Laundry	Balance	Total Balance C.F.	Remarks
Housekeeping												
Ladies Shirts												
Ladies Trousers												
Blouses												
Saris												
Dungarees												
Food and Beverage												
Cook Coats												
Cook Trousers												
Cook Caps												
Cook Aprons												
Cook Scarf												
Utility Worker Coats												
Utility Worker Trousers												
Utility Worker Caps												

totals of the above form with the totals in the second copy of the Linen Control Sheet (for room linen) and the Linen Exchange Register (for restaurant linen). These two figures (i.e. soiled/delivered to the laundry and fresh/received) are noted down in a register for every item every day. On the closing day of the month the total shortage from the laundry is worked out. The linen and uniforms are segregated and stored in their respective places.

Housekeeping Supply Room : This room should be under the direct supervision of the Executive Housekeeper and should be used to store all power cleaning equipment such as scrubbing and polishing machines and vacuum cleaners and their accessories. The room should also be used to contain one week's supply of cleaning materials such as soaps, detergents, and polishers and one week's supply of small cleaning tools such as mop handles, mop heads, sponges, chamois, brooms, brushes, carpet sweepers, buckets, etc. This room should also carry a week's supply of guest room standard supplies including soaps, matches, stationery, toilet paper, face tissue, laundry bags, etc. All of these items should be neatly arranged on labelled shelving so that replacements are always kept in the same location. This room should be stocked weekly from the General Store by written requisition. If the Housekeeper retains a copy of the requisition or requests that the store room return the duplicate requisition with each item properly priced, she will be in a better position to control her departmental costs and to assist in the formulation of forecasts for supplies consumption.

Floor Linen Room

The floor linen room is a store that stocks linen and supplies for rooms on a given floor. It is normally situated away from guest view such as the service elevator landing or the end of a floor. The room should be a cool, dry place away from the steam pipes and dust. The floor linen room normally has the following equipments.

Equipments

1. Cupboards for guest and cleaning supplies, blankets, pillows and mattress protectors.

2. Shelves for Linen Room and bath, used newspapers and magazines, used bottles and vacuum cleaners.
3. Janitors closet for cleaning equipments with long handles, e.g. mops and also waste baskets, buckets, etc.
4. Wooden linen hampers for coiled linen received from various maids carts on the floor, before sending the linen to the laundry.
5. Spaces for maids carts, baby cots and roll-away beds.
6. Sink for flower arrangements and disinfecting tumblers.

Basic Principles : The floor linen room should be kept locked at all times as expensive assets like linen, guest supplies, etc. are stored here. The room should be clean at all times especially when the staff go off-duty.

Procedure for Requisitioning Fresh Linen

1. Soiled linen is sorted according to types, counted and recorded in the room linen Control Sheet in triplicate. It is signed by the Floor Supervisor.
2. The Houseman takes two copies with the soiled linen to the laundry directly.
3. The Laundry Supervisor re-counts the items, and tallies with the Room Linen Control Sheet.
4. The Laundry Supervisor retains one copy after signing the Control Sheet and the Houseman takes the third copy to the Linen Supervisor for fresh supplies.
5. The Floor Supervisor replenishes fresh linen against figures indicated in the Room Linen Control Sheet. If there is a shortage of supply at that point of time, this is recorded in the "Balance" column of the Linen Control Sheet to be recovered whenever the Linen Supervisor has adequate stock.

Procedure for Requisitioning Guest and Cleaning Supplies

Basic Principles

(a) Requisitioning should be done strictly against consumption.

(b) Weekly Stores List must be prepared and presented on the day in the week specially designated for the purpose.

Notes:

1. Requisitioning is done on a weekly basis.
2. Each floor linen room is given a par-stock for each item of supplies.
3. The moment supplies in the floor linen room go below the par-stock the Floor Supervisor prepares a Weekly Stores List. The columns marked "consumed" and "required" are a control measure to ensure that what is requisitioned is not more than what is consumed.

The column "received" gives quantities actually issued by the stores. This is particularly useful when what is issued is less due to shortage of stock so that future claims can take this into account.

Hotel ABC

Room Linen Control

Floor No .... Bag No			Date .... Time	
Articles	Sent by Floor	Received by Laundry	Sent to Floor	Balance
1. Bed Sheets 2. L. Bed Sheets 3. Night Spreads 4. Large Night Bed Spreads 5. Pillow Slips 6. Bath Towels 7. Hand Towels 8. Face Cloth 9. Bath Mats 10. Mattress Protectors (S) 11. Mattress Protectors (D) 12. Bed Spreads 13. Shower Curtains 14. Blankets 15. Dusters				
	Signature	Signature	Signature	Signature ....

Fig. Room Linen Control

Food and Beverages Linen Exchange

Restaurant ....

Time .... Date ....

Description	Per Stock	Soiled linen	Fresh linen	Difference to be Rectified
" TABLE Cloth 240x90 yellow				
" 102x102 yellow				
" 160x60 yellow				
" 78x78 yellow				
" 72x51 yellow				
" 60x60 yellow				
" 60x60 cream				
" 51 x 51 yellow				
" 45x45 yellow				
" 40x40 yellow				
" 51 x 51 brick red				
" 45 x 45 brick red				
" 57 x 57 green				
" 45 x 45 green				
" 54 x 54 check				
" 48x48 check				
" 38x38 check				
" 39x39 green				
" 30 x 30 green				
NAPKINS 21x21 yellow				
" 21 x21 cream				
" 21x21 peach				
" 21 x21 green				
" 21x21 red				
" 16x16 yellow				
" 12x12 Tea Napkins				
" Tea cosy covers				
" Tea cosies				
" Tray covers				
" Table Mats				
" Waiter Cloth				
" Moultons				
" Dusters				

Floor Supervisor

items	Consumed	Date Reqd.	Date Recd.
Portfolio			
Guest Writing Paper			
Guest Envelopes			
Telegram Forms			
House Rules			
Picture Postcards			
Guest Comment Form			
Pen			
Pen Refill			
Beverage List/Room Serv ce menu			
Breakfast Knobs			
DND Cards			
TV Guest Comment Form			
Laundry List Pink			
Laundry List White			
Laundry Bags			
Scribbling Pads			
Service Directory			
Directory			
Gita			
Bible			
Hangers			
Hanger Hooks			
Ash trays			
Plastic Matches			
Matches			
Candle Stand			
Candles			
Sewing Kit			
Sewing Kit Covers			
Plastic Bags			
Soap			
Soap Dish			
Mugs			
Soap Suds			
Shampoo Sachets			
Tissues Large			
Tissues Small			
Hygienic Bags			
Shower Caps			
Shower Cap Covers			
Toilet Roll			
WC Band			
Shoe Shine Card			
Shoe Shine Strip			
Shower Curtain Hooks			
Paper Roll			
Occupancy List			
Linen Control Book			
Waste Paper Basket			
Plastic Bucket Small			
Plastic Bucket Large			
Trash Can			
Highball Glasses			

Items	Consumed	Reqd.	Recd.
Bathroom Tumbler			
Glass Cover (high ball)			
Glass Cover (bathroom tumbler)			
Rubber Gloves			
Air Freshener			
Naphthalene Balls			
Rubbing Compound			
Mansion Polish			
Boot Polish (black)			
Boot Polish (brown)			
Vim			
Sanifresh			
Brasso			
Dettol			
Anol			
Teepol			
Thinner			
Solvent Oil			
Feather Brush			
Shoe Polish Brush			
Upholstery Brush			
Scrubbing Brush			
Carpet Brush			
Long Brush Soft			
Long Brush Hard			
Fan Bottle Brush			
Bamboo			
Squeezer			
Compound Jharoo			
Phul Jharoo			
Coconut Jharoo			
Supils			
Mops Small			
Mops Large			
Coaster			
Flask			
Flask Refill			
Kaya Kalpa Tent Cards			
Bindya Tent Cards			
Weekly Store List			
Room Checklist			
Floor Public Area Checklist			
Late Duty Checklist			
Lobby Checklist			
Guest Lift Checklist			
Guest Outside Area Checklist			
Rear Entrance Checklist			
Amrapali Checklist			
Bukhara Checklist			
Mayur Checklist			
Shatranj Checklist			
Bali Hi Checklist			
Takshila Checklist			
Ghungroo Checklist			
Madira Checklist			

Fig. Weekly Stores List

4. This list is presented to the Executive Housekeeper for her approval which she indicates with her signature.
5. The designated person for stores requisitioning then fills a Stores Requisition Form in duplicate. The original goes to the store and the copy is kept in the Requisition Forms Book. For control the Executive. Housekeeper must sign all requisitions.
6. The supplies are drawn from the Housekeeping Store and the Storekeeper signs on both copies to acknowledge that items have been issued.
7. The supplies are brought to the floor linen room and checked against the Weekly Stores List.
8. Weekly Stores Lists are presented for at least a month. These lists also give an indication of consumption for future budgeting and planning.

Stores Requisition Date:					Department.	
S.No.	Item	Unit Reqd.	Units	Cost	Bin Card No.	Remarks
Authorised by:................		Received by:................			Issued by:..................	

Fig. Stores Requisition Form

Storage Tips

1. Brushes must not rest on bristles.
2. Cleaning sprays must be away from hot areas.
3. Dusters must be dried before storing. Buckets must be emptied of all water and dried before storage.
4. Polishes must be properly sealed to prevent drying.
5. At the end of the shift all used magazines, newspapers and empty bottles are taken to the garbage disposal area for resale.
6. Used soaps and candles are deposited at the Housekeeping Control Desk for reuse in offices, staff locker rooms, etc.

7. Garbage is examined by the Floor Supervisor for any "lost and found" items and then sent to the garbage disposal area.

Records Kept in Floor Linen Room

1. *Spring Cleaning Records* : for preventive cleaning cycle of rooms in the month.
2. *Floor Log Book* : which records:
   (i) duty roster for the floor;
   (ii) list of outstanding maintenances to be covered in the next shift;
   (iii) record of night cleared rooms and departure rooms;
   (iv) important messages for the Second Shift Supervisor.
3. *Guest Supplies Control Register* : to keep a control of guest supplies used in rooms. The consumption pattern helps the Housekeeper with future budgeting.
4. *Linen Control Book* : records movement of linen on a daily basis to and from floors.
5. *Weekly Stores List File* : for record of consumption and requisitioning of cleaning guest supplies from stores.

Item / Floor	Pens	Shower Caps	Soap Suds	Soaps	Others
First Floor					
Second Floor					
Third Floor					
Nos. Issued					
No. of Departures					
Consumption-morn.					
Balance					
Consumption-eve.					
Balance					
Floor Supervisor's Signature					

Fig. Guest Supplies Control Register

Left Luggage Procedure

The term "left luggage" is attributed to luggage left by a guest who checks out of the hotel but wishes to collect his luggage later. Guests who want to visit other cities in a country on a short tour may find it inconvenient to carry all their baggage with them or may find it uneconomical to retain a room in the hotel where they can keep their luggage. Hotels provide the left luggage facility to guests who are likely to check into the hotel after their return from a tour though this is not strictly necessary. There might be guests who check out but intend to eventually depart much later in the day and occupy their time sightseeing; they would find it inconvenient to cart their luggage with them. They leave their luggage in the hotel premises (normally a strongroom specially provided for this facility) under the guarantee by the management that the luggage would be safe. Some hotels may charge a fee for this facility, but most hotels do not. Given below is the step-by-step procedure for handling left luggage and the eventual delivery of the same to the guest on his return.

Receipt

Step 1 : Ascertain if the guest wishing to leave his luggage has paid his hotel bill.

Step 2 : String the baggage ticket on each piece of luggage separately. The baggage ticket has a number which is also printed on the counterfoil of the ticket .

Step 3 : Enter details in the left luggage register.

Step 4 : Tear off the counterfoil of each ticket and hand it over to the guest.

Step 5 : Keep the luggage in the left luggage area.

Delivery

Step 1 : Take the counterfoil of the luggage ticket from the guest.

Step 2 : Tally the same with the ticket attached to the luggage in the left luggage area.

Step 3 : Enter the date of delivery in the Left Luggage Register.

Step 4 : Retain counterfoils and tags of luggage.

HOTEL XYZ LTD.

Date .... Room No. ....

Baggage Check

No. 1234

Not responsible for
goods left over 30 days

Suit Case	Brief Case
Suit Box	Golf Bags
Umbrella	Overcoat
Package	
Others	

No. 1234

Not responsible for
Goods left over 30 days
(over)

Date .... Room No. ....

Left Baggage Register

Date	Room No.	Name of Guest	Bell Boy Name	Luggage Tag No.	Description of Luggage	Dt. of Delivery	Remarks

Scanty Baggage Procedure

A Guest with scanty baggage would have hand baggage or no baggage at all. Such guests are a hazard as they can slip out of the hotel without paying their bill. There is no way of determining whether a "scanty baggage" guest is walking out of the hotel with intentions of returning or not. Most managements stipulate a policy that "scanty baggage" guests are required to pay a deposit in advance as a safeguard against skipping out of the hotel. Guests who manage to check out of the hotel without intentions of paying the bill are called "skippers". There is a definite procedure to keep a control on guests with scanty baggage.

Step 1 : Notify the lobby manager and the front office as soon as a guest arrives with scanty baggage.

Step 2 : Stamp "scanty baggage" on the arrival errand card.

Step 3 : Stamp "scanty baggage" on the registration card.

Step 4 : Enter particulars in the "scanty baggage" register. The type of information filled is appended below.

Step 5 : Get the registration card signed by the lobby manager who has the discretion to ask for a deposit from the guest.

Step 6 : Get the Scanty Baggage Register signed by the lobby manager.

Scanty Baggage Register

Date	Name of Guest	Room Number	Name of Bell Boy	
Time	Description of Luggage	Remarks	Signature of Lobby Manager	Signature of Bell Boy

Wake-Call Procedure

A wake-call is a telephone call made by the telephone operator to a guest at a specific time, predetermined by the guest. By its very nomenclature a wake-call is a telephone alarm to wake a sleeping guest. Normally, the telephone department are fully concerned with wake-calls, but the lobby personnel are involved when wake-calls have to be made for airline crews and groups. All information regarding wake-calls is received by the lobby desk which in turn disseminates it to the telephone department. In the case of airline crews, the city airline operations office normally calls the lobby desk and conveys the time of pick up of the crew from the hotel. The wake-call time is thus 45 minutes to one hour before the pick up time. When airline operations give a pick up time, care must be taken to call back operations and re-confirm the pick up time, noting down the name of the person on the other end. It is customary for the lobby member receiving the pick up time to give his name to the airline operations officer.

In the case of groups, the group leader or travel agency would convey wake-up call timings to the lobby. The lobby would then prepare a wake-call list and forward the same to the telephone operator.

Crew/Group Wake-call List

Serial Number	Name of Guest	Room No.	Call time
Scheduled Call Time:			
Pick Up Time			
Amendments		Reference	
Call Time			
Pick Up Time			

Other Duties of Lobby Staff

The bell boys are officially appointed to carry out any errands desired by the guest or management in addition to baggage handling. They have additional responsibilities as well that are nevertheless important to hotel operations. Some of these are:

Postage : The bell desk is often the source for postage and handing over mail for posting. The bell captain would thus, have to ensure that he has adequate supply of postage of all denominations at all times.

Daily Newspapers : The bell boys are often responsible for the distribution of daily newspapers to all guest rooms. The bell desk should keep a stock for resident guests should they require another copy.

Security : While all hotels have their security department, the lobby staff have to keep a keen eye for unruly elements as they are stationed at a vantage position in the lobby. They may be called upon to physically tackle unruly guests.

Paging : Paging refers to a system whereby a guest identifies himself in such cases where hotel staff cannot identify him physically. Often callers on phone may like to speak to a guest who may be in the lobby. The bell desk has a mini-black board with a long handle and bells to attract the attention to the board. The bell boy would then write the name of the guest or his room number on the board which is held aloft. The bell boy then moves about the lobby ringing the bells to call attention. The concerned guest would then contact the bell-boy.

Processing Housekeeping Discrepancy

Thrice in 24 hours the housekeeping staff make a physical check of all rooms in the hotel to ascertain their status in terms of whether they are occupied or not. This status is entered into the Housekeeping List which is forwarded to the front office who tally the status with their racks. The morning housekeeping list may be tallyed with the night clerk's report. If there is a discrepancy the lobby staff are called to make a physical check of those rooms not tallying in status. The lobby member's finding is entered into a Room Discrepancy Report. To reduce verbage in all reports certain codes have been developed.

V Vacant

O Occupied (can be further categorised as SO= Single Occupancy, DO= Double Occupancy)

UR Under Repair another term used is OOO=Out of Order)

DND Do Not Disturb Housekeeping staff cannot enter to ascertain status. It normally indicates occupied but would have to be checked in the next shift.

DL Double Lock

L Luggage but bed not slept in

LB No luggage but bed slept in

SB Scanty Baggage

Practical Self-development Programme

The PSD programme is different from other programmes inasmuch as it works on the assumption that any individual when provided with a basic framework is intelligent and capable of training himself. Whereas all the cognitive inputs with some paper skills have been provided in the book earlier, learning is crystalised on-the-job, or practical training is given where a participant is made to come to actual grips with the situation, systems and methods. Large chain operations may have full-fledged training departments to guide a new recruit in the job. The PSD system is primarily meant for those who have to, or want to, develop themselves with their own individual efforts when the basic framework is provided.

What to Observe : The WTO lists all the tasks that exist in various job positions of the front office. From this list a participant can decide what he knows and more important what he does not know.

Weekly Training Schedule : After ascertaining what he does not know, the participant prepares his own training schedule. The participant decides how much time he would like to spend on learning a task. He may also decide to have meetings with concerned staff to sharpen his learning experience. These meetings may be fixed in advance and recorded in the Work Schedule. The schedule also has a column, Proposed Schedule of the task number as listed in the WTO and the title. The Actual Schedule column is the deviation from the proposed schedule. This is a personal record that indicates that proposed schedule must be covered later in the week.

Counsellor : The weekly training schedule has the signature of a counsellor. A counsellor is someone who is knowledgeable about a task and has authority in the work environment. He may be approached to give guidance and endorse the participant's level of learning. The counsellor provides the much needed feedback and recognition of a participant's attempt at training himself. Though having a counsellor makes the PSD Programme most effective, it is not absolutely essential.

Note: A participant may work on several tasks simultaneously or may work on a single task over a period of days.

Weekly Training Schedule

Name and Hotel.......................... Week of...............................

Number of Tasks Approved...... This Week............................

....To Date Counsellor's Signature

	Monday	*Tuesday*	*Wednesday*	*Thursday*	*Friday*	*Saturday*	*Sunday*
Hours							
Proposed Schedule Task No & Title							
Actual Schedule							
Other Tasks Approved							

Procedures for Emergencies

Lost and Found : This is a term used in hotel parlance to refer to any item temporarily misplaced or lost by a guest but traced later by hotel staff. Such articles are handed over to the housekeeping department who maintain a special locker for the same. If the item belongs to a guest who has checked out, then a letter is sent to the forwarding address left by the guest at the reception or to the address furnished on the registration card. If no reply is received within a specified time period stipulated by the management, the articles may be given away to the staff members who found the article, or auctioned to hotel employees. If "lost" guest belongings are found in public areas and the guest is still residing in the hotel, then the housekeeping keeps such articles till such time specific enquiry is made at the front office or lobby, in which case the guest would be required to give a description of the article before it is shown to him. By asking the guest to establish the identity of the article in the above manner, it is possible to accurately relate the lost article to him.

Fire in the Hotel : As soon as a fire is detected and intimated to the Front Desk, the first thing to do is to inform the telephone department. In most hotels the telephone department plays the pivotal role of alarming the hotel. In, smaller hotels which have the telephone function merged with the front office operations the procedure would be to call the fire department in the city for help. The front office should alert all guests and inform them to use the staircase and not the elevator. The telephone exchange should always be manned during the fire to facilitate communications from one point to another. If the front office staff have to get actively involved in the fire procedures then they should search each room thoroughly, especially under beds or in closets or bathrooms to ensure that no guests are left behind. They must guide the guest through the staircase, and help in extinguishing the fire by the use of appropriate fire extinguishers (foam for electrical fires and oil fires, water for general fires, and so on).

Death : The front office should inform the General Manager, the Security Officer and call for the hotel doctor or coroner of the locality. An alarm is not raised or any guests informed of the fact. The General Manager may decide to call the police. The body must be removed by the staff entrance and the room sealed till all police formalities are over. People known to the deceased are contacted through addresses entered on the registration card.

Accidents : The house doctor should be called immediately on phone and informed of the nature of the accident and the condition of the guest. The doctor's instructions must be followed immediately. Bleeding must be stopped by swabbing wounds with cotton wool and applying a coagulant such as iodine, alcohol, spirit or just plain after-shave lotion. If a fracture is suspected the guest is not moved till the doctor arrives. Burns are to be treated with creams meant for the purpose. Water is never poured on burns as this will surely lead to blisters. Hotels train their staff in First Aid for emergencies.

Vandalism : The front office staff must call the Hotel Security and order the main door to be locked. If things get out of hand the police must be called.

Damage to Property by Resident Guest : The front office cashier is instructed to raise a charge for the value of damages to property. A responsible guest will never argue but it should informed immediately to the General Manager.

Drunk Guest : It is prudent to never argue with a drunk guest. He must be politely led away from the public areas either into an office or his room. If he is boisterous or behaves unruly the Hotel Security must be called.

Theft : If a guest has stolen an item from the room then the value of the item is placed on the bill at the front office. This is a polite way of informing a guest of his misdeed. This must, however, be done only if one is absolutely sure that the guest is responsible. If a theft has taken place and the culprit is not known, the hotel security is informed giving all details.

Hotels often about certain precautions to avoid thefts: These are:

1. Self-locking room doors.
2. Safety deposit boxes for guests' valuables.
3. Watching guests with light baggage who could become potential skippers.
4. Watching a walk-in who is a potential thief against a guest who goes through the tedious process of making a reservation.
5. Avoiding giving room numbers to visitors or guest names to telephonecallers unless they give the name of the guest.
6. Training to associate names, physical features of guests to their room numbers in order to avoid giving the wrong key to the wrong guest.
7. Strictly controlling the master key. Housekeeping staff are forbidden to open guest rooms for them. Guests are directed to the front office who give a written authorisation to the guest to have the room opened by the guest.
8. Posting security personnel on floors.
9. Keeping all entrances, corridors and staircases well illuminated.
10. Reporting immediately any suspicious characters.

Room Key Record

Date :.....................

To : Housekeeping Time :...................

Please Open for the Bearer

Mrs. Mr./Miss ....

Room No. .... Thank you..................

Retain this Slip for the Record. Reception ....

Front Office Cashier

Job Description : Front Office Cashier

Category : Non-Supervisory

Reports to :

1. Income Accountant
2. Chief Accountant
3. Front Office Manager (Operationally)

Job Definition : Post all guest charges and credits on guest folios accurately and in time so as to properly settle guest accounts or receive payment upon guest departure.

Directly Controls/ Supervises : None, except when made shift-in-charge.

Assigned area of Activity : Front Office Cashier's cage.

Hours of Operation : One shift in 24 hours for 8 hours, or as per the policy of the management.

Authority : Refuse credit cards, currency notes or personal cheques as offered by guests. Give discounts as per policy. Hold back "credit cards" listed in the cancellation bulletin.

Work Performed :

1. Post all guest charges and credit into their respective folios.
2. Settle all guest bills upon departure.
3. Encash foreign exchange as per regulations.
4. Disburse petty cash to hotel staff and authorised paid outs.
5. Control Safety Deposit lockers.
6. Operate the accounting machine and be responsible for all postings in it.
7. Receive and hold in safe custody all cash payments made by guests till the account is rendered.
8. Render account through cash envelop at the end of the shift.

9. Maintain and turn in control records and reports specified by the management.
10. Note telephone meter reading on folios.

Coordinates with Front Office : Regarding arrivals and departures.

Coordinates with Lobby : Regarding arrivals and departures.

All other revenue producing departments such as restaurants, bars, telephones, etc. to collect charges to post into guest folios.

12

The Control Desk

The Housekeeping Desk is the nerve centre of the entire department and its efficiency determines the smooth operation and effectiveness of housekeeping. It is the focal point for the dissemination of information and communication to various points in the Housekeeping Department as well as other departments for coordination. The location of the control desk is normally adjacent to the Executive Housekeeper's office. This desk has to be manned 24 hours otherwise the life line of communication would stop. The area of the control desk must have a large notice board which serves as the main information display board for housekeeping staff. The board normally displays the following:

1. Room numbers of groups in the house.
2. Room numbers of crews in the house.
3. Night cleaning schedule.
4. VIP's in the house.
5. Weekly cleaning schedules.
6. Daily roster for supervisors and staff.
7. Any other general information.

The Role

Coordination with the Front Office : It is the Desk Attendant who receives departure room numbers from Front Office to transmit onwards to the appropriate floor so that the rooms can be cleaned and made ready for sale. Once the rooms are cleared, the Floor Supervisor calls the Desk Attendant handing over the cleaned rooms. The Desk Attendant informs the Front Office regarding the cleared rooms.

The desk also receives other information which requires special attention by Housekeeping such as:

VIP's in the House: With this information the Housekeeping can take a little extra time and care in cleaning the VIP rooms.

Groups in the House: Groups move together in terms of arrivals, departures, sight seeing tours and meals. It is thus important to clean their rooms together in view of strict time parameters.

Crews in the House: Normally airline crews are allotted a given set of rooms on given floors. Very often the arrival of a crew and the departure of another crew of the same airline may overlap. In such circumstances it is important for the allotted rooms to be cleared within a very short period of time. Also because of odd international timings, it is the crew rooms that display a "Do not disturb" sign at times others are normally out.

Flowers: Sometimes the management extends its compliments by a special gesture of a flower arrangement in the room as recognition of importance to a person. Such individuals are normally given the status of a VIP. Since flower arrangements come under Housekeeping, knowledge of who is to be provided that is received from the Front Office on a daily basis.

Coordination with the Engineering Department : All maintenance requirements in rooms are registered at the Control Desk. The Desk Attendant puts this information in the Maintenance Register giving the room number, nature of complaint and name of the Supervisor or Attendant who gave the complaint. The Desk Attendant makes a Maintenance Slip and forwards it to the Engineering Department. The Engineering Department then prepares a Work Order Slip and sends the concerned technician directly to the floor. When the work is completed satisfactorily the Room Attendant signs an acknowledgement of completion of the work order. This signed work order is then produced to the Desk

Attendant who enters this into the Maintenance Register against the appropriate complaint earlier registered.

Types of Registers and Files Maintained : In addition to the above, the following registers and files are maintained:

Register for Guest Messages: This register keeps all special messages/requests of guests. Messages could be requests for second service, additional blankets, etc.

Baby-sitting Register: The Housekeeping Department normally provides baby sitters to a guest. Requests for this service are filled into this register and the appropriate action taken.

Room Checklists File: All room checklists are deposited at the Control Desk and filed for one month. Should a complaint about cleaning in a room be received the Housekeeper would know exactly which attendant was responsible and whether she had checked the particular aspect under complaint.

Carpet Shampoo Register: This register has the schedule of carpet shampooing and the data whether the schedule is being followed.

Room Occupancy Reports File: All room occupancy reports are filed. The room occupancy reports are important to the Executive Housekeeper to determine the level of workload anticipated so as to provide the necessary staff to meet exigencies each day.

Duty Roster File: The duty roster is filed for information if required by any one in the department.

Log-book: It is the single most important register as it is here that instructions to staff of the next shift are written. This log-book is referred to by the Supervisors at the beginning of any shift for instructions by the previous shift. The log-book will also record room numbers of difficult guests, roll-away bed distribution, etc.

Memo Book: This book is maintained for outstanding maintenances not done. This information is made in copies so as to inform the concerned department to expedite the issue. This is important to ensure that the guest is not inconvenienced due to a lapse in maintenance.

Lobby

A Lobby is an area furnished with seating arrangements and is a meeting place common to all hotel guests whether residents or not, located immediately upon entry into the hotel building. The front office is located within the premises of the lobby. The lobby assumes importance as it is the first and last area of contact of a guest with the hotel. Thus, hotel managements spend considerable funds and efforts to make the lobby aesthetically attractive and rationally convenient.

Besides having the front office where all registration of guests is done into the hotel and final clearance is made at their departure, the Lobby Desk, situated in the lobby, is the heart of all coordination between guests and hotel services. The lobby desk is manned by a Lobby Manager who represents the management all 24 hours. He is a problem solver and has the authority to handle all guest grievances. The lobby manager would thus have to be a mature and experienced person, well conversant with hotel rules to be able to be effective in dealing with guest problems. He would have to be mentally alert and diplomatic in all his dealings as he is essentially a trouble shooter.

The lobby manager controls a team of lobby supervisors (called Bell Captains) and lobby attendants (who are often called Bell Boys or Bell Hops). This team is solely responsible for baggage handling at the time of guest arrival and departure or during their stay. The team also runs petty errands for guests. Members of the team would have to be well groomed, socially confident, physically strong and clear in communication as they are in constant contact with guests.

Lobby Departmental Hierarchy

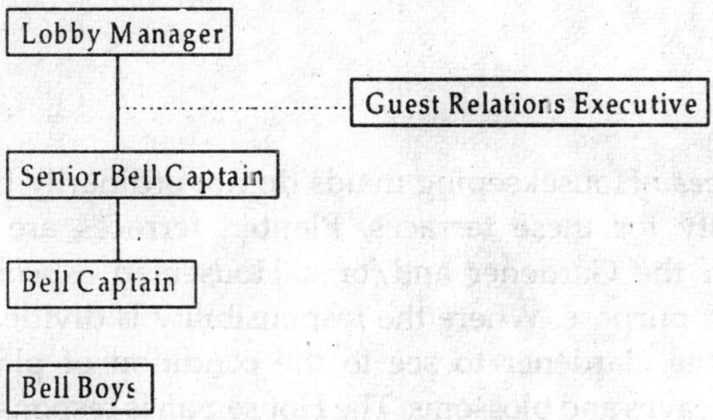

Large hotels may also have a Guest Relations Executive (normally a lady) located in the lobby to handle in-house public relations with guests. She is responsible for receiving VIPs and attending to any coordinational aspects regarding them.

The job descriptions in the subsequent lesson give a clearer perspective of what each member of the lobby team does.

Departments Coordinating with the Lobby

Front Office : To receive authorisation to take a guest's baggage to the allotted room at the time of guest arrival and to take the baggage out of the hotel at the time of departure.

To Inform Receptionist or Lobby Manager about any guest with scanty baggage.

To help in paging guests.

To help a residing guest to shift his room in case of a re-allocation of room.

To re-check status of rooms if there is a discrepancy between the housekeeping list and front office racks.

Security : To handle undesirable guests.

Telephones : To coordinate in crew-wake-call procedure.

Housekeeping : For errands in providing extra facilities to a guest in his room. For the requisition of personnel uniforms.

Engineering : For maintenance work in the lobby area.

Stores : For requisition of supplies, especially stationary.

All other Departments : In case of errands for guests which require coordination with a relevant department.

Public Area

Cleaning

Floor Terraces : Housekeeping maids do not ordinarily have the responsibility for these terraces. Planted terraces are the responsibility of the Gardener and/or a Houseman especially assigned for this purpose. Where the responsibility is divided, it is the duty of the Gardener to see to the condition of plants, removing dead leaves and blossoms. The Houseman is responsible for the removal of any debris. Cleaning is then to be carried out by the Houseman who must ensure that terrace floors, underplanters, tables or garden umbrellas are thoroughly cleaned and dried. The designated Houseman is also responsible for requisitions to the Maintenance Department.

Elevators : The Housekeeping Department is responsible for the cleanliness of the interior of elevator cars. A thorough cleaning of walls, ceilings and floors should be carried out at least once daily. The volume of traffic may require more frequent cleaning of elevator floors. In cleaning elevator car interiors, the car should be taken to the topmost floor for the cleaning procedure to be carried out. Cleaning and polishing must be done in the early hours of morning when guests traffic is low. Particular attention must be paid to recessed lighting troughs, ventilation louvres, door sills and grooves and the area around the operator's control panel.

Elevator Lobbies : The cleaning of elevator lobbies may be assigned to the Houseman responsible for the corridor or alternately to an individual responsible for elevator lobbies only. Mirrors, lights, promotional signs, upholstered furniture, door frames and sills, and sand urns must receive particular attention to ensure that they are clean and free of dust. Vacuum cleaning of carpets should be carried out every shift and as required in this area.

Corridors—Guest Floors : A Houseman is assigned to do this task and is responsible for the cleanliness of ceilings walls and floors. Carpeted floors should be vacuum cleaned daily, tile floors to be brushed, swept clean and then wet mopped. They should also remove stains. Floor tile edges, corners, baseboards and the immediate wall area above are to be inspected to ensure that there are no water marks. All corridor lighting fixtures are to be cleaned as often as required. It is also the responsibility of a Houseman to clean fire extinguishers and fire extinguisher recesses including glass doors.

Floor Linen Closets : One Maid/Houseman is assigned daily on a rotating basis to be responsible for each Floor Linen Closet. This procedure is carried out to ensure that the Linen Closet is kept clean and neat at all times. This assignment includes floor cleaning, dusting, and arrangement of shelving and freedom from dishes, silverware, bottles and trash of all kinds.

Mop and Janitor's Closets : The floor Houseman is assigned the responsibility for the maintenance of mop closets. This responsibility includes the total cleanliness of these areas—wall, ceiling, floors, sinks and light fixtures. No accumulation of bottles or other trash is to be permitted at any time. No mops should be permitted to remain in these areas unless they have been thoroughly washed, rinsed, and dried.

Service Lobbies and Service Stairways : The Floor Houseman is assigned the task of cleaning these areas on a daily or more frequent schedule depending upon traffic requirements.

Service Elevators : Most hotels give the responsibility of cleaning service elevators to the Kitchen Stewarding Department. However, some hotels may give the responsibility to Housekeeping in which case the same cleaning procedure as that established for guest elevators will apply to service elevators with the additional stipulation that floor cleaning must be carried out after each meal service.

Function Rooms : Complete cleaning schedule for daily cleaning of all Function Rooms should be prepared and assigned to the appropriate personnel. These cleaning schedules will include the procedure for daily inspection and cleaning if required of walls and ceilings, windows and window frames, floors and carpeting, lighting fixtures, draperies, pictures, lamps and furniture. Particular attention should be paid to legs of all chairs and tables and to the bases of floor lamps.

Lobbies : Lobby cleaning schedules should be prepared with due regard for the character of the lobby, the particular facilities provided, and the activity and volume of traffic. These schedules must include walls, ceilings and floors, all metal work, lighting fixtures and lamps, air-handling outlets, planters, windows and draperies, showcases, display boxes, cigar stands, Bell Captain's office, checkrooms and public toilets. The cleaning standard for all marble work and terrazo floors and stairways are to be separately set forth to ensure that the procedures followed will ensure meticulous cleanliness without damage to these surfaces.

Aluminium, bronze, stainless steel and cast iron metal work is to be kept highly polished.

Shopping Arcade : The responsibility for cleaning the shops varies in different hotels and is, usually dependent upon the type of rental agreement in existence between the hotel and shop lessors. The Housekeeper should check with the management to determine the area of responsibility and the housekeeping procedure necessary for the proper maintenance of these areas. In instances where the responsibility rests with the shops, management has the right and obligation to insist that the cleanliness and order of these shops is at least equal to the standard prescribed for other areas of the hotel. The types of concessions include Casinos, Barber Shops and Beauty Parlours, Gift Shops, Travel Bureaus, Offices and Show Rooms.

Cabanas : The cleaning responsibility for Cabana Terraces and Cabanas may be under the control of Housekeeping or the Maintenance Department depending upon who is given this responsibility. In either case, the cleaning procedure should be carried out with the same attention to detail as that used for guest rooms and guest room terraces.

Bars, Soda Fountains and Snack Bars : The cleaning of these facilities are generally the responsibility of employees assigned by the Food and Beverage Department. These people should be instructed, however, in proper cleaning methods by the Housekeeping Department in order to ensure clean, sanitary maintenance of these facilities, particularly floors, beneath and behind equipment.

Dining Rooms, Bar Rooms, Night Clubs, Grill Rooms and Coffee Shops : The basic cleaning of these areas rests with the Housekeeping Department and follows the same cleaning standards as those prescribed for Function Rooms and Lobbies. It is imperative that in these areas housekeeping personnel assigned must work in close cooperation with the employees of the Food and Beverage Department to ensure that the areas are clean serviceable well in advance of the time the room is actually required.

Dining Area Furniture and Equipment : Chair and table legs and bases must be thoroughly wiped down daily. Soiled-dish trollies, pastry carts, and other wheeled equipment should receive thorough daily cleaning with particular attention to castors to ensure that they are free of grease, food or mop strands.

Bandstands and Stages : These areas should be cleaned by housekeeping personnel assigned for the purpose. Cleaning procedures vary with the individual area but standards should be the same as those prescribed for other public areas of the hotel. Cleaning of stage lighting fixtures, light troughs, skylights and indirect lighting is to be the responsibility of the Maintenance Department personnel who are familiar with the care of such equipment and the inherent danger working with water around electrical equipment.

Offices : The Housekeeping Department is responsible for the assignment of personnel for office cleaning. Such cleaning should be scheduled at times when the offices are not in service. These cleaning procedures should include desks, chairs and other furniture such as tables and filing cabinets.

In order to facilitate this cleaning in good order in office areas, the hotel management requires that office personnel remove all loose papers, file folders, reports, etc. from the top of desks and filing cabinets at the close of each working day. Accounting books, records, purchase orders, invoices, payroll materials, etc. must not be permitted to accumulate. Items which the auditing procedure requires to be retained must be neatly bundled and labelled. Housekeeping employees should be requisitioned by Accounting and Auditing Department Heads on a regularly scheduled basis for cleaning these areas.

Uniform Rooms : These areas are the direct responsibility of the personnel employed in them. Uniform racks should be kept clean and in order. Shelving is to be kept free of uniform parts and pieces unless such material is wrapped and clearly labelled.

Tailor Rooms : The Housekeeping Department assigns personnel to keep these rooms clean. Cleaning is to be accomplished at the end of each working day. Sewing machines should be covered when not in service. Particular attention must be paid to the floor to prevent the accumulation of scraps, lint and thread.

Upholstery Shops : The Upholsterer is responsible for the maintenance, cleanliness and safety in the shop. The entire shop should be cleaned and in order at the end of each working day. Upholstery fabrics must be kept in closed cartons. Loose filling materials are not be permitted in the Upholstery Shop at any time. Scraps, waste and discarded materials should be kept in covered metal containers and removed from the shop at the close of each working day.

Store Rooms : All Store Rooms should constantly be maintained in a clean and orderly manner. Shelf cleaning and the condition of stored merchandise is the responsibility of the Department Head responsible for the Store Room. Floor cleaning and wall cleaning should be performed by housekeeping employees requisitioned for this purpose on a regularly scheduled basis. This provision is general for all stores except for refrigerated stores which are the complete responsibility of the Food and Beverage Department.

Swimming Pools : The bottom and sides of a swimming pool must be cleaned daily by pool personnel using standard vacuum cleaning equipment. In hotels which do not have filtration and water treatment equipment, pools should be emptied not less frequently than once each week and the walls and floors hand-scrubbed using wire brushes.

Pool edge tiles and overflow gutters should be hand scrubbed on a continuing schedule so that the total circumference of the pool is completed once every four days. All outside terraces including those surrounding swimming pools are to be swept and wet mopped at least once daily depending upon the type of surface. Serrated tiles which have a tendency to accumulate oily films from bathers' feet should be deck-scrubbed using strong detergent solution on a schedule which will maintain the area with its original colours intact. Cleaners responsible for terrace areas will be responsible for keeping fungus from growing between tiles. Growth of this nature can be successfully arrested by periodic applications of rock salt.

Employees responsible for the cleanliness of swimming pool areas will inspect diving boards, diving platforms and pool stairs daily to ensure that they are clean and safe. Pool personnel are responsible for all pool site furniture including chairs, lounge tables, sun mats and garden umbrellas.

Care and Storage of Out-of-Service Furniture : Each hotel possesses relatively large quantities of furniture which are not always in service. This furniture is most often associated with the Food and Beverage Department and is required for banquets and special functions. Upholstered chairs and sofas, dressers, desks, cribs, etc. usually complete the supply. Because of the large amount of money represented by this furniture and because its use is usually required on short notice it is important that few simple rules be observed in this care. They are:

1. The storage area should be out of the weather and in a clean well ventilated location.
2. No furniture should be placed in the storage area if it requires repair.
3. All furniture should be thoroughly cleaned before being stored.
4. All furniture should be covered during storage.
5. If space limitations require stacking, this should be done with care and with the provision of adequate padding or other surface guards to prevent marring surfaces.
6. Furniture destined for storage, but which require repair or renovation, should be the subject of a work order, with the work required to be completed prior to placing the furniture in storage.
7. No furniture should be stored in stair ways or on service landings.
8. If at all, possible decisions should be made promptly concerning the repair ability of furniture or its obsolescence. When these decisions have been made disposal should be prompt.

13

Guest Folio

A guest folio is the master bill in which all cash and credit transactions are recorded for each resident guest. All credit bills from various revenue outlets such as restaurants, bars, laundry, telephones etc. are received centrally at the cashier's cabin, either by hand or through pneumatic tubes. The pneumatic tube system consists of a series of tubes connecting all revenue outlets to the cashiers cabin. Bills are placed into carriers which are airtight, cylindrical containers that carry the bills through air suction to and from the revenue outlets and cashier's cabin.

It is a quick system necessitated by the fact that a guest could check out at any time, and bills pertaining to him/her must be presented upto the minute for recovery. These individual bills received from various revenue outlets are then posted through the NCR machine onto the guest folio. A guest folio is opened immediately upon a guest's arrival. The front office cashier is notified when the registration card of the guest is completed and presented to him by the receptionist. The registration card is then clipped onto the folio. When a folio is opened the following must be ensured:

HOTEL XYZ

Guest Folio

1	1
2	2
3	3
4	4
5	5
6	7
7	7
8	8
14	14
15	15
16	16
17	17
18	18
19	19
20	20
21	21
22	22
23	23
24	24
25	25
26	26
27	27
28	28

	DATE	
ARR		
DEP		
LOCAL CALLS		
CLOSING		
OPENING		
TOTAL		

RATE	ROOM NO			
CHARGE TO		RECEPTION	LOBBY MANAGER	CASHIER

Local Telephone Call Voucher

New Delhi	Guests Name	No. Room Nc Account No. Date
	Explanation	Charges
		Total
		Prepared by

HOTEL XYZ LTD.

RESTAURANT/BAR CHECK

GUEST NAME
(BLOCK LETTERS)

ROOM NO. ACCOUNT NO.

DATE	SERVER	TABLE	PERSONS	

SIGNATURE

(PLEASE DO NOT SIGN IF YOU HAVE PAID)

Server's Receipt

DATE	SERVER

Long Distance Telephone Call Voucher

New Delhi Guests Name	Room No.	Date
Station	Trunk Ticket No.	Charges
No. Called	Connected	
Particular Person	Disconnected	
Class of Call	Duration	Total

Room/Rate Change Notice

No.......................................

Name:...

Room : From .... To ....

Reason: ....

Rate : From .... To ....

Reason :......................................To....................................

Reception ....Authorised By:.......................

1. The guest name, room number, date of arrival and departure, address, source of reservation, opening telephone meter number and billing instructions are clearly mentioned on the folio from the registration card.
2. The registration card is completed in detail.

The telephone meter referred to in point 1, is a system used by hotels who have a PABX exchange board wherein a guest can make outside local calls directly from his room. The meter records each call. The difference between the opening meter reading at the time of a guest's arrival and the closing reading at the time of departure gives the number of calls made. Hotels that employ the PABX exchange board do not need meters as all outside calls are made through the operator. It must be noted that in either case all trunk calls are routed through the operator.

Once the above formalities are ensured, the folio is placed in pigeon holes located numerically, room-wise at the cashier's cabin itself.

The guest folio has debit and a credit column. All charges are posted in the debit column. There are only four circumstances when there are postings in the credit column:

1. When a guest has made payment towards his bill.
2. When a guest has made a deposit or advance.
3. When a guest is given a discount by the management or is complimented with free services or facilities.
4. When the cashier has overcharged and is required to make a correction.

Machine Posting into Guest Folio : The NCR 2000 has been referred to in all machine postings.

Posting Room Charges in Folios

1. Determine the guest name, room number and room rate from the registration card. Look for the room rate charge notice that may differ from the rate on the registration card.
2. Take the guest folio from pigeon hole.
3. Adjust the line-finding carriage of the machine to the number of the line on which the charge is to be printed, line number 1 for a new folio by sliding the carriage.
4. Insert the folio into the printing table with the front page facing upwards.
5. Set up the old balance amount, if any, and press the appropriate debit pick up keys
6. Set the room number on room keys by pressing the appropriate number of keys.
7. Set up the amount of room charge on 'amounts' keys by pressing the appropriate number of keys.
8. Move the appropriate control total key to the total position.
9. Upon completion move the control lever to 'clear' position.
10. Take out the folio and replace it in its appropriate pigeon hole.

Posting Departmental Credit Charges

1. Collect revenue department bills vouchers received from the pneumatic tubes or authorised person.

2. Arrange the bills vouchers department-wise, e.g. put all room service bills together separating them from others.
3. Arrange all departmental bills room-wise in terms of floors, e.g. 100 line, 200 line starting with 101, 201, etc.
4. Put these bills in pigeon holes specially made for bills needing to be posted.
5. Take all bills, vouchers pertaining to one floor at a time, e.g. 1st floor 100 line.
6. Take out the folios from guest pigeon holes pertaining to that particular floor.
7. Determine the room number and guest name by comparing the bill voucher and the folio.
8. Set the line-finding carriage to the number of line on the folio on which the charge is to be printed by sliding the carriage.
9. Set up the previous debit or credit balance on the amount keys.
10. Insert the voucher bill on the upper print with the front page facing downwards.
11. Insert the folio into the printing table with front page facing upwards.
12. Set up the room number on room keys by pressing them.
13. Press the particular department key. e.g. coffee shop, room service, etc.
14. Record the amount of guest charge on the amount key by depressing the necessary keys.
15. Press the control total key.
16. Take out the posted bill/voucher folio.
17. Move the control total key to clear position.
18. Attach bill/ voucher to folio and return folio to the appropriate pigeon hole.

Posting Guest Miscellaneous Charges

Guest miscellaneous charges include the following:

1. Shoe-shine

2. Laundry
3. Health club
4. Barber shop
5. Beauty saloon
6. Pastry shop
7. Other banqueting charges
8. Secretarial service charges
9. Postal charges
10. Any other charges to be realised from a guest for service rendered on credit.

The procedure is the same as for (5) to (12) in the preceding section. Miscellaneous charges are recorded in the Miscellaneous Charge Voucher.

HOTEL XYZ LTD.

Guests Name	Room or Acct. No. Date 20	
Explanation	Charge	
(Signed by)		

Guest Folios on American Plan and Modified American Plan : Processing (i) FIT on AP/MAP:

1. Mark the original folio AP/MAP.
2. Post room as well as food charges covered by the plan to this folio as per the procedure followed before.
3. Open another folio for incidental charges, e.g. tips, shoe-shine, laundry, telephones, etc. as these are not covered in the plan.
4. Post these charges to the incidentals folio.

Processing (ii) Groups on AP/MAP:

Room Transfer Folio

1. Ensure that the name of the group, number of pax, number of room, rate per room, total, date of arrival, date of departure, and billing instructions are clearly mentioned.

2. Post total room charges to the master folio for all rooms occupied by a group.
3. Note down the room number in the explanation column.

Meals Master Folio:

1. Refer to point (1) in the preceding paragraph.
2. Post total meal charges covered by the plan to this folio.
3. Give the breakdown in terms of breakfast, lunch and dinner.

Processing city ledger payment on behalf of guests.

1. Receive cash from, or on behalf of, guest for services rendered on a previous date on credit.
2. Prepare a cash receipt voucher (Fig. 18.7) in triplicate, fill in the required details.
3. Affix a revenue stamp and sign the voucher.
4. Give the original copy to the party making payments.
5. Extract and forward the second copy to the Account Department.
6. Leave the third copy in the book itself.

Cash Receipt Voucher

SI No./LL 20160 Date

Received from...

Address...

The sum of Rs...

Cash/cheque no...

Shri............on Account of................. Date................ Bank..............

Rs [ ]

A/c Code .... Cashier

City Ledger Payments from Company Employees

1. Receive cash from company employees for hotel services used by them on credit. Repeat (2), (3), (4), and (5) of the preceding paragraph.

Guest Departure

A guest departure is the most critical moment for the front office cashier. The cashier must ensure that the guest has paid his bill entirely or there is adequate information or authorisation to allow him to sign his bill. This is because the cashier is held responsible for any shortages which may be deducted from his salary. Some hotels insure cashiers to safeguard against shortages. Appended below is the procedure to handle guest departures.

1. Receive the intimation of a guest/ guests desire to leave the hotel from the lobby captain, or from the guest himself over the telephone or in person, and pull out the folio from the pigeon hole.
2. Note down the reading of the telephone meter applicable to the room number of guest checking out.
3. Substract the initial telephone meter reading taken at the time of the guest's arrival from the final reading.
4. Multiply the total number of calls by the amount for an individual local call charge as laid down by the management.
5. Fill in a Telephone Charge Voucher.
6. Post these charges to the guest folio in the debit column.
7. Find out if there are any cheques/ vouchers pending in the counter, if so, post them to the folio.
8. Ask the guest if he/she has signed any bills/vouchers in any of the service areas immediately before departure. If so, ring up the area cashier and find out the amount of charges. Ask for the voucher/bill immediately and post it to the guest folio.
9. Put the folio at the printing table of the machine and print the total debit as well as credit balances. Work out on the machine total debit balances to be recovered from guest.
10. Present the bill to the guest at the front office cashier's cabin only (in no case bills can be taken to guest rooms or elsewhere).
11. Collect the total amount of charges from the guest.

12. Mark the folio with the 'PAID' stamp and put down your initials.
13. Return the correct amount of change to the guest.
14. Tear off the first page of the guest folio and present it to the guest.
15. Keep aside the paid folios together for further processing by accounts.

Payment by Personal Cheques

1. Inform the guest politely that normally payments by personal cheques are not entertained.
2. In case of further insistence from guests, ask them to contact the lobby manager for a written authorisation.
3. At the receipt of the authorisation from the lobby manager, give the Application for Payment by Personal Cheques Form.
4. Check the details of the cheque and make sure that it has been marked "A/ C payee only" and is duly filled.
5. Compare the signature on the cheque with that of the application form.
6. Enter details in the front office cashier's report.
7. Settle the bill arrangements as in (12) to (15) in the preceding section.

Note: Encashing personal cheques of guests for purposes other than payment of bills will also require the authorisation of the lobby manager.

HOTEL XYZ LTD.

Application For Payment By Personal Cheques

Date: ....

Dear Sir,

I hand over to you at New Delhi the Cheque No........................... dated......................for Rs.......................(Rupees............................) drawn on..

(Name of Bank and Station)

for value received in cash and/or for the bills submitted to me for my Room, Meals and other amenities provided in your hotel.

I further confirm that I have sufficient fund in the above bank and that Cheque No..................... will be duly honoured by my Bank when presented for payment.

Yours faithfully,

(Signature)

NAME (IN BLOCK LETTERS)..

FULL ADDRESS...

....

Payment by Travel Agency Voucher : Travel agency voucher indicates that the guest has pre-paid to the travel agent amounts for accomodation etc. and the recovery of such amounts are made from the travel agent not from the guest.

1. Receive the travel agency voucher and see if such billing instructions are mentioned in the folio.
2. Read the voucher carefully and determine whether it has been issued from a bonafide travel agency duly recognised by the hotel, by referring to the list of bonafide agencies as issued by the accounts department.
3. See whether all the expenses/charges are covered by the voucher: if not, open and process guest folios, posting miscellaneous charges not covered by the voucher.
4. If the voucher is from a foreign travel agency, get it authorised by the lobby manager.
5. Ask the guest/group leader to sign the folio.
6. Do not give copies of signed bills.
7. Attach the voucher and the folio(s) together.

14

Information

The main functions of the information department are to:

1. maintain guest alphabetical index racks;
2. receive messages for guests on telephone or in person;
3. handle guest room keys;
4. handle guest mail/cables/telegrams;
5. handle guest packages/registered/insured mail;
6. handle paging; and
7. provide information to guests.

Maintain Guest Alphabetical Index (information racks) **:** The information section keeps track of guests resident in the hotel by keeping an updated "guest alphabetical index rack" also sometime referred to simply as the "information rack". This system consists of a frame which holds 35 to 40 movable carriers into which the copy of the arrival slip bearing the name of the guest is inserted. These names are alphabetically sequenced with the aid of a carrier.

At the beginning of each shift, the information assistants tally the information rack with the room rack located at the reception. The information rack is one in which the arrival slips of guests are stacked alphabetically so that when someone wants the room number of a guest it is easy to located the details provided the name given is correct. The reception section maintains the racks room-wise as they find it easier to allot rooms at the time of registration. During each shift any arrivals and departures are undated by cross-checking with the arrival and departure register. Latest arrival slips are inserted into the information rack while slips of guests who have checked out are removed after drawing a red line over the name in the slips. For missing arrival slips it is the responsibility of the information assistant to have them typed out from the slips in the room rack and inserted into the information rack.

Movable carriers permit insertion or removal of carriers with ease and thus render the easy updating of information rack. This system is called the Whitney rack system.

Receive Messages : When a person wants to leave a message for a guest staying in the hotel who is not available at a particular point of time, the information assistant hands over a message slip or assists the guest in recording details such as the name of the guest addressed his/her room number, time that message was recorded, the message, the visitor's name and the information assistant's signature. The message is taken down in duplicate. While the original is placed in the appropriate key rack the duplicate is sent to the room itself and slipped under the door. Modern hotels have a message light system. At the information is a panel with all room numbers listed each with a message button. Once each message botton is depressed a message light flashes in the room as well as on the panel. The message light is located at the room console or at the foyer light switches. This light that flashes in the room informs the guest that a message is awaiting at the information counter. The light that flashes on the panel behind the information section enables a guest to collect the message when he collects the key from the information rack. Once the information is conveyed to the guest the message button may be released. Sometimes a guest staying in the hotel may want to leave a message for a visitor who may come in person or may call. This message is recorded on a message slip of a different colour. This slip is inserted into the room slot in the key rack. The colour of the slip is a code to the information assistant to refer to the slip should someone wish to contact the guest. The message should also be informed to the telephone operator and the operators number and the time is recorded. The telephone operator informs the message over the phone to the expected visitor of the guest when he chooses to solicit the same over phone.

Message Slip

HOTEL XYZ

Date .... Time.......................................

To ....

Room No. ....

While you were out

Mr/Mrs./Miss ....

of ....

- Telephoned
- Please call back
- Called in Person
- Will call again
- Waiting to see you

....

....

....

....

....

....

Accomodation Assistant

Control Guest Room Keys : Absolute responsibility of guest room keys rests with the information assistants. It is vitally important that a strict control is maintained. Keys must be inserted into the correct room slot of the key rack. If this is not followed accurately, an unnecessary chaos could result. Guests would get wrong keys and discover this on reaching their rooms; keys would be declared inadvertently as lost; keys could get into wrong hands. It is important for the information assistant to try to remember faces of guests staying in the hotel. Thus, anyone asking for a room key is immediately identified. Some hotels have introduced key control cards. To ensure security for guests, issues of keys are made against these cards.

Handling Incoming Messages

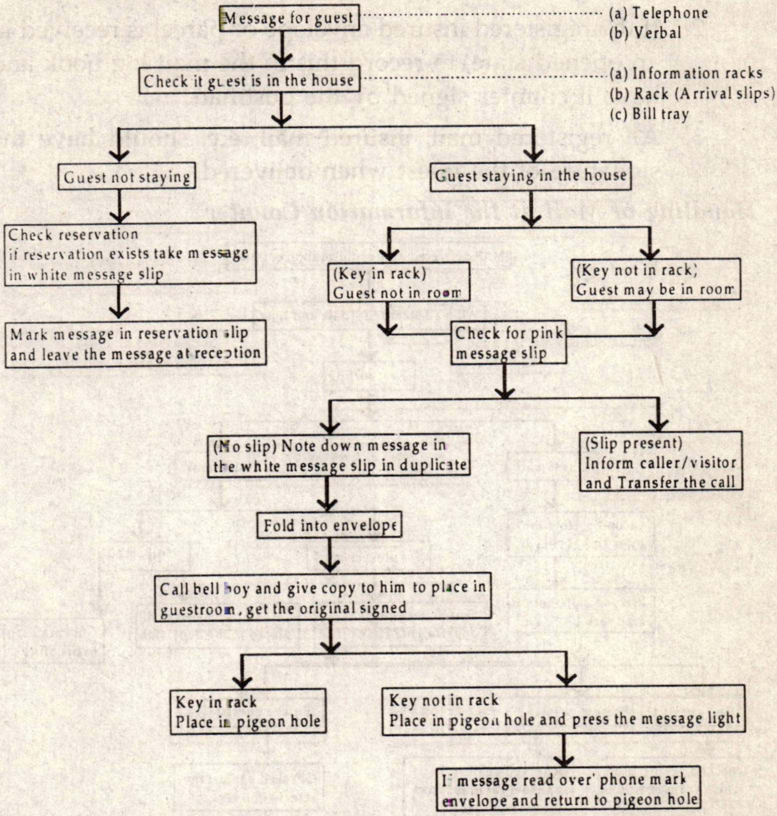

Handle Guest Mail. Cables. Telexes, etc. : See the activity flow chart which shows how mail is handled. Mail is often handled by the information assistant. If the hotel has a large number of rooms, the volume of mail received everyday may be appreciable enough to make the handling of it, one of the major and critical tasks of the front office. Mail may vary from letters, business and promotional material, cables and telexes, to large parcels. The timely delivery of the same to guests is important as it might influence his certain plans. Especially an executive could receive some critical or urgent information from his office that would bear on his decisions in connection with his work. To safeguard the hotel from guest complaints regarding mail, most hotels insist on the following:

1. Timing-stamp of all mail at the time of receipt.
2. If the registered insured envelope or parcel is received in an opened state, to record this in the mail log book and have it counter signed by the postman.
3. All registered mail, insured mail, etc. should have the signature of the guest when delivered.

Handling of Mail at the Information Counter

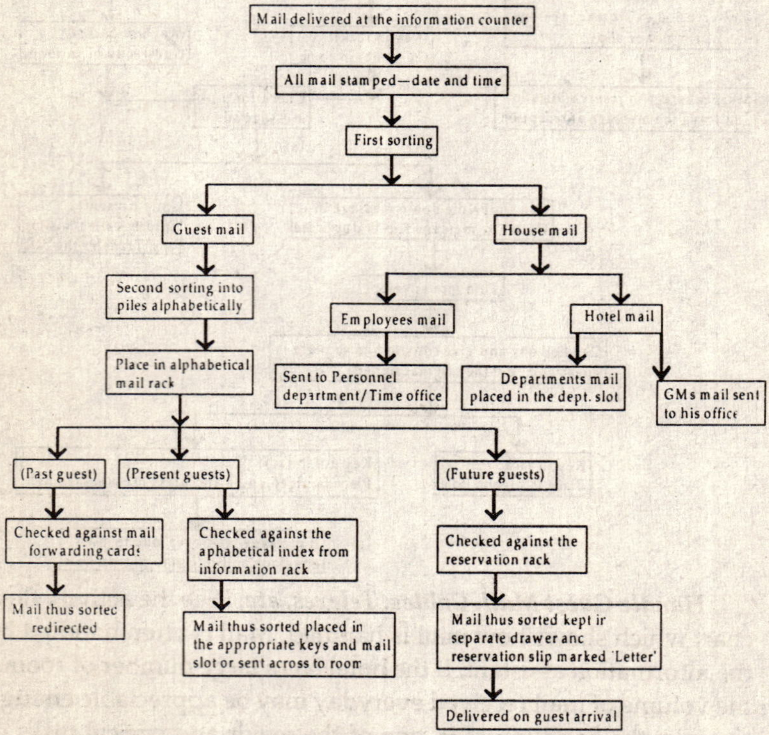

Handle Guest Packages/Registered/Insured Mail : Refer to the activity flow chart which illustrates clearly how special mail is handled.

Paging : Paging is the process of locating a guest in a given area within the hotel when a party calls a guest on the phone and the party specifically knows that the guest he a is contacting is in a specific area, then the information assistant writes the guest's name and room number on the paging board and deploys a bell boy to do the paging with this board. The bell boy then holds the board (which has bells with rings which draw the attention of the guest when shaken) above his head so that guests in an area can see. The bell boy walks through that specified area. The guest, if in that area, immediately contacts the bell boy who escorts the guest to the phone.

Sometimes a guest expecting a visitor or phone call may have left his where abouts in the hotel on a coloured message slip which is inserted in his room slot on the key rack and with this information the guest is paged as detailed above.

Handling Registered/Special Delivery or Insured Mail at Information

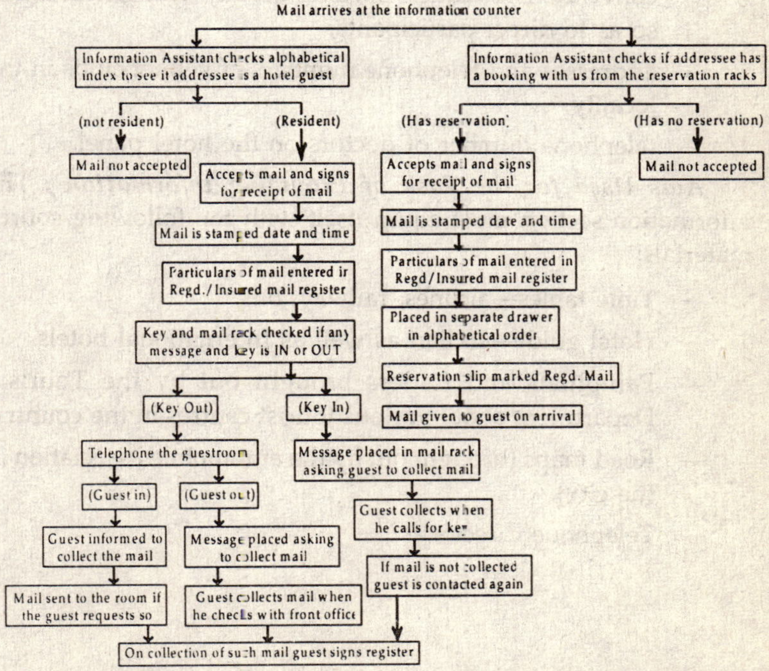

Provide Information to Guests : Guests can expect to find information at this counter, on must issues concerning their stay. The information assistant must know:

— the hotel facilities,

— hotel rules and regulations applicable to guests,

— names and addresses of travel agents for city tours and inter-city tours,
— name and addresses of private taxi agencies,
— location, distance and basic history of tourist spots in the city,
— map of the city,
— airline schedules, railway timings,
— city tour schedules and rates,
— in capital cities, the location and address of Embassies and Consulates,
— cultural events and movies running in the city,
— conventions, banquets fixed for the day with their location so as to direct participants,
— addresses and telephone numbers of kennel clubs in the locality,
— telephone number of doctors on the hotel panel.

Aids Used for the Task of Providing Information : The information section must equip itself with the following source materials:

— Time tables—airlines, railway, bus.
— Hotel guide—Indian as well as International hotels.
— Pamphlets and folders brought out by the Tourism Department about various tourist centres in the country.
— Road maps (brought out by the automobile association in the city).
— Telephone directory.

15

Role of Information Technology

Technology is becoming embedded in all sorts of products and services. It has become a part of our lives. In the field of information, the technology has revolutionised the way the services are provided to the consumers of various services. Different information technologies have now offered many opportunities for improving the delivery of different services. Rapid technological advances over the last decade have revolutionised the various information systems making functioning of these extremely easy, not only to the advantage of the industry, but for actual consumers of goods and services.

Arthur C. Clarke, world renowned space scientist, addressing the first meeting of the inter-governmental Council of the International programme for the development of communication in Paris in the year 1981, said, "In many ways and for many purposes, printed matter - books, newspapers and wallpapers will always be the best and the cheapest form of communication. But now electronics has given us tools that can perform miracles impossible to the printed word and which, of course, can reach millions who are unable to read. The newest and most powerful of these communication devices depend upon space technology, a fact that is not generally recognised". What Arthur C. Clarke had said almost two decades ago may seem to be history as so much has been done in so little a time that one really wonders about the various changes that have taken place since then. In fact, there has been a revolution in the various techniques in the field of information. The electronic gadgets have performed miracles in the last two decades. Today we find ourselves in the middle of a new era, an era of information revolution.

Modern techniques of data processing, mainly transmission of data and telecommunication, have already formed a new field of activity, characterised by an enormous potential for growth. These developments have greatly facilitated rational management of the business world. Telecommunication devices are in use today in almost all fields of economy. Be it in industry, agriculture, medicine, travel or any other field, these telecommunication devices are extensively used for the benefit of both the industry as well as the consumer.

Newer techniques of data processing, mainly transmission of data and telecommunication, have already formed a new field of activity, characterised by an enormous potential for growth and development. Telecommunication devices are in use today in almost all fields of economy. Telecommunication systems such as teletext, telecopy or videotex have given a very tough competition to earlier pioneer public communication means such as newspapers, magazines, etc. However, the new means of communication also offer great possibilities for improvement, rationalisation and the expansion of the existing facilities for data collection and transmission. Today the mass media the world over has immensely benefited from the new technology and information techniques.

Role of Mass Media

Understanding of the modern mass media techniques, as also the mass media means, are necessary for a person working in the travel and tourism field as knowledge of these will help in keeping pace with the fast changing scenario in the business of travel. The modern mass media techniques can be grouped as under :

(a) Satellite television

(b) Cable television networks

(c) Videotext

(d) Internet

All the four modern mass media techniques are widespread in the world and are considered to be crucial for business and industry.

These mass media techniques however have some limitations as far as their use for a specific person or an individual is concerned. Because of their widespread coverage and their technical methods of transmission these cannot be directed for the use of a specific person. Besides, the receiver of the information through these techniques cannot start a dialogue or communicate with another person. The communication, therefore, is limited to one way.

For the direct transmission of information, there are different modern means which have been developed and are quite widespread. The inter flow of information through these means is possible. These are :

(i) Teletex

(ii) Telecopy

(iii) Telebox

(iv) Videotex

(v) Telefax

(vi) E-mail

Teletex : Teletex is an improvement over telex and has in fact developed from it. The receiver for teletex is an electronic "typewriter", which can send electronically enriched "letters" to owners of ordinary telex equipment. The transmission of message time is usually shorter in comparison with time taken with telex. Besides, it is also possible to transmit more office typewriter symbols. A normal electronic typewriter can be used as a receiver for teletex.

Telecopy : Telecopy provides the possibility of exchanging photocopies through a data network. Information in the form of either written document or technical drawing is remote copied. This means that two facilities for copying are connected, one at the sender's end and the other at the receiver's end. Transmission time is only a few minutes.

Videotex : Videotex occupies a special position among the "new media". It plays a key role in the link between telecommunication and the computer sciences. Its advantages lie in the possibility it provides for linking computers, and also in its interactive dialogue capabilities. Using a videotex, information and communication systems can be converted into interactive systems capable of communicating with one another. In fact, the videotex is a multipurpose instrument with multiplicity of uses. It serves as:

(i) an instrument for data processing;

(ii) an information medium;

(iii) an organisational aid;

(iv) a communication system; and

(v) a marketing instrument.

This relatively new service connects various forms of use of the above-mentioned facilities and at the same time offers some other possibilities. To operate the service, a television set with a decoder and telephone is necessary without which the service cannot operate. In Europe, nearly all households have television sets and a telephone and, with the help of videotex, separate households can be reached in large areas. Members of German BTX service as well as Members of France Telecom Service can now obtain all kinds of information from external computers or use data bank, all through their television sets. In many other countries in Europe, USA, etc., similar systems are in use.

The use of videotex (VTX) is prevalent today in many fields. In addition to its use in the field of business as it allows fast message transmission, fast and inexpensive data collection and uptodate information which are crucial for advertising, the system is also used by specialised groups of users for collecting orders in the field. It is also used in the field of tourism as a one-way system, for receiving bookings. Because of its low unit costs, it is used extensively mainly in connection with personal computers. It has been found that videotex (VTX) is the most advantageous means of communication, taking into account its low cost and the wider range of its application.

Telebox : Telebox is an electronic post office box system. Each member of the system has his or her "post office box" in the computer, where other members can leave their message. The owner of each box can electrically contact the others.

Networking : All the above means discussed permit the exchange of information electronically through a data "network". The exchange of information between the members with the assistance of electronic transmission is very fast. The data are also available in written form in printouts. "Network" is a system of transmission linking facilities for automatic data processing. In this way different computers are connected, permitting data exchange and processing over long distances. Telecommunication is possible only when there is such a network available.

The telephone is the simplest and the best known network. In addition, there is also a separate clear data network for the exchange of data which works digitally. In this way a high transmission speed is achieved and there is a very low ratio of errors during transmission. There are different types of networks which can be used for telecommunication purposes either separately or combined. The text on the screen is provided by a telephone network or any other network. Communication with other members or computers in any place by anyone can be achieved by combining the telephone network with additional facilities provided.

A large number of enterprises as well as individuals are extensively using the communication techniques discussed above. In the field of tourism, in addition to travel agents, tour operators, hoteliers, airlines, travel journalists, etc., use these techniques. Travel journalists who especially travel extensively use the following facilities:

(a) Telecopy (sending previously prepared texts as originals)

(b) Teletex (for collecting and sending texts)

(c) Data banks (for collecting information)

The use of telecommunication techniques offers basic facilities and advantages in the following areas of work: i) collection of information, ii) processing of information, and iii) transmission of information.

Information Collection

The collection of information is the main part of the work carried out by journalists in connection with their work. A journalist, therefore, has to find reliable data in as short a time a possible. Besides, the data must be up-to-date. New means of communication as discussed earlier enable journalists to acquire the data in a short time. The data can also be obtained at any time regardless of restrictions of working hours. Hundreds of thousands of pages are stored in computers to which the journalist can have access. The data can be obtained through data banks which can be reached directly through a network that is used for most data banks.

A data bank is like a "master book" in which a mass of books newspapers, materials from different meetings and all kinds of published work is stored. All the relevant information can be collected in no time by means of an electronic data bank. Collecting the same information from a book and a visit to a library would be time - consuming and rather expensive. A journalist, seeking information on any subject for an article on tourism, can order the articles which are of interest to him through the record room of his own editorial office, or directly through the data bank, and these are recorded on the screen. He can also acquire a written article through a directly connected printing machine. In this way, in a matter of minutes, he can finish his search and the collection of data for his article. Considerable time is saved in this way.

Processing of Information : Information processing is an original and most crucial part of a journalist's work. A journalist has to evaluate collected information, combine the same with his new ideas and summarise the same in a compact form of an article. All this can be done only to a limited extent by means of telecommunication devices. For collecting data, the personal computer can offer new applications without much difficulty, as a journalist can process articles collected with the help of electronics. The wording of an article or the get-up can be changed as often as a journalist desires and it can be transmitted easily.

Transmission of Information : When the article is prepared on the basis of collected data, the same is to be transmitted to the editorial office or directly to the printers in their office. A journalist can do this personally by telephone call or in a written form. But the quickest and most simple method is to transmit the information with the assistance of telecommunication devices. If the article is written is the normal way on the typewriter, then it can reach the editorial office in no time. Provided the journalist uses telecopy facilities. The process of writing can be speeded up if the article is written using a personal computer, as this will not require additional printing. The article then can be transmitted directly to the computer available in the printing office.

Information Technology in Tourism : In the field of travel and tourism, communication plays a vital role as it is through communication that a potential customers obtains information about a product which, in the final analysis, is a destination which he proposes to visit. Travel and tourism being a service industry the need for not only accurate but rapid information about a destination becomes paramount for the satisfaction of the consumer. In tourism, especially in the area of travel trade and hotel industry across the world, what is being sold and distributed is primarily information about various facilities to be used by the tourist. These facilities and services required by a tourist prior to his departure, during his stay at a destination, and at the time of his departure until he reaches home, make his entire experience worth while.

Internet and Tourism Industry : The easy access to information and its worldwide dissemination have been decentralised with Internet taking big strides with each passing day and gaining immense popularity the world over. The invention of internet has opened a new world of information and ushered in a great knowledge era. Its effect has been felt in many sectors like health, commerce, education industry etc. The tourism sector has also felt its effects. Internet, in fact, has brought in a big change in the methods of sales and marketing of different tourism products, reservation systems in airlines, railway, hotels etc.

The Internet today caters to travel activity of all kinds ranging from virtual sightseeing and offering detailed information on travel sights to allowing users to plan their own itinerary, make travel reservations online, offering help with special needs and even maintain online travel diaries. Internet, by way of putting control in the hands of the users and offering discounts unheard of in real life, is fast tempting users to fulfil their travel-related needs online. Virtual sightseeing is the most simplistic form of using the Internet for travel. With users visiting several websites that offer detailed information about travel destinations, and virtually tour these places by pictures and commentaries offered by sites. This is also the fastest and most inexpensive way to go sightseeing today with the only cost being that of Internet access.

Computer Technology in Tourism : In the field of tourism, the computer has made entry in a big way. A computer is a managerial tool capable of processing large volumes of data rapidly. It can perform basic arithmetic functions (addition, subtraction, division and multiplication) and logical operations (sorting, ranking and assembling) in a fraction of a second. A computer dispenses results in a large variety of formats. These are capable of repeating programmed instructions almost endlessly without an error, and maintaining a vast database of stored information for possible future use. Today a computer can be put to a variety of uses in the day to day activities.

Although the computers were in use in some way or other in various branches of tourism industry since the early Sixties, today these are considered indispensable. These are extensively used in almost all branches of the travel industry. They are part and parcel of a travel agency and are playing a key role in making the task of providing travel services an easy affair. Computers lately are undertaking, among other jobs, the planning of vacations for an individual and his family through home terminals. The principal users of computers in the travel industry are:

(1) Airlines

(2) Hotels

(3) Cargo

(4) Travel Retailing

(5) Railways

Computer in Airlines : Today almost all the airlines use computers for their entire reservation work. The sudden growth, about forty years ago, in global travel, put a big pressure on the handling of air traffic, especially the passenger traffic for the airlines, both international and domestic. Growth patterns in passenger traffic had begun to indicate that handling reservation manually could not be sustained long without affecting efficiency in the customer service. It was then that a need to computerise passenger reservation systems was felt by the major airlines of the world. IBM took the initiative and developed a computerised reservation system known as Programmed Airlines Reservation System (PARS). This system was developed in the early 1960s. However, PARS was not developed exclusively for or with any one particular airline. The system was designed as an all-purpose software package that would fit the requirements of any domestic airline. It was designed around IBM's new hardware range system 360, which was subsequently to revolutionise the entire computer industry.

The first airline to use PARS was the United States based Continental airlines in the year 1967. This was followed by most major US airlines which used the system making PARS the most popular and successful software product of the time. This was a major achievement for IBM. The system later expanded to meet the needs of several other airlines outside the United States of America resulting in the creation of International Programmed Airlines Reservation System (IPARS). Initially this system was a joint venture between IBM and British Overseas Airways Corporation (BOAC) and aimed at adapting PARS to the needs of airlines that had mainly international operations.

Subsequently, many airlines adopted the system. The international package became almost as much of a standard as PARS. Although many airlines modified the system extensively, IPARS was at the base of most international airlines system. By the late 1960s, the system developed was known as CPARS (C for Compact). This system was followed by a system known as Univac Standard Airline System, USA. With the passing of the years more and more systems developed, incorporating more functions to enable the airlines to have more transactions and instructions. The functions of various systems are basically identical across all airline reservation systems. The differences between them are in areas not apparent to the passengers, such as the flexibility with which they can handle control of space of flights, particularly where multiple classes and multiple sectors are involved.

The popularity of any system to a large extent depends on its coverage and online reservation network. The number of terminals which a system has is also an important consideration. The more the terminals a system has, the larger will be the online reservation network. The number of reservation transactions carried out by a system in a given time is another important aspect. However, it became obvious that the system was too costly, for smaller international airlines developed their own IBM oriented reservation systems in the early 1970s to be considered by an airline before using a system. To sum up, the following main aspects are important to make a system perfect and universally acceptable:

(i) Number of reservation transactions to be handled,

(ii) Data links with other airlines,

(iii) Number of terminals,

(iv) Information processing capacity, and

(v) Data volume capacity.

Computers in Air Cargo : Most of the airlines are now using computers for cargo handling operations as well. The handling of cargo shipments on ground is a costly affair and the cost has been increasing over the years.

Almost 50 per cent of the handling of cargo shipment reflect the cost of manual information processing. Freight rate increases have not kept pace with cost increase, so airlines had either to accept reduced margins or take steps to reduce overheads. Computerisation of cargo has helped reduce costs as this speeds up the handling of information related to consignments and also reduces the time the cargo spends on the ground. The pioneer in cargo computerisation was Alitalia, whose PO 4-cargo system was adopted and modified by many major airlines, such as Swissair, TWA and British Airways. Univac's USAS has a fully developed cargo module. Almost all the major airlines in the world have now adopted one system or another of cargo computerisation.

Advantage to Travel Agents : Today several airlines have developed and adopted sophisticated computer systems for their use. The airlines also make available their system to their appointed sales agents who are equipped with an appropriate terminal and receive the necessary instructions and procedures. Airlines have thus greatly benefited from the use and adaptation of computers. Some of the major advantages of use of computers by airlines include:

(a) high profile applications like passenger reservations;
(b) applications of departure, control and cargo;
(c) accounting, budgeting, forecasting and planning;
(d) engineering management;
(e) cargo management;
(f) revenue accounting;
(g) fare quotations and construction;
(h) ticket printing;
(i) crew scheduling;
(j) crew management; and
(k) yield optimisation

Computer Reservation Systems (CRS) : Computer Reservation Systems (CRS) in recent years has made a major advance in the airline reservation system. Different Computer Reservation systems companies which are global giants in their own rights form a link between the airline and the travel agent by offering online flight bookings and availability details. This system was first introduced in Germany. A system capable of carrying out as many as one thousand reservation transactions every second involving data links with 28 airlines, a host of car hire agencies and hotels and about 20,000 travel agencies in Europe alone was set up in Erding in the southern part of Germany. The System known as "Amadeus" was developed jointly by four airlines-Air France, Iberia, SAS and Lufthansa. The information processing capacity of the mainframe IBM and Unisys computers installed at Erding, the world's largest computer centre involves a data volume of hundreds of thousands of books.

In addition to Amadeus, Galileo and Sabre are two other global giants in Computer Reservation System. CRS can now be used through Internet as well. This has brought the details of online flight booking and availability of seats within the reach of every passenger having an internet connection. The impact of the net can be gauged by the fact that CRS companies have now redesigned themselves as GDSs (Global Distribution Systems). The business is no longer limited to airline bookings alone but covers a broader horizon with value - added travel information.

Role of SITA : Airline industry had, however, laid the foundation for global communication long before the internet was even considered to be of any great value by its pioneers. It has been using networks like SITA 'Societe International de Telecommunications Aeronautiques' set up as early as the year 1949. The role of SITA in airlines automation has been very crucial. Automation is the key to achieving a higher level of productivity in any industry, especially in the airlines industry, and this will continue with more emphasis being put on achieving short-term benefits.

SITA is responsible for providing Data Processing Services. In fact, it is the major supplier of information - handling services for the airline industry. Its aims are to foster efficient telecommunications, data processing and transmission means for all categories of information required in the operation of air transport enterprises, with the specific aim of promoting safe and regular air transport in all countries.

There has always been a continued high growth of demand for the services offered by SITA. It provides data processing services in the following areas:

(i) Passenger Reservations
(ii) Departure Control
(iii) Meteorological Data
(iv) Credit Authorisation and Document Verification
(v) Baggage Tracing (BAGTRAC)
(vi) Share Cargo Service
(vii) Shared Flight Operations data base
(viii) Flight Planning
(ix) Baggage Handling and Management Service

(x) Common Customs Interface System

(xi) Fuel Management

(xii) Airline Schedules and Flight Availability database

(xiii) IATA Passenger Tariff Conference Support

SITA is providing a valuable service to the airlines. Almost all the information required in the operation of air transport in the world is being provided to the airlines industry. The range of services offered by SITA is very extensive and new services are being added as and when these are required. The network today is the world's largest private network serving a large number of countries.

Computer in Hotels : Like in airlines, the computer technology has entered the hotel industry in a big way. A hotel's most crucial internal resource is information and with the use of computers the information is available in a way that saves labour and ultimately increases the profits.

Although computers in the hotel industry started being used as far back as the late 1960s; it was only in the 1970s that the technological advances in computer technology made possible the right combination of compactness and versatility for different sizes of hotels. The lower cost encouraged many individual hotels to install the system. Today computers are installed in large numbers and are widely accepted in the hotel industry. One of the most important factors or its large-scale acceptance in the industry has been its reliability. The computer system has been found to be very reliable in the dissemination of the right kind of information at the push of a button.

Today, the hotel industry is a major market for the computer manufacturers and the software vendors. It has been increasingly realised that the hotel computer systems achieve better internal and external control and, through the use of analysis methods, provide the opportunity to improve the overall profitability of the unit. Like in the airlines, the computers offer substantial advantages for reservation systems in terms of speed and accuracy. The errors are almost negligible.

Application Areas : Hotel systems all over the world have traditionally been divided into the following two main areas:

(1) Front Office Application Areas.

(2) Back Office Application Areas.

Front Office Application Areas incorporate the following:

(i) Reservations

(ii) Registration

(iii) Guest accounting

(iv) Night auditing

(v) Communication operations (telephones, telex, fax).

Back Office Application Areas incorporate the following:

(i) Financial management

(ii) Inventory control systems accounts

(iii) Profit/loss accounts

(iv) General ledger

(v) Credit card verifications

The computer system streamlines the functioning of all the above areas in a hotel set-up. It helps in the smooth functioning of the hotel, better guest relations, increased efficiency of staff and the overall profitability of the hotel. The key to successful operation of a hotel lies in the operation of an efficient information system. With the introduction of computers in the hotel the information system has become more accurate and efficient. The guest has an access to the required information with a push button convenience. Since the computer is used as a communication medium, there is better coordination between various departments. The computer has relieved the staff of many routine jobs enabling them to devote more time and attention to the needs of the guests.

The computers have made guest accounting systems more sophisticated and reliable. It automatically collects and calculates, receipts and payments and consolidates and verifies credit card payments and cash controls. The sales outlets, like restaurants, automatically record the guest's expenditure at the point of sale, while direct electronic links to the telephone system in the guest rooms can monitor guest calls for instant charging to their accounts.

The computers have eliminated cumbersome accounting machines often seen at the cashier's desk giving a front office system a modern and sophisticated look, resulting in greater guest satisfaction and adding to the prestige of a hotel.

Back office systems have a large number of areas having great potential for cost control where computers are used to a great advantage for the hotel. With the use of computers, management can monitor the progress of individual restaurants and other sales outlets against targets and budgets which may be set for various items. Daily reports on inventory usage become available by way of organising input from each centre collected at regular intervals throughout the day.

Computer Terminals : The modern day business traveller is increasingly getting used to having a computer in his hotel room. In fact, many such business travellers in countries like USA, Belgium, Holland, France, Switzerland, Germany, Japan, Canada and many other countries are inquiring before booking a room as to whether guest rooms where they are planning to stay have an in-room computer terminal. The computer has thus entered the guest rooms of many hotels in the west and become the latest novelty of a luxury hotel. A number of individual hotels as well as hotel chains have introduced in-room terminals that are hooked by television and telephone into a data system that includes official airline guides, news agencies, stock market agencies, weather bureau, shopping services, travel, club, entertainment guide, electronic games and even job listing features. Access to the computer terminal is gained by the guest by way of punching a credit card number which is charged for their time at the terminals on sliding rates roughly equivalent to those for long distance telephone calls.

Global Distribution System

The hotel industry is today making extensive use of GDS internationally. The GDS basically is a whole gamut of providers who actually started off for the airline industry and then expanded to hotels and car-rental companies. Through GDS, the hotelier can get the customer or a travel agent to make bookings in his hotel. GDS offers more flexibility and instant reservation confirmation.

Travel Retailing

The profound changes over the years in travel services have made the use of computer technology in retail travel a necessity. The impact of computer technology on travel retailing made itself felt since the beginning of 1980 with the introduction of first-generation agency computer system. It was in the year 1983, that Thomas Holidays, a British company, first used computers. With the success of Thomas Holidays in introducing reservations via Prestel, several more leading tour operators introduced similar systems to sell their 1984 summer programmes. A Prestel set allows travel agents to make reservations with as many principals as agreed to it. The videotex technology which allows tour operators and travel agents to open reservations through Prestel sets is applied to airlines through British Telecom's Skytrack, an automated airline reservation system. This enabled travel agents to make bookings on several hundreds of the world's airlines, using the standard Prestel television set and a keyboard. Prestel was being used for the basics required in the travel industry like finding out airline schedules and fares, making reservations and getting information on a tour operator's holiday packages. The advantage of the system over the travel literature like brochures and books was that the information is automatically updated and only flights or packages that are available are shown.

New Systems-many new systems have been developed lately. There is an intense competition between various systems. Sometimes it becomes difficult for a tour operator or a travel agent to make a choice and decide about the merits and demerits of alternate systems. The new systems which are being used today are Sabre, Apollo, Dacoda, Trav Automation, Worldspan Galileo and Abacus. These systems allow travel agents to find the lowest costs for customers, identify promotions involving frequent flyer miles and free trips and tailormade trips to a customer's specific needs. All these services are available through a push button via the computer terminal.

Computer in Railways : In addition to use of computers by airlines retail agents, travel agents and tour operators, these are also being used directly by the railway systems.

The railway system in Europe and some other countries have now been using computers extensively. In countries like France, Germany, Switzerland and Belgium, to name a few, computers have been in use for over a decade. The most important use of computers in railways, however, is in the area of ticket reservation. The information regarding availability of seats is now available instantly in various networks. Railway systems now use computers for route planning, engineering, accounting, inventory planning and control, purchase and a host of other functions.

The most remarkable use of computer in railways has, however, been made by France. The metro system in Paris is one of the best in the world. France has been making great advances in the technology in its metro system. The latest technological marvel has been achieved beneath the surface of the earth through a concrete cylinder. No one on board is at the controls because there are no controls on board. Instead the sleek good looking aluminium and steel train is being guided by a computer from a distant command centre. Moving at 100 kilometres an hour the train suddenly stops as soon as bright lights appear ahead. Glass doors slide open and the passengers step on an immaculate platform awash in filtered daylight, tastefully decorated with mosaics and sculptures.

The train is the remarkable VAL (Vehicule Automatique Leger), the most ultra-modern futuristic subway system in the world inaugurated in the year 1983 in the Northern French city of Lille. Built by a French high technology giant Matra, the 20-mile network links Lille to the nearby cities. This is considered to be the most advanced automatic subway line in the world. VAL is distinguished from most conventional subway systems by its compact size, speed and computerised operating system. Each car is only 6.75 feet wide and 42.6 feet long as compared to 8 feet by 49.2 feet for a Paris metro car. Each train with two cars carries a normal capacity load of 124 passengers in clean, well-lighted comfort.

The system is operated from a control complex on the outskirts of Lille city. Two rows of television screens form an electronic tableau of the entire system. Four operators can call up images on the video monitors from 250 cameras installed in stations, tunnels and garages. The system's computer is programmed to run the trains at a rate of one train every minute during peak hours and every five minutes at other times. The computer is linked to about 200 microprocessors located in the stations and on board the train. In case of any mishap or accident, VAL operators can stop a train, slow it down or give any of the over 2,000 possible electronic commands.

The trains are equipped with telephones that enable passengers to report any crimes and summon the system's 20-member security force. The driverless system is almost foolproof as is claimed. Indeed, during one of the trial runs, a pigeon alighted on an elevated section of the line, tripping automatic detectors and stopping a train for only ten seconds before its on-board computer ascertained that it was safe to proceed. Railway systems, however, may not be able to indulge in such luxuries for a very long time. However, the importance of computers in railways has been more than emphasised.

Videotex System : This system invented by British Telecom is a way of providing computerised information without the expense of supplying a computer terminal. All that is required is a telephone line and standard colour television receiver with an adapter to link it to a keyboard and a decoder. The videotex system has been a great help to travel agents and tour operators in their day-to-day functioning. Videotex provides efficient, low cost information and reservation facilities which allows direct communications between agents and principals throughout the industry. Information is transmitted quickly and accurately via ordinary telephone lines to be visually displayed on a television type screen. At the touch of a button it displays information on holiday packages, airfares, accommodations, cruises, car rentals, insurance, and many other travel-related services.

The videotex system provides the following services to the travel agents/tour operators:

(i) fast and efficient means of obtaining accurate, updated information on every aspect of the travel industry with excellent visual capacity;

(ii) direct access to the information supplied by industry principals, thereby speeding up transactions and increasing both the efficiency of selling and the quality of customer service;

(iii) information on new product developments, fare changes, special offers and any other important information put into the system; and

(iv) display of tour itineraries, graphic illustrations of hotels, resorts and tourist attractions by selling staff.

Some other videotex system benefits to users include:

(a) key word-immediate access to a specific piece of information;

(b) increased sales-more sale conversations due to immediate access of information;

(c) increased productivity-more efficient customer servicing;

(d) cost efficient-reduced costs due to greater efficiency of communication

(e) up-to-date information-continued access to an entire library of travel-related information.

In the years to come, information and communication technology will play a very crucial role in the development and promotion of travel and tourism industry. New technology like on-line reservation systems in hotels and travel agencies, touch-screen information kiosks, interactive TV's virtual tours etc. have added new dimension to the concept of marketing. Information technology today has spread to all parts of the world and the tourism has been greatly affected by it. Communication and information technology has great capacity to accelerate the globalization of the travel industry.

Exercises

1. What are the components of the tourism infrastructure?
2. What are the six freedoms of the air?
3. What are the various basic market segments as delineated by airlines?
4. What is IATA and its role?
5. Make out the Housekeeping organisation chart of a large hotel.
6. What is a job description and what advantages does it offer management?
7. What are the 12 points in a job specification?
8. What are the activities prior to the actual interviewing process?
9. What are the departments that housekeeping coordinates with and how?
10. Why is tact and diplomacy important for Housekeeping staff?
11. What is the flow of laundry activity?
12. What are the different sections in an Engineering Department?
13. Describe the different type of fire extinguishers.
14. Describe the procedure to make a housekeeping operational budget.
15. Explain the "Lost and Found" procedure.

16. Explain how the following are cleaned:
    (a) Chromium plate
    (b) Galvanized iron
    (c) Leather
    (d) Wicker white furniture
17. Explain how the following stains can be removed:
    (a) Fresh black ink
    (b) Lipstick
    (c) Furniture polish
    (d) Iodine
    (e) Paints
18. What are the basic principles for using polishes?
19. What does 'sale of rooms' mean?
20. Why is the role of the front office important?
21. What are the basic components of front office operation? Explain these components.
22. What are the essential attributes of front office staff?
23. What is a job description?
24. What are the advantages of a job description?
25. Write out the job description of a front office assistant (reservations).
26. What are the various issues that should be included in a briefing?
27. Explain the following:
    (a) Twin room
    (b) Double suite
    (c) Cabana
28. What are the rules on a guest floor?
29. Explain the room cleaning procedure.
30. What do we mean by an evening service and second service?
31. What are the various codes in a room report?
32. What are the storage conditions for a linen room?
33. What are the equipment and accessories normally required in a linen room?

34. What do you mean by par stock? Explain its importance.
35. How is stock-taking done?
36. Explain the procedure for the exchange of linen and uniforms.
37. Explain the importance of a Housekeeping Control Desk.
38. What are the files and registers maintained at a control desk?
39. What is the procedure for requisitioning fresh linen?
40. Explain the basic storage rules in a floor linen room.
41. What are the records kept in the floor linen room?
42. A participant should not attempt more than two tasks a day.
43. Give a day off for recapitulation. This should normally be the working off day.
44. Spend a maximum of two hours in a day.
45. Fix meeting dates and time well in advance and with the approval of the department head.
46. Be careful in choosing a counsellor. He should guide you correctly. The department head would be the right person as he would be knowledgeable and also committed to your efforts.
47. Schedule those tasks in a day that give you flexibility to attend apart from the daily work.
48. Tasks should be related to each other.
49. Tasks undertaken in a day should be in the same section of the department.
50. Above all be honest with yourself right through the PSD programme.
51. How are the following cleaned:
    (a) Guest elevators
    (b) Restaurants
52. How is 'out of service' furniture stored?
53. Explain the "lost and found" procedure.
54. Explain the procedure in the event of a fire in the hotel.
55. What are the precautions adopted by hotels to avoid thefts.

Tick the Correct Answer

1. The hotel which is located in the heart of a city is referred to as
   - ❑ Motel
   - ❑ Downtown hotel
   - ❑ None of the above
2. A hotel may be categorised as 'medium' if it has
   - ❑ 25—100 rooms
   - ❑ 101—300 rooms
   - ❑ None of the above
3. A plan which includes charges for bed, breakfast and two meals is called
   - ❑ American plan
   - ❑ European plan
   - ❑ Continental plan
4. A commercial hotel caters mostly to
   - ❑ Tourists
   - ❑ Businessmen
   - ❑ None of the above
5. A 5 star hotel must have
   - ❑ Attached baths
   - ❑ Shopping arcade
   - ❑ Superior quality carpeting
   - ❑ All the above
6. As regards rooms, it is essential for front office staff to know the
   - ❑ Quality of carpets in the room.
   - ❑ Location of rooms.
   - ❑ The supplier of channel music.
7. As regards restaurants, it is essential for front office staff to know
   - ❑ The number of cooks in the kitchen.
   - ❑ Equipment used in the restaurant.
   - ❑ The type of menu offered in a restaurant.

8. Front office staff must know the following information on the city .
   - ❑ Church timings.
   - ❑ City tour facilities.
   - ❑ Locations of shopping centres.
   - ❑ None of the above.
   - ❑ All of the above.
9. Who escorts the guest from the main door to the registration area.
   - ❑ Information assistant
   - ❑ Bell boy
   - ❑ None of the above
10. The front office cashier normally gets to know of a guest's intention for check out from
    - ❑ Bell desk
    - ❑ Reservation assistant
    - ❑ Telephone operator

True or False

1. Always quote the highest rate for the room.
   ❑ True ❑ False
2. Offer a guest a choice of rooms.
   ❑ True ❑ False
3. A guest makes an emotional adjustment when checking into a hotel.
   ❑ True ❑ False
4. Abbreviations or colloquial slang is preferable in communication with guests.
   ❑ True ❑ False
5. A reception assistant's job is to calculate room availability.
   ❑ True ❑ False
6. A VIP Amenities Voucher is issued by an information assistant.
   ❑ True ❑ False
7. Pre-registration formalities are often done for VIPs.
   ❑ True ❑ False

8. The reservation assistant continuously updates the guest rack.

   ❑ True ❑ False

9. Information maintains room racks

   ❑ True ❑ False

10. A duplicate copy of the message slip is sent to the telephone department

    ❑ True ❑ False

Fill in the Blanks

1. The travel agent who deals directly with the consumer is called ....
2. A travel agent makes his money from hotels through ....
3. A tour group coming to visit only places of archeological interest may be termed group ....
4. An example of surface transportation is ....
5. Front office staff are .... for guests who want information or want to pass on information.
6. Front office staff are .... as they deal with other departments on behalf of a guest.
7. The front office receptionist reports to .... in a large hotel.
8. The room report is prepared by the .... department.
9. Flowers to VIPs are provided in the room by the............ department.
10. At a "check in" the guest folio is opened by............ .
11. Sales recapitulation is done by ....
12. All matters referring to credit are handled by ....
13. When a guest wants to leave a message, the information assistant hands him/ her a ....
14. A .... is used to locate a guest in a specified area.
15. Information and data on city tours may be got from ....

Appendices

Glossary

***A.A.U.I.* :** Automobile Association of Upper India.

***A.H.M.A.* :** American Hotel and Motel Association.

***A.I.I.* :** Air India International.

***A.M.* :** Anti meridian (before noon)

***A.S.T.A* :** American Society of Travel Agent. The largest worldwide trade association of retail and wholesale travel agent and allied industry service. Its headquarters are in New York.

***a'la carte* :** It is a type of menu which lists all the dishes available in the restaurant and each dish is priced individually.

***Account payable transaction* :** A financial procedure in which goods and services are received by the hotel before the hotel makes payment for them.

***Account posting machine* :** A device used to post, monitor and balance charges and credits to guest account.

***Account receivable load* :** Out of the total sales, that proportion of sales that are charged to accounts, and which are to be collected on later dates.

***Account receivable transaction* :** A financial procedure in which goods and services are provided to the consumer for which the payment shall be received in future. The consumer may be an individual or a company or an organization.

Account settlement : The payment of outstanding balance on the folio or city account by the consumer, either by cash or by credit (i.e. an agreement of the amount of outstanding bill at a later date).

Accountancy cycle : A period (can be daily, weekly, monthly, or yearly) from when a financial transaction occurs to the time it is reconciled and is shown on the financial report of the company.

Accounting system : A system of accounting for recording, analyzing and summarizing the

financial transactions of the company.

Accounts receivable ledger : A ledger of the aggregate of individual account receivable records.

Account : The way of first classifying and then summarizing of money transaction within the framework of an accounting system is called account.

Adds : Last minute reservations added to the list of expected arrivals on the day of arrival.

Adjoining rooms : Two rooms adjacent to each other and with a door in the common wall, maybe used for a family if the inside connecting doorway is opened or for two different guests if that door is closed. Also called connecting rooms, and inter-leading rooms.

Advance deposit : An amount of money that is sent by the prospective guest in advance generally deposited in the guest account. Also called as deposit reservation.

Advances : Any money disbursed for guests such as loans or payments made on behalf of the guests. This amount is charged to the account like other charges. Also called as cash paid out of cash disbursement.

Affiliate reservation network : A hotel chains reservation system in which all participating properties is contractually related.

Affiliated hotel : A hotel which is usually on franchise or referral system of another group or chain.

After departure : Also called as late charge and refers to any credit purchase money voucher which reaches the bills section after the guest has settled his bill and checked out. This requires late charge billing.

Agency ledger : That section of the city ledger where the travel agency transactions/ accounts are recorded.

Allocatable expenses : All those expenditure that can be classified or shared amongst various departments of the company.

Allowance : An accounts term which refers to the amount which is reduced from the guest folio as an adjustment against improper, unsatisfactory or no service to the guest. It may also be due to a posting error. Also called as account allowance.

American plan : Also called as en-pension, or full pension or a full board meal and bed and board plan. Here the room tariff includes the room charges and full meals i.e. breakfast (English), lunch and dinner (Table d'hote) charges. It may also include early morning tea and evening tea charges.

Arranging : A data processing function whereby data are sorted in a predetermined sequence.

Arrival date : A date when a prospective guest is expected to arrive in the hotel. Arrival time—The expected time of arrival of a prospective guest.

Arrival, departure and change sheet : A consolidated document prepared and maintained by the front desk staff recording all the arrivals, departures and change of rooms. In some hotels three separate sheets are maintained for each of these activities.

Audit : The review, test and verification of financial transactions in an accounting system.

Authorization approval code : It is the authorization approval by credit card company for the extension of credit limit facility in case the credit card holder's credit is about to exceed the assigned floor limit.

Available rooms : The number of rooms that the hotel has for sale out of the total number of rooms in the hotel. This figure may vary each day.

Average rate per guest : It is the average of the revenue earned per guest by the hotel for an accounting period. For example, average rate per guest for a day will be equal to the total room revenue collected for the day divided by the total number of guests accommodated for that day.

Average room rate/revenue : It is the average money collected from the sale of total number of rooms by the hotel for an accounting period. For example the average daily room rate is equal to total room revenue collected for a day divided by the total number of rooms sold for that day. This average is also referred to as sales per room occupied.

B.T.A. : British Tourist Authority.

Back office : It is that branch of the hotel which is responsible for coordinating all support services. All managerial activities and maintaining the ongoing status of the business and their activities are called back office functions.

Back to back : A travel trade term which refers to a sequence of consecutive group departures and arrivals usually arranged by tour operators so rooms are never vacant i.e. a manner of operating tourists on a consistent and continuous basis. For example a flight arriving with 250 passengers would pick up another 250 passengers who have completed their stay. This eliminates ferry mileage completely or reduces it to minimum possible.

Back-of-the-house : Those areas and sections of the hotel with which normally the hotel resident guest does not come in direct contact.

Bal : Balance.

Balance sheet : A statement of the financial position of the company at a specific time, showing the position of assets, liabilities and equity of the company.

Bank : Refers to the petty cash or float/imprest money given to cashier for making day-to-day small payments such as V.P.O. etc.

Bed and breakfast : Type of meal plan also called as continental plan where the room tariff quoted includes along with room rate the continental breakfast also.

Bed board : Usually a hardboard provided on the bed on

special request of the guest. Bed occupancy — A ratio of number of beds sold to number of rooms available for sale.

When the ratio is multiplied by 100 the figure obtained is bed occupancy percentage. Also called as guest occupancy.

Bell captain : Also called as hall porter and in charge of bell desk staff i.e. uniformed staff.

Bell desk/bell stand : The bell desk is a special desk located in the lobby from where the senior bell captain operates with his team. Also called as "porters' lodge."

Bell persons/boys slip : This is a slip which is prepared to communicate to the bellboy about the room of the guest which has requested for bell service.

Bench mark : A test or set of tests for assessing the performance of a computer programme.

Bermuda plan : A type of meal plan where the room tariff includes alongwith room rate the American breakfast rates.

Bill to account : This situation refers to the case when the unpaid bill or guest's account is transferred to a non-guest ledger for billing (of course approval of both parties is necessary).

Bin card : A stock card used in storekeeping which is attached to a bin, container or shelf.

On it are recorded receipts, issues and a running total of the particular item stored in the bin.

Container or on the shelf-black-listed guest : A list of unwanted guests. These may be those guests who make a lot of fuss and create problems for the hotel, (non-payment of bill, damage to hotel property, misbehave with its staff and/or other guests of the hotel etc.) FHRAI is usually informed about such guests.

Blanket reservation : A block of rooms held for a particular group with individual members requesting assignments from that block i.e. a unit that has been reserved for a specific arrival date but not for a specific guest, also referred to as blocked room.

Booked room : A room that is reserved for a specific guest.

Bounced reservation : Sometime due to some error in planning a guest with reservation may be refused accommodation. This situation is called bounced reservation situation; also called walking the guest.

Breakage : If an individual guest or a group does not avail of some services or amenities such as meals/food included in the package then the gain which accrues to the hotel is called breakage.

Brochures : Printed stationery, containing brief description of the services and facilities in the form of coloured photographs and nicely phrased text that the hotel is offering to its prospective guests. Generally given free to various travel agents, tourist bureaus, etc. for further distribution to prospective guests. An advertisement material in the form of folders, booklets, pamphlets etc.

Brunch : A meal served between breakfast and lunch and usually served in place of these two meals.

Bucket : It is a specially designed collapsible rack which is normally kept on the cashier's counter top for holding the guest folio. It is also called as 'cashier's well' and 'folio tray' and the 'tub'.

Budget : A statement of expected/projected expenditure constructed from anticipated/ projected revenue and available financial resources for a period of time, usually one year. The process of preparing budget is called budgeting.

Bumped reservation : Refusal of accommodation to a guest holding confirmed reservation and subsequently putting him in some other hotel.

C.I.P. : Commercially Important Person — A person who has influence over a large number of prospective buyers.

C.R.T. : Cathode Ray Tube.

Cabana : A room on the beach or near the swimming pool of a hotel, away from the main building.

Call sheet : A sheet which records list of room numbers, and times of the guests requiring to be called. Also called as wake-call-sheet. This also contains details such as newspaper, early morning tea or breakfast required by the guest.

Cancellation : A process of cancelling the reservation by guest before the date of expected arrival, made previously by him.

Cancellation code : A code number assigned to cancelled reservation to future references and a document listing all such cancellation codes is called cancellation record. Also a record or list of all guests who cancelled their reservation is called cancellation report.

Card key : An electronic or magnetic small plastic card used in electronic locking system that operates through a master control console at front desk which is wired to every guest room door. Also called as magnetic or electronic card.

Cash discount : An allowance offered by a creditor or debtor to encourage prompt payment.

Cash flow : It is the time period between the goods or service sold to a customer to the period actual cash for that sale is received.

Cash payout transaction : A cash transaction in which the hotel makes cash advance to a guest or non-guest account.

Cash register : A device used to record and maintain cash balances. The device may be mechanical, semi-automatic or automatic or electronic.

Cash sheet : A document in report form prepared by cashier, carrying all transactions against folio accounts, cash payouts, and departmental cash sales. This document serves as a primary cross-reference document in the hotel's audit.

Cash transaction : An exchange of goods or services for cash.

Casino hotel : A hotel with gambling facilities.

Chamber maid : A housekeeping staff normally responsible for cleaning of rooms and bed making.

Chance trade : Business done usually for cash with chance guests.

Change : Moving a guest from one room to another for various reasons.

Charge back : Sometimes the credit card company refuses the payment of a voucher signed by the customer which is sent by the hotel. This situation is called charge back.

Check-in : Procedure of receiving the guest, assigning and allocation of room and registering of a guest in the hotel.

Check-out : The procedure involved (baggage handling, bill settlement etc.) at departure time.

Check-out time/hours : It is the time by which the guest should check-out otherwise next day's charges will be charged. Usually it is 12.00 noon.

City account : Basically an account receivable for someone other than a registered guest.

City ledger : A collection of city, or nonguest, receivable account balances.

Cleaners : Members of housekeeping department who clean public areas such as corridors.

Close of the day : An arbitrary hour fixed by the hotel which separates the record of one day from the next day.

Closed : Dates for which a reservation system will not accept additional reservation.

Closet bed : A standard size bed that swings into a wall or cabinet in the form of a closet.

Commercial hotels : A hotel which is mainly patronized by businessmen and situated downtown usually.

Commercial rate : Special discounted rate offered to a frequently visiting hotel guest.

Commission : Amount payable to travel agents for arranging groups stay in the hotel. An amount payable to an agent, usually based on business given to hotel.

Commissionaire : Member of uniformed staff whose place of duty is outside the main entrance of hotel. Also called door man, link man and carriage attendant.

Commissioned sales : Materialized business given to the hotel by a third party such as travel agent for which the hotel has to pay commission to the third party.

Competitive price : Construction of room tariff based on the rates of the competitor. In this case the rate fixation is based on external rate structure criterions, rather than the inter-rate structure criterions.

Complimentary : Usually accommodation given to a guest free. Generally an abbreviated form 'comp' is used. A business promotional or goodwill activity. Complementary rooms are given by the hotel.

Computer system : An electronic system which comprises of an input-output device, a central processing unit and a memory unit called as hardware or the physical components and the programme and the instructions used called as software. This total system is used to either problem solving and or data processing functions.

Concessionaire : Abbreviated as concession sometimes refers to the shops providing services and amenities and facilities etc. to the resident guest. Generally they are not operated by the hotel, and are rented to experts. These are also called as rentals.

Concierge : A person usually found in American hotels responsible for providing guest services and needs etc. In some hotels concierge provides information service to guest also.

Confirmation notification : Also called as acknowledgement letter. Sometimes means the letter or other mode of communication such as phone, letter etc. by which the prospective guest (who has requested for room reservation) is informed of the acceptance of his request.

Construction cost : A sum total of all the initial/pre-opening expenses of a property. This is an important factor to be considered while calculating the room tariff.

Contribution margin : It refers to the difference between the sales and total variable costs of any item or group of items.

Contribution to profitability : It refers to the difference between contribution margin and fixed expenses or sales (variable cost + fixed expenses).

Control folio : Also called as master folio some time, refers to group folio.

Convertible bed : A sofa which can be converted into a single or double bed. The bed is also called sofa convertible into bed.

Corkage : Refers to charges made by a licensed establishment for providing service equipment and bottle, soda, etc. to customers who bring their own alcoholic beverage for consumption in the hotel.

Corner room : An outside room, i.e. a room on the corner of perimeter of the building, facing outward with two exposures.

Cost benefit : It is a financial analysis to determine if the benefits of the system are more as compared to the cost of the system or not.

Cost center : Also called as non-revenue departments of hotel and refers to all those operating departments of hotels which are non-revenue producing. These departments simply incur cost and have very little or no contact with the guests.

Cost effective : A system in which the benefits overweigh the costs. It is also called 'Justified'. Also called as 'Price Performance Ratio'.

Cot : In American terminology refers to an extra bed and in English terminology refers to child's bed. Sometimes Roll away beds are also called cot. (30"x72")

Coupons : These are documents issued by airlines or travel agents to their passengers or travellers, to be produced to the hotels and specifies the various services and facilities etc. which the guest can get on the basis of these vouchers and used by guests to settle their hotel accounts.

Coy. : Company

Cr.—Credit : An account term which means that the transaction will reduce the accounts receivable.

Credit card volume : That proportion of total sales which is on credit. This figure is an indicator of cash flow position of the hotel.

Credit limit : This is the limit of amount of money up to which the guest is allowed credit facility. After the limit is reached the hotel requests the guest to clear his bill either partly or fully.

Credit or credit entry : Writing of financial transaction of the right hand side of a "T" account. This transaction increases liabilities and revenue account while decreasing asset and expense account.

Cut-off-date : That date by which the confirmations should come otherwise after this date the block of rooms is released for general sale.

Cut-off-time/hour : It is the specified hour / time at which the unclaimed reservation are released and can be sold to any walk-in, i.e. if the guest who had booked the room comes after this hour, he may be refused accommodation.

D.G.C.A. : Director General of Civil Aviation.

D.N.S. : Did Not Stay.

D.O.T. : Department of Tourism.

Daily report of operations : After the daily audit a report is prepared which includes operating statistics, bank activity, revenue activity, transaction activity etc.,

Data processing cycle : Refers to time and procedures involved in the handling of data in a data processing operation.

Data processing : Input-process-output operation of data to achieve results.

Data : Raw, unevaluated fact that alone has no relevance but as a group can be used to draw conclusions.

Date and time punching machine : An equipment which is used for printing date and time on documents.

Day rate : Room tariff offered to a guest who stays only during daytime. Also called as 'Day use rate'.

Day use room : A status indicating that the room will be used for day only.

Debit/Debit entry : Recording of financial transactions on the left hand side of "T" account. These entries increase assets and expenses account and reduce liabilities and revenue accounts.

Demi pension : Also called half pension or modified American plan, which means the room tariff includes room rate, English breakfast and one major meal i.e. either lunch or dinner.

Departure date : The scheduled date of the check out of a guest.

Departure notification slip : A notification slip prepared at check-out time and circulated to all departments informing about the departure of the guest.

Difference returnable : Also called 'due back' or 'due bank' and exchange and refers to the excess turn-in over net receipts. The difference is returnable to front office cashier.

Direct expenses : An expense which is incurred only when goods or services are sold and would cease when the service or good is no more sold. For example expense or cost of food to a restaurant.

Discretionary income : Surplus income, after meeting the basic needs, which the guest can spend as he wants.

Dispense bar : A bar from where drinks are obtained by hotel staff for serving to guests.

DNA : Did Not Arrive.

Double occupancy : When a room is occupied by two persons it is called double occupancy.

Double up : When a room is occupied by two unrelated guests it is called as double up. For each of these two a separate Whitney slip is kept in the rack.

Double-double : Also called twin double. A room with two double beds i.e. sleeping accommodation for four persons.

Down grade : Moving the guest's reservation to a lower quality room is called down grade. Due out— Room that is expected to become vacant after the following day's check-out time.

Dunning letters : From time to time the outstanding bills statements sent by the hotel to former guests with delinquent accounts.

Duplex : A costly suite where the two rooms situated on successive floors are connected through an internal staircase.

Early arrival : A guest who arrives before his expected/ scheduled date/ time of arrival.

ECO : Express Check Out.

Efficiency accommodation : Accommodation that includes kitchen facilities.

Efficiency rate : Measurement of performance designed to measure variance between a desired standard and actual condition.

Electronic Cash Register (ECR) : An electronic cash control device

Electronic folio : The making and maintenance of guest folio in computer memory. A soft copy record.

Electronic fund transfer : The method of payment of goods or services in which the transfer of actual cash between two accounts is performed electronically.

Equity : Is the claim on business by the owners of the business. If the business is owned by one person the equity is called capital and earned surplus. A partnership will show the claim of each owner listed separately. A corporation will list its ownership claims as capital stock.

Equivalent occupancy : If the management plans a change in ARR (higher/lower) then the occupancy percentage needed to achieve the same net revenue as was achieved earlier by old price and occupancy percentage.

Estt : Establishment

Express check out : An activity which involves compilation and early morning distribution of guest folios to all those guests who are expected to check out that morning.

F.E.R.A. : Foreign Exchange Regulation Act.

F.F.I.T. : Foreign Free Independent Traveller.

F.H.R.A.I : Federation of Hotels and Restaurant Association of India.

F.I.T. : Free Independent Traveller (any individual who is not in a group) or a non-affiliated group member; also called as Free Individual.

Family plan rate : A special discounted rate for families.

Farm out : In case of a full house, assignment of guests with reservation to other units of chain or other properties.

Financial transaction : The sale of goods or services for cash, or deferred cash payments.

Fixed cost : All those expenses which are not dependent on sales volume. Also called as fixed overheads.

Fixed room rate : A room tariff which is fixed and does not change with the number of guests in the room. Also referred to as flat rate or "Run of the house rate".

Floor limit : The credit limit that the hotel allows to a guest. Also called as house limit in some hotels.

Floor porter : Male members of house keeping staff whose duty is lifting and moving of heavy articles within the department. Also called floor porters.

Folio header : Upper portion of folio showing columns such as room number and personal details like date of arrival, date of departure, room tariff etc.

Folio/Guest folio : A statement of guest account, shows the balance of guest's financial obligation to hotel. Also called as guest bill or account card.

Forecast : A future projection of estimated business.

Forecasted guest load : Forecasted occupancy for any given time of the hotel.

Forfeited deposit : The amount that the guest has paid advance for booking a room, may be forfeited in case of his 'no show' and is also called as retention charges.

Franking machine : A machine used for printing postage stamp value on the envelope. Free sale— Term used when rooms are available for sale.

Front : An American term which refers to the next bellboy available for rooming a guest.

Front of the house : Those parts of the hotel with which the guest comes in direct contact.

Front office cashier : Cashier who is responsible for all cash transactions at front office.

Full day : It is a way of measuring a chargeable day for accounting purpose for a guest. For example, it will be 3 meals for an American plan hotel and no meals and only overnight for European hotels.

Full house : A situation of 100% room occupancy in the hotel.

Fully automated : Refers to computerized electronic data processing (EDP) system in which data is handled automatically.

G.I.T. : Group Inclusive Tour.

G.O.I. : Government of India.

Garni hotels : A hotel which has no food and beverage service facility.

General cashier : The chief cashier of the hotel with whom deposits of all cashiers are made and who also issues floats.

Graveyard shift : A work shift which begins from midnight.

Green fees : An amount to be paid by guests using golf course.

Group plan rate : A special discounted rate offered to groups as an incentive to attract large number of guests and hence sell more rooms.

Guaranteed reservation : Where the hotel is sure to get room rate whether the guest comes or not.

Guest accounting : A process by which a guest's financial transactions can be monitored and controlled.

Guest : An individual client who has registered with the hotel.

Guest check : The voucher that are presented to a guest when he avails of services/facilities at various outlets such as restaurant, bar, etc. of the hotel.

Guest cycle : The concept of the guest movement to, through and from the hotel for the purpose of writing and monitoring guest and hotel transaction (pre-sale, point of sale and post-sale phases).

Guest day/night : Stay of one guest for one night also called as room night and bed night.

Guest history card : A card which is maintained for regular and VIP guests and the personal details such as his liking and disliking, birthdays, marriage anniversary etc. are recorded in. Any complaints, suggestions and number of visits are also recorded in it.

Guest ledger : The accounts of registered guests are recorded in it. It is also called as 'Room ledger' or 'Transit ledger'.

Guest profile : It includes things such as habits, likes, dislikes, etc. of a guest : (a) Geographic Analysis - like people, area etc, (b) Demorgraphic Analysis - like people their type and (c) Psychographic Analysis - like people and their needs.

Guest services : All the tangible and non-tangible amenities and facilities and services that the hotel offers its guest.

H.S.M.A. : Hotel Sales Management Association. An international organization of marketing which maintains liaison with all requests of the travel industry to discuss and implement areas of mutual interest. Its headquarters are in New York.

Handicap room : Room with specially designed features for handicapped guests.

Hard copy : A print out of information generated by computer system.

High balance : Means when the guest's outstanding bill is near or over the credit limit balance set by hotel, and such guests are called high risk guests.

Hollywood bed : When two twin beds are joined together with one common hard board to make one bed it is called Hollywood bed (the length of one twin bed is 80"-82" instead of the usual 75").

Hospitality services industry : All businesses involved in accommodation, food, entertainment, transportation, health care etc. to the guest.

Hot list : A list of lost/stolen credit card sent by the credit card company to the hotel. This is also called 'Stop Bulletin' and 'Cancellation Bulletin'.

Hotel Information System (H.I.S.) : An orderly arrangement of hotel data procedures and decision making criteria designed to increase managerial effectiveness through the proper handling arid flow of information.

House count : Total number of guest staying in the hotel at a particular time.

House phone : Telephone usually in the lobby of the hotel from where the visitor can contact the guest in the room.

House profit : The gross profit earned before deducting taxes.

Housekeeper's report : A report prepared by the housekeeper of the status of rooms.

Housing bureau : A reservation office like central reservation office.

Hubart formula : A formula developed by Ray Hubart for determining room rate keeping in consideration operating expenses, room sales, and a pre-desired return on investment (R.O.I.)

Human engineering : It is a new concept of replacing human resource by automated systems so that the human resource may be freed to provide more personalized service to the guest.

Human resource audit : An inventory of human power, i.e. how many were appointed, how many left and how many are still there. This also refers to 'Succession Built Up'.

I.A.A.I. : International Airports Authority of India.

I.A.C. : Indian Airlines Corporation.

I.A.T.A. : International Air Transport Association.

I.A.T.O : Indian Association of Tour Operation.

I.C.A.O. : International Civil Aviation Organization.

I.D.D. : International Direct Dialing.

I.H.A. : International Hotel Association.

I.L.O. : International Labour Office.

I.M.F. : International Monetary Fund.

I.S.D. : International Subscriber Dialing

I.U.O.T.O. : International Union of Official Travel Organization.

I.Y.H.F : International Youth Hostel Federation.

Ideal average rate : Point at which rooms are sold at the best rate possible.

Idle time : Also called hidden rest. This is the period that must be allowed during duty when a person does not work.

Imprinter : A special device/machine used for taking the impression of credit card on vouchers.

Incidental account : Charges which are guest's own responsibility; not paid by a company or travel agent.

Independent : An individual property not affiliated or a part of a chain.

Information dissemination : Flow of communications and documents throughout a department or unit.

Information rack : A rack which has Whitney slips arranged in alphabetical order of all

the guest staying in the hotel.

Information : This is which adds to what is known. It communicates knowledge, provides feedback and reduces uncertainty.

In-house guest : Refers to a guest who is registered and not checked-out.

Input data : Raw data which is to be processed by computer system.

Input : The first phase of a data processing or computer system.

Input unit : That part of computer system through which data/information are entered.

Input/output device (I/O) : The components of a computer system through which instructions/data are entered.

In-season rate : This is the maximum rack rate that is announced by a resort hotel in season as the demand of rooms is heaviest during this period.

Inside call : An intra hotel telephone call (call within the hotel only).

Inside room : A guest room that faces an inner courtyard of the hotel.

Integrated Circuit (I.C.) : A solid state electronic component of a computer system also called as chip.

Inter sell agency : A reservation system that handles reservation for many products such as airlines, car rentals and hotels etc.

Interface : Designing the ability of one computer to

communicate with another. Internal control— Verification of documentation of financial transaction.

Intuitive pricing : The pricing of accommodation or services of hotel done on the basis of what people are willing to pay and whatever the market will bear.

J.A.L. : Japan Airlines.

Journal : A date-wise record of financial transaction showing the result of various debit and credit entries.

Jr. : Junior.

Junior suite/petite suite/mini suite : A large room with partition for making separate bed room and sitting room.

K.L.M. : Koninklijke Luchtvaart Maatschappij nv (Royal Dutch Airlines).

Key and mail rack : A pigeon hole type rack used in old hotels for keeping the keys of guest room and the mail of in-house guest when he is not in the room.

Key card : A sort of an identification card given to guest by the receptionist at the time of check in. Usually contains general information facility, catering outlets, location of hotel, etc. should be produced when asked by the hotel staff. Also called as Room Key Card.

King size bed : An extra long, extra wide double bed (78" x 80-82"). An American term.

Lanai room : A room from the balcony of which a waterfall or a water body can be seen.

Late arrival : A guest with reservation who intimate in advance to the hotel about the late arrival i.e. after cut off time.

Late check out : A guest who with the permission of the hotel checks out of the hotel after the check out time, without extra charge.

Lead maid : An experienced maid who may compliment a Housekeeper's job on a floor.

Liabilities : Debts or financial obligations by the firm to a creditor.

Light baggage : Also called scanty baggage when the guest arrives with no or little baggage. Usually advance is taken from such guest and the departments should be informed not to give credit to him.

Lightning Call : Most urgent calls.

Line of authority : Hierarchy of administrative responsibility.

Lock out : When a guest is not allowed access to the room usually due to an unpaid bill.

Log book : A book/ register which is used to record activities and to communicate to the next shift.

Log book : Record of happenings.

Loss leader : A product which is priced below the break-even point price.

Lost and found : An area where all items found by the staff is stored.

Luggage pass : An authority for the guest luggage to be removed from hotel.

Machine-assisted : A hotel information system which is totally machine based.

Managerial reports : All documents providing feedback on financial status, productivity, and overall effectiveness of business operation.

Market mix : The distribution (percentage wise) of the hotel guests into various categories such as conventioneer, tourist and businessman, etc.

Market penetration : Going more and more into the market already achieved i.e. more and more exploring the area which has already given business.

Market share : Represents that share of market (in terms of revenue, number of guest, or any other index), which the hotel captures out of the total market.

Marketing : (i) From the point of view of philosophy marketing is looking at business from customers point of view. (ii) From function point of view it is identifying, anticipating and satisfying the customer's need for a profit.

Multiple occupancy : When the hotel room is occupied by more then one person it is called as multiple occupancy.

N.A.A. : National Airport Authorities.

N.C.R. : National Cash Register

Night audit : An activity performed by night auditor in the night to check that whatever has been done during the day is correct or not.

No post status : A term used to indicate a guest who is not allowed to charge purchases to his room account.

No show : A guest who does not arrive on the schedule date of arrival after making a

confirmed reservation is called 'no show'. Another term is DNA (did not arrive).

Objective and policy : Objective is 'what to do' and policy is 'how to do it'.

Occupancy load : Refers to occupancy percentage i.e. the ratio of hotel rooms sold to the number of hotel rooms available for sale.

Occupancy mix : Also referred to as profile of occupancy which means percentage break up of sold rooms on single, double and annual occupancy.

Occupancy : Sale of room and its occupancy status for a guest.

Off : Means that the room is off the list of rooms available for sale due to some reason. Also

called as 'Red Slip Room'.

Off-season rate : A special reduced rate offered by the hotels during off-season such as by hill resorts etc.

Omission error : By mistake omitting an important transaction.

On-the house : The term refers to complementary i.e. no charge.

Open : Date for the guest for which a reservation system can still accept reservation.

Opinion leader : A person who can influence the community.

Out of Order (O.O.O) : A room which is not ready for sale due to planned or unexpected shut down.

Outside laundry valet : A contracted laundry service (not operated by hotel)

Outside room : Room facing outside of the hotel with an exposure to the city.

Overbooking : A situation in which hotel books more room than available.

Overstay : A situation in which the guest does not leave on the day of scheduled departure and continues staying in the hotel.

P.A.T.A : Pacific Asia Travel Association.

Package tour : Usually refers to consolidated charges for services such as accommodation, transfers, meals and transport etc. Given to groups normally.

Paid in Advance (PIA) : Where the guest is required to pay the room rent in advance i.e. at the time of arrival.

Parcels book : A document where the record of parcels received and subsequently delivered to in-house guest is maintained.

Parlor : The living room part of the studio. The European term for this is 'Salon'. Also called as sitting room.

Penthouse : Luxury suite on the terrace of the hotel.

Plus position : When rooms available exceed guest arrivals.

Point of purchase/sale : Both the terms mean same. Refers to time and location of consumer's purchase during his stay at the hotel. From hotel's point of view it is called point of sales (POS) and from guest perspective it is called point of purchase.

POS terminal : A computer term for input equipment immediately accessible to the place of sale.

Position : Status of number of rooms available for sale.

Potential average rate : A statistics that combines the potential average single and double rates multiple occupancy percentage and rate spread to produce the average rate that would be achieved if all rooms were sold at their full rack rates.

Pre-arrival : That phase which is before the arrival of the guest and after the booking has been done. Activities during this period are called pre arrival activities.

Pre-assignment : Assignment of room to a prospective guest even before his arrival.

Pre-registration : An activity before the arrival of the guest where the guest's registration card is filled with all the information which is already available about the guest, i.e. registration before arrival.

Procedure narrative : Description or statement of what is to be done.

Psychological pricing : A system of pricing where the main consideration of costing is not the costs but the expectation of the customer's willingness to pay.

Quad : A room occupied by 4 persons.

Queen bed : An American term referring to a double bed of 60" x 80" size.

R.S.V.P. : Respondez Sil Vous Plail (Reply if you please).

Rack rate : This is the normal published room rate mentioned on tariff card and also written on the slip in the room rack.

Rate cutting : Reducing room tariff to attract more business.

Real time : A computer term which means very fast processing of data where there is practically no time gap between input and output.

Red book : A publication of AHMA of the member hotels, describing their facilities and tariff etc.

Refusal report : A report made by some hotels of the names of guests who were refused accommodation due to non-availability to know the excess demand.

Registration : A process of completion of check-in and the guest signing a registration card or arrival register.

Registration card : A document where a checking-in writes details such as name, address, passport details, nationality, date of arrival, date of departure, purpose of visit etc. and signs. Sometimes called as 'Reg. card' and 'G.R. card'.

Reminder-o-timer : A special alarm clock used for wake-up calls. It can be set forty eight times at fifteen minutes interval.

Reservation activity fee : The amount of money paid as commission to various agencies such as travel agents for giving business to the hotel.

Reservation : An activity of booking room in advance for a prospective guest on his request and mutual agreement whereby the hotel is bound to provide the guest accommodation on the scheduled day of arrival of the guest and the guest is bound to take it.

Reservation form : A document where all the detail information about the guest is recorded at the time of booking request.

Reservation horizon : The planning period throughout which the hotel will be willing to accept and confirm inquiries for available rooms i.e. the period up to which the booking for future can be accepted. Also called booking lead time.

Reservation rack : A part of Whitney system, where all the information of the prospective guest received from him is recorded. The slips are kept in alphabetical order. The racks are filed chronologically by arrival date order.

Resident manager : Usually responsible for the front of the house, and may act as hotel manager in the absence of GM.

Residential hotel : A hotel where long term guest on special terms and conditions stay. Guests are generally required to sign a lease bond.

Resort hotel : A hotel situated at resort places such as hills, beaches, winter sports, etc. Generally a centre of recreational activities.

Revenue centre : All those sections of the hotel which generate revenue.

Revenue forecast report : Expected future revenue calculated by multiplying forecasted occupancy by current room rate.

RNA : Room not assigned.

Room assignment : Allotting a specific room to a check-in guest.

Room availability : Those rooms which are available for letting.

Room count : The number of occupied rooms.

Room discrepancy report : A report showing the discrepancy as per housekeeping and front desk in occupancy status.

Room index : Room index is a chronological system of dates records of the occupancy of each bedroom and suite.

Room inspection report : A report of the inspection of room prepared by the floor supervisor after she inspects a room which has been readied by the chambermaid.

Room rack : A rack which is a part of Whitney system in which slips are arranged room number wise. The rack shows the rooms occupancy status.

Room rack slip : A paper slip used to display room status and guests assignments in the room rack.

Room rate variance report : A report listing rooms which have not been sold at rack rate.

Room revenue : The sum total of money generated by the sale of rooms for a given period of time. Also called as room sales.

Room service : Service of food and beverage in the room. Part of food and beverage department.

Room type : Various grouping of rooms such as standard, suites etc.

Rooming a guest : The procedure of escorting the guest and carrying of his luggage to the assigned room by the bellboy.

Rooming : A procedure of directing a guest and installation of his luggage to room at check-in time.

Rooming list : A list sent by the travel agent to the hotel of the names, nationality and other details of the group members in advance.

Rule of the thumb : A method of fixing room tariff. Here for each Rs. 1000 investment, Re. 1 per day will be the room rate.

Ryokan : A term referring to a traditional Japanese inn.

S.A.T.C. : South Asia Travel Commission.

S.I.T.S. : Special Interest Tours. (People who normally visit a place once only)

S.T.D. : Subscriber Trunk Dialing. By obtaining the correct code from the S.T.D. booklet, subscriber may dial to almost all places without having to ask the operator to connect call.

Safe deposit boxes : Individual lockers like bank vaults allotted to guests for keeping their valuables and documents etc.

Sales journal : A permanent summarized record of today's business.

Sample room : A room used to merchandise only.

Self check-out : Computerized system to allow the guest to review his folio and settle the account to credit card used at check in.

Self registering kiosk : A freestanding machine capable of registering a guest and dispensing a room key.

Self registration : A system that automatically registers a guest and dispenses a key, based on guest's reservation and credit card information.

Self registration/check out terminal/kiosk : A computer terminal located in the lobby, like a teller machine.

Sell up/up selling : Convincing a prospective guest to take a higher priced room.

Sells position : Refers to the rooms availability status.

Service charge : A certain percentage of bill amounts added to the bill of the guest. This amount is distributed to service staff in place of tips.

Service elevator : Back elevator used by hotel staff and for transportation of commodities of food to different floors.

Shoulder period : A mid-price period between full season and off season.

Siberia : A term normally used for inferior quality rooms, such as near the staircase etc. Guest must be informed about its situation and condition before selling it.

Single room : Meant for one persons sleeping, Bed size is 36"x75" approximately.

Six P.M. release : Means that the room for a guest with reservation will be held only up to 6 pm and released after that time. Usually done in case where there is no guaranteed reservation, (credit card guarantee or company or any other guarantee) or deposit reservation. Also called as time-cancelled reservation.

Sleep out : A sold room where the guest did not stay during the night.

Sleeper : Room available for sale but not sold out.

Sleeper : The American meaning of the term is that the room appears to be occupied although it is vacant due to the negligence of front desk staff and as per the English terminology the term means the guest staying in the hotel.

Sleepers list : A list of all occupants of sleeping accommodation in the hotel on any given night. An English term.

Slide : The transcription error caused by a misplaced decimal; for example 30.50 is written as 3.050.

Soft copy : Display on the computer screen.

Sold out : Rooms not available.

SPATT : A special attention guest, for example, a guest needing a wheel chair.

Split folio- Folio in which guest's charges are separated into two or more folios.

Star reservation : Means room is reserved for a VIP.

Statistics : Collection of quantitative data for analytical and interpretive purpose.

Stay over : A hotel guest who does not leave and continues staying.

Storage : A function in which the data are placed in a select area of the system for future access and retrieval.

Studio bed/sofa cum bed : A bed usually without head board and foot board which can also be used as sofa during the day (36"x75").

Suite : A combination of two or more rooms out of which at least one is used as sitting room and other as bedroom.

Supper : A term referring to a late night meal.

Swing : A work shift between the day shift and grave yard shift (4 pm - 12 night).

Synergy : A combined action where the total production of the combined parts exceeds by far from the contribution of individual parts composing the whole.

System : An orderly arrangement of components in an inter-related series.

Systems analyst : A person responsible for overall design of the system.

T.A.A.I. : Travel Agents Association of India.

T.W.A. : Trans World Airlines.

Tariff : The published room rate list.

Telex : A 24 hours teleprinter service which provides for instantaneous transmission of message in print.

Time lead : A coordinator of a team of maids of a particular floor to introduce team spirit, competitive spirit and sharing of tasks.

Time-shared hotel : A relatively new concept where an investor buys a unit which is shared by other users to whom it may be rented out when not in use by the investor. Also called condominium.

Time-sharing : Use of computer to process multiple requests by users.

TIPS : To Insure Prompt Service.

Trade discount : A reduction made on the list or advertised selling price to others usually in same line of business.

Traffic sheet : A telephone department control sheet usually used for long distance calls.

Transcript : A form which is used by the night auditor whereby he separates the day's charges by rooms and departments.

Transfer and transfer folio : A procedure of moving one figure from one form to another (carried over from first form and brought forward to another form). Generally used in case of guest folio amount when at the end of the week the outstanding figure is transferred to a new unnumbered folio. Another term used for this is "A Follow".

Transfer slip : According to English terminology it means a notification slip made when a guest changes the room. Also called 'Move notification slip' and 'Removal notification slip'.

Transformation error : Incorrect handling of a data procedure due to misconception or misunderstanding.

Transient hotel : A hotel catering to short stay guest i.e. a transient guest who stops en route to another destination.

Transposition error : A transcription error caused by wrong recording of sequence of digits, for example, 289 written as 198.

Travel agent : An entrepreneur who coordinates various contracted services (such as hotel, food and beverage, transportation, etc.) provided by various contractors to the traveller who needs them at various stages of his tour. For providing these services he gets commission form hotels and other contractors.

Trial balance : A list of all accounts in a ledger.

Turn around time : Time from when data was entered into a system until available as output information.

Turn away : To refuse accommodation to walk-in guest, because the rooms are not available. Also called as "Displacement".

Turn down : An evening service provided by housekeeper where she prepares the bed for night use. Turn in — The cash deposited by departmental cashier with general cashier at the end of the day.

Typsy guest : A drunkard guest who may misbehave with staff.

UNESCO : United Nations Educational, Scientific and Cultural Organization.

UNICEF : United Nations International Childrens' Emergency Fund.

UFTAA : Universal Federation of Travel Agent Association.

Underbooking : An erroneous belief that all the rooms are sold while in fact they are not.

Understay : A guest who checks out before his scheduled date of departure.

Upgrade : To move a reservation or staying guest to a better accommodation or class of service.

V.I.P. : Very Important Person.

V.P.O. : Visitors paid out. If petty payments such as taxi fare, cinema tickets, postage, etc. are made by front desk on behalf of the guest, then a V.P.O. voucher is prepared which is signed by the guest and debited to his account where the amount is entered into guest folio.

V.P.P. : Value Payable Post

V.T.L. : Also called the 'Tab', is ledger in tabular form used for recording all transactions with guests staying in the hotel.

Vacant and ready : Room status term indicating that the room has been cleaned and inspected and is ready for new arrival.

Variable cost : Costs that vary in direct proportion to sales (for example, housekeeping costs with rooms sales and food and beverage costs with restaurant sales).

Voice mail box : A device used for storing, recording and playing back messages through telephone system.

Voucher : The forms used by various departments such as food and beverage selling services to guests and signed by guests, transferred to front office bills section.

W.H.O. : World Health Organization.

W.T.O. : World Tourism Organization. Also World Trade Organization.

Wait-listed : Guest who could not be given confirmed reservation because of full booking.

Walk out : A guest who leaves the hotels without warning i.e. without settling his bill. Also called as Skipper.

Walk through : A thorough examination/inspection by a hotel executive of the whole property.

Walk-in : A guest who comes to the hotel without prior reservation. Also called as 'Chance guest' and 'Off-the-street guest'.

Walking a guest : Due to lack of availability of rooms, to refuse accommodation to a guest who is holding confirmed reservation; also called Bounced Reservation.

Wash factor : Deletions of unnecessary group rooms from a group block.

Watch : Another term for work shift.

Watch down : Blocking fewer rooms than the number requested by a group, based on previous group history.

Watch list : A list prepared by the night manager of people showing unusual behaviour such as suddenly placing large orders.

Whitney system : A proprietary system designed by the Whitney Duplicating and Check Company of New York for front office operations and records keeping.

Who : An unidentified guest in a room that is vacant as per front desk record.

Wholesaler : An entrepreneur who conceives, finances and services group and package tour and provides to the general public through retail travel agent.

Y.H.A.I. : Youth Hostel Association of India.

Y.M.C.A. : Young Men's Christian Association.

Yield management : A technique based on supply and demand used to maximize revenue by lowering prices to increase sales during periods of low demand and by raising prices during periods of high demands; also called as revenue management in some cases.

Yield : The ratio of actual revenue to potential revenue.

Youth hostel : A budget accommodation with limited services generally catering to shoestring budget traveller (students etc. travelling on bicycle or hitch hiking).

Z-bed : A folding and portable bed.

Zeroing out : At the time of departure to bring the account balance to zero debits and credits offsetting one another.

Bibliography

Alastair, M. Morrison : *Hospitality and Travel Marketing*, Delemar, New York, 1989.

Aldous, T. : *Battle for the Environment*, Collins, London, 1972.

Anand, M.M. : *Tourism and Hotel Industry in India*, Prentice-Hall of India, New Delhi, 1976.

Anderson, N. : *Work and Leisure*, Routledge and Kegan Faul, London, 1961.

Archer, B.H. : *Demand Forecasting in Tourism*, University of Wales Press, Cardiff, 1974.

Archer, B.H. : *The Impact of Domestic Tourism*, University of Wales Press, Cardiff, 1973.

Ashworth, G. J. : *Marketing in the Tourism Industry*, Routledge, London, 1990.

Ashworth, G. : *Recreation and Tourism*, Bell and Hyman, London, 1984.

Beazely, E. : *Designed for Recreation*, Faber, London, 1970.

Bernecker, Paul. : *Methods and Media of Tourist Publicity*, Austrian National Tourist Office, Vienna, 1961.

Bhatia, A. K. : *International Tourism : Fundamentals and Practices*, Sterling, New Delhi, 1991.

Bhatia, A. K. : *Tourism Management and Marketing*, Sterling, New Delhi, 1997.

Bhatia, A. K. : *Tourism in India : History and Development*, Sterling, New Delhi, 1978.

Boniface, B. and Cooper, C. : *The Geography of Travel and Tourism* Heinemann, London, 1987.

Brunner, E. : *Holiday Making and the Holiday Trades*, Oxford University Press, London, 1945.

Bryden, John M. : *Tourism and Development*, Cambridge University Press, Cambridge, 1973.

Bull, A. : *The Economics of Travel and Tourism*, Pitman, London, 1991.

Burkart, A.J. and Medlik, S. : *Tourism: Past, Present and Future*, Heinemann, London, 1976.

Burkart, A.J. : *The Management of Tourism*, Heinemann, London, 1975.

Burton, T.L. : *Recreation Research and Planning*, Allen and Unwin, London, 1970.

Calder, N. : *The Environment Game*, Panther, London, 1969.

Cherry, G.E. : *Town Planning and its Social Context*, Hill, London, 1970.

Chuck, Y. Gee. : *The Travel Industry*, Van National Reinhold, New York, 1989.

Clare, Gunn : *Tourism Planning*, Taylor and Francis, New York, 1988.

Clayne, R. Jensen : *Leisure and Recreation-Introduction and Overview*, Lea and Febiger, Philadelphia, 1977.

Cleverdon, Robert : *The Economic and Social Impact of International Tourism on Developing Countries*, The Economic Intelligence Unit Ltd., London, 1979.

Colley, G. : *International Tourism Today*, Lloyds Bank Review, London, 1967.

Cosgrove, Isabel and Jackson; R. : *The Geography of Recreation and Leisure*, Hutchinson, London, 1972.

Crampon, L.T. : *An Analysis of Tourist Markets*, University of Colorado Press, Colorado, 1963.

________, *The Development of Tourism*, University of Colorado Press, Colorado, 1963.

Dale, E. : *Management Theory and Practice,* McGraw-Hill, New York, 1973.

Davidson, R. : *Business Travel,* Pitman, London, 1994.

_______, *Tourism in Europe,* Pitman, London, 1992.

Davis, H.D. : *Potentials for Tourism of Developing Countries,* Finance and Development, London, 1968.

Donald, E. Hawking : *Tourism Planning and Development Issues,* George Washington University, Washington, 1980.

_______, *Tourism Marketing and Management Issues,* George Washington University, Washington, 1980.

Douglas Pearce : *Tourist Development,* Longman, 1989.

_______, *Tourism Today: A Geographical-Analysis,* Longman, New York, 1987.

Dower, M. : *The Challenge of Leisure,* Civic Trust, London, 1965.

Dumazedier, J. : *Towards a Society of Leisure,* Free Press, New York, 1967.

Ed Gell, D. L. : *International Tourism Policy,* Van Nostrand Reinhold, New York, 1990.

Edmunds : *Environmental Administration,* McGraw-Hill, New York, 1973.

Edward, J. Mayo : *The Psychology of Leisure Travel,* CBI Publishing Company, Boston, 1981.

Edwards, Francis, G. : *How to Focus ? Your Marketing Efforts,* Louis A. Allen Associates, London, 1976.

Engel, James F. : *Market Segmentation: Concepts and Applications,* Holt, Rinehart and Winston, New York, 1962.

Feiffer, M. : *Giving Places,* MacMillan, London, 1985.

Foster, D. : *Travel and Tourism Management,* MacMillan, London, 1985.

Frank, R.E. : *Market Segmentation,* Prentice-Hall, New Jersey, 1972.

Gearing Charles, E. : *Planning or Tourism Development,* Praeger Publishers, New York, 1976.

Gray, H. Peter : *International Travel-International Trade,* Health Lexington Books, Lexington, 1970.

Gunn, C. : *Tourism Planning,* Taylor and Francis, New York, 1988.

Heath, E. : *Marketing Tourism Destinations,* Wiley, New York, 1992.

Hibbert, Christopher : *The Grand Tour,* Weidenfel and Nicolson, London, 1969.

Hodyson, A. : *The Travel and Tourism Industry,* Pergamon, Oxford, 1987.

Hollander, S. : *Passenger Transportation,* Michigan State University, Michigan, 1968.

Holloway, J. C. : *Marketing or Tourism,* Longman, Harlow, 1995.

Howard : *Marketing Made Simple,* W.H. Allen, London, 1972.

Hurdman, L.E. : *Tourism : A Shrinking World,* Viley, New York, 1980.

Inskeep, E. : *Tourism Planning,* Van Nostrand Reinhold, New York, 1991.

Jefferson, A. : *Marketing Tourism-A Practical Guide,* Harlow, Longman, 1991.

Jenkins, J. R. Zif, J.J. : *Planning the Advertising Campaign,* MacMillan, New York, 1973.

John M. Bryden. : *Tourism and Development,* Cambridge University Press, London, 1973.

John, Lea : *Tourism Development in the Third World,* Routledge, New York, 1988.

Kaiser, Charles Jr. and Larry E. Helber : *Tourism Planning and Development,* CBI Publishing Company, Boston, 1978.

Katler, P. : *Introduction to Marketing Management, Analysis, Planning and Control,* Prentice-Hall, London, 1975.

Kerry Godrey and Jackie Clarke : *The Tourism Development Handbook,* Cassell, London, 2000.

Kotler P. : *Principles of Marketing,* Prentice-Hall, New York, 1999.

Lansing, J.B. Blood, D.M. : *The Changing Travel Market,* University of Michigan, Michigan, 1964.

Law, C. : *Urban Tourism: Attracting Visitors to Large Cities,* Mansell, London, 1993.

Laws, E.C. : *Tourist Destination Management: Issues, Analysis and Policies,* Routledge, London, 1995.

Lawson, Malcom : *Teaching Tourism-Education and Training in Western Europe : A Comparative Study,* Tourism International Press, London, 1975.

Leadley, P. : *Leisure Marketing,* Longman, Harlow, 1992.

Lickorish, L.J. and Kershaw, A.G. : *The Travel Trade,* Practical Press, London, 1974.

Lundberg, D.E. : *The Tourist Business,* Van Nostrand Rheinold, New York, 1990.

Lundberg : *International Travel and Tourism,* Institute of Certified Travel Agents, New York, 1970.

Mathieson, A : *Tourism: Economic, Physical and Social Impacts,* Longman, London, 1982.

McIntosh, R.W. : *Tourism Principles, Practices and Philosophies,* Grid, Ohio, 1977.

Medlik, S. : *Economic Importance of Tourism,* University of Surrey, Surrey, 1972.

_______, *Higher Education and Research in Tourism in Western Europe,* University of Surrey, London, 1966.

_______, *Profile of the Hotel and Catering Industry,* Heinemann, London, 1972.

Middleton, V.T.C. : *Marketing in Travel and Tourism,* Heinemann, London, 1988.

Mill, R.C. : *The Tourism Business: an Introductory Text,* Prentice-Hall, London, 1985.

_______, *The Tourism System,* Prentice-Hall International, London, 1985.

_______, *Tourism : The International Business,* Prentice-Hall, New Jersey, 1990.

Morisson, A. M. : *Hospitality and Travel Marketing,* Delmar, New York, 1989.

Murphy, Peter E. : *Tourism : A Community Approach*, Methuen, 1985.

Nicholson, M. : *The Environmental Revolution*, Penguin, London, 1972.

Norval, A.J. : *The Tourist Industry*, Issac Pitman and Sons Ltd., London, 1936.

Ogilvie, F.W. : *The Tourist Movement: An Economic Study*, Staples Press, London, 1933.

Parker, S. : The *Future of Work and Leisure*, Mac Gibbon and Kee, London, 1971.

Patmore, J. A. : *Land and Leisure*, David and Charles, London, 1970.

Peaker, A. : *"Holiday Spending by the British at Home and Abroad"*, National Westminster Bank Quarterly Review, 1973.

Pearce, D. : *Tourism Organisations*, Longman, Harlow, 1992.

_______, *Tourism Today*, Longman, Harlow, 1987.

_______, *Tourist Development*, Longman, Harlow, 1989.

Pearce, Sales, J. : *Travel and Tourism Encyclopedia*, Blandford, London, 1959.

Pigram, J. : *Outdoor Recreation and Resource Management*, Croom Helm, London, 1993.

Pudney, John : *The Thomas Cook Story*, Michael Joseph, London, 1953.

Rae, W.F. : *The Business of Travel*, Thomas Cook and Son, London, 1891.

Ram Acharya : *Civil Aviation and Tourism Administration in India*, National Publishing House, New Delhi, 1978.

Raymond, R. : *Ecological Principles for Economic Development*, John Wiley, London, 1978.

Reilly, R. T. : *Travel and Tourism Marketing Techniques*, Delmar, New York, 1988.

Richards, G. : *Tourism and the Economy*, University of Surrey, Surrey, 1972.

Robinson, H. : *A Geography of Tourism*, MacDonald and Evans, London, 1976.

Ross, G. F. : *The Psychology of Tourism*, Hospitality Press, Melbourne, 1994.

Rothfield, Crampon, Wahab : *Tourism Marketing*, Tourism International Press, London, 1975.

Ryan, C. : *Recreational Tourism :A Social Science Perspective*, Routledge, London, 1991.

Schmoll, G.A. : *Tourism Promotion*, Tourism International Press, London, 1977.

Sessa, Alberto : *Tourism in Developing Countries*, UNESCO, Paris, 1970.

Seth, P.N. : *Successful Tourism Planning and Management*, Cross Section Publications, New Delhi, 1978.

Sigaux, G. : *History of Tourism*, Leisure Arts, London, 1966.

Smith, S. : *Tourism Analysis*, Longman, New York, 1989.

_______, *Tourism Analysis*, Longman, Harlow, 1995.

_______, *Recreation Geography*, Longman, Harlow, 1983.

Susan Horner : *Marketing Tourism Hospitality and Leisure in Europe*, International Thomson Business Press, London, 1996.

Tull, D. S. : *Marketing Research: Measurements and Methods*, Prentice-Hall, London, 1993.

Wahab, Crampon Rothfield : *Tourism Marketing*, Tourism International Press, London, 1976.

Wahab, Salah : *Tourism Management*, Tourism International Press, London, 1975.

White, J. : *History of Tourism*, Leisure Art, London, 1967.

Young, George : *Tourism: Blessing or Blight*, Penguin, London, 1973.

Yukic, T.S. : *Fundamentals of Recreation*, Harper Row, London, 1963.

Zeithaml, V.A. : *Services Marketing*, McGraw-Hill, London, 1996.

